How Christmas Became Christmas

How Christmas Became Christmas

The Pagan and Christian Origins of the Beloved Holiday

Nathaniel Parry

McFarland & Company, Inc., Publishers
Jefferson, North Carolina

Library of Congress Cataloguing-in-Publication Data

Names: Parry, Nathaniel, author.
Title: How Christmas became Christmas : the Pagan and Christian origins of the beloved holiday / Nathaniel Parry.
Other titles: Pagan and Christian origins of the beloved holiday
Description: Jefferson, North Carolina : McFarland & Company, Inc., Publishers, 2022 | Includes bibliographical references and index.
Identifiers: LCCN 2022027101 |
ISBN 9781476688282 (paperback : acid free paper) ∞
ISBN 9781476647081 (ebook)
Subjects: LCSH: Christmas—Folklore. | Christmas—Social life and customs. | BISAC: RELIGION / Holidays / Christmas & Advent
Classification: LCC GT4985 .P3635 2022 | DDC 394.2663—dc23/eng/20220609
LC record available at https://lccn.loc.gov/2022027101

British Library cataloguing data are available

ISBN (print) 978-1-4766-8828-2
ISBN (ebook) 978-1-4766-4708-1

© 2022 Nathaniel Parry. All rights reserved

No part of this book may be reproduced or transmitted in any form or by any means, electronic or mechanical, including photocopying or recording, or by any information storage and retrieval system, without permission in writing from the publisher.

Front cover image © Maciej Es / ASTA Concept / Victorian Traditions / Shutterstock

Printed in the United States of America

McFarland & Company, Inc., Publishers
Box 611, Jefferson, North Carolina 28640
www.mcfarlandpub.com

To Eva and Lea

Table of Contents

Acknowledgments ix

Preface 1

Introduction 3

Part One—Origins and Evolution

1. Holiday Hype and Historiography 10
2. In Search of the First Christmas 22
3. Christmas in a Pagan World 34
4. Yule's Post-Pagan Metamorphosis 46
5. Repression and Resistance 58

Part Two—Curious Customs

6. Sacred Trees 68
7. The Man, the Myth, the Legend, the God—Santa Claus 83
8. Actual Christmas Magic 98
9. Children's Saturnalia 113
10. Ghosts, Goblins and Angels 127

Part Three—Enduring Legacies

11. Legacy of Miracles 142
12. Legacy of Misrule 158
13. The Halloween Connection 171
14. From Pagan to Secular 182

15. Reason for the Season 198
16. War Over Christmas 209

Chapter Notes 219
Bibliography 241
Index 245

Acknowledgments

Considering the subject matter of this book, perhaps it is appropriate to first acknowledge my ancestors for developing our wonderful Yuletide traditions and my family for providing me a lifetime of Christmas memories—my parents and grandparents for instilling a deep appreciation for this holiday, my siblings and cousins for sharing many special moments, and my children for rekindling the sense of magic and wonder that I had largely forgotten some time in adolescence. I also thank my wife, Malene, for putting up with me prattling on about the minutiae of Christmas history for the past year and for providing invaluable feedback on my ideas. Special thanks must also go to my teachers over the years who have imbued an appreciation for the learning process and the research skills to enable it.

The best thing about writing a book on Christmas history is the wealth and accessibility of historical sources spanning the ages, and for this I owe gratitude to countless historians, archaeologists, theologians, folklorists, and scholars, as well as the diligent archivists who have made so much information available online. In particular, I would be remiss if I did not acknowledge the good people who administer websites such as *Early Christian Writings*, *Hymns and Carols of Christmas*, *Forgotten Books*, *Internet Archive*, *Google Scholar*, *Google Books*, and *Academia.edu*. For images used in this book, I owe gratitude to the Getty Museum, the Metropolitan Museum of Art, the Cleveland Museum of Art, the Library of Congress, the Smithsonian Institution, the New York Public Library, the Web Gallery of Art, the Rijksmuseum, and Wikimedia Commons. Thanks also go to the very helpful and competent staff of the Danish library system for their assistance and to the whole team at McFarland.

I would also like to acknowledge historians such as Stephen Nissenbaum, Judith Flanders, Paul Frodsham, Ronald Sutton and Clement Miles, as well as folklorists including Jacob Grimm, Christian Ratsch, Claudia Muller-Ebeling and Linda Raedisch. Their work has been indispensable in informing my research but, I should say, these are just a few of the scholars, living and dead, who have been inspired to explore the mysteries of the Christmas season and the origins of our Yuletide traditions, building a rich historical literature, and exploring many of the same themes that I have focused on here.

Preface

There are two general views on Christmas that are as fervently held as they are diametrically opposed: one is that the holiday is a quintessentially Christian festival, rooted in pious observances of the birth of Jesus Christ on December 25 in or around year zero, but that the holiday's ecclesiastical characteristics have been eroded over time by secularism and commercial interests. The other is that Christmas is not Christian at all—that our Yuletide traditions are rooted in pre–Christian celebrations of the winter solstice and were essentially co-opted by the Church as it tried to spread the faith across Europe. According to this view, which is often colored by skepticism of religion in general or a hostility toward Christianity in particular, the holiday is actually pagan in nature and has nothing to do whatsoever with the birth of Jesus.

The truth, of course, is somewhere in between these extremes, and it is the intention of this book to fully explore this rich and fascinating middle ground. In doing so, I hope to both clarify the historical reality and hopefully help promote a mutual understanding that enables society to overcome the cultural tensions that too often sully the celebration of Christmas.

The two competing narratives about Christmas play out year after year in what is generally known as "the War on Christmas" or is sometimes called "the Christmas controversies." These controversies are characterized by legal fights over the separation of church and state and cultural battles about the role of religion in public life. But although the dispute today appears to generally fall down along "Christian vs. secularist" lines, it is in fact part of a long-running process of Christianizing pagan traditions and in some ways can be interpreted as the inability of the Church to fully establish its version of history over the past two millennia. This ongoing historical failure can be seen most clearly in the persistent questions about whether Jesus was even born on December 25 to begin with. Christian defenders of this date as the actual birthday of Jesus fail to appreciate the reality that it was likely chosen, at least partially, due to its significance in heathen celebrations of ancient Rome.

However, it should also be acknowledged that taking a stridently secularist approach to this history is fraught with its own problems—failing, for example, to appreciate the basic fact that regardless of the origins of selecting December 25 as the nativity, the date has come to hold intrinsic significance to Christians. Furthermore, the holiday—even if it has roots in pagan celebrations of the solstice—has been fundamentally influenced by Christianity, and therefore it is ahistorical to claim that "Christmas isn't Christian," as some are wont to do. It is a simple fact that the holiday has been known for hundreds of years as a Christian feast celebrating the birth of

Jesus, and there is no point in denying this. At the same time, there is also no point in denying the fact that as the world's dominant belief systems for thousands of years, pagan religions have had profound and lasting effects on our customs and views—including how we mark important turning points in the year.

This book tackles these issues in three parts. The first examines the origins and evolution of Christmas, as well as explores the historiography of the subject. Dealing with questions of why the Church decided to designate December 25 as Jesus's birthday and how pre–Christian winter solstice celebrations may have influenced the development of Christmas, Part One separates fact from fiction, tries to clearly establish what it is that we know and don't know about the roots of our Christmas customs, and offers a different take on the role of the sun in both Christianity and paganism. Part Two delves more deeply into those customs, exploring the origins of the Christmas tree, Santa Claus, and concepts such as "Christmas magic." Part Three demonstrates how the pagan influences of these traditions continue to have enduring impacts on Christmas and fuel the controversies that surround the holiday.

In structuring this book, I take a generally thematic approach. Instead of the chapters following a chronological progression, they tackle individual themes, taking a holistic look at the movements and ideas that have shaped the development of Christmas, which is closely related to broader concepts of the Christianization of Europe and the enduring influence of paganism over the centuries. Much has been written about the pagan influences on Christmas, with many writers taking an overly liberal approach to making unsubstantiated assertions, while some historians go in the other direction and refuse to draw conclusions unless backed by incontrovertible proof.

Since incontrovertible proof might sometimes be an unrealistically high bar, there is a need at times to make reasonable deductions based on available evidence, which due to the nature of the subject—being based on fragmented accounts from surviving historical documents and ancient religious tracts—is not always strong as some might like. That said, the reader should be confident that the sources cited in this book have been vetted and the facts assessed as well as can be reasonably expected.

Introduction

The holly! the holly! oh, twine it with bay—
Come give the holly a song;
For it helps to drive stern winter away
   —Eliza Cook, "The Christmas Holly"

A book exploring Christmas's pagan roots really should be nothing controversial. Although historians may dispute how much Norse or Celtic midwinter celebrations have influenced the development of Christmas in specific ways and there is still some disagreement about why precisely the Church designated December 25 as Jesus's birthday in the fourth century, it is widely accepted that pagan celebrations of the winter solstice have played some role in Christianity's observance of the nativity. But although the background of the holiday is relatively well known—as displayed by the clickbait internet headlines that pop up every December—and the pagan influences on Christmas have been generally appreciated both by historians and religious leaders for centuries, the subject is still sensitive to many who reject the notion that their cherished holiday may be fundamentally non–Christian in nature.

As someone who has long been fascinated by the history of Christmas, its pagan roots, and the historical questions surrounding the actual birthday of Jesus of Nazareth, I am acutely aware of how touchy this subject can be. Having found myself in many conversations over the years in which I gently point out that the historical reasons for celebrating this holiday may have more to do with the seasonal rotation of the earth around the sun than with Jesus being born in a stable, I have often encountered anger and incredulousness. Some people are unaware that Jesus may not have been born on December 25, while others will emphatically point out that his actual date of birth is irrelevant since this is the day that Christians have collectively decided to celebrate. Questioning the underlying assumptions about Christmas is often seen as hostile to the holiday, or more broadly, to Christianity itself.

So, first off, I would like to say that I love Christmas and respect all of the traditions associated with it, whether they are pagan, secular or Christian. This book is in no way meant to represent an attack on the holiday and hopefully is not seen as hostile to the Christian observance of Jesus Christ's nativity. As an occasionally practicing Christian, I make a point of attending church services during the Christmas season, and some of my favorite Christmas songs relate to the birth of Jesus. I would even say that Christmas is not complete without hearing Johnny Cash's rendition of "Little Drummer Boy" at least once.

If this book is an attack on anything, it is an attack on the distortion of history—an attempt to correct certain falsehoods and explore a rich historical narrative that has been overly simplified for hundreds of years. This oversimplification can be seen everywhere—from stories about "the first Christmas" that recall the narrative of Jesus's birth to the definition of Christmas offered by *Encyclopædia Britannica*, which calls it a "Christian festival celebrating the birth of Jesus"[1]—and has led to divisions marked by petty arguments about how it should be celebrated and the degree to which it should be infused with religious fervor. Between those who argue for purging all ecclesiastical connotations and those who insist on "keeping Christ in Christmas," it is a wonder how any of us can disregard all the noise and just enjoy the season.

The perennial Christmas controversies have taken this to the logical extreme, with arguments inundating the airwaves every year with complaints about nativity scenes being removed from public grounds or even Starbucks using holiday cups that aren't sufficiently "Christmassy." In 2004, Fox News' Bill O'Reilly launched his "Christmas Under Siege" segment with a dire warning that "Christmas is taking flak," noting that religious floats were being removed from holiday parades, "holiday trees" were replacing Christmas trees, and Christian symbols of the holiday were being prohibited in public schools. In 2006, an alarmist book was published called *The War on Christmas: How the Liberal Plot to Ban the Sacred Christian Holiday Is Worse Than You Thought* by John Gibson, backing up many of O'Reilly's claims about the supposed "secularization" of Christmas characterized by misguided attempts at multicultural inclusion and political correctness. Since then, Christmas crusaders have seized on any perceived attempt to minimize the Christian aspects of Christmas as an assault on religious freedom. The "PC police" who say "Happy Holidays" instead of "Merry Christmas" are undermining the very "reason for the season," according to these culture warriors and evangelical Christians.

On the other hand, there are overzealous secularists who object to the month-long celebration as an imposition of Christian doctrines on those who hold other beliefs, and at times, it does seem that they go too far pushing back against any imposition of this holiday in the public sphere. In 2017, for example, University of Minnesota officials distributed a memo to employees and students advising them to keep "inappropriate religious celebrations" out of public spaces. Among the "specific religious iconography" frowned upon by the university were Santa Claus, angels, Christmas trees, wrapped gifts, bells, and doves. They also warned against using the colors red, green, blue, white and silver, noting that "red and green are representative of the Christian tradition as blue and white/silver are for Jewish Hanukkah that is also celebrated at this time of year."[2]

Depending on one's political views, these incidents are either a sign of political correctness run amok, or a principled defense of the sacrosanct separation of church and state. Because Christmas is seen primarily as a Christian occasion, secularists insist that there must be strict limits on how the holiday is recognized so as not impose religious doctrines on those who are atheist, agnostic, Muslim, Hindu, Jewish, Buddhist or Sikh. Why, these secularists ask, are we compelled to recognize a Christian feast when there are so many other religious festivals that are ignored? Meanwhile, Christmas enthusiasts resent that they can't freely and openly celebrate this most sacred occasion.

With a deeper understanding of Christmas, an appreciation for how it developed and its context in the broader narrative of human history, these disputes over how to celebrate the holiday appear trivial and contrived. When its development as a cultural and spiritual phenomenon is understood, it becomes clear that it is not simply a Christian holiday, but rather a blend of various traditions rooted in pagan celebrations of the winter solstice. Despite its name, at its core, the holiday is not exclusively a celebration of Christ, but rather an end-of-year celebration intrinsically linked to the earth's rotation around the sun and corresponding seasonal changes. This is ultimately why the holiday resonates so widely and why there is no need to argue about the correct way to celebrate it.

Although some secularists and modern-day heathens may take the "Christmas is really pagan" argument too far and offer sensational claims that sound true-ish but are not supported by the historical record, the reality is that midwinter festivals have existed in one form or another for millennia, and it wasn't until some 300 years after Jesus was born that the Church claimed this holiday as "Christmas." It is a matter of debate why December 25 was chosen as the date of Jesus's birth, but two things are clear: (1) the date cannot be found in the Gospels or other historical records and (2) the date closely coincides with ancient Roman holidays Dies Natalis Solis Invicti, Saturnalia and Kalends, from which many of our Christmas traditions are derived.

There is some irony in the way that it is now considered "controversial" to acknowledge Christmas's pagan influences because in earlier times this was relatively common knowledge, and it was widely accepted that the Church shrewdly selected December 25 for the nativity because this day was already being celebrated by pagans. As Syrian Christian Bishop Dionysius Salibi explained way back in the 12th century: "It was a custom of the Pagans to celebrate on the same 25 of December the birthday of the Sun, at which they kindled lights in token of the festivity. In these solemnities and revelries the Christians also took part. Accordingly, when the doctors of the Church perceived that the Christians had a leaning to this festival, they took counsel and resolved that the true Nativity should be solemnized on that day."[3]

So, even some 900 years ago, it was appreciated that Christmas was actually an amalgamation of pagan traditions that had been infused with Christian themes, rather than being a genuine celebration of the savior's birthday that grew organically out of Christian doctrines. The Church, according to this once commonly held view, bestowed religious significance on a pre-existing celebration that had no real relation to the Christian faith in order to help convince pagans to join the flock and to help establish Christianity as the dominant religion and social order of Europe. The roots of the holiday are the pagan traditions of the winter solstice, and the "nativity" recognized as the birth of Christ was originally the *natalis invicti*, or birth of the sun god, worshipped in third-century Rome as Sol Invictus.

More broadly, the traditions are related to the seasonal realities of life in the northern hemisphere, where the days grow depressingly dark at this time of year and midwinter celebrations have always played an important role, particularly in pre-industrial (and pre-electrical) agricultural societies. The seasons were central to the lives of ancient peoples, who therefore had a special reverence for the sun and celebrated its return with vigor.

* * *

Having lived in Denmark for over a dozen years, after growing up in the mid–Atlantic region of the United States, I have come to intimately appreciate the importance of the sun and its return. While days of course are shorter in December throughout the northern hemisphere, the lack of sunshine in Nordic countries is particularly pronounced. Being this far north, it is dark until well after 8:00 in the morning and dark again by 3:00 or 4:00 in the afternoon. The brevity of the day is compounded by the reality that the weather in this part of the world tends to be overcast and gray throughout the winter, so glimpses of the sun are exceedingly rare even during those few hours of "daytime."

Once you experience this yearly cycle a few times, it begins to make sense on a visceral level why our ancestors attached so much significance to the winter solstice and why they would celebrate the return of the sun with such enthusiasm. It also hits home why they would engage in traditions such as lighting candles and using evergreens for decorations, which must have been a pleasing comfort during a long, cold, dark winter—perhaps even a necessity to keep spirits up at an otherwise grim and bleak time of year.

Indeed, it has occurred to me over the years that if Christmas did not exist, we would have to invent it, simply to make it through the doldrums of midwinter. Or, more accurately, it's not that we would *have to* invent it—we simply *would* invent it. It would evolve naturally because enduring the cold, gray, sunless month of December would be intolerable without some kind of respite. The horrifying prospect of a Christmas-less world was captured by C.S. Lewis in his book *The Lion, the Witch and the Wardrobe* with a one-sentence description of the White Witch's rule: "It's always winter, but never Christmas." To escape that nightmare scenario, we would surely devise some method to brighten up the days—not to mention a way to celebrate the end of the year and usher in the next one. Perhaps we wouldn't think up the exact same traditions that we enjoy today, but we would definitely come up with something.

Luckily, we don't have to invent Christmas, because it already exists.

We have wonderful traditions of music, lights, foods, festivities, gift-giving, and stories. There are special plants that we use to decorate our homes, magical elves who perform miracles, and arcane symbols whose origins are obscure but are widely embraced nonetheless. How many people know the historical background of gingerbread houses, for example, or the significance of holly? Even the Christmas tree is something of an enigma: it is one of the most quintessential and recognizable symbols of Christmas and yet no one can say with certainty where the tradition comes from or why it is that we engage in it. Upon examining these customs and traditions more closely, it is astounding how many of them are throwbacks to earlier, pre–Christian beliefs, only to be gradually incorporated in the Christmas celebration over a long period of cultural and religious blending. It also becomes clear why certain activities at Christmas, such as eating and drinking in abundance, seem to contravene traditional teachings of Christianity of moderation and humility, and why so much of our popular culture focuses on Christmas's secular aspects rather than its religious side. How many of your favorite Christmas movies, for example, tell the story of the birth of Jesus?

* * *

Although some may get defensive when it is pointed out that the Christmas celebration may not actually be rooted in Christianity, seeing it as an attack upon their faith, the reality is that the layers of traditions—dating back centuries before the birth of Christ—are what make this celebration so rich. When seen in all of their historical complexity, these traditions can be more deeply appreciated. Christmas, quite simply, is one of the greatest things that humanity has ever produced—the most wonderful time of the year—and no particular culture or religion can claim ownership over it. It is, by its nature, an inclusive celebration rooted in ancient celebrations of the return of the sun, incorporating traditions developed by many different cultures over the course of millennia, and infused with a mysticism that transcends any one religion.

With this deeper appreciation, arguments over the true "reason for the season" become trite. There is no single reason to celebrate this holiday, nor is there any particular reason not to, regardless of what religion you may subscribe to—or whether you subscribe to none at all—because this holiday does not actually belong to Christianity; it belongs to humanity. This isn't to say that Christians cannot also celebrate the birth of Christ, but it should be appreciated that historically speaking, it is very unlikely that Jesus was born at this time of year. Therefore, it is unreasonable to insist that anyone else should be compelled to recognize his nativity or to incorporate Christian doctrines in these traditions, most of which are fundamentally pagan or pre–Christian in nature to begin with.

In fact, it was because of its known pagan origins that the holiday was banned by the Puritan-led English Parliament in 1647, as well as by the original English settlers of Massachusetts. Even today, there are Christian denominations, such as the Quakers and Jehovah's Witnesses, that reject the celebration of Christmas on religious grounds. The Seventh-Day Adventist Church does not recognize Christmas or any other religious festivals throughout the calendar year as holy feasts. As strict adherents to the teachings contained in the Bible, the Seventh-Day Adventists emphasize that while there is nothing wrong with having a day when Christians remember the birth of their Savior, the festivity is not ordained by Scripture, and therefore it is not considered to be binding on believers. "We recognize only one holy day, the Sabbath; and we keep it holy in obedience to our Creator and Redeemer," their website states.[4]

So, considering the disagreements that exist even within Christianity about the celebration of Christmas—and have existed for hundreds of years—it should not be considered controversial to acknowledge that the holiday's roots historically have very little to do with Christianity. Recognizing this does not diminish or devalue Christmas; it accentuates and clarifies Christmas by helping to appreciate it in all of its historical richness. In addition to helping to resolve age-old controversies about the "reason for the season," developing this appreciation could also help people to reconnect with ancient beliefs and to understand the significance of certain customs. What becomes clear with a deeper understanding of this history is that when we engage with these traditions, we are engaging with some of the oldest continuing traditions that exist in the world. In this way, Christmas allows us to recall ancient belief systems that have otherwise been forgotten. This is one reason that it is indeed the most wonderful time of the year—it reconnects us with ancestors and reminds our modern society of bygone eras when magic was considered a fact of life and rituals were performed to ensure the return of the sun and a prosperous new year.

When looking at Christmas history, then, it is important to try to avoid taking a "side" in the contrived controversies that have come to characterize this discussion.

Although the debate has largely fallen into a "Christian vs. secularist" framework, as a matter of historical inquiry, this is simply not the way to understand the issue. While we might ultimately identify with a particular worldview, whether it is "Christian" or "secularist" or even "neopagan," historically speaking we are all cut from the same cloth—we all descend from pre–Christian peoples, from hunter-gatherers who venerated trees and pagans who worshipped various pantheons of gods. Examining the pagan roots of Christmas in this sense is not an affront to Christianity, but simply an examination of our common past.

Part One
Origins and Evolution

1

Holiday Hype and Historiography

And bid good-morrow to the sun;
Welcome his safe return
To Capricorn.
And that great morn
Wherein a God was born
 —Jeremy Taylor,
  "A Hymn for Christmas Day"

There is an intensity with which people push back on claims of the pagan origins of Christmas that is rather peculiar. In some ways it is understandable that Christians would want to defend the ecclesiastical basis for celebrating the nativity, but at the end of the day, it is simply a fact of life that many of our customs have been handed down from pagans and this should not be considered particularly contentious. After all, pagan survivals can be seen everywhere—from days of the week and the months of the year that are named after Norse and Roman gods, to the names of the planets in our solar system and popular commercial brands such as Nike and Ajax—which is an enduring testament to the historical fact that for thousands of years paganism dominated the world. It is only natural that remnants of pagan belief, particularly those related to the yearly cycle and the changing of the seasons, would be passed on through traditions such as midsummer and midwinter celebrations. Perhaps this is why many people—particularly those of a secularist, neopagan or atheist persuasion—readily embrace claims that Christmas is little more than a Christian adaptation of heathen customs.

But despite the pagan influences of the Christmas celebration being widely accepted and relatively well known, something that becomes clear rather quickly is that as a matter of historical inquiry, there is a lack of certainty on core questions. In fact, it seems that while there are many assumptions and conclusions that people draw about Christmas's origins and the roots of our Yuletide traditions, almost nothing is known for certain and historical records are non-existent or incomplete on the most pertinent issues—with ancient (and sometimes dubious) written accounts and scant archaeological findings serving as the basis for much of our knowledge.

The Christmas tree is a case in point. Various explanations for this tradition point either to a Christian basis for the custom or to pagan origins, but the lack of clarity on the topic reminds us that the evidence for specific transmissions of customs is not always as strong as it could be. Considering the spiritual significance of trees in the pre–Christian world, it is generally safe to assume that there is some pagan connection to the Christmas tree, but the fact is there is no solid documentary evidence for this. At the same time, of course, it should be acknowledged that a lack of strong evidence does not necessarily mean that there is no connection at all. In some cases, pagan beliefs and practices may have been absorbed into the Christian celebration and their original meanings simply forgotten over time.

The lack of clear evidence may also be due to the fact that many pre–Christian societies were essentially illiterate, but it should also be acknowledged that even if they were literate, they probably wouldn't have thought to keep written records of each and every one of their customs and beliefs—such as why, exactly, they burned Yule logs or decorated their homes with evergreens. In some cases, the absence of strong documentary evidence could also be the result of conscious decisions of ancient civilizations to suppress or bring to the fore certain aspects of history. For example, following the Roman Empire's conversion to Christianity in the fourth century, non–Christian writings were destroyed in great bonfires in the center of the town square and scribes were threatened with having their hands cut off if they attempted to recreate these documents.[1] Meanwhile, the works of early Christian writers were allowed to be passed down from generation to generation, many of which continue to inform us today.

Scholars who follow the available evidence continue to intensely debate the origins of Christmas and the roots of various traditions. Employing the highest principles of historiography, their work stands in marked contrast to the abundance of "information" out there that essentially serves as propaganda for one side or the other. Depending on which "side" you are on, you may be inclined to dismiss arguments about the holiday's pagan origins or embrace every spurious claim regardless of whether it is backed up by documentary or archaeological evidence.

Evangelical Christians will insist, for example, that pro–Church narratives regarding how December 25 was selected as the date of Jesus's birth are the unvarnished truth, while neopagans or free thinkers skeptical of religion will insist that every custom that we enjoy on Christmas was basically a hostile takeover by a corrupt and opportunistic Church. Caught in the middle are diligent historians who attempt to separate fact from fiction and follow the available evidence, which in some cases is lacking. The assiduousness of historians trying to piece together an accurate picture of the past may lead in some cases to an overly cautious reluctance to engage in speculation about matters that are not fully supported by the data.

In her book *Christmas: A History*, for example, Judith Flanders flatly states that "no convincing evidence of winter solstice celebrations in pagan Europe has survived."[2] Strictly speaking, there is a good deal of truth in this statement, at least when it comes to evidence of solstice celebrations by the ancient Celts, Teutonic tribes, and the Norse. (There is actually a good deal of evidence of solstice celebrations by the pagans of ancient Rome.) But although Flanders is technically correct in pointing to a paucity of verifiable information about early pagan winter solstice celebrations, including those of the Norse and Celts, there is indeed *some* information, and the best we can do is use what we know to draw reasonable conclusions. At the same time, of course, it is important to exercise caution and diligence to avoid overstating—or simplifying—certain claims.

This tendency of exaggeration and simplification can be all too common in sources on the internet that make bold claims without solid proof to back them up and can unfortunately be seen on both sides of the debate. One typical article, titled "Christmas Isn't Christian," contends that Jesus was born in the springtime, and that Christian missionaries, who were "fascinated by the rural, rustic pagan traditions," simply gave pagan holidays such as Yule and Saturnalia "a makeover" as a way to "appease and convert pagans who were deeply, spiritually attached to their own holidays."[3] Another piece, at *History of Yesterday*, claims that the Norse celebrated Yule "around the 21st of December," when "fathers and sons would bring home evergreens" and "families would sit together in a fire both for warmth and as a ritual for good fortune come spring."[4] While some of these claims may well be true, it must be acknowledged that an examination of the historical record provides little in the way of proof to back them up. In some cases, the actual data directly contradicts some of the assertions, such as the date of the pre–Christian Yule celebration, for example.

Other dubious claims relate to Santa Claus being a representation of the Norse god Odin, while the actual history is far more nuanced. As an article by Judith Gabriel Vinje at *The Norwegian American* confidently declares, Odin and his eight-legged horse Sleipnir provided the basis for the modern Santa Claus myth. "Clement C. Moore replaced Sleipnir with eight flying reindeer in his 18th-century poem, and the image stuck," she states without any real evidence to bolster the assertion.[5] These sorts of unsubstantiated statements, even if they are not completely baseless, can lead to widespread misunderstanding and often have the appearance of being more the stuff of urban legend than actual history—opening up the whole line of inquiry to ridicule and dismissal. As Nick Page puts it in his book *Christmas: Tradition, Truth and Total Baubles*, "Time and again, we are told that Christmas customs are really pagan—or even pre–Christian—practices," but "an investigation of the facts shows no actual line of connection between the pagan past and the pagan-but-in-a-different-way present."[6]

Some Christians meanwhile deny the pagan origins of Christmas altogether, pushing back on the claims that the date of Jesus's birth was chosen simply because it was already being celebrated by pagans. Skeptics of this theory point out that no direct evidence has ever been produced indicating that Christmas was derived from these sources and offer countervailing justifications for the selection of December 25 as grounded in Christian doctrine. As Kurt Simmons writes in the *Journal of the Evangelical Theological Society*, "The whole theory rests upon inference and the unhappy history and reputation of the Roman Catholic Church vis-à-vis accommodating and appropriating pagan traditions." He notes that claims of Christmas's pagan origins have been around since the Reformation, but so far not a single piece of documentary evidence—no epistle, historical account, or decree by council—has ever been uncovered that establishes this as fact.[7]

Instead, Christians point to evidence that the date was selected for purely ecclesiastical reasons. An article at the website *The Good Shepherd* by Father Geoff Harvey offers the Christian argument for celebrating the nativity on December 25, insisting that there is no relationship at all to the winter solstice or pre-existing Roman holidays. "People pushing the pagan conspiracy theory argue that December 25 is the date of a pagan festival," Harvey writes. "But they never bother to explore the series of Christian dates from which December 25 is derived."[8]

The date of birth of Jesus is central to the argument of Christian defenders of the holiday's ecclesiastical origins, with several explanations offered as to why early

Church leaders chose December 25 independently of pre-existing pagan observances. Essentially, the argument goes, the date of December 25 is derived from the date of Jesus's conception, with various calculations made to arrive at this date offered in the third century by early Christian writers such as Irenaeus, Hippolytus, and Sextus Julius Africanus. Writing in the Catholic magazine *Inside the Vatican*, for example, Hugh O'Donnell acknowledges that pre-existing pagan festivities may have served as a catalyst for certain Christmas traditions, but nevertheless argues that the selection of the feast for this day had a firm basis in Christian theology. He cites St. Hippolytus who noted in 202 CE: "For the first advent of our Lord in the flesh, when he was born in Bethlehem, was December 25th, a Wednesday." The method for calculating this date was apparently by working backwards from the date of Christ's death. Based on details in the Gospels, Christ is believed to have died in the middle of the Jewish month of Nissan, and according to the calculations of Tertullian, a contemporary of Hippolytus, this day would have been in late March—approximately nine months before December 25. "The importance of Christ's death in correlation to his birth is revealed by another ancient tradition: that Christ was conceived and crucified on the same calendar day," O'Donnell writes. "It was a common belief that the Messiah fulfilled his mission on the anniversary of its inception."[9]

Another view suggests that December 25 became the date of nativity by reasoning that identified the spring equinox as the date of the creation of the world and the fourth day of creation, when the light was created, i.e., March 25, as the day of Jesus's conception.[10] Essentially, the world was thought to be created by God at the spring equinox, so therefore this must also be the date of conception, with the nativity naturally following nine months later.

But while these religious arguments might help convince the faithful that the reasons for selecting December 25 are actually rooted in Christian doctrines, for historians the story is problematic on a number of levels. For one thing, it requires the suspension of critical thinking to accept the claim that the calculation for December 25 was made for purely theological reasons and had nothing to do whatsoever with the fact that this date coincided with a popular pagan holiday. It would be one of the greatest historical coincidences that a humble religion competing with well-established and long-cherished traditions such as Saturnalia just happened to choose the same date for one of its main feast days out of pure happenstance.

This would also require ignoring evidence that early Church leaders were in fact preoccupied with pagan traditions such as Saturnalia and were anxious about how these holidays could provide an obstacle towards building the Christian faith. Tertullian, a prolific Christian author who advanced the notion that Jesus was born on December 25, lamented in 230 CE—a century before the first official Christmas observance—that the pagans' adherence to their traditions contrasted markedly with the lack of similar devotion demonstrated by the Christian faithful. "By us, to whom Sabbaths are strange," he wrote, "and the new moons and festivals formerly beloved by God, the Saturnalia and New Year's and Midwinter's festivals and Matronalia are frequented, presents come and go, New Year's gifts, games join their noise, banquets join their din! Oh better fidelity of the nations to their own sect, which claims no solemnity of the Christians for itself! Not the Lord's day, not Pentecost, even it they had known them, would they have shared with us; for they would fear lest they should seem to be Christians."[11] These concerns, openly expressed by early Church leaders regarding the popularity of heathen festivals, indicate that there was at least a motive to replace pagan festivals with Christian ones.

A sermon by early Church Father John Chrysostom, titled "On the solstice and equinox of the conception and birth of Our Lord Jesus Christ and John the Baptist," also provided a hint of the threat to Christian doctrines posed by the Roman holiday of Dies Natalis Solis Invicti, or birthday of the invincible sun, celebrated on December 25. "They also call this the birthday of the invincible one (Invictus)," fretted Chrysostom. "But who then is as invincible as our lord who defeated the death he suffered? And if they say that this is the birthday of the sun, well He Himself is the Sun of Righteousness."[12]

As these accounts make clear, there is no doubt that the early Church leaders who designated December 25 as Christ's nativity were fully aware of this day's significance in the cult of Sol Invictus and were generally concerned with the popularity of Roman pagan customs such as Saturnalia. As Steven Hijmans, a professor of Roman art and archaeology, has asked, "the question is whether they chose it because of or despite that pagan significance." Noting that the two most likely possibilities are that the early Church chose December 25 either to emphasize the incarnation of Christ (as opposed to his baptism date on January 6), which would make it primarily an intra-Christian polemical move, or that it was an inter-faith power play to co-opt an important date on the pagan calendar, Hijmans concludes that "it is obvious that the nature of the pagan feast in honour of Sol which is recorded for December 25 will have played some role in the considerations."[13]

It should also be pointed out that while Christians may now hold up the writings of Irenaeus, Hippolytus, and Sextus Julius Africanus in their efforts to debunk the "conspiracy theory" that December 25 was chosen in order to co-opt a pre-existing celebration, these three writers were only a handful of early Church leaders to offer

Icon depicting Emperor Constantine, who converted the Roman Empire to Christianity in the early fourth century, accompanied by the bishops of the First Council of Nicaea. Artist unknown.

possible dates of Jesus's birth. As historian Clement Miles explained in his classic 1912 work *Christmas Customs and Traditions*, "there is not a single month in the year to which the Nativity has not been assigned by some writer or other" and December 25 "is only one of various guesses of early Christian writers."[14]

This reality was alluded to by American Puritan clergyman Increase Mather in his 1687 screed against Christmas, published as *A testimony against several prophane and superstitious customs now practised by some in New-England the evil whereof is evinced from the Holy Scriptures and from the writings both of ancient and modern divines*. In this pamphlet he notes that "the particular Day of Christs Nativity is now unknown unto the world, yet it seems most probable that He was born in the latter End of September, or in the beginning of October." Pointing out that "[t]here hath been great Variety of Opinions amongst Christians concerning the time of our Lords Nativity," he highlights several of the most well-known estimations, including those of Paulus de Middleburgo who placed the date at March 26, Clemens Alexandrinus who believed it was on April 22, and others who placed it at May 22 or the beginning of November.[15] Providing a hint of the inherent difficulty in establishing an agreed upon date, to this day the Eastern Orthodox Church recognizes the date of Jesus's birth on January 7 instead of December 25.

The fact that there were so many different approximations of Jesus's birthday is one reason that the nativity was not recognized until three and a half centuries after he was born. Besides the fact that they generally didn't place much emphasis on birthdays, even if they wanted to the early Christians could not celebrate it because they couldn't agree on the date. But if they were truly attempting to establish an honest approximation of Jesus's birth based on information available in Scripture, it must be asked, why would they work backwards from the crucifixion? Why wouldn't they look at the actual clues offered by the two nativity accounts in the Gospels, as scholars have done over the centuries? This would be the most logical approach if they were genuinely interested in attempting to pinpoint the time of year of Jesus's birth and if they did, they might have come to a different conclusion.

* * *

Historians and archaeologists have long sought to follow the evidence to determine when Jesus was actually born. There is earnest disagreement about the most likely time of year, but there does seem to be near universal consensus that it was not at the end of December. The Gospels are the primary sources of historical information about Jesus, and despite the fact that they were written well after his crucifixion, they are generally considered useful by scholars as a historical guide. "The category of testimony is probably the most useful way to think of the kind of material we read in the Gospels," writes biblical scholar Richard Bauckman.[16] This doesn't mean that everything in the Gospels should be taken at face value, but that is not how historians assess historical documents in any case, Bauckman explains. Since it is never possible to verify every aspect of what someone claims, historians look for reasons for trusting or distrusting sources and assessing whether testimony is trustworthy or not, and ultimately there is enough reason to consider many of the accounts in the Gospels to have historical value.

The Gospels, written over a period of four decades in the first and second centuries by several followers of Jesus, offer some contradictory details but also share a good deal of general information, much of which has been subsequently confirmed by archaeological finds. The cities of Capernaum, Chorazin, Tiberias and Bethsaida, for example, which were described in the Gospels but then lost to history for centuries, have since been rediscovered, some quite recently. Bethsaida, home of the apostles Peter, Andrew and Philip, was only excavated in 2017.[17]

The nativity accounts of Jesus come from the Gospels according to Matthew and Luke, which differ in some ways from each other, but do share consistent elements. Notably, both claim that Jesus was born under the Judean king Herod the Great in Bethlehem and his birth was a virgin birth conceived by the Holy Spirit. As for the time of year, however, there are just a few clues to follow. The Gospel of Luke says that Joseph and Mary traveled from Nazareth, where they lived, to Joseph's hometown of Bethlehem to register in a Roman census, and it was there that the baby Jesus was born. As written in Luke's Gospel: "And she gave birth to her firstborn, a Son. She wrapped Him in swaddling cloths and laid Him in a manger, because there was no room for them in the inn. And there were shepherds residing in the fields nearby, keeping watch over their flocks by night. Just then an angel of the Lord stood before them, and the glory of the Lord shone around them, and they were terrified."

There are a number of anomalies in this story, as has been widely documented by historians. For one thing, although there was a census taken in the year six CE, this was a decade after the death of Herod. There is also no record of any requirement for people to return to their place of birth to be counted, and furthermore, only the head of household was required to register with the censor, which means it was probably unnecessary for the very pregnant Mary to ride a donkey 70 miles from Nazareth to Bethlehem.[18] What's more, these censuses, which were deemed important by the Roman authorities for levying taxes, only enumerated property owners, so even if they had been compelled to return to Bethlehem, Joseph and his wife logically would have lodged at his property rather than in a stable.[19]

These anomalies suggest that Luke and Matthew, writing decades after the events, did not have first-hand knowledge of the birth and may have been embellishing the story to provide a reason for Jesus being born in Bethlehem rather than Nazareth. The reason for doing this was that Bethlehem had significance in ancient religious Hebrew writings by the Israelites as the future birthplace of the Messiah. Luke's account of the census might have been something of a "plot device" to place the birth of Jesus in Bethlehem in order to fulfill the ancient prophecy of Micah. The inconsistencies in the story, revealing a lack of a firm grasp of the historical facts, may also explain why the details about the time of year of Jesus's birth were left out. Considering that the Gospel writers were unclear about the year of the birth and perhaps even where the birth took place, it is no wonder that they wouldn't offer a specific date or month.

But if we were to accept the general premises of the nativity story, as Christians generally do, we would have to conclude that the birth most likely did not take place on December 25. It is unlikely that his parents would have gone to Bethlehem to register in a census in December, because Roman authorities didn't take censuses during winter, when temperatures often dropped below freezing and roads were in poor condition. Scholars have also pointed out that since December is cold and rainy in Judea, the shepherds probably would have sought shelter for their animals rather than "keeping watch over their flocks by night." As archaeologist and biblical scholar

Jim Fleming has noted, shepherds' flocks may not have even been permitted on fields after they were plowed in October or November to allow the winter rains to soak into the parched ground. Shepherds were encouraged to graze their sheep before autumn to eat the stubble of sown crops and fertilize the fields, suggesting that—if the account in the Gospel of Luke is any guide—Jesus was probably born in summer or early fall.[20]

Neopagans, atheists and secularists have seized on this history and extrapolated from it that December 25 was chosen specifically in order to replace pre-existing pagan celebrations of Saturnalia and Yule. But to be fair, just because Jesus's birthday is more likely to be August 25 than December 25, it should be acknowledged that this does not necessarily mean that the date for Christmas was picked solely to appropriate solstice celebrations, or because the Persian god Mithras and the Roman god Sol Invictus had previously been celebrated on this date. Although it does appear that early Church leaders were attempting to supplant Roman celebrations and provide Christians in Rome with an ecclesiastical rationale for participating in traditions of revelry and gift-giving, ultimately their motives are unknown. Moreover, in other parts of Europe, the date of midwinter festivals may not have always taken place in late December, as is widely assumed.

It appears, for example, that the ancient Nordic celebrations of Yule (the precursor of Christmas in Scandinavia) may not have coincided neatly with the winter solstice. Venerable Bede, an eighth-century Anglo-Saxon scholar, diligently recorded the calendar as kept by pagans living in Denmark.[21] He notes that the Danes began the year on the "8th kalends of January," which according to the Latin calendar was December 25, "when we celebrate the birth of the Lord." Each season consisted of three months when it was a common year, Bede explains, but when an embolismic year occurred, i.e., when there were 13 lunar months, the extra month was assigned to summer. Building off of Bede's observations, in 2006 Swedish archaeologist Andreas Nordberg published *Yule, Disthing and pre–Julian Time-Reckoning*, which demonstrated that it is possible to reconstruct the old lunar-solar system fairly precisely. Based on his model, Nordberg argues that the celebration of Yule in pre–Christian times would not have fallen at the same time every year. Because the annual cycle was divided by seasons, the calculating of which was based around the lunar-solar calendar, the nature and timing of annual festivals and celebrations would have varied from year to year, with the pre–Christian Yule feast occurring at the first full moon after the first new moon following the winter solstice. This would put the celebration alternatively at sometime in January or February.[22]

If this is true, then it appears that the reason for Scandinavians celebrating Yule in late December probably had more to do with adapting to the established celebration of Christmas during Christianization. This, of course, doesn't mean that pre–Christian Yule customs didn't influence the celebration of Christmas, only that the fixing of the date at December 25 was an adaptation these pagans likely borrowed from Christians rather than the other way around.

Ultimately, in dealing with questions related to ancient history, particularly when they pertain to relatively illiterate cultures, there is necessarily much left to speculation and logical deduction. This can be frustrating at times, particularly in our smartphone-dominated culture of immediate answers and easily accessible information. People tend to prefer simple explanations to their questions, which is one reason the myth of Jesus being born on December 25 is so widely believed in the first place. When children ask their parents why Christmas is celebrated on this date (or when their parents ask Google or Siri), it is far simpler to say that this is the birthday of Jesus Christ than it is to get into a lengthy explanation of ancient pagan rituals that were absorbed by the Church in the fourth century. Likewise, those who reject

This etching represents a mosaic from the Santa Maria Assunta Cathedral in Aosta, Italy, depicting the months of the year. In the center is a figure labeled "Annus," or "year," holding two spheres marked "Sol" and "Luna," or "sun," and "moon." The yearly cycle is depicted as circular and marked by anthropomorphized months. Etching by C. Martel after E. Aubert (Wellcome Collection).

the traditional Christian narrative of Christmas may opt instead for simple, alternative explanations regarding pagan celebrations of the winter solstice. The truth, however, is not always so neat and tidy, and the nature of the decision to replace pagan traditions with Christian traditions might not conform with commonly held assumptions. When some people imagine how the decision was made by early Church leaders to designate December 25 as Christmas, for example, they might picture some men sitting around a table hatching a plan for eliminating pagan celebrations of gods such as Sol and Saturn in order to eradicate polytheism and replace it with the Christian faith.

It is possible, however, that the beliefs of polytheists and Christians were not actually so diametrically opposed, and that the nature of supplanting paganism with Christianity was less of a hostile takeover than it was a natural evolution. This more nuanced view can be appreciated by looking more closely at the way that the sun is viewed in both Christianity and paganism, and more generally how much importance was attached to the role of astral bodies in the ancient world.

* * *

Believed to influence the growth of crops and to govern human affairs, the sun, moon, planets and stars were studied with great care by the ancients. The sun was revered as both a cosmic body and as a god, playing an ambiguous but important symbolic role in both the polytheistic religion of Roman pagans and the monotheistic religion of early Christians. This, ultimately, could explain why both of these belief systems attached importance to celestial events such as the equinox and solstice, offering some context both for pagans' solstice celebrations and the calculations of early Church leaders debating Jesus's birthday. There are at least 80 references to the sun contained in the Bible,[23] both in the Old Testament and New, with passages such as Psalm 113:3 which reads, "From the rising of the sun to its setting, the name of the Lord is to be praised!" According to Psalm 84:11, "the Lord God is a sun and shield; the Lord bestows favor and honor." Matthew 14:33 states that "the righteous will shine like the sun in the kingdom of their Father."

As the birthday of various sun gods, the date of December 25 should not be seen in isolation or as something unique to either pagans or Christians, but as part of a cosmic-symbolic system. Not unlike the connections pagans drew between the winter solstice and their sun gods, who naturally would have manifested on the day the sun "died" and was "reborn," the birth of Jesus was also likened by the early Christians to the rising of a sun, or as referred to by the prophecy of Malachi, the "Sun of Righteousness." This was alluded to in a Christmas Day sermon in the late fourth century by Church Father John Chrysostom, who asked his congregants to imagine the glory of Christ's birth, comparing it to "the sun coming down from the heavens, running on the earth and sending out its beams on everybody from here." To have witnessed the birth of Jesus, he said, was "to see the sun of righteousness sending out beams from our own flesh and illuminating our souls."[24] An indication of Jesus's symbolism as representing the sun can also be found in early images of Jesus that bear a striking resemblance to the sun gods Helios, Apollo and Sol Invictus of Greco-Roman mythology.[25]

Clearly, the sun, as both a celestial body and a symbol of divine righteousness, holds great importance in the belief systems of both paganism and Christianity, and

Jesus depicted as the sun is a common motif in Christian art. In this artwork, from late 15th-century Germany, the Christ child and Virgin Mary are surrounded by billowing rays of sun. The image refers to a passage from the Book of Revelation, which reads, "And a great sign appeared in heaven: A woman clothed with the sun, and the moon under her feet, and on her head a crown of twelve stars." Artist unknown. Germany, late 15th century (J. Paul Getty Museum).

this ultimately may be why December 25 was selected as Jesus's birthday despite the accounts in the Gospels suggesting a birth in summer instead. As the 20th-century theologian Frank Homer Curtiss explained, "there was a fundamental and scientific reason to adopt December 25th as the date, for it is the date of the birth of the physical Lightbringer in Nature, the Sun. And since Jesus is the spiritual Lightbringer or the manifestation of the Spiritual Sun to humanity, the day of his birth should very properly be celebrated on the solar date of the Sun's birth, as was the case with all previous Lightbringers."[26]

The sun's symbolic significance and its actual importance as the giver of life is ultimately why it has been celebrated by so many different religions, and why early

Christian writers attributed prominence to the spring equinox as the time of Jesus's divine conception and the winter solstice as the time of his birth. In this sense, establishing December 25 as Jesus's birthday was logical from both an ecclesiastical and a practical perspective, and therefore the arguments over precisely why the early Church decided on this date are somewhat off-base. While it may very well have been a shrewd political play to help replace pre-existing traditions and draw pagans into the new faith, it also held significance in Christian theological thought, and therefore the either-or approach that many people take in addressing this issue is not the best way to understand it. Instead, it is more likely that the early Christians—taking cues from both the Bible and Greco-Roman mythology—attached the same sort of cosmic symbolism to the sun and other celestial bodies that pagans did. This symbology was central to their ancient understanding of the universe and its cosmic patterns of time, space, heaven and earth, with the winter solstice playing an integral role.

But of course, this more charitable explanation for why the early Church settled on December 25 doesn't change the fact that the date already held significance as a holiday that would eventually come to be supplanted by Christians' observance of the nativity.

2

In Search of the First Christmas

Through our great gate at Pompeii, at the third hour of the day,
The slaves run, leaping, dancing, in frolicsome array,
Some playing flutes, some shaking wands, or clicking horny thumbs,
Because at last the winter feast, the reign of Saturn comes.
  —Walter Thornbury, "The Saturnalia"

The designation of "the first Christmas" is typically bestowed on the story of the nativity—the day that Jesus was born and the subsequent days when the magi came to pay homage. A 2009 book, for example, *The First Christmas: What the Gospels Really Teach About Jesus's Birth*, tells the Christmas story through the eyes of Matthew and Luke, exploring religious themes such as Jesus's birth as a fulfillment of prophecy and the spiritual meaning of the Gospels. There is also a 1998 claymation short film depicting the birth of Jesus Christ by the name of "The First Christmas," a 2005 live-action film by the same name, and countless children's books that also use this title. Invariably, these accounts of the first Christmas tell the story of a virgin birth in a stable in Bethlehem, with Joseph and Mary in the main roles and a cast of supporting characters of shepherds, kings, donkeys, cattle, sheep.

But is this accurate? Can we really call the birth of Jesus "the first Christmas"? After all, many of the traditions associated with Christmas precede Jesus's birth, the date of which was not even agreed upon until hundreds of years later. With this in mind, perhaps it would be more accurate to look further back in time for the story of the first Christmas, back to ancient pagan celebrations of the winter solstice that were later absorbed into the observance of the nativity. But of course, these festivals can't really be considered "Christmas" because they went by other names and didn't contain the Christian elements that are so integral to the holiday. In that case, perhaps it would make sense to skip ahead a few hundred years after the birth of Jesus when the Church finally decided on a date to observe the event, or perhaps, a thousand years after his birth when the holiday received its name. But then again, those early observances would likely be unrecognizable to modern eyes as "Christmas" because they didn't contain all the fundamental ingredients that we consider necessary for the holiday.

So, would it make more sense, perhaps, to place "the first Christmas" sometime in the modern era, when it finally evolved into the holiday as we recognize it today? This is the approach taken by the makers of a 2017 movie, *The Man Who Invented Christmas*, a biopic about Charles Dickens who is credited with launching our modern holiday. But not to diminish the role of Dickens in cementing the humanitarian impulses of goodwill and charity that have come to characterize Christmas at its best, is it fair to say he "invented" it when so many came before him who also contributed to establishing the holiday by writing hymns and carols, for example? Or what about his contemporaries who established the Santa Claus myth? After all, is it really Christmas without Santa Claus?

What these questions bring to mind is that the concept of Christmas is malleable and that its definition depends very much on one's perspective on what the holiday's fundamental elements are. Notwithstanding the many stories and films that confidently declare the birth of Jesus as "the first Christmas," as if it all started the day that Mary gave birth in a stable in the year zero and simply grew from there, actually there is no clear point of departure for the holiday. Christmas was not established in a linear fashion with a logical progression and growth stemming from any single event—with the magi initiating the practice of gift-giving and other customs and traditions developing organically along the way—but rather, developed from many different cultural and spiritual strains over the period of a couple millennia. Therefore, it may ultimately be ahistorical to even use the term "first Christmas" at all.

When considering the context in which Christmas was established as a Christian feast in the fourth century, it is worth remembering that Christianity's growth from a minor religious sect to a major religion took hundreds of years and the religion that ultimately established the Christmas holiday bore little resemblance to the religion of the previous three centuries—when the faith may not have even had a name and was practiced by its adherents at great personal risk and largely in secret.[1]

As a religious community, the early Christians lacked the arts of drama and celebration that other faiths enjoyed. There was no such thing as Christian poetry, architecture, painting, art, music, and dance that had served to establish the older faith as both a belief system and rich cultural milieu.[2] In fact, in ancient Rome, Christians were considered criminals and lived beneath the city in Catacombs that were shared with escaped slaves and gladiators. As Rome's most despised religious outlaws, the early Christians kept a low profile and would not have brought attention to themselves through outward displays of worship, such as celebrating the birth of Christ. They may have even participated in pagan celebrations to avoid detection as Tertullian alluded to in the early third century. Christians, he wrote in *On Idolatry*, have "induced the belief in their mind that it is pardonable if at any time they do what the heathen do." Providing rationales for frequenting the Saturnalia and midwinter festivals, Tertullian says, "[t]o live with heathens is lawful, to die with them is not."[3]

The cautiousness of early Christians even extended to how they communicated with each other, avoiding obvious symbols such as the crucifix or writing in Latin, and instead using a range of cryptic signs that they would paint on the Catacombs walls such as stylized fish and symbols that secretly spelled out prayers. The obscure symbols would help other Christians find their way through the dark labyrinth and, it was hoped, help to spread the faith.[4]

One of the main sources of conflict at the time between Christians and Roman pagans was their different approaches to religious tolerance and the Christians' perceived lack of respect for pagan beliefs. Pagans, despite their reputation for persecuting Christians, were generally rather tolerant of other faiths. Romans regularly welcomed new cults devoted to foreign or newly discovered deities, as long as these cults were approved by the Senate, didn't break the law or cause too much disturbance. The only religion that was not tolerated was Christianity, and this was due to the fact that the Christians were seen as hostile to the entire premise upon which the Roman religious system depended: respect for pagan gods. The point of contention when it came to Christians was how they cast all spiritual beings except God and his servants as forces of evil, with this hostility even extending to a refusal to recognize the emperor's divinity. This refusal to honor the emperor was viewed by most Romans as a forfeiture of rights as citizens of the Roman state.[5]

Because of their disrespect to the Roman pantheon, Christians were blamed for all disasters brought against the human race by the gods, so when a fire destroyed much of Rome in 64 CE, the Roman emperor Nero ordered that Christians be rounded up and executed.[6] This was the first recorded mass persecution of Christians, but it would be far from the last. Persecutions took place sporadically throughout the first three centuries of Christianity, until the conversion of the emperor Constantine to Christianity in 312 CE. This event had a profound impact, with legitimacy immediately bestowed on the faith along with significant and previously unknown privileges to its practitioners. The following year, Constantine issued the Edict of Milan, which granted legal status to Christianity, and ten years later, the Roman Empire adopted Christianity as its official religion. In 336, a Roman bishop noted: "25 Dec.: natus Christus in Betleem Judeae" or "December 25, Christ born in Bethlehem, Judea." This day, December 25, 336, is the first recorded celebration of Christmas, but it would take another decade and a half to make it official.[7] Pope Julius I declared December 25 a nativity celebration around the year 350—three and a half centuries after Jesus was born—and in the Codex of 354, the Church year was marked as beginning on the date of December 25.[8]

As Rome began to recognize the nativity on December 25, other centers of Christianity resisted the festival and only grudgingly began to accept the designation of Jesus's birthday. It wasn't observed in Constantinople until 373, more than 40 years after the city became the site of Emperor Constantine's "New Rome." Antioch, the second oldest Christian center after Jerusalem, first observed Christmas in 376. A decade later, it was still far from accepted by all Christians, with stiff opposition to the holiday in eastern Christendom.[9] Even when churches accepted the premise of observing the festival, they often continued to dispute the date. In 386, the date for observing Christ's birth was January 6 in Bethlehem, and at the end of the fourth century, Epiphanius, the bishop of Salamis, argued that January 6 is Christ's "Birthday; that is, His Epiphany."[10] In the fifth century, the feast was still repudiated in Egypt because it was believed that a single festival—Epiphany—should mark the Lord's nativity and baptism on the same day. It was not until the middle of the fifth century that most churches—with a few notable exceptions, such as the church of Armenia—accepted December 25 as the day of the nativity.[11]

So, for the first several centuries of Christianity, Christmas did not exist. This is because early Christians were focused more on spreading the gospel and initially were reluctant to place emphasis on birthdays—not even the birth of Christ. Most early Christians seem to have followed the thinking of Frater Origen, a Church Father who in 245 CE denounced the celebration of Jesus's birth "[a]s if He were a King Pharaoh."[12] As the 1911 edition of *The Catholic Encyclopedia* explained, "In the Scriptures, no one is recorded to have kept a feast or held a great banquet on his birthday. It is only sinners like Pharaoh and Herod who make great rejoicings over the day in which they were born into this world."[13] The day of martyrdom held more significance to early Christian believers, as it ushered him or her into the kingdom of heaven, so more attention was given to observing Jesus's crucifixion and resurrection through Easter and Ascension feasts. In contrast to the dearth of information about early nativity celebrations, evidence for the celebration of Easter begins to appear in the mid-second century,[14] a full 200 years before the first Christmas observance. However, because early Christian scholars determined that they could not pinpoint the exact date of Jesus's resurrection, Easter has been marked over the centuries at different times within a five-week span in the spring.[15]

Considering the difficulty in establishing the nativity as a Christian feast, a process marked by doubt and disagreement within the Church and initial hesitancy among the people to observe it, it's worth stepping back to examine more closely the social and religious context in which Christianity and Christmas emerged. This context helps explain the foundational basis for the rise of Christmas as a cultural phenomenon.

* * *

The society in which Christianity emerged was characterized by extreme class divisions. The rich in ancient Rome lived in beautiful houses—often on the hills

This 19th-century painting by Roberto Bompiani illustrates a Roman feast, conveying their opulence and extravagance. Note the greenery that adorns the walls. "A Roman Feast." Artist Roberto Bompiani. Oil on canvas (J. Paul Getty Museum).

outside of the city, away from the noise and smell, frequently holding lavish dinner parties and serving their guests the exotic dishes of the day. They enjoyed an extravagant lifestyle with luxurious furnishings, surrounded by servants and slaves to cater to their every desire.[16] Although some upper-class homes had only a few slaves, others boasted up to several dozen, many of whom were highly specialized, serving as administrators, domestics, personal attendants, entertainers, and manual laborers. Subsisting on the most meager provisions, slaves spent countless hours night after night serving extravagant dishes in extended dining sessions.[17] Slaves were routinely abused and cruelly punished for the most minor infractions, such as sneezing or preparing food that wasn't satisfactory, so they lived in a perpetual state of unease, knowing that at any moment they could be subject to violence at the hands of their masters. Domestic slave labor was geared towards meeting the slaveholders' desires and the slave was always vulnerable to the master's exercise of power.[18]

Free-born lower-class Romans, while enjoying more rights than slaves, also had it pretty rough. They endured squalor in crowded, crime-ridden neighborhoods, living in shabby houses infested with vermin, in constant fear of disease and fire. Destitute families would often leave newborn babies on the streets, in the hopes that someone would take them in as a servant or slave. The plebeians forgot their troubles by enjoying the popular entertainment of the time—chariot races and gladiator fights to the death—and by savoring the many days of respite offered by the ruling class. It has been estimated that there were over 100 days a year set aside for holidays and religious festivals, which helped to keep the mob mollified and to prevent trouble from erupting.[19]

The most popular of these holidays was Saturnalia, which is said to be derived from older farming-related rituals of midwinter. Originally a celebration of the bounty of the harvest while pacifying the darkness of winter with revelries and games, Saturnalia officially was marked on December 17 and, in Cicero's time, lasted seven days, limited by Augustus to three days but then extended by Caligula to five. During this period, Roman social norms were turned on their head, and for the period of festivities, criminals could not be convicted, nor wars started. The celebration of Saturnalia coincided with other observances around the same time: the celebration of the solstice, Dies Natalis Solis Invicti, Opalia, and Kalends, which marked the beginning of the new year.

Occurring in quick succession, the holidays generally merged together, and it may have been difficult to say when one ended and the other began. The celebration of the winter solstice appears to have been influenced by the spread of Mithraism in the first century from the Middle East to the Roman Empire, and came to represent the birth of Mithras, but by the third century, Sol Invictus had become the central god of the empire.[20] Following the Battle of Emesa against Zenobia in 272 CE, where troops had been inspired by a "divine form" believed to be Sol, Emperor Aurelian returned to Rome triumphantly and erected a magnificent temple to the god. A new college of pontiffs was established to serve the god, who was to be the supreme deity of Rome, and Dies Natalis his main festival. Meaning "the birthday of the Unconquered Sun," the festival celebrated both the sun god and the winter solstice—in which the sun stops moving south, when it was believed to "die," and then "returned to life" when it begins its journey north again.

This was also a time for worshipping Saturn, the god of seed-sowing and wealth.

2. In Search of the First Christmas 27

REGIONES			CIVITATES
Æmilia, Alpes, Apulia, Bohemia, Calabria, Gallia, Italia, Phœnicia Sabina, Sicilia, Thracia.	Sidera per duodena regit Sol aureus orbem. Cavior at reliquis illi Leo flammiger. Alpes, Et regit Italiam, Siculos, Apulosq; Bohemos, Phœnissas gentes, Apamenaq; rura, Sabinos.	Æmiliam, Orchiniam, et vallatæ mœnia Romæ, Acq; Syracusas, ↄↄↄ Stagna vadosa Ravennæ, Ille noua imperya, et magna cum laude triumphos Claraq; constituet deuicto ex hoste Tropæa.	Confluentes, Cremona, Damasc: ena, Lingona, Praga, Ravenna, Roma, Syracusa, Ulma.

This illustration, a 16th-century engraving by Johannes Sadeler, depicts Saturn presiding over his Golden Age. "Saturn," ca. 1585 (Los Angeles County Museum of Art, Mary Stansbury Ruiz Bequest).

Possibly a version of the Greek god Kronos as well as the Punic deity Baal, Saturn was thought to have ruled when the world enjoyed a Golden Age of prosperity and was believed to have taught important agricultural skills to men. Saturn was the husband of Ops, the Roman goddess of sowing and harvest, and the father of Jupiter, the god of the sky and thunder. Saturn's reign was considered a period of equality and universal happiness without sorrow, a time when neither slavery nor private property existed, until he was betrayed by Jupiter and deposed. But during the Saturnalia festival, which started with a public banquet at Saturn's temple on December 17, Saturn was again king.[21]

A Roman state official and Latin scribe named Macrobius, writing around 431 CE, offers some of the most detailed information about the holiday. In *The Saturnalia*, Macrobius provides an explanation for the varying lengths of the celebration. Originally, he explains, the festival was celebrated on only one day, but with the Julian reform of the calendar, two days were added to December, and since Saturnalia was celebrated 16 days before the Kalends "the result [was] that, since the exact day was not commonly known—some observing the addition which Caesar had made to the calendar and others following the old usage—the festival came to be regarded as lasting for more days than one." The original day then was given over to Opalia, honoring Ops. The two deities represented the produce of the fields and orchards and were also

This engraving was done as an illustration for the poem "The Saturnalia" by Walter Thornbury, appearing in *Once a Week* magazine in 1863. "The Saturnalia." Artist George John Pinwell, engraved by Joseph Swain (Internet Archive).

thought to represent heaven and earth. It was for this reason, says Macrobius, that the two festivals were celebrated at the same time.[22]

Saturnalia entailed a good deal of intoxication and included a practice in which masters and slaves switched roles. It was a time when "[l]icence is given to the general merrymaking," when "the whole mob has let itself go in pleasures" and "is drunk and vomiting," according to Seneca the Younger, a Roman philosopher, in his Moral Letters to Lucilius written in the mid-first century.[23] Citizens abandoned the usual toga in favor of more informal cloths, especially a brightly colored dinner suit called the synthesis. A feast, often lasting two or three days, was central to the celebration, with a variety of status inversion practices marking a temporary departure from social norms: masters would dine with their slaves, slaves would dine first after masters served them meals, the children of the house would entertain the slaves,[24] and gender roles were sometimes swapped.[25] Often wearing the traditional slave's hat, the pileus, masters would wait on their servants hand and foot,[26] and slaves had freedoms that otherwise were denied to them the rest of the year, including the freedom to speak freely and rebuke their masters with impunity. Freed from the decorum and deference to their social betters that they were otherwise expected to show at all times, slaves enjoyed their time playing games, gambling, eating and drinking.[27]

During Saturnalia, people made offerings of gifts to one another, especially clay dolls and candles symbolizing "life lights." Work and business came to a halt, with slaves enjoying some well-earned leisure time, and the wealthy were expected to pay the rent for those who couldn't afford it. People decorated their homes with wreaths and other greenery, and apparently sang songs in the nude, in a possible precursor of modern-day caroling. A mock "king" was chosen among friends, known as "Lord of Misrule," to lead in pranks, mischief, and merrymaking. As Lucian of Samosata (120–180 CE) wrote in his poem *Saturnalia*: "[T]he serious is barred; no business allowed. Drinking and being drunk, noise and games and dice, appointing of kings and feasting of slaves, singing naked, clapping of tremulous hands, an occasional ducking of corked faces in icy water—such are the functions."[28] According to Lucian, Saturnalia was a time to remember what life was like during the reign of Saturn, "when all things grew without sowing or plowing of theirs … and there were fountains of milk and honey; all men were good, and all men were gold." As the poet Catullus described it, Saturnalia was "the best of times."[29]

* * *

As administrators of a vast empire, the Romans would have brought Saturnalia traditions to other lands that they occupied and ruled, such as Britain following its conquest in the first century. Under the Roman occupation of England and Wales (and, for a short period, southern Scotland) from 43 to 410 CE, a distinctive Romano-British culture emerged as the Romans introduced improved agriculture, urban planning, industrial production, and architecture. They also brought the god Saturn and traditions of revelry and egalitarianism during Saturnalia.[30] During this holiday, Britons may have enjoyed some of the luxury foods the Romans introduced, such as figs, dates, pine nuts, and snails, and drunk imported wine.[31] Other Roman customs that found their way into British culture include social inversion and the practice of selecting a Lord of Misrule during Saturnalia celebrations, with this becoming a prominent feature of later Christmas observances in Britain.

Scandinavians, too, while never falling under Roman rule, often worked as mercenaries for the empire and brought back ideas, customs and objects from the Romans. According to archaeologists, there is evidence that Norse religions were influenced by the ancient Roman pantheon,[32] which for its part was influenced by other belief systems. Certain emperors were known to have particular passions for various foreign gods, with the ancient historian Tacitus relating how Vespasian was partial to the gods of Memphis while Nero worshiped the Syrian goddess Dea Syria, and Marcus Aurelius, Severus, Commodus, Caracalla, and Heliogabalus were followers of Isis, Serapis, and Mithras.[33] Indeed, Saturnalia itself may have been an adaptation of Carthaginian celebrations of Baal, resulting from the cultural exchanges that took place between Rome and Carthage as a result of the Second Punic War.[34] Essentially, there was a constant flow of information and views of the world, and just as eastern gods may have influenced the Roman pantheon, it is likely that Roman and Greek gods may have filtered into the Norse pantheon, along with some customs relating to the celebration of the winter solstice. As the German medieval chronicler Adam of Bremen described his visit to the temple of Uppsala in central Sweden, the gods worshipped by the Vikings bore striking resemblance to more familiar Roman gods. Odin, in particular, was depicted "as our people depict Mars," Adam notes, while Thor resembled the Roman god Jupiter.

The Roman pagan beliefs also influenced Christian practices, particularly during the fourth century when the religions briefly co-existed on a relatively equal basis. Following the transition to Christian rule, it appears that the pagan religious elements were firmly re-established with the text of the Codex-Calendar of 354 reflecting contemporary cult practices,[35] a trend that continued through the century. The calendar used a figure celebrating Saturnalia as the emblem for December—despite the fact that Pope Julius I had declared December 25 a nativity celebration four years earlier.[36] While continuing to recognize pagan feasts, the calendar did not list any Christian holidays, as they still did not hold any civic significance.[37] It wasn't until 529 that Christmas was declared a civic holiday, by Emperor Justinian,[38] and not until 567 that the 12 days from Christmas to Epiphany were declared a sacred and festive season.[39]

Meanwhile, imperial festivals continued to be held under the Christian emperors, who followed the same logic of pagan emperors of earlier centuries: they wanted their names, achievements and fortune associated with the social groups served by the festivals themselves. Indeed, the far greatest recipient of festivals was the emperor and his family. In the Codex-Calendar of 354, most *ludi* and *circenses*, i.e., the games and circuses, were devoted to honoring the imperial cult, which accounted for 98 days of celebrations. The remaining 69 days were devoted to holidays in honor of gods of the Greco-Roman pantheon,[40] with two Christian feasts coinciding with these pagan festivals. On February 22, the day of Caristia, a pagan tradition that honored family and ancestors with banqueting and gifts, a Christian feast was held called "Natale Petri de Cathedra," and on December 25 the nativity was recognized on the same day that a large number of chariot races were held in honor of Sol Invictus. These Christian festivals were exceptional since most others were concentrated between July and September and none occurred on the same day as any pagan celebrations.[41]

The Roman festival calendar was alternatively tolerated grudgingly by the early

Christian emperors, with the thriving ceremonial practices used by the Constantinian dynasty to promote its interests or modified in order to neutralize the pagan celebrations. This is particularly true from 375 to 400, when the laws of the emperors began to attack the temples and the beliefs of paganism on an unprecedentedly broad front,[42] while religious leaders emphasized to the faithful the solemn significance of the nativity.

Churches decided that the nativity deserved a preparatory period like Easter's Lent, and so in the late fourth century, they initiated Advent, first in northern Italy and then in Rome.[43] Advent had been proposed by church leaders at the Council of Saragossa, Spain, in 380, when they defined a 21-day period of fasting beginning on December 17, which of course, also happened to be the first day of the Saturnalia festival. It was also in the year 380 that Emperor Theodosius I signed a decree that punished the practice of pagan rituals.[44] As the Western churches elevated December 25 over January 6 (the date observed as Jesus's baptism), they launched the Midnight Mass tradition, the first of three separate Christmas masses, traditionally beginning at midnight when Christmas Eve gives way to Christmas Day.

In a Christmas Day sermon in 386 CE, Church Father John Chrysostom reminded his congregants that the birth of the Messiah was something "which long ago patriarchs painfully longed for, prophets foretold and the righteous set their hearts on." His sermon, titled "On the birthday of our Savior Jesus Christ, which was still unknown at the time, and was made known a few years ago by some believers who came from the West and announced it," emphasized that the nativity is the consummation of those ancient prophecies, "a day God was seen on earth through flesh and dwelt among humankind." Chrysostom urged the faithful to "rejoice with great gladness" and "be full of wonder and astonishment at the grandeur of God's plan which exceeds all thought."[45]

* * *

In recognition of Christians' opposition to ancient Rome's public games—events that could entail horse races or gladiator fights and were understood as part of the worship of the traditional gods—Emperor Theodosius restricted the games beginning with a series of laws in 392. First prohibiting the *ludi* on Sundays and then on holidays such as Christmas and Epiphany, the laws specifically stated that the prohibitions were implemented "out of respect for religion," i.e., the Christian religion.[46]

By the late fourth century, artistic representations of the nativity began to appear, with writers such as Ephrem the Syrian, Ambrose of Milan, and the Spanish layman Prudentius producing nativity poems, hymns, and prayers. Frescoes, wall paintings, and sarcophagi depicted nativity scenes, and when popular curiosity pressed for more answers about the nativity than the text of the Gospels provided, Church leaders filled in the details—giving the magi names and explaining their origins, for example.

But even as the Church endeavored to solidify the ecclesiastical basis for the nativity celebration and as Christmas took on nearly as much importance to Christians as Easter, Saturnalia continued to impact the Christmas feast, and bishops grew increasingly impatient with the excessive eating and drinking that characterized the period. Church leaders strove to develop the nativity observance as a distinctly Christian affair, but the influence of pagan traditions continued to deeply

This panel from a Roman sarcophagus, dating from the fourth century, depicts the Adoration of the Magi. It is located in the cemetery of St. Agnes in Rome. Artist unknown (Museo Pio Christiano, former museum of Benedict XIV).

affect the popular celebration. A Christian scribe named Scriptor Syrus noted in the late fourth century that pagans and Christians celebrated together on December 25. "It was a custom of the pagans to celebrate on the same December 25 the birthday of the sun," he wrote. "In these solemnities and revelries the Christians also took part."[47] Even when the Roman empire dropped the midwinter celebration as an official festival, Saturnalia survived by bestowing many of its elements to the celebration of Christmas.[48]

Just about half a century into the Christian feast, Bishop Asterius of Amasea complained how the customs of the Christmas season were blurred with the practices of Saturnalia and Kalends. In a New Year's sermon in the year 400, titled "On the Festival of the Calends," Asterius railed against gift-giving, which he warned corrupts the minds of the youth with greed and materialism. "This festival," he said, "teaches even the little children, artless and simple, to be greedy, and accustoms them to go from house to house and to offer novel gifts, fruits covered with silver tinsel. For these they receive in return gifts double their value, and thus the tender minds of the young begin to be impressed with that which is commercial and sordid."[49]

He also criticized elements of misrule and lamented how the festival "renders the city a place to be shunned rather than visited." Those who "are found within it are flogged, treated with drunken violence, what they have in their hands is snatched from them; they are warred upon in time of peace, are jeered at, and mocked with words and deeds." Asterius argued that the revelries should not be called "a feast" because they are "full of annoyance." "Going out-of-doors is burdensome," he said, "and staying within doors is not undisturbed. For the common vagrants and the jugglers of the stage, dividing themselves into squads and hordes, hang about every house." He complained in particular how public officials are "besieged with especial persistence," how revelers would shout and clap their hands until their target acquiesces and "throws out to them whatever money he has and even what is not his own." This goes on "until late in the evening [and] there is no relief from this nuisance. For crowd succeeds crowd, and shout, shout, and loss, loss."[50]

The debauched Roman pagan customs of Saturnalia continued for centuries after the official transition to Christmas took place. All the way into the eighth century, Church authorities were complaining that remnants of Saturnalia tainted the nativity celebration,[51] and the suppression of these customs was just one of many tasks that the Church viewed as priorities in its efforts to transform a pagan society into a Christian one.

The new Christian establishment turned its attention towards conversion of pagans beginning in the fifth century. Rome's urban and administrative elites had by and large adopted Christianity, mostly out of social and material expediency, but the population residing in the countryside, far from imperial control, maintained its pagan practices and required coercive measures. Pagans were persecuted with increasingly draconian force and although the rural population eventually converted, their pagan rituals were sometimes allowed to be assimilated into Christianity, enduring as both cultural and religious survivals.[52] Saturnalia was one of these survivals which continued to influence the secular revelry of Christmas and some newly converted Christians retained external symbols of sun worship on Christmas Day. According to writings of Saint Augustine and Pope Leo I, these transgressions were immediately rebuked and suppressed.[53]

Christians sought to eliminate pagan practices through legislation and coercion, with emperors issuing laws and imperial officials implementing them, aided by mobs that systematically attacked pagan holy sites and temples.[54] Perpetrators of anti-pagan violence were mostly young men who didn't share the commitment to nonviolence of earlier generations of Christians, considering some degree of force as justified in spreading the Good News of the coming of the Kingdom of God.

This meant that from the very beginning of Christianity's founding as the religious and political order of the Roman Empire, Christians and pagans were in conflict. The conflict played out in many ways, including in the observance of the Christmas feast, which became a push and pull between piety and revelry, with the Church striving to emphasize the solemnity of the occasion and the people continuing to celebrate in their old-fashioned ways.

Over the centuries this would continue to fundamentally impact the celebration of Christmas, with the development of the holiday loosely falling into two tracts: the "secular" traditions, influenced by pagan celebrations such as Saturnalia, and the "religious" traditions, influenced by Church teachings. This differentiation, however, was not always clear, and there was always a certain degree of overlap between the two.

3

Christmas in a Pagan World

Heap on more wood!—the wind is chill;
But let it whistle as it will,
We'll keep our Christmas merry still.
Each age has deem'd the new-born year
The fittest time for festal cheer:
Even, heathen yet, the savage Dane
At Iol more deep the mead did drain
   —Sir Walter Scott, "Old Christmastide"

Although Saturnalia, falling so precisely at the time of Christmas, is widely cited as the main inspiration for our modern holiday, it was not the only celebration marking the winter solstice. Christmas, like Christianity itself, developed within a pagan world, and in weighing the holiday's influences from pre–Christian cultures, it is important to keep in mind that Christianization did not take place in a vacuum. Christianity was just one of many competing belief systems, all of which had long-established customs, rituals and holidays, and before establishing itself as the dominant social, religious and political system of Europe, the adoption of Christianity was a very slow process, with much overlap between the old beliefs and the new. These old beliefs were influenced by the new one—as well as by each other—even as they influenced Christianity's development.

As the shortest day and longest night of the year, the solstice has long symbolized the sun's rebirth from the womb of darkness and has been recognized in various ancient cultures as Hökunótt, Lucina, Lenacea, Zurram, Dōngzhì Festival, Inti Raymi, Soyal, and Shab-e Yalda. In ancient Greece, the sea god Poseidon was celebrated around the time of the winter solstice,[1] while in the tradition of Modranicht, Old English for "Night of the Mothers," Anglo-Saxon pagans would celebrate on what is now Christmas Eve by offering sacrifices to the gods.[2] Modranicht was also observed in southern Denmark, as the scholar Venerable Bede recorded, noting that on December 25, "when we celebrate the birth of the Lord ... they used to call the heathen word Modranecht, that is 'mother's night,' because (we suspect) of the ceremonies they enacted that night."[3]

In central Italy, on December 24, the Nocturnal Procession of the 'Ndocciata celebrated the birth of the pagan sun god with a procession of farmers carrying tall fire torches and a bonfire lit in the main square of the town Agnone.[4] Romanians, meanwhile, would light cartwheels wrapped in straw and twigs at midwinter and roll them down hills, with youths running alongside them jingling bells and yelling:

"Look out, the fire wheels roll and roll / They bring good luck, rich store." The sparks from the burning wheels were believed to make the fields more fruitful.[5] The Chumash, a Native American people who inhabited coastal regions of California, performed rituals at the winter solstice to keep the spirit world in an equilibrium, with a shaman watching the sun each day as the solstice approached and ensuring that the people took necessary actions to honor the sun and harness its power.[6] Many peoples at the end of the year have an annual expulsion of ghosts, devils, and evil spirits, sometimes using fire and loud noise.[7]

In the British Isles, pre–Christian peoples made gifts at mid-winter and decked their homes and holy places with greenery, particularly holly and ivy. The ancient Celts considered holly sacred, and their priestly class, the druids, used it in healing the sick. It was widely used for ceremonial purposes before the Christian era, believed to repel evil spirits and protect houses from lighting. People adorned their barns and stables with holly at midwinter, as it was believed that cattle would thrive if it was placed where it could be seen at Yule.[8] Gift-giving was done as a blessing rite to open the new year following the solstice when the days begin to grow longer. From very early times, the midwinter festival was a time of feasting, entertainment, rest from work, charity, and merriment. These celebrations likely included various types of dancing and plays.

* * *

The Celts were known to worship the sun and built massive structures such as Stonehenge which appear to have had functions related to solstice rituals. The tallest stone of Stonehenge lines up with the sunrise on the winter solstice, and it is believed that Neolithic people held great feasts there at this time of year. Archaeological finds have shown that at some point between 2600 and 2400 BCE, as many as 4,000 people gathered at Stonehenge for midwinter festivals at which animals were slaughtered,[9] and likely enjoyed products like fermented milk and cheese, as well as beer and mead. Archaeologists have long speculated that the purpose of Stonehenge was related to the commemoration of the death and rebirth of a divinity at midwinter, and it was far from the only site in ancient Britain serving this function. Evidence of excavation suggests that ceremonies were held at many similar sites such as Durrington Walls and Dorset Cursus, which appear to have significance for the winter solstice based on their alignment with midwinter sunsets and sunrises. At the Durrington Walls henge, evidence of midwinter celebrations has been discovered such as pits, hearths, animal bones, pottery, flint tools, and pig fat residue.[10] As archaeologist Paul Frodsham notes in *From Stonehenge to Santa Claus*, "complex cosmologies must have existed in association with the observance of the winter solstice at Stonehenge and the other great Neolithic monuments."[11]

Considered leading experts in religion, magic and the supernatural, the druids are largely shrouded in mystery, with fragmented accounts of their practices handed down from ancient sources such as Julius Caesar, Cicero, Dion Chrysostom, Clement of Alexandria, Hippolytus, Diogenes Laertius, Pliny, Lucan and Tacitus. The druids emerged as major figures in national histories during the Renaissance and still capture the modern imagination today. Ancient depictions portray the druids variously as impressive philosophers and scientists, or as bloodthirsty savages who relished in human sacrifice. Caesar, the only one of the ancient sources who had the opportunity to extensively observe the druids in their own society, took a middle ground—considering them capable of great learning but generally exerting a malign influence because of the brutal nature of the religious rites that they practiced.[12] As Caesar described the druids, they were members of a national order produced by a rigorous training process, but according to Irish texts, the term *driudecht*, or "druidcraft," is simply a term for magic. The Irish view of druids, therefore, was basically a group of full-time magicians, those who understood and deployed supernatural power.[13]

In the mid-first century, the Roman conquest suppressed the druid class and brought a new pagan belief system to Britain. Itself a cosmopolitan hybrid of influences from various pagan religions including from Greece, Egypt and Persia, the Roman pantheon of gods would soon be making an enduring impact on Britain as well. Within 50 years of Roman arrival, two-thirds of Britain was under Roman control,[14] leaving a rich archaeological record that reveals a mix of native and imported cults, with the Roman religion having a major influence on cultural and religious customs. Roman religion introduced an enormous number of divine beings with special attachment to particular natural forces or places, imbuing the political, military and administrative structures of Romano-British rule with spiritual meaning. Jupiter, Mars and Mercury were most represented, covering human affairs such as government, weather, travel, farming, trade, war, and death.[15] There also appears to have been a vibrant cult of Mithras, the Persian god whose birthday was marked on December 25. Shrines to Mithras have been uncovered in London and York, as well as on the defensive fortification known as Hadrian's Wall, and temples to Mithras have been found at Musselburgh, just east of Edinburgh. Bacchus, the Roman god of wine, was also well represented in the Romano-British pantheon, and his mystery religion was apparently the most widespread in Britain.[16]

Roman religious belief appears to have impacted the year-end customs of the British people. The custom of marking the New Year's Day celebration of January 1 is believed to be a survival of the Roman occupation, and specifically the transmission of the festival of Kalends. The date of the year did not officially change until March 25, but January 1 was considered among the most important of the 12 days of Christmas due to the older Roman tradition of ringing in the new year on this day. In line with the older Roman customs, gifts were exchanged, including in the royal household where kings, queens, servants and courtiers all gave each other presents. Some nobles gave gifts to the servants of the king and religious houses exchanged gifts with their staff.[17]

There is evidence of the presence of Christianity in Britain from the year 314, but it would take another few hundred years before Christian missionaries focused fully on ensuring that the Britons became a Christian people. They utilized the nativity celebration toward this end, with Saint Augustine baptizing more than 10,000 people in England on Christmas Day in 597, the very year that he had arrived to begin his missionary work.[18] By the end of the seventh century, Christianity was the official faith of every community in the British Isles, but regions adapted differently to the new religion, with the Picts for example rejecting Roman forms of literature, art and monument, and preferring alternatives such as symbol stones.[19] But even as Christianity was taking hold in Britain, paganism continued to flourish

3. Christmas in a Pagan World   37

This image depicts Bacchus and his leopard on a pedestal, with a man playing a pipe and a woman crouching before a basket. "Offering to Bacchus" (detail), ca. 1688–1711. Artist Bérain, Jean (the Elder) (J. Paul Getty Museum).

nearby and would soon come back to the British Isles in the form of invasions and foreign settlement.

* * *

While Christmas was first celebrated by Christians in Rome around 350, pagan celebrations continued throughout the Empire. Pagan Libanius of Antioch said later in the fourth century that "Kalends is celebrated everywhere as far as the limits of the Roman Empire extend." He noted that "luxurious abundance is found in the houses of the rich, but also in the houses of the poor better food than usual is put on the table." People spent their money freely, and "he who erstwhile was accustomed and preferred to live poorly, now at this feast enjoys himself as much as means will allow." There was an unusual generosity shown to others during this festival, he noted. "A stream of presents pours itself on all sides," according to Libanius, and "[i]t may justly said that it is the fairest time of the year."[20]

The Roman Emperor Theodosius issued an edict against paganism in the empire at the end of the century, thus banning pagan festivals such as Kalends and Saturnalia, but far to the north of the Roman borders, Germanic peoples continued to mark the rebirth of the sun in their traditional pagan fashion with intoxicating drinks and roasted meat from animal sacrifices—practices that continued for centuries alongside celebrations of Jesus's birth.[21] As explorers, conquerors and traders, the Saxons and later the Vikings brought their beliefs and customs to other peoples, including the Britons.

As Roman legions left Britain, the Germanic-speaking Angles, Saxons, Jutes and Frisians began arriving beginning in the early fifth century, originally in small invading parties but in increasingly larger numbers. Meeting little resistance from the locals,[22] they soon began establishing settlements of their own, introducing new pagan ideas even as the Christianization of Britain was underway. This led to an amalgamation of beliefs and customs that would have an enduring impact on the celebration of Christmas. For example, the development of Father Christmas in England was probably influenced by the invasion of the Saxons, who were known to anthropomorphize seasons. The Saxons may have also introduced the god Odin, who wore a cloak and long white beard,[23] not unlike the depictions of Father Christmas that would later begin to emerge in Britain. It is known that the English particularly venerated Odin, or as he was known in England, Woden. Evidence for this includes the prevalence of place names incorporating variations of "Woden," as well as the fact that the word "Wednesday" borrows his name and six of the eight Anglo-Saxon royal houses traced their descent from him.[24] The second most popular god in the Anglo-Saxon pantheon was Thunor, better known by his Norse name Thor. As a god of the sky and thunder, Thunor was closely associated with the Roman god Jupiter.[25]

Even after Britain converted to Christianity, another wave of paganism would return with the Viking invasion in 800, both suppressing the development of Christianity by attacking churches, killing and enslaving monks, and reintroducing heathen beliefs and a pagan pantheon of gods in the nascent Christian society. These pagan raiders, who frequently became settlers, added another layer of tradition to the already multilayered religious belief system in Britain—by then incorporating indigenous pagan beliefs, the pantheon of Greco-Roman gods, Christianity, and the first wave of pagan conquest. The impact of the Viking invasions on the development the Christian faith was considerable, with dioceses in parts of England disappearing entirely, and apparently no high-level Church activity from the years 880 to 920. Great Christian centers such as Iona and Lindisfarne were relocated to the mainland, and others were abandoned permanently.[26]

While leaving an enduring imprint on the Christianization of Britain, the Vikings also appear to have been influenced by the Christian customs that they encountered, and indeed began converting in large numbers to Christianity in the ninth century. One practice that the Scandinavians adopted was the making of monumental sculpture. Such monuments are found mainly in northern England and southern Scotland, with Cumbria and Yorkshire boasting more than 600 Viking monuments between them. The monuments feature motifs taken from Norse mythology, suggesting that for a period Christian and pagan beliefs co-existed on a relatively equal basis. On some of the monuments, Christ's crucifixion is depicted in parallel with imagery from the Norse end-of-world myth of Ragnarok. Sigurd, the Norse dragon-slayer, is also depicted alongside Christian saints celebrated for vanquishing evil beings, and a church at Andreas in the far north portrays Odin accompanied by his raven, plunging a spear into the wolf Fenrir. It is open to interpretation whether this represents a Christian appropriation of pagan stories or whether the pagans were appropriating Christian symbolism, but what is clear is that there was much mixing of religious beliefs at the same time that Christmas was developing as a holiday in Britain.[27]

* * *

Although Christianity had spread to Britain and most parts of southern Europe by the fifth century, it would take another five or six hundred years to come to Slavic lands and six or seven hundred years for the religion to establish itself the Nordic countries. Scandinavia's neighbors to the south—the Frisians and the Saxons—converted in the 700s and 800s, while Poland and Kievan Rus became officially Christian in 966 and 988. Denmark officially adopted Christianity in the late 900s, Norway in the early 11th century, and Sweden adopting Christianity very gradually, finally converting in the late 12th century.[28] The missionaries who brought Christianity to the pagan tribes also introduced the celebration of Christmas. It came to Ireland through Saint Patrick in the late 400s, to England through Saint Augustine of Canterbury in the early 600s, and to Germany through Saint Boniface in the mid–700s. The Scandinavians received it through Saint Ansgar in the 860s.[29]

Conversion was an arduous process full of rejection and defeat for the Christian missionaries, who learned to employ a variety of strategies in convincing pagans to adopt the new faith. Frankish conquerors of the Saxons, for example, used force against the heathens, with King Charlemagne issuing an unprecedented series of legal decrees in the 780s that provided for their forcible conversion. He ultimately offered a baptize-or-die ultimatum against the reluctant converts, with many choosing death.[30] As this draconian method failed to produce the desired results, more creative forms of persuasion were developed, including the publication of an epic poem called the *Heliand* in the first half of the ninth century. Meaning "savior" in Old Saxon, the *Heliand* was written at the request of Charlemagne's son, Emperor Louis the Pious, to overcome Saxon ambivalence toward Christianity. It adapts the story of Jesus to fit the worldview of the pagans, making the New Testament relatable by providing recognizable parallels to Teutonic mythology and Germanic culture, depicting Jesus more as a wise chieftain than a divine teacher. His 12 apostles are presented as loyal vassals who fight to defend their lord from his enemies,[31] the disciples have distinctly Germanic virtues and are rewarded by Jesus with arm bands, and the Feast of Herod is recast as a drinking bout.[32]

In a retelling of the nativity story, the *Heliand* describes the message of "Mighty God's angel" to the shepherds (who are depicted as watching over horses rather than sheep):

> Then he spoke and said there would come a wise king,
> magnificent and mighty, to this middle realm;
> he would be of the best birth; he said that he would be the Son of God,
> he said that he would rule this world,
> earth and sky, always and forevermore.
>   He said that on the same day on which the mother gave birth to the Blessed One
> in this middle realm, in the East,
> he said, there would shine forth a brilliant light in the sky, one such as we never had
> before between heaven and earth nor anywhere else,
> never such a baby and never such a beacon.[33]

Around the same time that the *Heliand* was written, the Stuttgart Psalter was published. Depicting the Book of Psalms in pictorial form, the Stuttgart Psalter

Stuttgart Psalter image depicting Christ as a heroic warrior. Illustration from Psalm 91, verse 13, ca. 820–830 (Württembergischen Landesbibliothek Stuttgart).

offered a wide array of monsters, unicorns, animals, and allegorical figures. Much like the *Heliand*, this collection of illustrations helped establish an image of Jesus as an all-powerful warrior, slaying beasts such as dragons and lions.[34] With these creative adaptations of the Bible, the Saxons were introduced to Christianity in a way they could relate to, and these more pagan-friendly versions of Scripture soon spread to neighboring regions. Nevertheless, in some heathen strongholds, particularly to the north, pagans continued to reject the new faith.

* * *

In a 1926 account of the efforts to introduce Christianity to Sweden, the Rev. Berndt David Assarsson calls the period from 830 to 1160 "the period of struggle, during which the Christian preachers, at the cost of innumerable sacrifices, and surrounded by all kinds of dangers, advanced step by step toward victory over the deeply rooted paganism." Many of the missionaries lost their lives trying to spread the faith in Sweden, but over a period of more than 300 years, the country eventually converted. "The provinces of the south and the southwest were the first to embrace the Faith," recalls Assarsson. "After them came the provinces of the north. The far-off provinces remained pagan until the end of the eleventh century. Then it was that for the first time Sweden saw its king baptized at Husaby in Westgothland."[35]

In Slavic lands, vestiges of heathenism persisted even following formal conversion with a phenomenon called *dvoeverie*, meaning double faith, posing a challenge to Christian priests and monks as various peoples were Christianized between the seventh and 12th centuries. While Christianity took hold among the nobility and in the cities, among the rural majority of the Slavic population, old myths remained strong. These include beliefs in a deity known as Perun, who crafted thunder and lightning, as well as deities such as Hors, Dažbog, Stribog, Simargl, and Mokosh, in addition to various nymphs. As Christianity reached rural areas, farmers gladly accepted baptism and welcomed new holidays such as Christmas, but they still persisted in performing ancient rites and participating in old pagan cults. This was the case even after the ancient deities and myths upon which they were based had been completely forgotten. To the peasants, Christianity was not a replacement of their mythology, but rather an addition to it.[36]

"Christianity may have offered a hope of salvation, and of blissful afterlife in the next world, but for survival in this world, for yearly harvest and protection of cattle, the old religious system with its fertility rites, its protective deities, and its household spirits was taken to be necessary," writes scholar Liliana Damaschin. "This was a problem the Christian church never really solved; at best, it could offer a Christian saint or martyr to replace the pagan deity of a certain cult, but the cult itself thrived, as did the mythological view of the world through which natural phenomena were explained."[37]

In this regard, seasonal changes were recognized in the old ways and marked every year with a series of festivities. An important Slavic festival at the winter solstice, which later became associated with Christmas, was called Božić, simply meaning "little god." The festival celebrated the birth of a new god of the sun (a little god) to replace the old and weakened solar deity during the longest night of the year. Known as Svarog, the old sun god was replaced by his son, the young and new sun, known as Dažbog. Though rooted in paganism, the Christian version of the holiday simply supplanted the concept of a new sun god being born with the birth of Jesus Christ, and the term "young god" was applied to Jesus instead of Dažbog.[38] Božić, incidentally, is still the word used for Christmas in some Balkans countries.

All over Europe, similar overlapping of old and new religions was taking place even as Christianity spread far and wide and as Christmas developed as one of the most important holidays on the Christian calendar. As folklorist Jacob Grimm documented in his seminal work *Teutonic Mythology* in 1835, paganism remained prevalent in parts of the continent into the 16th and 17th centuries and, indeed, "the remotest Laplanders cling to it still."[39] Grimm is credited with salvaging many pagan customs and as much of the lost and disappearing knowledge as possible, including by documenting customs such as the sacrifice of boars to the Norse god Frey, which was adapted after the adoption of Christianity into the practice of baking loaves and cakes on Yule-eve in the shape of a boar.[40] He also recorded a ceremony related to the Yule boar sacrifice that involved "rubbing the sacred flame, running through the glowing embers, throwing flowers into the fire, baking and distributing large loaves or cakes, and the circular dance."

These dances evolved into plays and dramatic representations with performers in disguise, with blackened and rouged faces. "One, wrapt in fur, sits in a chair as the victim, holding in his mouth a bunch of straw-stalks out fine, which reach as far as his ears and have the appearance of sow bristles," Grimm writes.[41] These boar-related customs reflected the special status of the animal in Norse mythology. The boar was the companion animal to the god Frey, who represented sunlight, peace, prosperity, and fertility. The sun was likened to Frey riding his shining, golden boar across the sky, and the boar's golden bristles represented the sun's

42 Part One—Origins and Evolution

The god Frey riding his boar, Gullinbursti. Artist Ludwig Pietsch. Illustration for the 1873 book *Manual of Mythology: Greek and Roman, Norse, and Old German, Hindoo and Egyptian Mythology* by Alexander Murray (Internet Archive).

rays.[42] In Norse belief, the boar was also associated with the dead, with the souls of fallen warriors feasting on freshly cooked wild boar every day.[43]

* * *

As a mostly illiterate people—save the rudimentary writings on Runic stones—the Scandinavians' pre–Christian religious practices are not fully known, but there are some indications of how they may have communed with the gods at religious festivals such as Yule. The most important source for this information is the *Poetic*

Edda, a collection of Old Norse anonymous poems that were passed down orally for centuries until they were put to paper in the ninth century. Considered the most valuable source on Norse mythology and Germanic legends, it is supplemented by the *Prose Edda*, which was compiled by Icelandic poet Snorri Sturluson in the 13th century,[44] as well as the accounts by the 11th-century chronicler Adam of Bremen and earlier chronicles by Christian missionaries in the ninth and tenth centuries.

From these sources, we know that celebrations of the winter solstice (as well as other celestial events) were important to ancient Scandinavians, but there are some discrepancies about when precisely the Yuletide celebration may have taken place. Some sources claim that beginning on the night of the shortest day of the year, people would drink and swear oaths for three nights, but other accounts suggest that the festivities may have taken place at some point after the winter solstice. Sixth-century Byzantine chronicler Procopius mentioned that Scandinavians celebrated a feast for the returning sun,[45] but accounts in Sturluson's sagas seem to imply that the main event occurred several weeks after the solstice. The saga of Hervor placed Yule in February, while the chronicler Thietmar of Merseburg claimed that the feast took place in January.[46] The various times for the festival probably relate to the fact that the ancient Scandinavians followed a lunar-solar calendar and may have marked the solstice at the first full moon (or the first full moon after the first new moon) after the shortest day, rather than on the shortest day itself. As explained by Swedish scholar Goran Henriksson, "People of today may find it difficult to understand why such an exact rule was needed to determine the day for the sacrifice to the gods, but there seems to have been a long tradition in Europe that the gods must be worshipped on specific days."[47] This is because while the years were determined precisely according to the sun, the months and the days were set according to the moon, and therefore the same sacrifices to the gods must be made at the same time of the year based on the lunar cycle. It wasn't until Scandinavia converted to Christianity that the celebration of Yule was set at December 25.

While the precise date of ancient Yule celebrations is difficult to pinpoint precisely, one thing that is relatively clear from the historical record is that it involved the consumption of alcohol, with celebrants drinking mead and beer in honor of the gods. A ninth-century poem described King Harold Fairhair's intention to observe Yule by drinking on a ship rather than in the comfort of his home. "He wants to drink Yule out at sea, if he alone should rule, the brave King, and practice the sport of Freyr," reads the skaldic poem Hrafnsmál by Torbjørn Hornklove.[48]

The Yuletide celebration included feasting, games, and gift-giving,[49] as well as the burning of large logs on the central hearth of the longhouse, a tradition that emerged from the ancient realm of tree worship and was practiced in various forms not only Scandinavia but throughout Europe. The Yule log was considered the embodiment of the sun god,[50] symbolizing the continuation of light despite the darkness outside and may have also been believed to release ancestral spirits in the burning fire. These spirits, considered souls of the dead who returned at the New Year, had to be mollified with drinks and offerings,[51] and oaths sworn in front of them were considered sacred.

Yule oaths were marked by a custom of leading a boar around the longhouse for people to set their hands upon to make promises. "And they would sacrifice a boar in the *sonarblót*," reads *The Saga of King Heidrek the Wise*. "On Yule Eve the sonar-boar was led into the hall before the king; then people laid their hands on its bristles and made vows."[52] Some scholars cite this practice as possibly an ancient precursor to New Year's resolutions. Other survivals of the custom can be seen in the way that pork dishes continue as Christmas favorites and how Scandinavian Christmas cookies are often shaped like a pig.

The festivities were celebrated with the plentiful, well-prepared food and drinks from the winter stores. Ancient Scandinavians lit large bonfires to scare off evil spirits and to alter the course of the sun,[53] consumed horse flesh (prohibited at other times of year) and sprinkled themselves with the blood of sacrifice. Sacrifices could include both animals and humans, and as Adam of Bremen notes, at the great shrine at Uppsala, "each and every tree is believed divine because of the death and putrefaction of the victims hanging there." When a sacrifice was to be made, ancient custom held that all farmers were to come to the temple with the food they needed while the feast lasted, and all were to take part in drinking ale.[54]

The Norse believed that 12 gods in particular were superior and resided in 12 celestial dwellings. There were also 12 names by which Odin was designated, leading to speculation among scholars that this number had significance due to the divisions of the year and the reckoning of the sun's course. Each of the 12 gods, or Æsir, was designated a month, and the second month of winter was known as Ýlir, a variation of one of Odin's many names, Jólnir,[55] which means "Yule lord" in Old Norse. Powerful gods like Odin and Thor and fertility gods like Frey and Freyja were especially celebrated at the turning points of the year, midsummer and midwinter.

Odin in particular was the god of Yule, but other gods were also offered sacrifices, to help ensure that they provided everything one could need for a lucrative and happy year. The feast held in Odin's honor was called *jólablót*, which takes its name from Jólnir, and was a multi-day event. Some sources say it lasted for three days while others claim as many as 12, which would coincide with the number of superior gods and could be related to the 12 days of Christmas. With the borders between the physical and spirit worlds thinnest at the time of Jól, different nights were dedicated to honoring various deities and the dead were also believed to more active at this time, with copious ale drunken and toasts made in their honor.[56]

* * *

Although kings and nobles throughout Scandinavia officially adopted the Christian faith and pagan subjects were baptized by the end of the 11th century, many pagan elements remained. Some gods may have been Christianized as saints (or reinterpreted as demons), and paganism itself became subsumed within the broader categories of superstition, magic, and witchcraft. As Grimm pointed out in 1835, Catholicism "includes a good many and often graceful and pleasing relics of paganism," particularly in the adoration of saints.[57]

But while Christianity was influenced by these relics of paganism, so too had pagan beliefs been influenced by Christianity—largely due to Vikings' contacts with other cultures—prior to conversion.[58] Christianity provided its own set of notions and practices that served similar uses as the pagan religions. Elements of pagan practices, for example, were sanctified by some cultures, such as the reinterpretation of the ancient Celtic feast of Samhain into the celebration of All Saints and All Souls, later forming the basis for our modern Halloween. This is called syncretism, or the combining of different beliefs, which is a process that was advocated by early popes to incorporate pagan lore into Christianity, known by its Latin name *Interpretatio christiana*.[59] As Augustine of Hippo (354–430 CE) declared: "Do not kill the heathens—just convert them; do not cut their holy trees—consecrate them to Jesus Christ."[60]

This is why many customs from pre–Christian times have become ubiquitous—notably the use of evergreens such as holly, mistletoe and trees. The use of many of these common Christmas decorations can be traced to pagan practices throughout Europe. The mistletoe, for example, was sacred to the ancient druids and at Saturnalia, Roman homes and temples were decorated with evergreens. Bacchus wore wreaths of ivy in his hair, providing a possible inspiration for evergreen wreaths at Christmas. In pre–Christian Scandinavia, holly was hung on doors and windows to keep wandering winter spirits out of the house.[61]

Other customs are less ubiquitous but nevertheless demonstrate how syncretism continues to affect modern-day observances of midwinter festivities. For example, Serbians prepare a ceremonial, round loaf of bread called česnica for the Christmas dinner, which is steeped in pagan traditions. The preparation of the bread is often accompanied by rules and rituals, including a coin that is placed into the dough during the kneading, which is supposed to bring luck and prosperity to the person who finds the coin in his or her piece of the bread. Although the tradition is now incorporated into Christian rites, in pagan times, the česnica was used in folk magic for divining or influencing the amount of crops.[62] Many European cultures also still utilize pre–Christian gods in their Yuletide celebrations, with Germany, Austria and the Czech Republic featuring characters like Krampus and Knecht Ruprecht, who accompany St. Nicholas to threaten to thrash or abduct disobedient children.

Considering this deeply layered background, it becomes clear that Christmas is more than just a time to enjoy the company of loved ones, exchange gifts, or for the faithful, to solemnly celebrate the birth of Christ. It is also a time to recall customs and beliefs of ancestors going back longer than recorded history and reconnect with a spirituality that is deeply connected to seasonal cycles. The way that Christmas resonates so deeply with so many people should be understood within this deeper context. Even when direct lines are not easily drawn between pre–Christian customs and the customs that we continue to perform every year during the dark days of December, the sense of awe, comfort and wonder that we experience when engaging in arcane traditions is proof that these practices are deeply rooted in our past, even if their true meaning is not fully known.

4

Yule's Post-Pagan Metamorphosis

> *We'll twine the fresh green holly wreath,*
> *And make the yule-log low;*
> *And gather gaily underneath*
> *The winking mistletoe;*
> *All blithe and bright*
> *By the glad fire-light;*
> *For this is Christmas morning!*
> —Edwin Waugh, "Christmas Morning"

Originally known as Yule, then dubbed Midwinter-Mass and the Nativity, the holiday that we celebrate today as Christmas received its name in the early 11th century. *Crīstesmæsse*, as it was called in Old English, evolved as Christendom was establishing itself as Europe's political and social order, absorbing and suppressing heathen practices as the Christian faith spread across the continent. As the Roman empire dissolved, bishops came to replace imperial governors as primary tax collectors, using the funds to fortify cities against attack, ensure water and grain supply, build churches, and eliminate remnants of pagan worship.[1] Christian leaders employed their education and skills toward celebrating and enhancing their religion as it reached new peoples.

But Christianity, as a foreign religion that aimed to replace time-honored gods who were revered and loved, was not universally embraced. Pagan gods and their worship were integral to the people's traditions and customs, with roots in local languages and hallowed by antiquity. As Jacob Grimm explains in *Teutonic Mythology*, "kings and princes traced their lineage back to individual gods; forests, mountains, lakes had received a living consecration from their presence."[2] Christian missionaries came with a bible and a cross, telling people that their gods either didn't exist or were personifications of evil, urging them to renounce their beliefs as a sin and to abandon customs that they had held dear for generations. This did not always go over well. In St. Patrick's attempts to convert pagan Ireland to Christianity in the mid to late 400s, for example, he was so initially despised that he was temporarily imprisoned, and several attempts were made on his life, leading him to carry a dagger for self-defense.[3]

Patrick, however, understood enough about local customs to know that he would have more success converting Irish pagans by convincing them that Christianity was not all that much different from their beliefs. He deftly merged Christian and pagan symbols, using the three-leaf clover, which resembled the pagan Triskelion, to help explain the Christian belief in the Holy Trinity, and moved the dates of early Christian celebrations to dates that were sacred to the pagans so that the new religion could be more easily assimilated. In the *Annals of the Kingdom of Ireland*, published in the mid–19th century, John O'Donovan notes that "Patrick engrafted Christianity on the Pagan superstitions with so much skill, that he won the people over to the Christian religion before they understood the exact difference between the two systems of belief." O'Donovan called the result a half-pagan, half–Christian hybrid that could still be found in the superstitions of the peasantry at the time of his writing.[4]

With these sorts of concessions and compromises proving more effective than coercive techniques, from Late Antiquity through the Middle Ages, conversion employed a tactful blending of Christianity and paganism in which old customs were allowed to remain despite their heathen origins. Pope Gregory the Great, who was the bishop of Rome from 590 to 604, insisted that pre–Christian practices should not be suppressed but instead should be converted from "worship of devils to the service of the true God."[5] In a letter to Abbot Mellitus in 601, Pope Gregory provided instructions on how heathen sacrificial feasts should be turned into Christian festivals, advising that special care should be made to infuse holy themes into pagan practices. "Because they are wont to slay many oxen in sacrifices to demons, some solemnity should be put in the place of this, so that on the day of the dedication of the churches, or the nativities of the holy martyrs whose relics are placed there, they may make for themselves tabernacles of branches of trees around those churches which have been changed from heathen temples, and may celebrate the solemnity with religious feasting," the Pope instructs. "Nor let them now sacrifice animals to the Devil, but to the praise of God kill animals for their own eating, and render thanks to the Giver of all for their abundance." Pope Gregory added that it is "undoubtedly impossible to cut off everything at once, because he who strives to ascend to the highest place rises by degrees or steps and not by leaps."[6]

Essentially, renaming festivals and giving them a veneer of Christian respectability was considered more effective—and more feasible—than total eradication. This is precisely what happened in Norway, when King Haakon I, ruler of Norway from 934 to 961, scheduled ancient celebrations of Yule to coincide with Christian celebrations. A baptized Christian, Haakon issued a decree that Yule celebrations were to take place at the same time as the Christians celebrated the birth of Christ, "and at that time everyone was to have ale for the celebration with a measure of grain, or else pay fines, and had to keep the holiday while the ale lasted."[7] In other words, everyone had to drink beer in honor of baby Jesus or they were slapped with a fine. One of Haakon's successors, Olafur Tryggvason, who ruled Norway from 995 to 1000, continued these practices by removing heathen sacrifices known as *blot* and drinking connected with the sacrifices, and instead convinced the common people to take up festive drinking at Christmas, Easter, St. John's Eve, and Michaelsmas.[8]

But while the Scandinavian peoples may have converted to Christianity and nominally adopted customs such as celebrating Jesus's nativity, the pagan religion—with its pantheon of gods such as Thor, Odin and Frey—colored their way of thinking for the next several hundred years.[9] When pagans received the sign of the cross as a first step towards conversion, they were not prohibited from worshipping their old gods, and quite often, continued to do so. To the extent that they were worshipped, Norse gods were worshipped on the battlefield, with Vikings believing they could enter Valhalla and commune with Odin and Thor if they died gloriously in battle. In contrast to Christianity, the customs of the Norse did not involve moral codes proscribed by divine law, nor did they really believe in divine authority at all. The gods were considered powerful beings whom it was necessary to accommodate in order to survive and prosper but were not seen as moral arbiters passing judgment on human behavior.[10] But while seemingly having very little to do with Christian beliefs, the worship of these gods may also have already been influenced by Christianity by the time conversion formally took place.[11]

Many Vikings on military expeditions, diplomatic missions and trading journeys had seen churches and monasteries, heard the singing of hymns, and listened to sermons. Impressed, they may have brought back some of these Christian customs and adopted them.[12] For instance, the temple, priests and statues at Uppsala, described by Adam of Bremen in 1075, were possibly adaptations of Christian practices, as there is no evidence of these religious customs in earlier sources.[13] Moreover, by the time of conversion, Jesus Christ may have already been incorporated into the pantheon of Nordic gods, at least by some pagans.[14] This meant that the transition to the worship of Jesus was already underway before conversion, helping to more smoothly enable the shift from solstice celebrations to the Christmas feast.

* * *

Soon after the date for Christmas had been established in the mid-fourth century, religious leaders began to teach that for four weeks, beginning on the first Sunday after November 30, Christians were to sedately observe the Advent by repenting and asking God to forgive their sins.[15] Advent (a word deriving from the Latin *adventus*, meaning arrival) may have been kept by monks in the Roman Church as early as the sixth century and was seen in Late Antiquity as a time for Christian converts to prepare for Baptism on Epiphany. Extended to span the course of five Sundays by the Early Middle Ages, it was a period of fasting, with Christians expected to eat only one meal a day for three days a week, and to generally refrain from meat, dairy products, wine, fat, ale and mead, as well as gambling, sex, getting married or unnecessary travel.[16]

As it got colder and darker throughout the month of December, the faithful solemnly anticipated the Lord's coming on Christmas, a day to be celebrated with pious rejoicing, singing and worship—not to mention enjoying a good meal after a month of deprivation. Advent was a time of reflection and waiting as the days grew darker for Jesus to come and lighten the world, which due to the winter solstice taking place at the same time as the nativity, had both a literal and a figurative meaning. The mood of the season is captured in the words of the hymn "Oh Come, Oh Come Emanuel," with its lines, "Come, O Bright and Morning Star, and bring us comfort from afar! Dispel the shadows of the night and turn our darkness into light."

Yet, some pagan customs persisted even though they apparently mocked ecclesiastical rituals and were characterized by blasphemous excess. In a loose adaptation of the pagan Saturnalia, the Feast of Fools, a popular festival in France taking place on January 1, would elect a mock bishop, and those of low status switched places with high officials. By the 13th century these celebrations came to openly ridicule Christian morality and worship, and despite increasing disapproval from the Church, continued until the 16th century.[17]

4. Yule's Post-Pagan Metamorphosis

This 16th-century engraving depicts characters dancing, playing music and participating in a bowling game. It is generally seen as an indictment of the folly and misrule associated with the Feast of Fools. Artist Pieter Breugel (The Metropolitan Museum of Art, New York, Elisha Whittelsey Collection, the Elisha Whittelsey Fund, 1969).

Meanwhile, some popular pagan practices were transformed into pious Christian observances, with the Church focusing efforts on eliminating remnants of paganism and consolidating Christianity by consecrating heathen traditions as part of the Christmas feast. The St. Lucia tradition is one of these pagan survivals. What had been a day in ancient times in which the Norse marked the winter solstice by lighting bonfires meant to ward off wandering spirits, this practice was converted into a solemn celebration of the legend of St. Lucia—a victim of fourth-century Roman persecution—around the year 1000 and is still practiced in Scandinavian countries today.[18]

But while the Church may have absorbed—or at least permitted—some of the heathens' practices, others were outlawed, and religious authorities tried to suppress unruly pagan tendencies by force and with fines. At the same time, the Christian faithful added many new traditions throughout the Middle Ages and secular forces also helped the holiday evolve by contributing songs, foods and stories.

* * *

As Christianity spread across Europe and pagan traditions of the solstice celebrations were transmitted into the Christian celebrations of the birth of Christ, Church leaders intensely debated how many of the newly converted pagans' pre–Christian customs should be allowed to continue after they had received the cross. Questions such as whether to allow decorating spaces with greenery at Christmas time, or whether these pagan traditions should be eschewed altogether, were the source of much disagreement among the Church hierarchy. Some clerics argued against adopting the use of evergreens in particular and attempted to prohibit these supposed pagan relics, but eventually the assimilators won out over the suppressers and by the late Middle Ages, virtually all churches in England were decorated with holly, bay, rosemary, and laurel at Christmas time.[19] Ivy was considered objectionable due to its pagan association with the Roman god Bacchus (and its use in orgies in honor of him), but it was nevertheless also widely used by churches. Only mistletoe was shunned completely.[20]

Despite their well-known pagan origins, once adopted by Christians, evergreens took on a holy meaning for believers. Laurel and bay, although traditionally the symbolic flower of Apollo, came to symbolize Jesus's triumph over death. Holly, which in pagan times was seen as a powerful fertility symbol and was used to ward off witches and evil spirits, became associated with Christ's crown of thorns, with its bright red berries symbolizing his blood and the white flowers representing the immaculate conception.[21] More generally, evergreens came to "signify and put us in mind of His Deity, that the Child that now was born with God and man, who should spring up like a tender plant, should always be green and flourishing, and live for evermore," according to an anonymous English writer in the 16th century. Another medieval chronicler wrote in the *Survey of London* that during "the feast of Christmas every man's house, as also their parish churches, were decked with holme, ivy, bayes, and whatsoever the season of the year afforded to be green." He noted that in 1444, a storm had torn down some Christmas decorations in Cornhill, and it was believed that this was the work of a malevolent spirit that had been offended by the holy adornments.[22]

On the surface, the question of whether to allow the use of evergreens may seem to be a rather cosmetic issue, but it was actually part of a more fundamental struggle over the degree to which Church leaders felt it necessary to compromise with pre–Christian customs in order to welcome former pagans into the flock, and countervailing concerns over whether this would be a corrupting influence on the religion they were trying to build. From the time that Constantine established Christianity as Rome's official religion, Church leaders focused on Christianizing the classical world's poetry, law, philosophies, and traditions, which were all very much at odds with Christian teachings. This was particularly relevant to the Yuletide celebrations, as these customs were held dear by pre–Christian peoples, but it was also understood that many of the pagan practices were decidedly un–Christian in nature.

Christian denominations took varying views on the suppression or assimilation of paganism over the centuries, with Protestantism, and particularly its Calvinist and Puritan confessions, taking a harsher approach toward purging relics of paganism, especially those related to Christmas, and Catholicism generally seeking to "baptize" these customs rather than eliminate them. Lutheranism, as practiced in the Scandinavian countries, generally left standing many of the practices of Catholicism as well as the Christmas customs that were pagan in origin.[23]

But while different approaches were taken toward seemingly symbolic issues such as evergreens, one common dilemma that affected religious leaders throughout Europe was how to deal with some of the more unsavory customs that surrounded the Yuletide. Devout and reverent Christians may have piously observed Advent, but the period was also characterized by excessive eating and drinking, rowdy and gluttonous displays, aggressive begging, the mocking of established authority, and the invasion of wealthy homes.[24] As early as the fourth century, Church leaders found it necessary to issue warnings about dancing and "feasting to excess" on Christmas.[25] And as Frankish King Childebert complained in the sixth century, "on Christmas Day ... female dancers are abroad in the town" and "the populace is committing many blasphemous acts," including "nocturnal drunkenness, misplaced jokes and songs." He noted that God would surely be insulted by these practices, and therefore a punishment of 100 lashes was in order.[26]

The competing worldviews between pagan irreverence and Christian piety led to a long-running tug of war between the more unruly tendencies that characterized Roman and Viking festivities and the Church's aspirations for a subdued and solemn observation of Jesus's nativity.

* * *

Competing against belief systems that used human sacrifices to satisfy powerful and fickle gods, Church leaders were principally preoccupied with demonstrating that Christian rituals were at least as effective as heathen practices, and that Christianity would triumphantly lead its followers to glory in this world and the next.[27] To do so, religious leaders devised new and elaborate ways to observe the nativity in order to demonstrate the majesty of Jesus. In the ninth century, churches began adding extra dialogues and songs to Christmas services to celebrate the birth of Christ in a practice called "troping," which entailed half the church choir singing a question and then the other half responding. Choristers, dressed as midwives, sang "Quem quaeritis in praesepe, pastores, dicite?" (Whom seek ye in the manger, shepherds say?), to which other choristers, dressed as shepherds, would answer, "Salvatorem Christum Dominum, infantem pannis involutum" (Christ the Saviour, the infant Lord wrapped in swaddling clothes). Then a curtain would be pulled aside to reveal an image of the Virgin Mary with baby Jesus lying in a model of the crib, illuminated by tall candles.[28]

In time, this practice led to dramatization using individual speakers and actors and eventually to the presentation of nativity plays prominently featuring the magi and King Herod. A play that became popular in church services was The Prophets, in which a priest conducted a dialogue with various prophets such as Jeremiah, Daniel and Moses, and choir boys played bit parts like a donkey or devil.[29] Other popular medieval Christmas plays dealt with subjects such as the Creation, Fall, and the End Times, and all the plays featured devils, including Lucifer himself. In a 13th-century Bavarian Christmas play, there was a scene featuring demons hauling King Herod to hell, and in another scene, Lucifer mocks the shepherds at the nativity, claiming the good tidings of the angels are lies.[30]

Closely related to the nativity plays, mystery or miracle plays focused on the story of Adam and Eve and were commonly presented during Advent. Considered by the Church an important means of teaching the people about the fundamental beliefs of Christianity, these performances evolved from simple presentations with few props to elaborate productions with an ever-increasing cast of characters. They also expanded their storytelling scope from depictions of the Fall of Man to more comprehensively covering the Old and New Testaments, from the story of creation to the Resurrection. While the original performances were done in a solemn and somber tone, and initially were performed in Latin, later productions incorporated humor to make the plays more relatable for common people, and were done in local languages such as English, German and French. A favorite scene from the telling of the story of the Great Flood was the depiction of the domestic troubles that Noah faced with his wife scolding him for wasting his time building the ark. To escape his nagging wife, Noah went off into a corner, which always brought hearty laughter from the audience.[31]

* * *

Popular entertainment was an important component of the medieval Christmas celebration, with monks and medieval guilds touring and performing plays that depicted key episodes from the Gospels. Wagons carried people through the streets dressed as figures from the Bible's Christmas story and bands of musicians accompanied troupes of masked pantomime artists known as mummers. These entertainers performed dances, songs, and plays, which were quite varied but typically entailed some kind of miracle being performed, such as someone being brought back to life from the dead.[32]

Dressed in outlandish costumes as lords, cardinals and knights, these troupes could number over 100 revelers, and would sometimes go into people's homes to dance

This engraving was featured in an 1847 gift book called *My Own Treasury*. It depicts disguised Christmas mummers, wearing bells, waving rods, and dancing in the streets. Artist unknown.

in exchange for food and drink. The performers hoped to elicit laughter and admiration with their ridiculous antics and costumes. Mummers often performed short plays with scenes from legends such as Saint George and the Dragon, a narrative with pre–Christian origins which tells the story of taming a dragon that demanded human sacrifices. These entertainers appeared in dramatic performances at the royal court, passing through the streets on their way to private parties and amusing townsfolk as they travelled.[33] As described in *The Book of Days*, "Christmas mumming was in many respects a kindred diversion, though it appears to have partaken less of the religious element, and resembled more nearly those medieval pageants in which certain subjects and characters, taken from pagan mythology or popular legends, were represented."[34]

As urban populations grew and became more educated, plays extended their range and by the late 14th century, England had a particularly rich tradition of theater. Brief biblical episodes, such as 11 verses of Luke's Gospel, were expanded by clerical authors into entire theatrical performances, with the two "shepherds' plays" becoming the most popular.[35] Some Christmas plays combined elements of paganism and Christianity, such as "The Pleasant Comedy of Old Fortunatus." Originally a biblical figure—one of the 70 Disciples of Jesus Christ—Fortunatus also became known as a magical fulfiller of wishes in medieval Europe. One of the best-known stories involves Fortunatus acquiring a magic purse from Lady Fortune that continuously refills itself, which enables him to marry and start a family.[36] A play that was apparently performed before Queen Elizabeth I at Christmas in the late 16th century featured allusions to paganism, including the lines

> Peace foole: tremble, and kneele: The Moone saist thou?
> Our eyes are dazled by Elizaes beames,
> See (if at least thou dare see) where shee sits:
> This is the great Panthaeon of our Goddesse,
> And all those faces which thine eyes thought stares.[37]

When Fortunatus meets Lady Fortune, he says to her, "Dread Goddess, how should such a wretch as I be known to such a glorious deitie?" to which she replies, "Where I and these with fairie troops abide, Thou canst not stir, unlesse I be thy guide."[38] There are numerous other references throughout the play to supernatural creatures such as nymphs, fairies, demigods, and angels.

Along with Christmas plays, displays of the manger scene where Jesus was born also grew in prevalence at this time. According to some sources, it was in 1223 that St. Francis of Assisi, founder of the Franciscan order, conceived the idea of celebrating the nativity "in a new manner," by recreating the manger scene of Jesus's birth in a church at Greccio. This is generally regarded as the first time that Christians saw a replication of the Infant Savior laying in his crib surrounded by Mary and Joseph, as well as animals such as ox and lamb, and is credited with having inaugurated the popular tradition of singing and dancing around cribs at Christmas (although there are some scholars who argue that nativity scenes may have been used in Italy as far back as the 12th century). St. Francis also urged the emperor to make a special law that the poor should be well provided for at Christmas time, so that all were able to rejoice in the birth of Christ.[39]

* * *

Hymns and carols developed in this period, growing in complexity as well as in popularity. Derived from pagan festivals, carols arose as an art in the 13th century and could be sacred or secular. Conceived as songs that celebrate the Christmas season in a joyous manner, they were typically accompanied by dancing[40] and were initially condemned by the Church as obscene and lustful.[41] The carol's more pristine cousin was the hymn. Deriving from the Greek word *hymnos* meaning "a song of praise," a hymn typically would have a deeply spiritual component. While Christian hymns are modeled on the Book of Psalms and other poetic passages in the Bible, and by definition are considered as praise to Jesus and the Christian God, the origins of singing hymns—like carols—are actually pagan. Ancient hymns include the Egyptian Great Hymn to the Aten, written for the sun-disk deity Aten in the 14th century BCE, and the Homeric Hymns, a collection of Greek hymns from the seventh century BCE praising deities of ancient Greece.[42] A hymn to the ancient Mesopotamian sun god Shamash, who was also worshipped by the Sumerians and was considered the deity of justice, celebrates his power of light over darkness and wickedness:

> O ever-renewing light, who brings happiness to the people, who sets free,
> O Shamash, who brings order to the dead and the living, who sees everything,
> O Shamash, light of heaven and earth, radiance of the lands....
> May the heavens rejoice in you; may the earth be jubilant in you.
> May the whole pantheon bless you.
> May the great gods make your heart content.[43]

Christians have sung psalms and hymns since the time of the early Church, with historians pointing to the fourth-century composition "Jesus Refulsit Omnium," or "Jesus, Light of All the Nations," as perhaps the first nativity-themed hymn. Sharing similar themes as ancient heathen hymns of praise, the lyrics depict the moment that the magi find the stable where the infant Jesus lay:

> Jesus, devoted redeemer of all nations, has shone forth,
> Let the whole family of the faithful celebrate the stories
> The shining star, gleaming in the heavens, makes him known at his birth and, going before, has led the Magi to his cradle
> Falling down, they adore the tiny baby hidden in rags,
> as they bear witness to the true God by bringing a mystical gift.[44]

In the medieval period, the tunes became more elaborate and a whole genre of lyrics developed devoted to the birth of Christ. Hundreds of hymns were written to be sung at Christmas time, with titles like "A Child Is Born in Bethlehem," "Worship Be the Birth of Thee" and "When Jesus Christ Incarnate Was." In "Hail Mary Full of Grace," medieval worshippers sang, "The Holy Ghost is to thee sent, From the Father Omnipotent, Now is God within thee went, The angel said Ave."[45] In "Good Day Sir Christmas," the text included the lines "Heaven and earth, and also hell, And all that ever in them dwell, Of Your coming they full snell. Good day. Of Your coming, this, clerks find, Ye come to save all mankind, And from their balas them unbind. Good day."[46]

From the mid–12th to the mid–14th century, Christmas carols followed the monophonic dance-song structure, meaning all the singers were singing a single melody. By the 15th century, carols had become more sophisticated, following a polyphonic structure, with multiple melodic lines sung at the same time. Hymns and carols also increasingly used the macaronic style, mixing languages such as English and Latin, which reflected the contemporary reality that Latin was still the working language of scholars and clerics, but minstrels and storytellers increasingly preferred to use the vernacular in their work. A popular macaronic carol in the 15th century was "The Boar's Head Carol," which many believe is related to the ancient Norse tradition of sacrificing a boar for the god Frey in the hopes that it would bring fortune in the new year but could also be related to the story of the Calydonian boar hunt as told by Ovid in *The Metamorphoses*. Whatever its origins, the custom entailed medieval Christmas celebrants carrying a large platter with a boar's head as its centerpiece, parading into a banquet hall while singing: "The boar's head in hand bring I, Bedeck'd with bays and rosemary. And I pray you, my masters, be merry." They would end with "*Quot estis in convivio*," Latin for "as many are in the feast."[47]

While many medieval carols focused on religious themes such as the birth of Jesus, others were simply celebratory and intended to spread good cheer, with some appearing to have origins in ancient pagan beliefs.[48] The first collection of carols appeared in England in 1521 but publishing quickly moved to continental Europe and soon carols were everywhere, with hundreds of verses written in every language. All over Europe, Christmas revelers were singing songs such as "Deck the Halls with Boughs of Holly," "The First Nowell," "God Rest You Merry, Gentlemen," "We Wish You a Merry Christmas," and "The Cherry Tree Carol."[49]

This artwork, illustrating a man carrying a platter with a boar's head adorned with holly, appeared in the January 1873 edition of *Harper's New Monthly Magazine*. "Bringing in the Boar's Head." Artist J. Gilbert. Illustration for "Christmas Throughout Christendom."

When the Reformation came to the Nordic countries in the mid–16th century, Scandinavians warmly welcomed the new wave of congregational hymn singing that came with it. The widespread translation of hymns and the Bible in this period had an enduring impact, influencing not only religious life and the celebration of holidays such as Christmas and Easter, but also in the development of language and literacy. The growing popularity of hymns in Scandinavia was initially sparked by the use of translated works of Martin Luther, but it soon featured works written by native Scandinavians.[50] Thomas Kingo, for example, was one of Denmark's most famous hymn writers, contributing about a quarter of the Danish hymnal.[51] In the 17th century he wrote numerous Christmas hymns such as "Sweet Jesus, Christmas Prince," with its lyrics "We yesterday among angelic sounds sang your birth in with joy; shall we weep now and weep today a hymn?" In the 19th century, Hans Christian Andersen, author of such classics as "The Ugly Duckling" and "The Little Mermaid," contributed to the Danish Christmas hymnal with "Infant Jesus in a Manger Lay."

In colonial America, one of the most popular genres of books—together with the ubiquitous farmer's almanac—was the hymnal. As historian Stephen Nissenbaum points out, the very first book printed in New England was a hymnal, essentially a rhymed version of the Old Testament Book of Psalms, published in 1640 as the "Bay Psalm Book."[52] Revised editions came out every so often and were soon joined by other collections, but it wasn't until 1702 that one of them contained a hymn related to the nativity. Written by Nahum Tate, it begins with the lines "While Shephards watch'd their Flocks by Night / All seated on the Ground / The Angel of the Lord came down / and Glory shone around."[53] Over the next several decades, this hymn was joined by others to be sung in American churches on Christmas, including "Hymn on the Nativity," "An Anthem for Christmas-Day" and "An Hymn for Christmas Day," all of which were based on the nativity accounts in the Gospels.

* * *

The increasingly popular Christmas hymns and carols were a sign not only of devotion to Jesus Christ as the savior of mankind but also Christians' embrace of Christmas in its development as a Christian feast. In earlier centuries, with hymns solely in Latin, only the clergy could fully participate in liturgical devotions, but the vernacular Christmas poetry of later ages made it possible for common people to partake as well. During the darkest time of the year, many happily joined in the celebration of the Old Testament's prophecy of the coming of the Sun of Righteousness, as brought to mind in the popular English carol "Hark! The Herald Angels Sing." Recalling the prophecy of Malachi, with its admonition that "for you who fear my name, the Sun of Righteousness shall rise with healing in its wings," "Hark!" includes the lines "Hail the Sun of Righteousness! Light and life to all He brings."

It was becoming clear that although the date of December 25 may have been initially chosen as Jesus's birthday because it coincided with a popular pagan festival that Church leaders were trying to supplant, the conjunction of the date with the winter solstice also fit in well with biblical themes of Jesus as the bringer of light, warmth and healing to all who follow him. It also aligned with the outlook held by Christians that there was a dualistic struggle between light and darkness, that God and Satan were equally powerful entities who grappled for control of the world, with the image of Jesus as light found throughout the Bible. The Book of Isaiah for example reads that "darkness shall cover the earth ... but nations shall come to your light, and kings to the brightness of your rising." The Book of Revelation offers a promise that night will no longer exist after the coming of the Lord. "And night will be no more," it reads. "They will need no light of lamp or sun, for the Lord God will be their light, and they will reign forever and ever." At a time before electricity when people had only fire to create light and during the time of year when days grew extremely short, this promise of eternal light was surely a consolation and comfort.

The introduction of hymns and carols, along with the widespread use of evergreen decorations and the development of Christmas plays, the crib, and the general growth of myths and customs associated with the holiday, helped establish a rich tapestry of traditions to help cement Christmas as a beloved date on the Christian liturgical calendar. But even as the holiday evolved during the Middle Ages as a Christian feast, elements of paganism continued to influence the celebration in ways that the Church often found objectionable. This challenge would eventually come to a head in a series of conflicts and controversies in subsequent centuries.

5

Repression and Resistance

Then came the merry masquers in,
And carols roar'd with blithesome din;
If unmelodious was the song,
It was a hearty note, and strong.
    —Sir Walter Scott, "Christmas in the Olden Time"

The medieval Church took great pains to emphasize the solemn nature of the nativity and the need to observe it sedately but ultimately couldn't change the fact that the celebration took place in a historical and cultural context that had as much to do with living in an agricultural society dominated by seasonal realities as it did with religious beliefs. Particularly for pre-industrial (not to mention pre–Christian) societies, December was a time to gorge and to blow off steam. Regardless of what God or gods people worshipped, it was bound to be a time of merrymaking which could easily degenerate into rowdiness and disorder. The farmers' crops had been harvested and most work was done by this time, and it just so happened that this was when the year's supply of beer and wine was ready to drink, so it was widely considered a good time to indulge. Since farmers generally waited until winter to slaughter animals in order to prevent the meat from going bad, December was also the first time in months that it was possible to enjoy a proper meal with some pork or a nice goose.[1]

But at the same time, Christians were expected to observe the fasting requirements of Advent, which, although not as strict as the fasting of Lent, were still rather restrictive. During this solemn occasion, Church leaders pointed to passages of the Bible that warned against excessive drinking and eating, such as Proverbs 23:20, which advises: "Do not join those who drink too much wine or gorge themselves on meat, for drunkards and gluttons become poor, and drowsiness clothes them in rags." Another useful admonition from the Bible during this time of fasting and penance was Ephesians 5:18: "Do not get drunk on wine, which leads to debauchery. Instead, be filled with the Spirit."

Often though, for those who did refrain from meat, alcohol, gambling and sex during the month of fasting, it only ensured that when Christmas Eve finally arrived, the feast would be all that much grander. Records kept of typical Christmas feasts reveal that massive amounts of food and alcohol were consumed. At a Christmas feast held by Richard of Swinfield, Bishop of Hereford, in 1289, for example, some 40 guests ate two carcasses and three-quarters of beef, two calves, four does, four pigs, 60 fowls, eight partridges, two geese, as well as a good amount of bread and cheese, with a boar's head as the centerpiece of the table. Records show that they drank 40 gallons of red wine and four gallons of white, and although no one apparently kept track of the amount of beer consumed, it was probably quite a bit.[2]

Feasts among the peasants were naturally more modest, with the local lord supplying special Christmas foods for both people and animals. Typical were the rations given to three tenants on a manor in Somerset, England, in the 13th century: a chicken, cheese, two loaves of bread, a mess of beef and of bacon with mustard, and as much beer as they could drink during the day. A shepherd on the same manor received a loaf of bread and a dish of meat on Christmas Eve, as well as a loaf for his dog on Christmas Day.[3]

According to Troels Frederik Lund, a Danish historian writing in 1914, the 16th-century Christmas celebration began at the end of November, when households started preparing for the party. Among the most important tasks were baking and brewing, and the Christmas beer was to be made with special care. "Even the poorest household," Lund writes, "where the beer was thin enough on a daily basis, had to brew a stronger stock for Christmas." This was called the "Christmas barrel," and to have "tasted the Christmas barrel" was the popular expression for being drunk.[4]

The feasting and drinking that characterized the midwinter period was at odds from the beginning with the efforts of religious leaders to convince the faithful to observe with fasting and penance. This was particularly the case where celebrations had long been carried out in pagan societies that did not recognize divinities in the same way that Christians did or place the same emphasis on social mores such as moderation and humility. According to Christian norms of behavior as described in popular medieval texts like *How the Goode Wife Taught Hyr Doughter* and *How the Goode Man Taught Hys Sone*, ideal behavior is to be moderate, prudent, and to show restraint in one's emotions. The *Goode Man* says, "Laugh not too much, for that is waste," and the *Goode Wife* says that laughing too loudly makes one look like a "gyglot," or a "loose woman."[5] These values of restraint and modesty stood in marked contrast to pagan customs, which continued to hold sway over many common people in the Middle Ages.[6] While Christians believed that God considers gluttony and lust as deadly sins that could prevent one from entering the Kingdom of God, Nordic pagans believed that their gods, also known as Æsir, were delighted by boisterous feasts where alcohol flowed freely. As explained in *The Viking Gods*, "Happy gatherings at the banquet, where the flowing mead-horn was passed freely round, and where words of wisdom and wit abounded, or martial games with sharp swords and spears, were the delight of the Æsir."[7]

The jocular nature of Scandinavian celebrations is revealed by the origins of the word that they have used for centuries for the midwinter festivities. Yule, spelled *jul* in Nordic languages, comes from the Old Norse *jól*, which comes from the Proto-Germanic *jehwlą*, meaning "festivity," which in turn originates from the Proto-Indo European *jekə*, meaning "joke, play."[8] This means that the Scandinavian word for Christmas is basically "joke." Etymologists also believe that the word "jolly" shares the same root, coming from the Old French *jolif*, meaning "festive, merry; amorous; pretty."[9] According to some sources, *jolif* was borrowed from Old Norse *jól*, which might explain why the word "jolly" is so closely associated with Christmas time.

* * *

In Denmark, the pagan solstice celebration became a Christian Christmas feast around the year 1000, nearly 700 years after it was established in Rome. As described in the book *The Family's High Times in Olden Days*, the Danish Church ordered that the birth of Jesus should be celebrated on December 25 and tried to have the ancient name of Yule changed to Christ Mass. Danes rejected the name change and stuck with Yule, which is still the name used to this day. The celebration continued to combine pagan and Catholic customs, with Christmas Eve generally observed as a quiet vigil ending with the Catholic Midnight Mass. But the following days were largely spent on drinking parties, wild games, dancing and fights. "Drinking Christmas," or *drikke jul* in Danish, was the Viking Age expression to celebrate Christmas and was commonly used all the way up until the 16th century.[10]

The pagan-influenced festivities were so wild that the Church had to issue laws that prohibited raucous celebrations during the Christmas days. After Denmark became the seat of an independent province of Scandinavia in the early 12th century, the Church issued one of its earliest ordinances, which was to command absolute peace and quiet from December 25 to January 6. Indeed, laws adopted across Scandinavia during the Middle Ages declared a "Christmas peace" that began in the days leading up to Christmas and continued for weeks after the holiday. All disturbances and unrest were strictly forbidden during this time and any violence was punished with an increased fine. The Christmas peace mandated that as long as Christmas lasted, no courts could be in session, and no work should be performed except that which was absolutely necessary. Even chopping wood was frowned upon, with all firewood for the house needing to be chopped in advance of Christmas time. The Christmas peace extended to animals, with people required to show tolerance to wolves, bears, rats, and mice.[11]

Nordic peoples, however, with a predilection for indulgence, had a hard time understanding the Church's restrictive attitude, and largely continued to celebrate the solstice in their old-fashioned ways. One of the pagan traditions that remained was the Yule log. As was the custom in large parts of Europe, a tree trunk was dragged inside and laid on the hearth where it was to burn until Christmas ended.[12] As it burned, revelers engaged in extended periods of feasting and drinking. Scholar Rudolf Simek has noted that "it is uncertain whether the Germanic Yule feast still had a function in the cult of the dead and in the veneration of the ancestors, a function which the mid-winter sacrifice certainly held for the West European Stone and Bronze Ages." But it is clear that well into the Middle Ages, ancient customs such as the Yule log and Yule boar continued to be reflected in celebrations even after the Reformation.

Meanwhile, the laws mandating peace and quiet at Christmas time remained in full force. In Norway, Bergen's town hall protocol stated: "Anno 1593 on St. Thomas Day, which is the 21st of December, Christmas peace was set according to the City Act." Citizens participated in watchkeeping patrols, armed with knights and lanterns in hand, in order to uphold the Christmas peace.

* * *

Despite the best efforts of the Church to ensure that Christmas celebrations were respectable and dignified, rowdy customs continued to characterize the festivities throughout the Middle Ages and beyond. Indeed, a certain amount of legitimized disorder was considered an important component of the medieval Christmas celebration. In medieval England, a Lord of Misrule—also known as an Abbot of Misrule and the Christmas Lord—was appointed at the royal court and provided with all the elements of kingship, including a gibbet to perform mock executions of those who offended him. Lords of Misrule were also a feature of universities and law schools known as Inns of the Court. Chosen from the student body or sometimes the faculty, the Lord of Misrule would initiate pranks and lead schoolmates in wild behavior. In one incident at Christmas in 1516, the Lord of Misrule and his entourage broke down doors and invaded rooms at the Inn, resulting in a fine and dismissal.[13]

Another rowdy custom was wassailing. The word wassail comes from the Old Norse *"ves heill"* and originally was a greeting but also came to be known as a beverage made from hot mulled cider and spices. The roots of the tradition in Britain likely date back to many years before Christianity began to spread from around 600,[14] when farmers would sing to their orchards, animals and fields, and originally may have been intended as a blessing rite to encourage livestock, grain fields and trees to be productive and to ensure a plentiful harvest the following year.[15] As a 17th-century poem by Robert Herrick described the tradition, "Wassail the Trees, as they may bear You many a plum, and many a pear."[16]

Wassailing became widely popular in the medieval period as a Yuletide drinking ritual and salutation, as well as a common practice for peasants to express goodwill to their lords in exchange for material goods. The custom migrated to colonial America and evolved into a kind of aggressive begging mixed with caroling heavily influenced by excessive consumption of alcohol.

In the Middle Ages, the wassail was a reciprocal exchange between the feudal lords and their peasants, but while lords may have generally been glad to gift their peasants with food, drink or money, there was always a bit of a menacing aspect to the practice. Indeed, if the lord refused to offer something, he was usually cursed and could see his home vandalized. This more sinister side of wassailing can be detected in the lyrics of carols that wassailers sang. The familiar tune "We Wish You a

An illustration for the Christmas Eve 1842 issue of the *Illustrated London News*, depicting Father Christmas in a wassail bowl. Artist Alfred Henry Forrester.

Merry Christmas," for instance, contains both an innocuous demand and an ominous threat, when the carolers sing "now give us some figgy pudding," only to add "we won't go until we get some." But wassailers also emphasized that they should not be seen as beggars, a point that is made clear in the song "Here We Come A-wassailing," when the lord of the house is assured that "we are not daily beggars that beg from door to door, but we are friendly neighbours whom you have seen before."

In a 13th-century song, wassailers would implore the lords of the manor to chug a glass of wine, threatening to curse those who didn't:

> Lords, by Christmas and the host
> Of this mansion hear my toast
> Drink it well
> Each must drain his cup of wine,
> And I the first will toss off mine
> Thus I advise,
> Here then I bid you all Wassail,
> Cursed be he who will not say Drinkhail.[17]

For wassailing to work, both sides had to understand the "rules," and sometimes, if one side failed to live up to their side of the arrangement, it could go very wrong. In one such incident, in 1679 in Salem, Massachusetts, four young men entered a house singing and demanding pear cider, but the homeowner refused and forced them out, despite their insistence that "it was Christmas Day" and they only came "to be merry and drink perry." They demonstrated their anger over the rude treatment by throwing "stones, bones, and other things." They damaged the exterior of the house, knocked down a fence, and broke into a cellar to steal "five or six pecks of apples."[18]

In *The Battle for Christmas*, Stephen Nissenbaum traces the wassailing tradition to the earlier custom practiced in ancient Rome of turning social norms on their head during the annual Saturnalia celebration. "Christmas was a time when peasants, servants, and apprentices exercised the right to demand that their wealthier neighbors and patrons treat them as if *they* were wealthy and powerful," Nissenbaum writes. "The Lord of the Manor let the peasants in and feasted them. In return, the peasants offered something of true value in a paternalistic society—their *goodwill*." Nissenbaum notes that depending on the circumstances and the level of aggression on the part of the wassailers, this exchange could have been a voluntary and gracious offering or a forced concession to a hostile confrontation.[19] In other words, the practice of wassailing was not too far removed from what we might think of today as extortion or aggravated robbery.

* * *

These sorts of customs, the concept of "misrule" and the ritualized reversal of social norms, were seen by some as important elements of Christmas but by others as rather un–Christian remnants of heathen practices, causing Christmas to become increasingly unpopular among the more pious elements of society. First and foremost to object to the holiday were the Puritans who arose as a religious movement in the late 16th century in an effort to "purify" the Church of England by eliminating remnants of the Roman Catholic "popery" that had stayed in place following the end of the English Reformation. While the primary source of dispute between Puritans and the authorities was initially over the appropriate form of church government, particularly the perceived need for bishops to be replaced with government by elders, the Puritans also sought to reform the church to make their earnest and devout lifestyle the basis for the whole nation.[20] They launched a campaign to purge the relics of paganism that the early Church had incorporated into its liturgy, convinced that these compromises with heathens had weakened the Christian faith and allowed forces of the Devil to wield influence over Christians. Much of the Puritans' energy was spent on demonstrating that most Catholic rites were thinly veiled mutations of earlier pagan ceremonies, for example, that holy water was the Roman *aqua lustralis*, that wakes were the Bacchanalia, and that Christmas was Saturnalia.[21]

To the chagrin of the Puritans, the Elizabethan Religious Settlement of 1559 had preserved certain characteristics of medieval Catholicism, including cathedrals, church choirs, and Christmas. The Puritans strongly objected to this celebration, considering it a Catholic invention and having the "trappings of popery" and the "rags of the Beast."[22] They generally condemned its waste, extravagance, disorder, and sinfulness, and also pointed out that nowhere in the Bible can it be found that God had called upon mankind to celebrate Christ's nativity in this way.[23]

After they came to power in the mid–17th century, the Puritans moved to suppress Christmas, stressing that if "Christ-tide" (which is what they preferred to call it so as to avoid the Catholic overtones of using the word "mass") is kept at all, it should merely be a day of fasting and atonement. In 1644 the Puritan-led English Parliament published an "Ordinance for the better observation of the Feast of the Nativity of Christ," emphasizing that the Christmas celebration, as widely observed, was "contrary to the life which Christ himself led here upon earth, and to the spiritual life of Christ in our souls." Therefore, Parliament declared "that this day particularly is to

In this cartoon, the man on the left, presumably a Puritan, tells Father Christmas, "Keep out, you come not here." Father Christmas responds, "O Sir, I bring good cheere." The passerby on the right says, "Old Christmas welcome; Do not fear." Frontispiece to John Taylor's pamphlet *The Vindication of Christmas*, printed 1653.

be kept with the more solemn humiliation because it may call to remembrance our sins and the sins of our forefathers, who have turned against this Feast, pretending the memory of Christ, into an extreme forgetfulness of him, by giving liberty to carnal and sensual delights."[24]

But the suppression of Christmas was resisted by the English people. Although Parliament pointedly met on Christmas Day in 1644, the shops in London were closed in observance of the holiday. In 1646, many shops did stay open in line with the Puritans' wishes, but these businesses were so vandalized that the shop owners petitioned Parliament to provide them with protection in the future. The following year, the Puritan-led Parliament took the step of banning Christmas altogether, denouncing it as "a popish festival with no biblical justification" and a "wonton Bacchanalian feast."[25] But while shops were indeed open this year, people continued to observe Christmas by hanging evergreen decorations, which the Lord Mayor and City Marshal dutifully destroyed. Pro–Christmas riots even broke out in the countryside, most notably in Canterbury. The so-called Plum Pudding Riot was sparked by a Canterbury shopkeeper being put in the stocks for refusing to keep his shop open. Disaffected citizens protested by smashing windows of Puritan homes and shops, and the mayor was forced into hiding while his house was looted. Soldiers were dispatched to Canterbury in January 1648 to put down the mob, but the pro–Christmas riot had led to a general royalist revolt throughout Kent and the second round of the English Civil War.[26]

The Puritan ban in England was short-lived and Christmas was restored as a legal holiday in 1660, but the disagreements over religious issues including the observance of holidays substantially contributed both to civil strife and to the establishment of colonies in America. Although few would argue that the celebration of Christmas played a central role in the English Civil War from 1642 to 1651 or provided the main impetus for the Puritans to set sail for the New World to found their model of the Puritan way of life, the general dispute over how Christianity should be observed—with Yuletide festivities seen as an unholy blend of popish and pagan traditions—certainly played a role in these historic developments. There is some irony in the fact that the Mayflower, the vessel carrying 102 settlers fleeing religious persecution in England, deposited its passengers at the site of Plymouth Rock the day after Christmas in 1620.[27]

* * *

Just a year later, in 1621, Governor William Bradford of the Plymouth Colony reprimanded several colonists who maintained that it was against their conscience to work on Christmas day, and soon the Puritans were moving to prohibit observing the holiday altogether.[28] Like their predecessors in England, the American Puritans stressed that there is no reference to this celebration in Scripture, which only mentions the Sabbath as a holy day, with its required prayers, readings and rituals. Since the Bible did not prescribe special religious feasts, the Puritans rejected them as "devices of men," including the observance of Christmas.[29] They were also offended by the secular reveling at Christmas and understood that they were rooted in heathen customs.

Just as they had done in England, the Puritans initiated a ban on Christmas in the Massachusetts Bay Colony in 1659. According to a public notice posted that year, "the exchanging of Gifts and Greetings, dressing in Fine Clothing, Feasting and similar Satanical Practices are hereby FORBIDDEN." The case that the Puritans made for prohibiting the Christmas celebration included specific references to the holiday's pagan roots. As Puritan the Rev. Increase Mather of Boston observed in 1687, "the early Christians who first observed the Nativity on December 25 did not do so thinking that Christ was born in that Month, but because the Heathens' Saturnalia was at that time kept in Rome, and they were willing to have those Pagan Holidays metamorphosed into Christian ones."[30]

Puritans denounced Christmas as "Foolstide" and suppressed any attempts to celebrate it in colonial Massachusetts by making it a criminal offense. Citing the need to prevent "disorders arising in several places within this jurisdiction, by reason of some still observing such festivals as were superstitiously kept in other countries, to the great dishonor of God and offence of others," the General Court of the Massachusetts Bay Colony declared that "whosoever shall be found observing any such day as Christmas or the like, either by forbearing of labor, feasting, or any other way" would be subject to a hefty five-shilling fine.

The ban was revoked in 1681 by the English-appointed governor Edmund Andros, but New England officials continued to frown upon gift-giving and reveling. Evergreen decorations, widely understood as holdovers from pagan times, were forbidden in Puritan meeting houses and discouraged in homes.[31] As James Howard Barnett notes in *The American Christmas*, the Puritan view prevailed in New England for almost 200 years and against this backdrop, observing the holiday was taboo in former Puritan colonies until the mid–19th century. There were pockets of resistance that celebrated the holiday in Puritan-dominated areas but based on court records it appears that over the period of the 22 years that Christmas ban was in effect, no one was ever brought up on charges of enjoying Christmas. This probably indicates that those who did celebrate it did so discreetly.[32]

Besides the Puritans, other religious denominations including the Baptists, Congregationalists, Quakers, and Presbyterians also opposed the holiday. As

Born in 1639, Increase Mather was a highly influential Puritan minister in the Massachusetts Bay Colony who proselytized against the observation of Christmas. Portrait of Increase Mather. Artist H. Hopwood (Wellcome Collection).

Presbyterian minister Samuel Davies argued in a 1758 Christmas Day sermon, the licentious and superstitious use of the day was in general contrast to teachings in the Bible. He noted that based on his reading of the Scripture, there is no reason "to set apart this day for public worship, as though it had any peculiar sanctity, or we were under any obligations to keep it religiously." He pointed out that no human authority has the power to make one day holier than another. "And as for divine authority," he said, "to which alone the sanctifying of days and things belongs, it has thought it sufficient to consecrate one day in seven to a religious use, for the commemoration both of the birth of this world, and the resurrection of its great Author, or of the works of creation and redemption."[33]

With demographics heavily shaped by the early waves of English immigrants, much of post-colonial America shunned Christmas and its churches declined to recognize Christmas as a holy day well into the 19th century. An account in the New York *Daily Times* on December 26, 1855, noted that "the churches of the Presbyterians, Baptists and Methodists were not open on Dec. 25 ... but the Episcopalian, Catholic and German Churches were all open [and] decked with evergreens."[34] Also supporting Christmas were the Anglicans and Lutherans.[35] What appears to have turned the tide in favor of the Christmas celebration in America were the large numbers of immigrants arriving from Holland and Germany, as well as members of the pro–Christmas Church of England. The new colonists brought many Christmas-related customs from their homelands, including the Yule log, the Christmas tree, wassailing, and caroling, as well as variations of Father Christmas, St. Nicholas and Kris Kringle.

But while the Christmas celebrations were widely practiced in various American communities, it would take generations before Christmas established itself as a national tradition. It wasn't until nearly 100 years after the signing of the Declaration of Independence and five years after the Civil War ended that Christmas was declared a national holiday in the United States, in 1870. It would continue to become a widely celebrated holiday over the next few decades.

By this time, however, there were already those who were lamenting that people were losing the Christmas spirit. A book published in 1888 called *The Book of Christmas: Descriptive of the Customs, Ceremonies, Traditions, Superstitions, Fun, Feeling, and Festivities of the Christmas Season* complained that the "hearty festivity in which our ancestors met this season has been long on the decline; and much of the joyous pomp with which it was once received has long since passed away."[36] In other words, Christmas just wasn't what it used to be.

Part Two
Curious Customs

6

Sacred Trees

Cold and wintry is the sky,
Bitter winds go whistling by,
Orchard boughs are bare and dry,
Yet here stands a faithful tree.
 —Louisa May Alcott,
  "A Song for a Christmas Tree"

Wherever Christmas is celebrated, even in the middle of summer in countries of the southern hemisphere such as Australia, you will find evergreen trees standing tall in living rooms, decorated with ornaments, tinsel, and lights. There is a deep sentimentality bordering on reverence that many attach to this tradition, captured well by the German carol "O Tannenbaum," which is essentially an ode to the Christmas tree: "O Christmas tree, O Christmas tree / Your boughs can teach a lesson / That constant faith and hope sublime / Lend strength and comfort through all time." Yet, while the Christmas tree serves as the focal point of countless families' festivities and is seen by many as something of a necessity to celebrate the holiday properly, its origins are shrouded in mystery. Some might have a vague recollection of a story relating to the Protestant reformer Martin Luther initiating the practice while others might assume that it is a holdover from pagan practices, but the truth is, the origins of this custom are murky at best. Religious teachings offer possible inspirations for the tradition, but ultimately their usefulness is limited because no single religion can be seen as the spiritual basis for the significance of trees.

It is true that pagans had special reverence for trees, but trees of course hold symbolic meaning in many religions and cultures. There is for example the "tree of life," or "world tree," which is a bedrock of ancient belief systems from Mesopotamia to Persia to China to Mesoamerica, holding significance in Buddhism, Manichaeism, Islam, and Judaism to name a few. In the Norse religion, it is called Yggdrasil, which is known to be an ash tree, but Norse peoples and Germanic tribes also honored Thor's Oak and the sacred tree at Uppsala. Numerous biblical passages refer to trees, including Chronicles 16:33, which states that "the trees of the forest sing before the Lord, for he comes to judge the earth." The Gospel of Matthew uses trees a metaphor for righteousness, advising that "every healthy tree bears good fruit, but the diseased tree bears bad fruit." And then of course, there is the tree of knowledge in the Book of Genesis, which is the source of man's Original Sin.

In heathen beliefs, the importance of trees was alluded to in the Old Testament's Book of Jeremiah:

6. Sacred Trees

> Learn not the way of the heathen, and be not dismayed at the signs of heaven; for the heathen are dismayed at them. For the customs of the people are vain: for one cutteth a tree out of the forest, the work of the hands of the workman, with the axe. They deck it with silver and with gold; they fasten it with nails and with hammers, that it move not. They are upright as the palm tree, but speak not: they must needs be borne, because they cannot go. Be not afraid of them; for they cannot do evil, neither also is it in them to do good.

Some have seized on this biblical passage as proof that the Christmas tree is pagan in origin. Indeed, the line about heathens "cutting a tree out of the forest" and "deck[ing] it with silver and with gold" sounds curiously familiar and could provide some insight into the practices of pagan peoples, specifically how they may have venerated trees and decorated them with ornaments. But since the Book of Jeremiah covers events leading up to the fall of Jerusalem to the Babylonians in 587 BCE, it may be a stretch to cite this as the origins for our modern custom of decorating evergreen trees at Christmas time.

* * *

Others cite the wreath as an ancient pagan precursor to the Christmas tree, noting that it was an important symbol of victory and power in Greco-Roman beliefs and was associated with the god Apollo. In Ovid's poem Metamorphoses, written in the year eight CE, the nymph Daphne rejects Apollo and turns into a laurel tree. Apollo tells her that since she will not be his wife, she will be his tree. "O laurel," he says, "I shall for ever have you in my hair, on my lyre and quiver." This poem inspired art related to Apollo crowning himself with the wreath, possibly providing inspiration for this Christmas tradition. Wreaths, however, were also used throughout Europe in pre–Christian societies as symbolic of harvests, associated generally with the changing seasons and fertility.[1] It was after Pope Gregory I advised bishops to encourage such popular customs as decorating with greenery that they began to take on meaning as Christian expressions of faith,[2] and wreaths in particular came to be associated with Advent.

But while wreaths and the use of other greenery may provide some general context, they don't explain the specific practice of decorating evergreen trees at Christmas time. When it comes to this custom, there is a good deal of disagreement where and when it may have started, with some countries taking it as a matter of national pride in staking claim to it. Although Latvians insist that they initiated the practice in Riga in 1510 and neighboring Estonians claim that the first Christmas tree was erected in Tallinn in 1441,[3] it seems that the first written record of people decorating trees in their homes is from 1605. A contemporary chronicle from Strasbourg reported that Protestant artisans brought fir trees into their homes in the holiday season and decorated them with "roses made of colored paper, apples, wafers, tinsel, sweetmeats, etc." The specific practice may have originated with a decoration commonly used in Germany called a candelabrum. This pyramidal wooden structure was often elaborately decorated, containing family mementoes, Christmas decorations and candles, with the whole family participating in constructing and decorating it.[4] Similar in shape to a small evergreen tree, the practice of decorating trees may have started with this activity, beginning in the upper classes of Germany and moving to lower social strata, from urban to rural households, and from the Protestant north to the Catholic south, and from Germany to the rest of Europe.[5]

This drawing for Dickens' *A Christmas Carol* captures the essence of a traditional Christmas wreath. Wreaths can be traced back to ancient Greece and in pre–Christian societies were seen as symbolic of harvests and fertility. Artist Everett Shinn. Illustration from Dickens' *A Christmas Carol*, ink on paper and board (Smithsonian American Art Museum, Gift of Fred D. Bentley, Sr.).

"The Christmas tree is genuinely German in its origin," reads an account from 1865. "Thence it happens that it is found among the Germans alone, and that, like a stranger, it has wandered from Germany to all other lands." According to this writer, who notes that the symbolism of the Christmas tree has both a heathen and biblical background, German emigrants and sailors from merchant vessels spread the custom far and wide. The Germans, who retained their collective memory of ancient veneration of trees while also embracing their Christian symbolism, manifested their respect for trees in the Christmas tree tradition which they then shared with others when they migrated to other countries. "Wherever you trace the origin of the Christmas-tree outside Germany, you will find that it has been introduced from the Fatherland."[6]

But rather than originating from any one particular place or time, decorating trees in the dark days of winter may have actually sporadically taken place throughout the ancient world long before anyone thought to take note of the practice. "The establishment of the Christmas tree as the central symbol of German celebration had no obvious historical trajectory," Joe Perry writes in *Christmas in Germany: A Cultural History*. "Rather, the custom emerged out of divergent and dispersed practices, which in Early Modern and central Europe included the use of indoor greenery to celebrate the various December festivals that marked the end of the harvest season."[7] Small evergreens known as Yule trees were brought into homes during winter as a reminder that nature was only dormant, not dead, and that it would eventually return. The overlapping of pre–Christian and Christian practices as related to trees could be seen as recently as the mid–20th century. In his *Handbook of Christian Feasts and Customs*, published in 1952, Francis Weiser points out that "Yule trees may still be found in some sections of central Europe, standing side by side with the Christmas tree in the homes of rural districts." He notes that their symbolism has "remained entirely separate" from that of the Christmas tree.[8]

Perhaps, however, the symbolism was not as separate as Weiser believed, with both customs rooted in the veneration of trees that extends back to prehistoric times when nomadic tribes made up the world. The religious significance of trees to pre–Christian peoples is hard to overstate, and the residual customs related to these beliefs may have survived even if their one-time sacred status has largely been forgotten.

* * *

For Neolithic people, clearcutting trees for farming would have had a profound impact on their relationship to the world, revealing details of the land and enabling humans to shape it even as natural forces had done before. Natural marks in the land such as rock formations and great trees, which had been important to nomadic hunter-gatherers, would have retained their sense of wonder for people raising livestock or tilling crops.[9] Therefore, when a wandering group of tribespeople cleared the land to establish a village, they would leave a group of trees in the center of the clearing, and in the center of those trees would be a "mother tree." The tribespeople focused their pursuit of religious belief on this mother tree, and as settlements grew and additional communities were formed, the pioneers would take with them their gods and their customs.

The ancient Celts believed that ancestral ghosts sometimes assumed the form of trees, as well as other objects such as stones, and sometimes animals. All the Celtic tribes had a sacred tree and their intellectual class, the druids, particularly venerated the oak tree. Indeed, the druid caste's origins can be traced back to the hunter-gatherer age when forests covered Europe and early Europeans saw the oak, in particular, as a symbol of plenty. This tree was considered the hardiest and most useful of all the trees, and to have knowledge of it endowed one with survival abilities and wisdom. This led to the rise of the "wise ones of the oak," and the important role played by the woodsman in ancient barbarian civilizations for thousands of years.[10]

In pagan times, the changing seasons were of enormous significance, with the shift in weather affecting the availability of certain foods and marking important breaks in the yearly agricultural cycle. Trees were venerated as symbolic of the various seasons, with evergreens specifically associated with the winter solstice, but trees in general holding significance at all times of year. The oak tree was particularly important at the summer solstice, representing strength and endurance, and symbolic of summer's abundance which later gives way to winter's desolation. In some parts of Germany there was a custom of dancing around a tree to celebrate the longest day of the year,[11] and in Finland branches from birch trees were placed on both sides of the front door during the summer solstice to welcome visitors.[12]

In Adam of Bremen's 11th-century description of the temple of Uppsala, he noted that near the temple stood "a very large tree with wide-spreading branches, always green in winter and summer." Trees adorned with bodies of human sacrifice victims were considered holy, Adam reported, while other trees acquired sacred status due to their proximity to springs, which were venerated as the givers of life and others were worshipped as representing particular gods. Sacred trees were lavishly

A robed man sits in the shade of a giant tree, with a group of three robed figures surrounding a smaller tree in the background. "Old England: A Pictorial Museum," 1845. Artist Charles Knight.

decorated, a practice that was decreed a treasonable offense in Rome under the reign of Theodosius after he made Christianity the official state religion.[13]

The ash tree was important to the Gaels, who believed it had protective properties, and in British folklore, it was believed to promote children's health.[14] This tree was also sacred to the Nordic peoples and, according to the *Poetic Edda*, was called Yggdrasil, or the world tree. Binding together nine magical realms, the world tree was also known as the tree of life or the tree of destiny and had a special relationship to the human spirit. The tree grew in the middle of the world and had roots that spread to the home of the gods, the home of the giants, and to Hel's realm of death.[15] Travelers could move between the worlds on sacred rivers and lakes and across a "Rainbow Bridge," known as Bifrost.[16] Beneath each root was a spring and under the root of Jotunheim, home of the giants, was the water of wisdom. Under the root of Asgård was a holy place where the gods gathered.[17] As described in the 1854 study *The Religion of the Norsemen* by Rudolph Keyser, "the element of evil gnaws continually at its deepest root" but the trunk of the tree "is sprinkled over with the sacred, purifying waters of the celestial fountain, and Yggdrasil, with all its sufferings, stands forever green."[18]

Associated with the goddess Freyja, the beech tree was sacred to the Germans, who would cut twigs from the branches and write upon them mysterious signs known as runes. These sticks would then be scattered on the ground, and from their arrangement, the future could be ascertained by a diviner. From this ancient practice derives the German word *buch*, or its English counterpart "book." The Germans also attached special significance to the linden tree, which was considered a symbol of love, fertility, prosperity, fidelity, friendship, peace, justice, altruism, and good luck. People were known to celebrate and dance under a linden tree, as well as hold judicial proceedings there in order to restore justice and peace, as it was believed that the tree would help unearth the truth. Thus the tree became associated with jurisprudence even after Christianization, with the term "under Tilia," i.e., under the linden tree, inscribed on judicial verdicts in some German regions up until the Enlightenment. Linden trees also have a special place in popular traditions due to their perceived protective traits, helping to keep away evil spirits, as well as their healing properties and many uses for raw material. The symbolism of the linden tree is detailed in various religious doctrines, not only German mythology but also Slavic, Baltic, Romanian, and Greek.[19]

The significance attached to trees was not limited to one region or another, nor to one pantheon of gods or another. In ancient Greco-Roman mythology, various deities such as the god of the sun and light Apollo, the goddess of wild animals Diana, the water nymph Egeria, and the woodland god Virbius[20] were believed to reside in groves, which were therefore considered sacred. If the sanctity of a holy grove was violated in the ancient Roman world the punishments could be severe. In Attica, those who were caught in the act of cutting trees in a sacred grove or carrying away timber, firewood, or fallen leaves, could be punished with flagellation or a fine. Similar customs prevailed in Italy, where those who took wood from a sacred grove were required to sacrifice an ox to Jupiter. In one grove, which was believed to be the sanctuary of the goddess Dia, sacrifices of sows and lambs had to be offered when a branch fell to the ground or when an old tree fell.[21]

Providing an indication of the intrinsic sacred nature of trees and forests, in northern Europe, the heathen word used for "temple" was synonymous with "wood," and similarly, the Celts used the word *nemeton* for "sanctuary," which seems to be identical in origin and meaning with the Latin word *nemus*, which meant "forest."[22] This shared etymology underlines the profound religious significance of trees, forests, and groves for pre–Christian peoples. Indeed, as Grimm explains in *Teutonic*

Published in Wilhelm Wägner's 1886 book *Asgard and the Gods*, the caption reads, "The world tree Yggdrasil and some of its inhabitants." "The Ash Yggdrasil," 1886. Artist Friedrich Wilhelm Heine.

Mythology, groves were considered the homes of the gods, who would veil their forms "in rustling foliage of the boughs."[23] The forest was not the only the place that deities dwelled, he explains, but it was the principal one. "Here and there a god may haunt a mountain-top, a cave of the rock, a river," writes Grimm, "but the grand general worship of the people has its seat in the grove." Divine worship was therefore typically associated with trees and performed in groves, a practice that existed for many centuries, "down to the introduction of Christianity," Grimm writes.[24]

Indeed, it was precisely because of pagans' veneration of trees that they were systematically targeted for destruction by missionaries during Christianization. Part of the missionaries' task was to make the figure of Christ appear to be almighty and majestic, which is something that they did through dramatic displays of Jesus's power and divinity, including by chopping down sacred trees. This was an important tactic to both suppress pagan customs and to demonstrate the miraculous power of Jesus. St. Martin of Tours, for example, exploited pagans' veneration of trees in his efforts to convert them in fourth-century Gaul. After he had demolished a temple, he set about cutting down a pine tree nearby, only to be surrounded by a "crowd of heathens" who angrily protested.[25] According to a 19th-century account by Father Francis Xavier Weninger,

> One day, he was about to fell a tree, because the heathens used it for their idolatry. They opposed him, most violently; at length, one of them said: "Behold! we ourselves will fell the tree if you promise that, as it falls, you will support it in your hands. By this sign we shall be convinced of the might of the God whose word you preach." The Saint promised without any hesitation, to do as they desired. The tree was cut so that it would fall towards Martin; and when it came down, he made the sign of the Cross and stretching out his hands, not only received the tree into them, but threw it back to the opposite side, without injuring anyone. By this and several other miracles, the holy bishop ... converted a great many heathens.[26]

The general beliefs about the sanctity of trees combined with the spiritual importance attached to seasonal changes and the path of the sun led to observances using evergreens and trees at the winter solstice. This could help explain not only the origins of the Christmas tree, but other tree-related Christmas traditions such as the Yule log,[27] or a pre–Christian custom in Poland of hanging a branch of an evergreen tree from the ceiling during the winter festival. It is why, as Clement Miles describes it in *Christmas Customs and Traditions*, the Christmas tree was seen as "a kind of sacrament linking mankind to the mysteries of the woodland." Unlike the British, to whom the Christmas tree was considered a luxury (at least at the time of Miles' writing in the early 20th century), to the Germans, the Christmas tree was a necessity, and no one was too poor to have one. "The Germans have quite a religious feeling for their *Weihnachtsbaum* [Christmas tree]," Miles writes, "coming down, one may fancy, from some dim ancestral worship of the trees of the wood."[28]

But while these ancient origins of the Christmas tree may help explain the underlying context for this custom, they don't provide a solid basis for understanding why the tradition specifically developed in Germany and spread from there. To appreciate how this happened, it is worth looking at the story of the Christianization of the Teutonic tribes.

* * *

A well-known legend traces the Christmas tree's origins to the conversion of Germany to Christianity in the early 700s, when St. Boniface used the fir tree to replace the heathens' sacred oak, noting that its shape pointed to God in heaven and its evergreen leaves signified eternal life.[29]

This account was recalled in a short story by a 19th-century Presbyterian minister named Henry Van Dyke who made a habit of reading his Christmas stories to his New York City congregation in the 1890s. His tale, called "The First Christmas Tree," told the story of Boniface, whom Van Dyke described as "[f]air and slight, but straight as a spear and strong as an oaken staff." It is a story of the triumph of light over darkness, in which "the cross of Christ [breaks] the hammer of the false god Thor." According to legend, Boniface and his traveler companions came across an assembly of a pagan tribe in the forest on Christmas Eve. "All who swear by the old gods have been summoned," Boniface's companion tells him. "They will sacrifice a steed to the god of war, and drink blood, and eat horse-flesh to make them strong." He warned that it would "be at the peril of our lives if we approach them" and urged Boniface to hide his cross in the hopes of escaping certain death at the hands of the hostiles. But Brave Boniface would have none of it and insisted that he would show them the cross to "make these blind folk see its power."

After introducing himself, Boniface was told by one of the heathens, an old priest named Hunrad, that they had gathered around a great oak tree for the death night of the sun god, Baldur the Beautiful. "This night is the hour of darkness and the power of winter, of sacrifice and mighty fear," Hunrad said. "This night the great Thor, the god of thunder and war, to whom this oak is sacred, is grieved for the death of Baldur, and angry with this people because they have forsaken his worship." He claimed that a sacrifice was needed to appease the god and chose a young boy from the crowd to be the unfortunate victim, telling him that he would soon be on his way to Valhalla. But Boniface intervened, declaring that the birth of Christ had heralded the end of "bloody sacrifices":

> Not a drop of blood shall fall to-night, save that which pity has drawn from the breast of your princess, in love for her child. Not a life shall be blotted out in the darkness tonight; but the great shadow of the tree which hides you from the light of heaven shall be swept away. For this is the birth-night of the white Christ, son of the All-Father, and Saviour of mankind. Fairer is He than Baldur the Beautiful, greater than Odin the Wise, kinder than Freyja the Good. Since He has come to earth the bloody sacrifices must cease. The dark Thor, on whom you vainly call, is dead. Deep in the shades of Niffelheim he is lost forever. His power in the world is broken. Will you serve a helpless god? See, my brothers, you call this tree his oak. Does he dwell here? Does he protect it?

Boniface proceeded to chop down the sacred oak tree to demonstrate the power of Christ over Thor, shouting, "Tree-god! Art thou angry? Thus we smite thee!" After the tree was felled, the missionary gazed upon a young fir tree nearby, with its top pointing towards the stars, and said, "here is the living tree, with no stain of blood upon it, that shall be the sign of your new worship."

Amazed that Boniface was not struck down by Thor for destroying the sacred tree, the pagans immediately converted to Christianity and began venerating the fir tree. "I think the day is coming when there shall not be a home in all Germany where the children are not gathered around the green fir-tree to rejoice in the birth-night of

Christ," Boniface said.[30] And hence, according to the legend, the Christmas tree was born.

* * *

It is a matter of speculation whether these events happened precisely as the story has been handed down, but nevertheless, due to this story Germans most often get the credit for initiating the tradition of the modern Christmas tree, which was adopted throughout Europe and was brought to America with the waves of European emigration in the 17th and 18th centuries.

But although it generally establishes the Christmas tree as a quintessential Christian tradition, a symbol of Christ's triumph over false pagan gods and a heartwarming story of the benevolence of the "birth night" of Christ contrasted with the heathen "death night of the sun god," the legend also confirms that there are strong elements of paganism in this beloved Christmas tradition. If we are to accept it as true, or at least loosely based on actual events (Boniface for what it's worth was a real missionary who was consecrated as a bishop by Pope Gregory II in gratitude for his success in converting the Frisian Saxons[31]), its underlying implications are that the Christmas tree's origins are at least partially heathen. After all, if trees were not sacred to the pagans, neither Boniface's destruction of the oak tree nor the fir tree that he pointed to would have had any significance. The fir tree was only relevant to the pagans because they had previously venerated sacred trees and groves. This is why, following the destruction of Thor's Oak tree, the pagans "took the little fir from its place, and carried it in joyous procession to the edge of the glade," placed the tree inside one of their houses and "kindled lights among the branches until it seemed to be tangled full of fire-flies."

The fact that trees and groves were so important to the pagans is precisely why they were so enamored by missionaries' displays, and according to the legend of St. Boniface, why it is that they embraced the fir tree as the symbolic embodiment of life. It took on significance following conversion as a holy display of devotion to Christ because underlying heathen ideas remained largely intact—covered with a veneer of Christian belief—among many former pagans. As the Church had rededicated the trees to Christ,[32] in later years, Christians could continue the practice of decorating trees as an expression of their faith.

This more nuanced perspective, however, is missing from many mainstream accounts that can be found related to the Christmas tree's origin. For example, while acknowledging that evergreens have always had a special meaning for people in the winter, and that ancient peoples may have hung evergreen boughs over their doors and windows, *History.com* credits Germany with starting the Christmas tree tradition when devout Christians brought decorated trees into their homes in the 1500s. "It is a widely held belief that Martin Luther, the 16th-century Protestant reformer, first added lighted candles to a tree," according to the website. "Walking toward his home one winter evening, composing a sermon, he was awed by the brilliance of stars twinkling amidst evergreens. To recapture the scene for his family, he erected a tree in the main room and wired its branches with lighted candles."[33] This is the same general approach taken by the British periodical *History Today*, which defers to legend in claiming that Luther "invented the Christmas tree" in 1536 while walking through a pine forest, "when he suddenly looked up and saw thousands of stars

78　　　　　　　　　　Part Two—Curious Customs

This illustration depicts a scene in a forest where evergreen trees are chopped down and wreaths are fashioned with branches. Artist Winslow Homer (Smithsonian, gift of John Goldsmith Phillips, Jr.).

glinting jewel-like among the branches of the trees." It was this awe-inspiring sight that gave him the idea to set up a candle-lit fir tree in his house that Christmas "to remind his children of the starry heavens from whence their Saviour came."[34] However, although Luther died in 1546, the first confirmed Christmas tree in his hometown, Wittenberg, only appears in the 18th century, raising considerable doubt about the veracity of the claims that he invented the tradition.[35]

Other accounts point to earlier sources for the tradition but focus just as much on its purported Christian origins. In his book *The Christmas Tree*, for example, Daniel J. Foley traces the tradition to the "paradise plays" that were popular in the 15th century. These plays depicted miracle scenes from the Bible, including the story of the nativity, and used evergreens as props. A popular medieval play about Adam and Eve used the fir tree adorned with apples, representing the tree of knowledge. Watching these plays, Foley claims, people were inspired to use fir trees in their own homes.[36] This is certainly a plausible explanation, and, incidentally it is the same general version of the Christmas tree's origins offered by *Encyclopædia Britannica*, which also cites the Christmas pyramid as an inspiration:

> The Germans set up a paradise tree in their homes on December 24, the religious feast day of Adam and Eve. They hung wafers on it (symbolizing the host, the Christian sign of redemption); in a later tradition, the wafers were replaced by cookies of various shapes. Candles, too, were often added as the symbol of Christ. In the same room, during the Christmas season, was the Christmas pyramid, a triangular construction of wood, with

shelves to hold Christmas figurines, decorated with evergreens, candles, and a star. By the 16th century, the Christmas pyramid and paradise tree had merged, becoming the Christmas tree.[37]

Britannica, however, also concedes that there may be a pre–Christian element to the practice, noting that "[t]ree worship was common among the pagan Europeans and survived their conversion to Christianity."

Scholar Bernd Brunner has also investigated the origins of this tradition and in his book *Inventing the Christmas Tree* identifies the first known Christmas tree as being erected in the Strasbourg Cathedral in 1539. But while this is the first example of a public display that he was able to decisively document, Brunner stresses that this was probably not the first instance of the practice, and ultimately—despite the name of his book—the custom is not something that was simply invented. Rather, "it was the product of centuries of custom, myth, vivid imagination, craftsmanship and iconography." Summing up the roots of this holiday icon, Brunner defers to German historian Alexander Demandt, who points out that the roots of the Christmas tree are many and reach deep into the past. "The meaning is Christian, the origins are ancient, and the form of the Christmas celebration is Germanic," Demandt argues.[38]

* * *

What the various accounts of the Christmas tree's origins demonstrate is that, like many Christmas customs, the ultimate source of the tradition is not known for certain but likely incorporates various strains of spiritual belief including paganism and Christianity. In some ways, it could be said, tracing this custom's origins is similar to tracing the origins of pizza. While Italy's Naples generally lays claim to this beloved food, the reality is that pizza-like dishes were eaten by many peoples, including the ancient Greeks and Egyptians, in the Mediterranean and probably other regions throughout history. After all, it is a pretty simple concept to put items such as cheese and vegetables on top of bread, and variations of this practice may very well have existed as far back as people figured out how to bake bread and make cheese.

Likewise, while it is difficult for historians to pinpoint the exact moment that the Christmas tree tradition was initiated, and although history may record the first trees being decorated in the Middle Ages out of Christian piousness, the custom—in one variation or another—likely has its roots in practices that go much further back in time. While Germany generally receives the credit for initiating the custom, the reason it caught on and spread so widely, and continues to deeply resonate to this day, is because both tree worship and decorating homes with greenery at midwinter were widespread in the ancient world.

In fact, it was due to its perceived heathen connotations that some religious authorities frowned upon the custom of decorating trees, urging the faithful instead to use the crèche to express their devotion to Christ at Christmas time. Protestant theologian Johann Konrad Dannhauer condemned the Christmas tree custom in his book *The Milk of the Catechism* in 1657, calling it a "trifle" that "overtak[es] the word of God." He stressed that it would be "much better to direct children towards the spiritual cedar tree of Jesus Christ."[39] Dannhauer's condemnation of the Christmas tree calls into question the supposed Christian roots of the tradition and specifically

This wood engraving depicts a 19th-century family gathered around a Christmas tree. It appeared in the December 25, 1858, edition of *Harper's Weekly*. "The Christmas Tree." Artist Winslow Homer (Smithsonian, Gift of John Goldsmith Phillips, Jr., Harris Brisbane Dick Fund 1936).

the dubious claims that it was initiated by Martin Luther. Despite being an Orthodox Lutheran theologian and educator, writing just a century after Luther supposedly invented the tradition after his stroll through the forest on a starlit night, Dannhauer admits: "Whence comes the custom, I know not; it is child's play."[40] Catholics, meanwhile, considered Christmas trees as little more than a Protestant fad, deriding them as *Lutherbaums*.

So, considering the objections of contemporary Christian leaders and their doubts about its origins as a Christian practice, why then does history generally record the Christmas tree as being a product of devout Christians decorating trees in the spirit of devotion to Jesus Christ? It is difficult to answer this question with any certainty, but it is possible that medieval Christians and subsequent generations of theologians may have exaggerated the role of Luther and other devout believers in initiating the practice. These accounts served to gloss over the heathen influences and provided Christians the assurances they needed to enjoy the custom without troubling themselves with concerns about the custom perpetuating pagan superstitions. This doesn't change the historical reality, however, that Roman pagans once decorated homes with laurels and evergreens during the Kalends, or that pagans venerated trees in the ancient world.

* * *

Although it may not be possible to draw direct lines from one ancient practice such as adorning trees with victims of sacrifice or dancing around trees at the solstice to modern rituals of picking out an evergreen tree at a gas station parking lot, hauling it home, and hanging ornaments on the branches, there is a particular historical context that is relevant. Whether or not connections can be made decisively between one practice and another, the reality is that pagans, including pre–Christian Teutonic tribes, were particularly partial to tree worship, believing that trees provided links between humans and the gods. And while convincing documentary or archaeological proof might be lacking, there is a good chance that the practice of decorating trees during the period of the winter solstice is something that was taking place long before the chronicle in Strasbourg recorded it in 1605.

In this sense, when a family makes a tradition of trimming the tree together, it is more than just a cozy and fun thing to do. It is in fact a continuation of traditions and ancient beliefs that stem from a time when people venerated trees as givers of life. The ancient link between humans and the woods, which is represented extensively in oral traditions, mythologies and pagan beliefs, have been passed down in various symbols and rituals over the centuries, one of these being the tradition of the Christmas tree. As Christian Ratsch and Claudia Muller-Ebeling write in *Pagan Christmas*,

> Whenever we decorate the evergreen tree and make it the center of a Christmas feast, we are engaging unconsciously with very ancient ideas. ... We engage with the cyclical events in which we are bound, which are reinforced in our minds by the recurrent Christmas ritual. We engage with times long past, when natural events that we now take for granted were holy to human beings.

Or, as Paul Frodsham explains the growing popularity of decorating Christmas trees in Victorian England, it "was surely the (perhaps subconscious) desire to perpetuate ancient traditions associated with evergreens and fire (represented by candles or fairy lights) at midwinter."[41]

In this sense, perhaps these customs are neither pagan nor Christian, but simply human. The fact that people have been using evergreens at midwinter since the time of the ancient Egyptians, and that there are references to wreaths in the ancient records of the Romans, Hebrews and Persians, could be an indication that this practice is just something that people do as a method of self-expression and to raise spirits at an otherwise bleak time of year. "This practice among men is obviously a kind of universal expression of joy mingled with devotion, and can hardly be described as either a pagan or a Christian custom," writes Daniel Foley in *The Christmas Tree*. "Living plants exemplifying the essence of beauty helped to dispel the gloom of winter, and the evergreens particularly symbolized eternal life." The long-running debate over who initiated the Christmas tree or whether it is a pagan or a Christian tradition might therefore miss the point about the underlying significance of these customs.

The same goes for many other Christmas traditions that recall ancient beliefs. While there is some disagreement and sometimes the historical evidence is less than clear on certain points, one conclusion that can reasonably be drawn is that Christmas owes much—if not everything—to pre–Christian traditions. Regardless of the particulars of how each religion may have influenced the others, and precisely how specific customs may have been affected, what is clear is that the history of Christmas is closely related to pre-existing beliefs and practices that dominated Europe prior to Christianization. Customs such as the Christmas tree, even if they might also have some relation to Christian practices such as the paradise plays, are nevertheless intertwined with Christianity's intermingling with other religions and beliefs. This reminds us that the celebration that we enjoy every year would simply not exist as we know it, were it not for our pagan predecessors such as the Romans, the Celts, and the Norse.

7

The Man, the Myth, the Legend, the God—Santa Claus

He rides to the East, and he rides to the West,
Of his goodies he touches not one;
He eateth the crumbs of the Christmas feast
When the dear little folks are done.
Old Santa Claus doeth all that he can;
This beautiful mission is his;
Then, children, be good to the little old man,
When you find who the little man is.
  —Anonymous, "Santa Claus"

Our modern Christmas celebration is personified by a character who at first glance appears to have nothing to do with either Christianity or paganism, but upon closer inspection may be the product of both. Seen today as a generally secular figure who is heavily utilized by commercial interests for selling consumer goods during Christmas time, Santa Claus is actually an amalgamation of ecclesiastical and pagan myths, reimagined by writers, artists, and marketers to reflect contemporary realities and values. The legend has been enthusiastically embraced by popular culture which has enabled it to grow and develop into a comprehensive and cogent narrative that appears unique to Christmas but harkens back to a time when humans widely and earnestly believed in supernatural beings and magic.

The historical backdrop for the Santa Claus myth is most often traced to a third-century monk called Saint Nicholas, who was known for his piety, generosity, and kindness. There are no written references of St. Nicholas until approximately 250 years after his death, so much of what is known about him is more the stuff of legend than history, and consequently there are some who claim that he never actually existed as a human.[1] According to this view, St. Nicholas was an invention of the Church, a Christianized version of various pagan gods, in particular the Greek god Poseidon and his Roman equivalent Neptune. This, however, appears to be a minority view and most scholars seem to believe that Nicholas (probably) existed,[2] although this does not preclude the possibility that he was given certain attributes by the Church that would help supplant these pagan deities.

Reliable information about Nicholas's life—assuming he existed—is scarce, and while historians dispute the "facts" related to his life,[3] he is said to have been born in 270 CE near Myra in Greece, now part of modern-day Turkey, as the son of wealthy parents who died when he was still young. Following the admonition of Jesus to "sell what you own and give the money to the poor," legend has it that Nicholas donated his entire inheritance to assist the needy and the sick. He was reportedly made Bishop of Myra and was apparently imprisoned under the rule of Roman Emperor Diocletian.[4] He is also said to have participated in the first Council of Nicaea in 325, where the creed establishing that God the Son and God the Father are of the same substance was affirmed, but scholars disagree about whether Nicholas was actually there. Some skeptics have noted that his attendance was not mentioned by the historian Eusebius, who was present at the council.[5]

Known for his love of children and concern for sailors and ships, Nicholas has been venerated for centuries as the protector of orphans and sailors, and is the patron saint of several port cities, as well as the Hellenic Navy. In centuries of Greek folklore, Nicholas was seen as "The Lord of the Sea," which has led some scholars to speculate that Nicholas is in fact a Christianized version of Poseidon.[6] Indeed, the date of his death, given as December 6, "may be an adaptation of Poseidon's feast day to connect Nicholas with the ocean and mariners," according to anthropologist Benjamin K. Swartz, Jr.[7] Supporting this theory, an archaeological discovery in Bulgaria of what is believed to be the remains of an altar to Poseidon's temple is located adjacent to a Christian church dedicated to Saint Nicholas. This suggests that Nicholas's sainthood may have functioned as a replacement for pagan deity worship.[8]

As early as the sixth century, St. Nicholas had become widely revered throughout much of Europe. Legends were told of his miraculous feats, including how he would force storms to subside in order to save ships from being sunk and how he could walk on water to assist drowning sailors, as well as stories of him protecting children from harm. In one legend, St. Nicholas decided to help a poverty-stricken family whose father could not afford to pay the dowries needed to marry off his three daughters. Rather than allow the three girls to be sold into prostitution, St. Nicholas left bags filled with gold for the family. Believing it was more virtuous to make the donations in secret without receiving accolades for his generosity, Nicholas anonymously threw the bags of gold through the window and

This coin, from ca. 300–295 BCE, depicts Poseidon hurling a trident. Many scholars believe that the legends of St. Nicholas served as a replacement during the Christianization period for pagan legends of Poseidon. Poseidon coin from Greece. Silver (Cleveland Museum of Art).

ran away. This story led to the practice in medieval times of children hanging up stockings on the Eve of St. Nicholas's Feast on December 6. Children would awaken the next morning to find small gifts in the stocking like nuts and figs.[9]

Being so closely associated with sailors and ships, St. Nicholas was especially venerated by the Normans, who were descended from Viking pagans. In the 11th and 12th centuries, the Normans were among the most influential forces in Europe and with roots as seafaring people, they were attracted to the legends of St. Nicholas performing miracles at sea.[10] As recent converts to Christianity, they also may have been impressed by his miraculous powers, which resembled the abilities of pagan gods from the Norse pantheon. Normans who hadn't adopted Christianity, particularly in the land known as Kievan Rus (comprising parts of the modern nations of Belarus, Russia, and Ukraine), were receptive to the story of St. Nicholas, which proved to be an effective tool of conversion by Byzantine missionaries. The Normans embraced St. Nicholas as their favored saint and spread his name everywhere.[11] Merging with the pre–Christian figure known as Morozko, described in Slavic mythology as a "snow demon,"[12] the St. Nicholas myth gave rise to Ded Moroz, or "Grandfather Frost," which would become the Eastern European version of the midwinter gift bringer.

The detail from "The Story of St Nicholas: St Nicholas saves the ship" shows one of St. Nicholas's many miracles at sea. Artist Fra Angelico, 1447–48.

St. Nicholas became the most popular saint in Europe by the 15th century, and even after the veneration of saints began to fall out of favor during the Protestant Reformation, he maintained a large following, especially in Holland. According to most historical accounts, in the 17th and 18th centuries Dutch, German and Swiss colonists brought the tradition of St. Nicholas (known to the Dutch as Sinterklaas, or as the Swiss-Germans called him, Samichlaus or Santi-Chlaus) to America where he was adopted by the American colonists and in the process lost many of his ecclesiastical characteristics.[13] The German version was assisted by his partner Belsnickel, also known as Knecht Ruprecht, a somewhat menacing figure who punished bad children and gave presents to good children. With a face darkened with burnt cork, a wig, carrying a switch and wearing bells, Belsnickel visited homes to check up on the behavior of the children, showing up at houses a week or two before Christmas and often inspiring fear because he always knew who had been a naughty child. Entering the house, he would scatter sweets over the floor and the children would have to dodge his switch as they attempted to collect the treats.[14]

❋   ❋   ❋

While St. Nicholas is widely considered the primary inspiration for Santa Claus, like many Christmas traditions, the origins of the myth are multilayered and are as varied as the many names that he goes by around the world: Father Christmas, St. Nick, Ded Moroz, Papai Noel, Julemand, Mikulás, Hoteiosho, Père Noël, and Noel Baba to name a few. As British historians A.W. Purdue and J.M. Golby have explained, "Every European society had ... some legend of a spirit or personification of Christmas, legends that were almost certainly part of the southern European Saturnalia or the Yuletide of the Teutonic north before they took on a Christmas guise."[15] Indeed, many of these origin stories are influenced by pagan traditions in one way or another, and striking similarities can be found in depictions of them compared to Slavic, Egyptian, Greek, Roman, and Germanic gods associated with the winter solstice. Much like these various gods, the Slavic Ded Moroz, American Santa Claus and Scandinavian Julemand, for example, all tend to be old men with long white hair and beards, wearing long robes, and donning hats or hoods.[16]

The British Father Christmas, while apparently originating in the Middle Ages, appears to be an outgrowth of the Lord of Misrule tradition that can be traced back to the Roman Saturnalia. Other Lord of Misrule characters were known as "Prince Christmas" and "The Christmas Lord," who presided over feasting and entertainment in medieval Britain. The tradition was later popularized in the 17th century following the English Civil War as a response to Puritan efforts to abolish Christmas, with defenders of the holiday adopting Father Christmas as the symbol of old-fashioned Yuletide feasting and good cheer. Father Christmas was a larger-than-life figure, and indeed was sometimes portrayed as a giant wearing a crown of holly, ivy or mistletoe, carrying a Yule log and a bowl of punch.[17] Initially, Father Christmas was known more as a chief reveler than a gift bringer, leading merrymaking and eating and drinking to excess. In a 1616 performance for King James I, he was accompanied by his children, Mis-Rule, Carol, Minc'd Pie, Gamboll, Post and Paire, New-Yeares-Gift, Mumming, Wassail, Roast Beef, Plum Pudding, Offering, and Babie-Cake.[18] Later, in the Victorian era, Father

This illustration of Father Christmas depicts him with a crown of holly, holding a wassail bowl and carrying a Yule log on his back. It was made for the *Illustrated London News* in 1848. Artist Alfred Henry Forrester.

7. The Man, the Myth, the Legend, the God—Santa Claus

"HERE WE ARE AGAIN!"

In this wood engraving by Thomas Nast, Santa encounters another nocturnal visitor by the fireplace. The caption reads, "here we are again." From *Thomas Nast's Christmas drawings for the human race*, published in 1890 by Harpers & Brothers in New York.

Christmas developed into a more family-friendly version bringing gifts to children while they slept.

In the 19th century, the British Father Christmas came to be very much influenced by new stories and images being produced in America, particularly the writings of Washington Irving and the popular poem by Clement Clarke Moore, "Twas the Night Before Christmas," published originally as "A Visit from Saint Nicholas" in 1823. In his satirical work *Knickerbocker's History of New York*, published on St. Nicholas's feast day, December 6, 1809, Irving described an impish, pipe-smoking Nicholas who flew "jollily among the tree tops or over the roofs of the houses, now and then drawing forth magnificent presents from his breeches pockets and dropping them down the chimneys of his favorites." Irving provided much of the lore of Santa's Christmas Eve travels, leading Charles Jones, a mid–20th-century scholar who wrote an article for *The New-York Historical Society Quarterly* called "Knickerbocker Santa Claus," to conclude that "without Irving there would be no Santa Claus."[19] Irving's *History*, Jones points out, introduced readers to the idea of Santa Claus bringing gifts, parking his wagon on the roof while he slides down the chimney. As a bestselling and highly influential book, Irving's *History* would have been well known to Moore, writing his poem a decade or so later, and many of the attributes Moore gives to Santa were borrowed directly from Irving.

Moore's story described "a right jolly old elf" who flies around on a sleigh pulled by reindeer, visiting homes and leaving presents. Although there is an ongoing dispute about who wrote this poem, with some pointing to Henry Livingston, Jr., as the rightful author, the historical consensus still seems to be that it was in fact Moore who wrote it. (Although, it should be acknowledged that as an ordained minister and respected academic, the poem was somewhat out of character for most of Moore's published writings. Then again, perhaps that is why the piece was originally published anonymously, leading to the ongoing controversy over authorship.)

The poem provides details on St. Nick's appearance, and in a number of ways, it seems that Moore is redefining his look. While in previous centuries he was seen as wearing the cloak of a bishop, as he is still depicted in The Netherlands, Moore described him as "dressed all in fur, from his head to his foot," which is closer to the attire of the Belsnickel than the traditional St. Nicholas. He was also described as being a bit overweight, or in the words of the poem, "chubby and plump," a departure from earlier depictions of St. Nicholas in which he was generally rather slim.

The poem also includes a number of possible allusions to Norse mythology, leading to speculation that his depiction of St. Nick was at least partly inspired by Norse gods. In describing St. Nick as a "jolly old elf," Moore is including two possible references to the Old Norse language. Moore's modern audience might not appreciate the significance of his choice of words, but as a professor of ancient languages, there is a good chance that Moore would have known that the word "jolly" is derived from the Old Norse *jól* and the origins of "elf" are in the Old Norse word *álfar*. In early Norse mythology the *álfar* were supernatural beings divided into two categories: the "light elves," or *Ljósálfar*, that lived in Alfheim (one of the nine worlds in Norse mythology), and the "dark elves," or *Dökkálfar*, that lived underground. As some have speculated, it is possible that according to this differentiation, St. Nicholas could be seen as a light elf and his partner Belsnickel as a dark elf.[20] The *álfar* were also known to enter homes through chimneys and to offer gifts such as money or grain, but if offended might take revenge by burning down the house.[21]

Whether intentional or not, by calling St. Nicholas an elf rather than a bishop or a monk, Moore is—knowingly or unknowingly—harkening back to a pre–Christian era in which the supernatural was considered part of everyday life. This allusion appears more likely when considering other possible references to Norse paganism in the poem, such as the line "More rapid than eagles his coursers they came," as eagles are a common theme in Norse mythology. Eagles accompany the valkyrie on the battlefield, and in Snorri Sturluson's *Prose Edda*, the *Hræsvelgr* is a member of a race of nature spirits with superhuman strength, known as a *jötunn*, who takes the form of an eagle. The most famous eagle in Norse mythology, though, was *Veðrfölnir*, who lived on the top branch of Yggdrasil. The eagle is therefore seen in ancient Norse belief as a symbol of leadership and vision.

Moore's poem also for the first time indicates St. Nick's mode of transportation being a magical sleigh pulled by reindeer, or as Moore describes them "eight tiny reindeer"—an indication that St. Nick himself was a small elf rather than a full-grown human. Furthermore, Moore's choice of the number of magical animals has led some to wonder whether he may have been inspired by Odin's eight-legged horse Sleipnir.[22] While these possible connections are dismissed by most scholars as fanciful speculation, noting that the number of reindeer probably had as much to do with the number of legs on a spider as it did with the number of legs on Odin's horse—in other words, nothing at all—it is true that during the Christianization period, many people came to associate Odin with Saint Nicholas,[23] and there are a number of other interesting parallels between the two figures that are worth considering.

* * *

In ancient Scandinavia, Odin was believed to ride through the woods from November through the end of December,[24] his long white beard flapping in the wind as storms howled over the land, leading a ghostly hunting party on a search for the sun. As the father of all the gods as well as the father of the slain, Odin was both revered and feared—when he and his hunting party rode past, people would run for cover. Anyone who was spotted by his ghostly procession might be carried away and dropped miles from where they had been picked up, but practitioners of various forms of magic may have joined in it voluntarily in order to have a sort of out-of-body experience flying together with Odin and his eight-legged horse.

There are also accounts of children filling their boots with carrots, straw, or sugar and placing them near the chimney for Sleipnir to eat, with Odin rewarding these children for their kindness by leaving gifts.[25] This custom has obvious similarities with the modern-day tradition of leaving Santa cookies to eat and carrots to give to the reindeer, but some scholars have raised doubts about whether it was actually practiced in pagan times, as there seem to be no records of stocking-filling until the cult of St. Nicholas emerged during the Christianization period. However, there may yet be a connection between St. Nicholas and Odin in that the Norse identified the bearded, cloak-wearing bishop with the bearded, cloak-wearing god. As the Norse adopted Christianity, St. Nicholas and Odin seem to have merged, which could help explain some of the similarities between the two. Prior to the makeover he was given by Moore, as a writer at *History Daily* points out, "Santa Claus was depicted as a tall, gaunt old man with a long, white beard wearing

Appearing in an 1893 Swedish translation of the *Poetic Edda*, this image depicts Odin in one of his disguises. "Odin as Wanderer," 1886. Artist Georg von Rosen.

a fur coat and wide-brimmed hat, which just happens to match the description of one of Odin's favorite disguises."[26] Furthermore, just as Santa is seen as all-knowing, assisted by his legions of elves who keep tabs on children and helps keep the Naughty and Nice List up to date, Odin was also considered omniscient, assisted by two ravens—Huginn and Muninn—that fly around the world and feed information to the god.

As a force that works for the fertility of the fields and helps people reach material fortune, pagans considered it important to keep Odin happy by offering sacrifices—particularly at the end of the yearly cycle in order to ensure a prosperous new year. As observed by Christian Ratsch and Claudia Muller-Ebeling in *Pagan Christmas*, "In his role as a mythical fulfiller of wishes, one might very well see Wotan [Odin] as an ancestor of that famous bringer of presents, Santa Claus himself."[27]

* * *

Odin, of course, is not the only pagan god Santa has been associated with over the years. In 1872, an article in *Harper's New Monthly Magazine* suggested that by travelling through the skies in a sleigh, Santa's yearly voyage closely resembles those of the deity Thor, who flew in a chariot pulled by two white goats.[28] Similarly, the traditional English Father Christmas was also known to ride a goat and the Finnish name for Santa is *Joulupukki*, which literally translates as "Yule goat," suggesting a possible link with Thor.[29] Another possible connection is that Thor was famous for battling the ice-giants, which some have argued is symbolic of man's constant battle with winter, and he was believed to live in a palace in the "Northland," surrounded by icebergs—a possible inspiration for designating Santa's home at the North Pole.

Santa's supposed links with Thor have been a recurring theme throughout much Christmas scholarship, with Francis Weiser writing in 1958 that, like Santa, "Thor was the god of the peasants and the common people." Not only that, but he was also depicted as a jovial and friendly elderly man of a heavy build, with a long white beard. Thor's color was red, like Santa's, and was said to come down through the chimney into his element, the fire.[30] The names of Santa's reindeer as given by Moore also back up the Santa-as-Thor theory, with "Donner" and "Blitzen" similar to the Germanic words for "thunder" and "lightning," both of which were commanded by Thor.[31] Some have also pointed out that the names of Thor's goats, Tanngrisnir and Tanngnjóstr, can be translated roughly as Tooth-cracker and Tooth-gnasher, or Cracker and Gnasher for short. These names don't sound too dissimilar from the reindeer names Dasher and Dancer, although, admittedly, it might be a stretch to claim any direct connection. Another name that Moore gave Santa's reindeer, however, is clearly derived from paganism, albeit the Greco-Roman pantheon rather than the Norse pantheon. The Roman deity Cupid (or as he was known ancient Greece, Eros) was the god of love and sex, appropriated by Moore as the sixth reindeer in Santa's fleet.

Another possible pagan inspiration for Santa Claus can be found in the Roman god Bacchus, known in ancient Greece as Dionysus, a nature god of fruitfulness and vegetation, and famous as a god of wine and ecstasy. The son of Zeus and a mortal woman named Semele, Dionysus was said to be born on December 25 and was raised in a cave by nymphs surrounded by abundant wild vines. His life and adventures were the inspiration for the development of the satyr play and the theater. Wandering aimlessly from place to place, he was often seen clad in a deer skin, wearing a wreath of

7. The Man, the Myth, the Legend, the God—Santa Claus 91

This 16th-century engraving by Enea Vico depicts a debauched bacchanalian revelry with the god of wine riding a donkey. "Triumph of Bacchus," 1543. Artist Enea Vico (Los Angeles County Museum of Art, Mary Stansbury Ruiz Bequest).

vine-leaves and dancing with the nymphs. Those who welcomed him during his travels were rewarded with wine, and to the ancient Greeks he came to be known as the patron of viticulture, wine, and fertility and vegetation. Through drunkenness and dancing, he offered freedom which released people from their everyday troubles.[32] He also presided over an ancient midwinter festival called Rural Dionysia, which was held during the month of Poseidon, from December to January.

As a 19th-century poet using the pseudonym "Rip Van Dam" described Santa Claus—or "Saint Claas," as written in the poem—the primary function of the figure seems to be leading Bacchus-like orgies of drinking, dancing and sexual escapades. The 1828 poem, "Ode to Saint Claas, Written on New Year's Eve" presented Santa as the "king of good fellows" who brought not only treats such as sugar plums, but also mulled cider and spiced rum. "Jolly Saint," reads the poem, "Come then with thy merry eye, / And let us bouse [booze] it till we die! / Come and o'er my thirsty soul / Floods of smoking glasses roll!" The poem describes Santa as an "imp" who encourages others to dance and perform "merry pranks," such as women stealing kisses from their male counterparts. The bacchanalian nature of this hedonistic Santa was alluded to in the closing lines of Rip Van Dam's poem in which the poet declares his reverence for him: "I bow the reverent knee, / And shout Saint Claas, all hail to thee!"[33]

Giving credence to the Santa-as-Bacchus theory, when cartoonist Thomas Nast immortalized Santa Claus's current look with a series of drawings from 1862 to 1886,

Two cartoons by Thomas Nast, "King Death's Distribution of Prizes. Bacchus Takes the First Premium" from 1870 and "A Merry Christmas" from 1880, demonstrate that Nast's inspiration for Santa's look likely came from the Roman god of wine. In the 1870 wood engraving (left), Nast is using Bacchus as a warning of the excessive use of alcohol. In the 1880 relief print (right), Santa is dressed in a fur suit with a wide belt with pieces of mistletoe. Note their similar features and the wreath that Santa is wearing. Both of these images appeared in *Harper's Weekly*.

he drew obvious inspiration from the god of wine.[34] Nast had used a likeness of Bacchus in an 1870 cartoon called "King Death's Distribution of Prizes Bacchus Takes the First Premium," and it is impossible to deny the similarities with his later depictions of Santa. Nast gave Santa Claus a crown of holly, similar to the crown that Bacchus was known to wear, and for his part, the cartoonist conceded that his depiction of Santa's rosy face came directly from Bacchus, providing confirmation to some critics that the American Santa Claus is essentially a god of materialism and hedonism.[35]

Finally, by bringing not just gifts but also merriment and good cheer, Santa Claus has also been seen as the modern equivalent of the Roman god Saturn, or at least as the Lord of Misrule associated with the celebration of Saturnalia. In *Santa Claus: A Biography*, historian Gerry Bowler draws connections between the chief reveler of Saturnalia and later figures associated with Christmas such as Father Christmas and Santa,[36] and in *The Battle for Christmas*, Nissenbaum notes that the version of Santa depicted by the poet Van Dam "was no other than the Lord of Misrule, master of the Christmas carnival."[37] Or, as a scholar named L.D. Johnston wrote in 1936, it is "by no means impossible that St. Nicholas had absorbed some of the ancient Roman

Saturnus and I am inclined to think that our modern St. Nick, Kris Kringle or Santa Claus, goes back to that ancient figure."[38]

* * *

There are also those who argue that Santa Claus is neither a Christian nor pagan invention but is instead inspired by shamanism and the use of "magic" mushrooms. This theory was advanced by a book written in 1967 by R. Gordon Wasson, who claimed that shamanistic reindeer herders of Siberia ingested the red and white psychedelic mushroom caps in their ceremonies and their psilocybin-induced visions inspired stories of reindeer flying. Despite being dismissed over the years by historians who have tried to follow the actual evidence of Santa's origins and have found no connection between remote reindeer herders in the Arctic Circle and the St. Nick stories of writers such as Irving and Moore, the theory is still popular in some quarters. Anthropologist John Rush, for example, asserts that Santa is essentially a modern counterpart of a shaman "who consumed mind-altering plants and fungi to commune with the spirit world."[39] Drawing a loose connection with Norse mythology, proponents of this theory claim that shamanism was closely associated with Odin who was considered the shamanic god of ecstasy and knowledge.

Lending some credibility to this idea is the fact that ornaments shaped like the red and white psychedelic mushrooms and other depictions of the fungi are prevalent in Christmas decorations, particularly in Scandinavia and northern Europe. This appears to be a holdover of the ancient use

This typical Scandinavian ornament resembles the mushroom *Amanita muscaria* and suggests a strong historical connection between psychedelics and Christmas. Several possible explanations have been offered for this association, including the fact that in the wild these mushrooms grow under conifers that are commonly used as Christmas trees and reindeer are known to eat them, which may provide an explanation of the myth of Santa's flying reindeer. Also, Siberian shamans were believed to use magic mushrooms at the winter solstice (photograph by the author).

of psychedelics, with some historians believing that everyone from Celtic druids to Scandinavian Vikings may have ingested the red fly agaric mushroom to commune with spirits, have visions, and in the case of Viking berserkers, to help them fight on the battlefield. It has also been pointed out that Arctic shamans gave out mushrooms as gifts on the winter solstice, and because snow often blocked the doors of homes, they used an opening in the roof, which is a possible explanation for the story of Santa using chimneys to enter homes. "At first glance, one thinks it's ridiculous, but it's not," says Carl Ruck, a professor of classics at Boston University. "Whoever heard of reindeer flying? I think it's becoming general knowledge that Santa is taking a 'trip' with his reindeer." These shamans "also have a tradition of dressing up like the [mushroom] ... they dress up in red suits with white spots," Ruck pointed out, providing a plausible explanation for Santa's iconoclastic outfit.[40]

Historian Nick Page dismisses the idea as nonsense, writing facetiously that besides "the fact that the shamans didn't travel by sleigh, that they didn't wear red and white, and that the connection between Santa and reindeer was invented in the mid–1800s in America," it is "a watertight case."[41] Ronald Hutton, a history professor at the University of Bristol and author of several books on pre–Christian European history, agrees. "If you look at the evidence of Siberian shamanism, which I've done," Hutton said in 2010, "you find that shamans ... didn't usually deal with reindeer spirits [and] very rarely took the mushrooms to get trances." Hutton credits Moore almost exclusively for creating our modern Santa Claus figure. "It was the work of Clement Clarke Moore, in New York City in 1822, who suddenly turned a medieval saint into a flying, reindeer-driving spirit of the Northern midwinter," Hutton said.[42]

But even if we do accept that Santa is nothing but Moore's creative adaptation of St. Nicholas, this fails to appreciate the historical reality that St. Nicholas himself was likely inspired by ancient Greek and Roman gods Poseidon and Neptune. It also downplays the possibility that as a scholar of religion and literature, Moore may have taken inspiration from a variety of obscure sources in developing his ideas. And while many dismiss the idea that Santa Claus is a manifestation of hallucinogenic mushrooms or that he is based on pagan gods such as Odin and Thor, it is undeniable there is some mystical quality to Santa that people universally identify with. Indeed, the very fact that there has been so much speculation regarding Santa's origins is a testament to the reality that people widely (even if unconsciously) recognize the influence of paganism in his magical attributes. The image of Santa Claus flying through the sky has been seen throughout the years as a perhaps not-so-subtle extension of mystical beliefs from an earlier time, and love him or hate him, it is noteworthy that so many people over the years have associated Santa Claus with various gods, either welcoming this as a throwback to an earlier, more magical time, or opposing it as an undesirable demonic influence from heathen belief systems.

In the final analysis, whether Santa Claus was inspired by shamanism or by a particular god from one or another pagan pantheon—or by several—is somewhat beside the point. He is not a Siberian shaman, nor Odin, nor Thor, nor Bacchus, but ultimately a unique figure who represents the spirit of Christmas through concepts of selflessness and magic, and whether he is specifically associated with one deity or another, his persona is clearly something of a modern-day equivalent of a god. By "believing" in Santa Claus, whether earnestly and sincerely as millions of children do, or acquiescently and grudgingly as many adults claim to do—at least when they are discussing the matter with their kids—21st-century mankind is engaging with belief systems not unlike those before us who genuinely believed that Odin flew through the night's sky during December and that he was responsible for increasing the fertility of the fields. Instead of Odin flying on his eight-legged horse or Thor being pulled by two goats, it is Santa on a sleigh pulled by eight reindeer. Instead of Bacchus, assisted by his band of satyrs, roaming the countryside gifting peasants with wine, it is Santa, assisted by his elves, traveling the world gifting children with toys. Whether or not a direct line can be drawn from one to the other, the concepts are rooted in the same basic belief system.

* * *

Yet, while some of us might nostalgically embrace this pagan-influenced history of Santa as evocative of our shared primordial past, his association with paganism has also led Santa to be vigorously denounced by Christian leaders over the years. Wilbur Glenn Voliva, the one-time head of the Catholic Apostolic Church and despotic "general overseer" of the town of Zion, Illinois, announced publicly in 1921 that Santa Claus was not real and banished him from Zion, declaring that "gifts come from above" and that "fathers and mothers will pass them along" to children who behave well.[43] Not to be outdone, an indignant the Rev. Martin F. Clough scolded parents in 1949 for teaching children the Santa Claus myth. "Santa is the most popular hoax of the age," he wrote in the *Hartford Courant*. "Around the globe so-called Christian parents are deceiving the children about Santa Claus. Santa Claus is a modern representative of the heathen god Nimrod who is a defiant hater of God and Satan's earliest effort to produce Anti-Christ."[44] Santa Claus was even burned in effigy by priests of the Dijon Cathedral on December 24, 1951, in front of hundreds of French children attending Sunday school. The executioners condemned Santa as a usurper and a heretic who was paganizing Christmas and pushing Jesus out of the observance of the religious feast.[45]

Christians today who object to the use of Santa Claus in our modern celebration of Christmas might not be quite as strident, but generally argue that the character is simply unnecessary and detracts from what should be a solemn and holy observance. Critics argue that Santa distracts from the religious aspects from Christmas and point out that in many ways, he actually represents the polar opposite of Jesus Christ, who should be the focal point of the festival. Not only are there numerous cosmetic differences between the two figures, with Santa being portrayed as elderly and portly, and Christ as youthful and slim, and Santa dressing in ostentatious red fur and Jesus wearing humble white robes, but more importantly, they use their supernatural powers for very different purposes. The miracles of Christ, for example, provided health and necessities to the infirmed and were used by the Messiah to signify the much greater gift of eternal life that comes through believing in him. The miracles of Santa Claus, on the other hand, provide toys and luxuries, the very material goods that Christ often condemned as diversions from following the path to heaven. As Jesus told a wealthy man according to the Gospel of Matthew, "go, sell your possessions and give to the poor, and you will have treasure in heaven."

Not quite the same message as Santa, who is best known for asking, "What do you want for Christmas?"

Websites such as *Jesus Is Savior* therefore denounce Santa Claus as a "great impostor," calling him "a subtle, deadly attack on our children to confuse, doubt and rob their God-ordained 'child-like' faith." According to this view, he is a tool of Satan to fool children and push them away from Jesus Christ, with the goal of condemning them to eternal damnation.[46] Central to this critique is the idea that Santa is in fact a repackaging of pagan gods and that his entire persona is virtually an inverse of what Jesus Christ represents.

Some reject the comparison altogether, claiming that Santa is not a descendant of pagan gods, but is actually a deformed and distorted version of St. Nicholas to whose legacy we should return. The St. Nicholas Society, for example, stresses that it is "not opposed to celebrations, gift-giving or other holiday activities, but it does encourage a sanity in the amount of gifts bought and exchanged as well as allowing Christmas to remain a day of Christian celebration," all of which are undermined by Santa Claus. Denouncing Santa as "a commercial invention," the Society points out that as "a servant of Christ and an example for us all to enjoy and emulate," the ecclesiastical version of St. Nicholas "is a perfect model for care and gift-giving."[47] (Never mind the possibility that St. Nicholas may in fact have been an invention of the Church to supplant the cult of Poseidon.)

* * *

But while it is likely that the Santa Claus figure might draw some inspiration from Odin, Thor, Bacchus, Saturn and Poseidon, he also shares some important characteristics with Jesus that shouldn't be overlooked. Despite his many critics among devout Christians who worry that Santa has come to represent the materialism that Jesus warned against, in some ways, Santa also epitomizes the spirit of generosity, selflessness and unconditional love that Jesus championed. Possessing magical powers of flight and omniscient knowledge, as well as a deep sense of moral righteousness and certitude, he is a modern-day god-like figure personifying charity, goodwill, peace and kindness. Although he is said to keep a list of naughty and nice children, at the end of day, pretty much every kid gets a present even if they have misbehaved once or twice—which is not unlike the spirit of unconditional love that Jesus preached and the forgiveness for one's sins that comes with belief in him.

This is one reason that some churches have embraced Santa Claus and include him in services at Christmas time. As far back as the 19th century, churches began incorporating Santa in Christmas Day services, with clergy reckoning that distributing gifts on Christmas could draw the focus towards the religious festival and away from the more secular New Year's Day.[48] A 2019 survey of evangelical leaders found that a small majority (52 percent) felt that Santa could be used in church services, if done appropriately. The Salvation Army's David Hudson, for example, said that "[s]ome of the most meaningful events I've attended have included Santa kneeling at the feet of the manger." Rich Nathan, a pastor in Ohio, said that his church utilizes Santa for outreach and to provide charity to needy families. "We always have Santa there for the kids," he said.[49] Randy Heckert, director of leadership development for the Evangelical Friends Church, noted that Santa Claus can be seen as a human example for giving, "much as we might honor Mary and Joseph, or other models of faith."

Others, however, continue to object to including Santa on religious grounds. John Stumbo, president of the Christian and Missionary Alliance, said that Santa could be used as a bridge "to the secular community who understands little or nothing of the spiritual significance of our holidays," but ultimately, he believed that the message would be lost, especially in young minds. "Let the world have their fairy tales," he said, "let the Church stay faithful to our grounded-in-historical-events faith."[50]

8

Actual Christmas Magic

Noël! Noël!
Carols each Christmas bell.
What are the wraiths of mist
That gather anear the window-pane
Where the winter frost all day has lain?
They are soulless elves, who fain would peer
Within, and laugh at our Christmas cheer:
Ring fleetly, chimes! Swift, swift, my rhymes!
They are made of the mocking mist.
   —Edmund Clarence Stedman, "Guests at Yule"

Today, the term "Christmas magic" is used more or less interchangeably with "Christmas spirit" and is generally thought of as a metaphor. We might talk about "the magic of Christmas" when the faces of children light up sitting on Santa's lap, when we gaze upon a beautiful tree decorated with lights and ornaments, when we feel a certain giddiness opening a special gift, or when we're surprised by someone displaying an uncharacteristic kindness during the holiday season. There is also "magic" associated with the holiday in the way our stories incorporate fantastical feats, such as flying reindeer pulling a sleigh through the sky and a jolly old elf who can somehow deliver presents to a couple billion children around the world in a single night. When kids ask how Santa could possibly visit so many homes and leave presents even in apartment buildings where there is no chimney to go down, parents will respond with a one-word answer: "magic."

But while we might use the word "magic" these days as shorthand for "something that is physically impossible," or the word "magical" as a synonym for "delightful," there was a time when it was taken quite literally. Rather than being a metaphor, for thousands of years, magic—the practice of beliefs and rituals to manipulate natural and supernatural forces—was considered a very real phenomenon by both pagans and Christians. Priestly classes such as the druids and the magi were renowned for magical abilities, both feared and respected for their skills. Irish chronicles and folklore described the druids as diviners and conjurors who served pagan Celtic kings, while the magi were Zoroastrian priests primarily responsible for ceremonial tasks such as overseeing sacrifices and tending to sacred flames but were also known as practitioners of sorcery.[1] In ancient Mesopotamia (comprising parts of modern-day Syria, Iraq and Iran), many kinds of rituals and incantations were used to alter reality, with magic invoked to counteract evil omens and defend against demons, ghosts, and evil sorcerers. In ancient Egypt, magicians recited a spell following the winter solstice called "The Book of the Last Days of the Year" in order to protect against demonic messengers who were known to wreak year-end havoc.[2]

Ancient civilizations such as the Sumerians, Akkadians, Assyrians and Babylonians considered rational science and magic as virtually indistinguishable, with medical treatments consisting of both medicine and magical formulas. Cults and rituals invoking deities were useful methods of seeking protection from fire, flood and crop failure,[3] and those who were proficient in these skills often served as advisors to kings and emperors.[4] It was common for powerful people to consult astrologers, for example, to divine the knowledge for the most favorable days to sign contracts, make treaties, betroth their daughters, or to get married.[5] At times though, astrologers could also be blamed when things went wrong, leading to a number of purges of these diviners from ancient Rome—in 139 BCE, 33 BCE, 16 CE, 69 CE, and 89 CE.[6] Astrology was also closely related to astral magic, or the harnessing of celestial power from the divine realm of the stars and planets to manipulate human behavior and control earthly events.[7]

In ancient Greece and Rome, no clear lines were drawn between astronomy and astrology, science and superstition, and religion and magic. As scholar Malcolm Gaskill writes, "For all its grandeur and glory, the classical world was steeped in the dark manipulation of spirits; here was the means to alleviate anxiety, deploy anger, and satisfy desire."[8] Formal religion and magic were interlinked, with divine influence believed to impact everyday events, and certain people were empowered to communicate with the gods, including priests, philosophers, physicians, and poets. This elite class sometimes performed ritual magic, but personal requests to employ black magic to harm others or for personal gain were often carried out by soothsayers and others on the margins of society, such as prostitutes. Greek philosophers claimed to reject magic, but ancient Greeks at all

This illustration appeared in the book *The Wonder Clock*, published by Harper Brothers in 1888. It depicts a king being presented with a hen by a magician. "The Master of the Black Arts Bringeth a Curious Little Black Hen to the King," 1887. Artist Howard Pyle (The Metropolitan Museum of Art, Rogers Fund, 1926).

This image is from Olaus Magnus's *History of the Nordic Peoples*, published in 1555. The witch to the right develops a powerful storm by emptying her pot with a magic potion into the sea, causing a shipwreck. From *Historia de gentibus septentrionalibus*, Book 3, Ch. 15. On Women Skilled in Magic (Lars Henriksson, http://www.avrosys.nu/).

levels of society turned to various magical remedies to secure the favor of Eros, the god of love, or Hekate, the goddess of witchcraft.[9]

The theme of magic is found throughout the Bible, with more than 100 references in both the Old and New Testaments.[10] Numerous passages warn against divination, necromancy (the conjuring of spirits), fortune-telling, and sorcery. John 4:1 advises that people should be careful when communicating with spirits, as "many false prophets have gone out into the world." Despite these admonitions against magic, it was a common practice to consult magicians well into the Christian era in Europe. As Bishop Hugh Latimer stated in 1552, "A great many of us, when we be in trouble, or sickness, or lose anything, we run hither and thither to witches, or sorcerers, whom we call wise men ... seeking aid and comfort at their hands." During the 16th and 17th centuries, popular magicians provided many services, ranging from healing the sick and finding lost items to fortune-telling. They were known by a variety of names, such as cunning men, wise women, charmers, blessers, conjurers, sorcerers, or witches, which indicated the various views held about their practices, ranging from sympathetic to reverential to scornful.[11]

As to the question of where magic originated, there were many erstwhile views on this as well. In his work *Natural History*, Roman philosopher and author Pliny the Elder wrote in 77 CE that magic began in Persia with Zoroaster between 1500 and 1000 BCE.[12] Some early Christian writers also ascribed the origin of magic to Zoroaster, but in the fourth century CE, Bishop Clement of Rome claimed that fallen angels or demons had taught it to men.[13] Other Christians claimed that Ham, son of Noah, had learned magic and, having survived the Great Flood, passed this knowledge to his descendants the Egyptians, Persians and Babylonians.[14] In Norse mythology, Odin learned magic by venturing into Nifelheim, the realm of ice, where the wicked go when they die. To discover its secrets, he thrust a spear through his body and into Yggdrasil, the world tree. For eight days and nights, his body hung from the spear while his spirit was in the realm of the dead. There he discovered the workings of magic and on the ninth day, he came back to life, newly armed with an array of magical powers.[15]

Vikings utilized sorcery for many purposes, but it seems that two themes were dominant: magic for aggressive ends and for love. Most Viking-Age magic was performed by women, but the practice was so common that there were nearly 40 different terms for sorcerers of both sexes.[16] On the battlefield, which was seen as the home of supernatural beasts and dark spirits, specialized military sorceresses cast spells of defensive and offensive magic to aid in the fighting. The famous berserkers who terrified their enemies with their fanatical, fearless intensity on the battlefield were believed to be aided by magical spells (as well as, perhaps, magic mushrooms).[17]

* * *

During the Christianization of Europe, and particularly during the medieval period, pagan beliefs in magic and the supernatural were incorporated into the Christian faith. Church leaders and missionaries placed enormous emphasis on the miracle-working of saints and disseminated stories of the superiority of Christian miracles to heathen magic. Early Christian leaders were more than willing to assimilate elements of the old paganism into Christianity, which proved effective in winning new converts but also may have been confusing to some. The worship of trees and beliefs in supernatural beings were modified by turning pagan sites into Christian ones and associating them with saints instead of heathen deities.[18] Similarly, fertility rites associated with important days on the calendar such as the winter solstice were adopted into Christian traditions, some of which maintained explicitly magical purposes.[19] The day of the week upon which Christmas fell, for example, was believed to affect its magical powers, with Sunday the preferred day in this regard.[20]

Many curious customs have been documented related to Christmas magic. As late as the 19th century, it was common in Europe to perform rituals on Christmas that were intended to increase the productivity of gardens and orchards. In one such rite, a garden would be thrashed with a flail on Christmas Eve in order to ensure that the grass would grow the following year. People would also tie wet straw bands around the orchard trees, or place stones on them, on Christmas Eve to make them more fruitful. Another custom was to beat the trees on Christmas night and in some parts of England the peasants would also salute or sing to the apple trees on Christmas Eve, in what is widely regarded as an ancient precursor to wassailing and caroling. In Germany it was believed that a washcloth hanged on a hedge on Christmas Eve would cause horses to grow fat when they are groomed with it. At their core, these and many other apparently superstitious customs are, as Hamilton Mabie describes it in *The Book of Christmas*, published in 1909, "rites and solemnities of passing heathendom, with its recognition of the kinship of all nature, out of which grew astrology, magic, and other pseudo-sciences."[21]

Pagans employed magical practices in observing the winter solstice to repel evil spirits, and similar Christian rituals were adapted for use at Christmas time. The Blessing of the Waters has particular significance in the Orthodox Church, and in Russia has had a function of great magnificence. Following conversion from paganism to Christianity, the ritual was seen as vital in chasing away the gods that the

This woodcut from 15th-century Germany depicts the Virgin Mary, baby Jesus, angels, and several saints. During the Middle Ages, traditional folk magic increasingly became viewed as heretical and was associated with the Devil, while the miracles of saints and "angel magic" grew in both popularity and legitimacy. "Madonna and Child with Three Members of the St. Augustine Order: Saints Augustine, Nicholas and Clara" (Cleveland Museum of Art, Gift of Leonard C. Hanna, Jr., 1928).

peasants had once worshipped. It was believed that after these gods had been displaced by conversion, they came back during the dark days of December to haunt former pagans as demons. In order to repel these malevolent spirits, people erected a cross constructed of ice, and herded the sprites, fairies and wood nymphs using singing and waving banners. Once collected they were cast into a lake.[22]

Magic has also been seen in certain arcane Christmas customs such as one in Germany of moistening bread with dew on Christmas morning in order infuse it with magical powers,[23] and in more well-known traditions such as the use of bells and certain plants. These customs generally have long-since lost their supernatural significance in the minds of Christmas celebrants today, but they remain as residue of a time when magic was considered a fact of life.

* * *

In pre–Christian times, the 12 days between December 25 and January 6 were known as the "rough nights" (later to be dubbed the 12 Days of Christmas). On these days, the veil between our world and the spirit world was at its thinnest, and the natural world came to be ruled by elemental energies. Odin's Wild Hunt would ride across the northern skies, uncanny spirit beings would fight battles between light and darkness, and the living energies of other planes of existence were ever present. As described in *Pagan Christmas*:

> Rituals were in order to ward off the demonic influences and to conjure a rebirth of the sun after the dark days. At nightfall, "house and stable were smudged with healing herbs." Because of these smudging rituals (originally pagan and later performed by Catholic priests), these nights were known as "smudging nights." People burned juniper and many other aromatic substances to drive out demons. The smoke transformed the aromatic woods and herbs into scent that was supposed to implore the gods to take mercy on human beings and to keep away all evil. They also placed various combinations of magical herbs in their beds for protection and mixed them into their animals' food.[24]

In central Italy, to this day, an ancient rite called 'Ndocciata uses fire to ward off witches. Following the tolling of bells, a procession begins with hundreds of porters carrying tall torches made from white fir branches, dry brooms, and twine. The ancestral tradition takes place every year on December 8 and is repeated on Christmas Eve. In pagan times the torches were lit in honor of the sun god on the longest night of the year but have since been adapted by Christians to honor Christ's birth.[25]

Bells have long been used to keep away malevolent spirits and utilized by both pagans and Christians, as well as other faiths, in religious rites. In folklore, bells were considered to possess something like a lifeforce or a soul, and were believed to ring of their own accord to warn of impending disaster.[26] In Wicca, small hand bells may be rung in rituals to enhance harmony and augment power, to cleanse homes of negative energy, to banish unwanted spirits, to call in positive energetic influences, or to invoke the goddess in rituals.[27] In folk magic, the ringing of bells wards off the "evil eye," or the misfortune caused by malicious glances from strangers. Bells have been attached to clothing, worn as amulets, tied to children and hung from the necks of animals important to a community.[28] In ancient Roman times, people used to ring bells to scare away demons and herdsmen used them to keep away evil spirits from their flocks.[29] According to folk belief, on Christmas Eve, bells would ring even if they were underwater or buried underground.[30]

Churches use bells for funerals, to summon people to worship, and historically have used them to counter the diabolical aspects of lightning storms. In Catholicism, bells are said to be despised by demons because they are used to draw attention to the divine worship of God, and for this reason they are considered an effective tool in exorcism rituals to counter demonic influences.[31] According to *The Golden Legend* of Jacobus de Voragine, archbishop of Genoa (printed around 1483), "the evil spirits that be in the region of the air doubt much when they hear the bells ringing; thus the bells are rung when it thunders, or when great tempest and outrages of weather happen; to the end that the fiends and wicked spirits should be abashed and flee, and cease of the moving of tempests." Church bells included inscriptions that described their power to "ward off lightning and malignant demons" or to "affright the demons." Another inscription promised that the bell "vanquishes tempests, repels demons, and summons men."[32] Churches came to ring bells to alert parishioners of the beginning of the Advent season, and people believed that their magical powers were augmented at this time.

As described by Linda Raedisch in *The Old Magic of Christmas*, "The wearing of bells and other jangling things is a universal means of protecting the wearer from evil or simply opportunistic spirits. ... Wherever there have been bells, they have been used to ward off unseen and undesirable influences."[33] This is why bells have come to be associated so ubiquitously with Christmas, which falls at a time of year that our ancestors believed that spirits had unusually easy access to our temporal realm. They have been used, for example, by men and boys who dress up as perchten in Austria, wearing horned masks and ringing bells to drive out the demons of winter.[34] They have been used on the Scandinavian Yule goat, a wooden beast with a goat's skull and a tail fastened with bells.[35] In England, mummers used bells in their performances, especially the morris dance and the sword dance,[36] and in Switzerland, in the Samichlaus processions on St. Nicholas's Day, boys were known to chase the saint through villages ringing bells.[37] The figures of Knecht Ruprecht, Belsnickel and Krampus also wear bells, and of course, so do Santa's reindeer. Santa Claus himself is known to ring a hand-held bell, particularly those Santas that are seen in shopping centers collecting donations for the poor.

The association of bells with Christmas

This vintage Christmas card features mistletoe, holly and bells, all of which were believed to hold magical properties in pagan beliefs. Evergreens such as holly and mistletoe were used as sacraments to ensure growth and fertility, while bells were used to frighten off spirits. "Christmas Greeting." Artist Ellen Clapsaddle (photograph of a vintage Christmas card from the personal collection of Nancy Oram).

has led to many popular songs being written over the years such as "Christmas Bells Are Ringing," "Silver Bells," and, of course, every child's favorite sing-along "Jingle Bells." With their cheerful lyrics such as "jingle all the way" and "ring-a-ling, hear them ring," these joyful songs actually have deep roots in ancient beliefs about the power of magic to repel demons and other malevolent spirits.

* * *

Many plants and herbs associated with Christmas also had significance in ancient times as holding magical powers. Evergreens such as holly, ivy and mistletoe, which all bore fruit in winter time and therefore were considered manifestations of abiding life at a time of year when everything is dead, were used by pagans as sacraments to ensure growth and fertility.[38] The red and green poinsettia plant, named for American ambassador Joel Roberts Poinsett, who introduced the plant to the United States in the 1820s, was once used in shamanic rites to give humans "blossoming dreams"[39] and was offered in war rituals as a portent of victory.[40] A botanical native of the Mexican state of Chiapas, this plant was known by the Aztecs as *cuetlaxochitl*, which has been translated alternatively as "mortal flower that perishes like all that is pure," "leather flower," and "flower that grows in residues or soil." It was considered a gift from nature and was not to be touched, its bright red color considered a sign from the gods of the blood of human sacrifice.[41]

The poinsettia plant was repackaged for Christmas by 17th-century Christian friars who added the plant to their nativity processions. This spawned a folk tale, "The Legend of the Poinsettia," in which two children, Maria and Pablo, brought a handful of weeds as gifts to lay down at a church manger scene on Christmas Eve. "When the children entered the church, many of the villagers turned to stare," the story goes. "As they began placing the weeds around the manger, some of the villagers laughed at them." Maria and Pablo began to feel embarrassed for their gifts of weeds to the infant Jesus, but then the green leaves began to turn to red, inspiring awe at the miracle unfolding inside the church. "The laughing villagers became silent as they watched the green plants transform into the lovely star-shaped crimson flowers we call poinsettias," according to the legend.[42]

Another magical plant associated with Christmas is the mistletoe. A parasitic plant that grows on a variety of trees and causes growths that deform the branches, mistletoe has been utilized for miraculous purposes by many cultures over the centuries. It features prominently in Norse mythology, particularly in a story about the god Baldur being pierced and killed by mistletoe thrown by a blind god named Hodur, sending Baldur to the realm of Hel, where he would remain forever in "darkness, dampness, and cold."[43] Mistletoe was also considered by the ancient druids the most sacred plant with both magical attributes and medicinal properties. In Pliny the Elder's *Natural History*, he writes:

> The druids—that is what they call their magicians—hold nothing more sacred than the mistletoe and a tree on which it is growing, provided it is a hard-timbered oak.... Mistletoe is rare and when found it is gathered with great ceremony, and particularly on the sixth day of the moon.... Hailing the moon in a native word that means "healing all things," they prepare a ritual sacrifice and banquet beneath a tree and bring up two white bulls, whose horns are bound for the first time on this occasion. A priest arrayed in white vestments climbs the tree and, with a golden sickle, cuts down the mistletoe, which is caught

in a white cloak. Then finally they kill the victims, praying to a god to render his gift propitious to those on whom he has bestowed it. They believe that mistletoe given in drink will impart fertility to any animal that is barren and that it is an antidote to all poisons.

Druids believed the magical power of the mistletoe was strongest when growing in oak trees, but if the plant touched the ground after being cut, the magic would be lost.[44] The mistletoe was so sacred to the druids that if two adversaries met beneath a tree on which it was growing, they would lay down their weapons, exchange greetings, and observe a truce[45]—a possible precursor from ancient times to the modern practice of exchanging kisses under the mistletoe at Christmas. Other theories about the origins of the kissing tradition relate to its supposed fertility-increasing properties, but it should be noted that the first records of this practice only appear in the 19th century and ultimately the reasons for this tradition are unknown.

Although the druids were suppressed by the Romans, traditions of mistletoe lived on and began to appear in recorded Christmas customs in the 17th century. The poet Robert Herrick, in his poem "Ceremonie upon Candlemas Eve," described the practice of taking down Christmas decorations on February 1 with the lines

This 1752 engraving illustrates a druid up an oak tree harvesting mistletoe, with a contingent of Christian priests at the bottom of the tree. "The druids; or the conversion of the Britons to Christianity," 1758. Artist S.F. Ravenet (Wellcome Collection).

8. *Actual Christmas Magic* 107

"Down with the Rosemary, and so / Down with the Baies, & mistletoe." As historian Judith Flanders notes, although Herrick is the first source to associate mistletoe with Christmas, "what we don't know was whether Christmas mistletoe was a 17th century novelty, or if earlier references just failed to survive."[46] Nevertheless, some mistletoe customs were revived by aficionados of antiquities, known as antiquarians, during a period of nostalgia in the early 19th century. These antiquarians studied ancient historians such as Pliny and adopted some of the customs that he had documented,[47] possibly embellishing the magical properties of the plant and exaggerating

CHRISTMAS FLIRTATION.

In this late 19th-century drawing, a woman is standing under a mistletoe bough with a flirtatious look in her eye. From Thomas Nast's *Christmas drawings for the human race*, published in 1890 by Harper & Brothers in New York (Getty Research Institute).

its importance. In *The Golden Bough: A Study in Magic and Religion*, published in 1913, James Frazer claims that to the druids, "the growth of mistletoe on an oak was a sign that the tree was especially sacred; and the rarity of this feature—for mistletoe does not grow commonly on oaks—would enhance the sanctity and mystery of the tree." He notes that it is "the rare, not the familiar and commonplace, which excites the religious emotions of mankind."[48]

Whether they are survivals from the times of the ancient Celts or from more recent times, there are many arcane mistletoe-related rituals that have been recorded, some of which persisted into the 20th century and remnants of which survive to this day. The plant was thought to assist in attaining riches and since it was also believed to boost fertility, women would tie a sprig of mistletoe to their waists in order to increase chances of conceiving.[49] A mistletoe bough was often cut and hung up inside the house as the clock struck 12 on New Year's Eve, while the bough that had been hanging there for the past year was set on fire in a practice called "Burning the Bush." Adorning a home with mistletoe was believed to prevent the house being struck by lightning, to keep away witches, and to ensure that the household would have sufficient food. The magical plant was also believed to treat epilepsy, dispel tumors, protect crops, and to divine treasures.[50]

As Richard Mabey writes in *Flora Britannica*, "Mistletoe traditions are amongst northern Europe's last surviving remnants of plant magic."[51] Because of its pagan and magical associations, mistletoe is rarely allowed inside a church.

* * *

The Christmas elf is another relic of a time when people widely believed in magic. Although it has been modernized for a more temporal culture and reimagined as a friendly, hardworking toymaker in Santa's workshop, the concept actually has its roots in ancient pagan beliefs—dating back to the Norse myths about the *álfar*.

In pre–Christian times, elves were thought of as supernatural beings with magical power and were commonly offered sacrifices such as the sprinkling of blood in order to curry their favor. Practiced at the beginning of winter, the sacrifice known as *álfablót* was a highly private affair in which people would make offerings of food and drink to the álfar, which were considered related to the gods associated closely with health, fertility, and sorcery. The sacrifices were hoped to ensure a fruitful and peaceful new year.[52]

As folklorist Armann Jakobsson has pointed out, the Old Norse term *álfar* probably encapsulated a wide variety of "paranormal others." The sagas depict elves as possessing magical powers and the eddic poetry associates *álfar* with the Norse gods. Whether *álfar* were good or evil is ambiguous, to the extent that Snorri Sturluson invented categories of "light elves" and "dark elves." This firm classification was probably not widely accepted, even in the context that Sturluson was writing in medieval Iceland, but it does seem that elves were generally ambivalent towards everyday people and capable of either helping or hindering them. Elves had a reputation for pranks and mischief, and anomalous daily occurrences were often attributed to them. According to folklorist Carol Rose, elves were sometimes friendly toward humans, but they were also known to take "terrible revenge on any human who offends them." They might, for example, steal babies or enchant young men under their spells for years at a time.

Elves were believed to live in the ground[53] and different varieties have been known as kobolds in Germany, nisses in Scandinavia, brownies in Scotland, and boggarts in England. In Faroese folklore, the *huldufólk*, or "hidden people," are also referred to as elves, and are believed to dislike symbols of Christianity such as crosses and churches.[54] In the Celtic world, the ancient gods that were driven underground by Christian missionaries became known as *aes sídhe*, which are comparable to fairies or elves.[55] The *aes sídhe* were feared as ardent guardians of their territory, and were believed to retaliate against trespassers by kidnapping them. Some considered elves to be Europe's first settlers, who buried themselves in the mountains and hills to flee Christianization, hiding in dark holes so that they could continue to practice their magic.[56] In medieval Europe, elves were seen as nefarious and were often linked to demons. They kept mostly to themselves, but might venture out at night to steal butter, milk, or even a cow from the farm.[57]

*   *   *

Despite their mischievous reputation, elves and their various iterations were considered a necessary member of the home in the old days. Believed to live in barns, the Scandinavian nisse guarded farms and there was a time when every homestead had a tiny nisse to help with the chores, or, if he was feeling naughty, to play tricks on the household. The roots of the nisse are found in pagan beliefs in "house gods" that protected the household, similar to the Christian belief in a patron saint.[58] Over time, the nisses were joined by julenisses, or Christmas elves, who both played pranks and left gifts for the family.[59] In Sweden, the tomte followed a similar path. These were fearsome creatures who were responsible for the protection and welfare of a farmstead and its buildings. They demanded respect and if they felt they had been insulted, might take revenge by killing a cow or breaking things. As lovers of tradition they eventually became associated with Christmas and were known to emerge as the days grew darker and the winter solstice approached to assist with the preparations for the holiday.[60]

Popular German folktales collected by the Grimm brothers in the early 19th century demonstrated the dualistic nature of elves, and how they might help or harm people depending on their mood. In one story, a mother's child had been taken away by elves, and replaced with "a changeling with a large head and staring eyes, which would do nothing but eat and drink." The distraught mother sought advice from her neighbor who told her that if she could make changeling laugh, "all would be over with him." So, the woman boiled water in some eggshells, a sight that was so unusual it elicited the laughter she was looking for. "I am as old now as the Wester forest," said the imp, "but never yet have I seen any one boil anything in an egg shell!" While the changeling was laughing uncontrollably, a host of little elves came with the child they had taken, set it down and took the changeling away with them.

Another story collected by the Grimm brothers demonstrated the elves' helpful side. In the Christmas tale "The Elves and The Shoemaker," a group of elves came to visit a shoemaker's home in the middle of the night to "stitch, and sew, and hammer ... until all [the work] was done." In gratitude for their much-needed assistance and helping to make the shoemaker rich, his wife decided to make them gifts of little shirts, coats, vests, trousers, as well as stockings and shoes. When the elves came back the next night, they were delighted to discover the clothes that had been left for them, quickly dressed themselves and sang, "Now we are boys so fine to see, Why should we longer cobblers be?" Although they never returned to assist the shoemaker again, he was prosperous for the rest of his life thanks to the aid of his little helpers.

This story may have helped inspire the concept of a Christmas elf, which developed a few decades later. The idea of these diligent little workers happily toiling away in Santa's workshop was popularized in magazines during the mid–1800s. In 1857, *Harper's Weekly* published a poem titled "The Wonders of Santa Claus," which included the lines "In his house upon the top of a hill, And almost out of sight, He keeps a great many elves at work, All working with all their might, To make a million of pretty things, Cakes, sugar-plums, and toys, To fill the stockings, hung up you know, By the little girls and boys."[61] From this account grew a whole genre of stories and artwork featuring Santa's workshop and his band of elves. A 1932 Disney short film, "Santa's Workshop," for example, depicted a happy team of elves working in perfect unison on the assembly line, and singing and whistling as they prepare Santa's sleigh for his Christmas Eve journey.

The Christmas elf has evolved today into the popular "Elf on the Shelf" product, enjoyed by many families in the United States and increasingly in other countries as well. The practice consists of "adopting," i.e., purchasing, a "Scout Elf" who reports to Santa Claus and helps manage his naughty and nice lists. "When a family adopts a Scout Elf and gives it a name, the Scout Elf receives its Christmas magic and can fly to the North Pole each night to tell Santa Claus about all of the day's adventures," the Elf on the Shelf website explains.[62] Each morning, the Scout Elf returns from the North Pole and takes a place in a different spot to watch the family's activities. According to the rules of the Elf on the Shelf tradition (albeit a relatively new tradition, beginning

In the center of the drawing, a nisse is tidying up a stable. This is the oldest known image of a nisse, found in a story by Olaus Magnus from 1555. Nisse. From *Historia de gentibus septentrionalibus*. Olaus Magnus—History of the Nordic Peoples (detail) (Lars Henriksson, http://www.avrosys.nu/).

with the publication of a children's picture book in 2005), if children touch the elf he will lose his magic, which can only be regained by giving him cinnamon.

Although Elf on the Shelf has been dismissed as "a marketing juggernaut dressed up as a tradition,"[63] it actually resembles a more authentic tradition rooted in genuine folk customs, that of the drillenisse, as long practiced in Scandinavia. This tradition relates more closely to the elves' historical role as mischief makers. In countries such as Denmark and Norway, during Christmas time a drillenisse, roughly translated as a "teasing elf," moves into the home and throughout the month of December plays pranks on the household. The nisse is never seen but children might wake up, for example, to find their shoes full of rice, furniture turned upside down, or a carton full of green milk. To keep the drillenisses happy, it is common to leave food for them, including their favorite dish—rice pudding with cinnamon on top.

In this Christmas card drawing by Peter Nicolaj Møller, a drillenisse appears to be conniving with Cupid, the son of Mercury and Venus known to shoot arrows at unsuspecting victims to induce states of love and passion. Late 19th century, Denmark (Heimskringla, https://heimskringla.no/).

* * *

These traditions remind us of the broader context in which the concept of Christmas magic developed, with magical beings, magical charms, and magical plants ubiquitous during the festive season. These can be actual physical objects such as bells and poinsettias but can also be beliefs and customs that have been popularized and have consequently lost their one-time magical characteristics. With an appreciation for how these magical traits of Christmas date back to ancient times when belief in the supernatural was widespread, it begins to make sense how "Christmas magic" continues to be such an enduring theme in popular culture. A whole genre of film and literature has developed to explore the theme of magic at Christmastime, with stories as "The Nutcracker and the Mouse King" and "Frosty the Snowman" becoming perennial Christmas favorites. "The Nutcracker," an 1816 short story by E.T.A. Hoffmann which was later adapted into a popular seasonal ballet, tells the story of a young girl's favorite Christmas toy coming to life and taking her away to a magical kingdom, while the 1969 cartoon *Frosty the Snowman* tells a similar tale of a snowman coming to life after putting on a magical silk hat and taking a trip with a young girl to the North Pole. More recent contributions include the 2003 Will Farrell movie *Elf*, which ends with all of New York City uniting in singing "Here Comes Santa Claus" in order to generate the Christmas spirit needed to fuel Santa's magical sleigh, and the 2011 Hallmark Channel movie *Christmas Magic*, in which a woman is tasked by an angel with serving as a spirit guide to a young restaurant owner who is contemplating suicide.

The Polar Express, a 2004 film that people seem to either love or hate, explores the theme of Christmas magic through the story of a boy who is so consumed with anxiety over the holiday that he worries that even asking his parents about the nature of Christmas could destroy whatever magic it has. Seizing on the opportunity to take a trip to the North Pole on a train, he makes his way to the center of town where he is surrounded by elves and has Santa Claus in his sigh but is still so filled with doubt about Christmas that he is unable to hear Santa's sleigh bells. Others around him marvel at how beautiful the bells sound but he is unable to hear them until he finds one on the ground, picks it up and whispers, "I believe. I believe." Finally, through the sheer will of his desire to believe, he is able to hear the beautiful sound and to experience the magic of Christmas.

These films and stories are a reminder that while people in the Western world today generally may not believe in actual magic—as in the use of ritualistic practices to manipulate the natural and supernatural world—Christmas is the one time of the year that this word is commonly used and generally sensible people entertain notions that they would usually reject, like the idea that miracles are possible. Indeed, at Christmas time, it is almost obligatory to concede that miracles happen and failing to believe in the "magic of Christmas" is practically considered sacrilege. While at other times of the year, parents teach their children that magic isn't real, at Christmas, they try to convince them of the opposite, sincerely telling them how Santa uses magic to make his reindeer fly and how the impossible is possible if you just believe. Without some "Christmas magic," the holiday feels incomplete.

The reason for this is that our ancestors heartily believed in magic, and this time of year was particularly uncanny—with increased spiritual activity, Odin's Wild Hunt, and the corresponding need to ward off evil spirits with incense, bells and plants. While we might use terms like "Christmas magic" metaphorically, its historical origin is anything but a metaphor: magic was quite real and it was particularly relevant during the 12 days of Christmas and the rough nights. Whether we realize it or not, this is why we tell our children fantastical stories of flying reindeer and little elves who perform miracles—and why this actually seems plausible, at least for a month or so every year.

9

Children's Saturnalia

> *It was the eve of Christmas day,*
> *When rigid rules aside were cast*
> *By such as walked the wicked way:*
> *His sober household kept a fast*
> *He wished the day were past!*
>   —Helen Gray Cone, "The Elfin Bough"

In 1997 an annual television event was launched that would quickly become an integral part of millions of Americans' holiday traditions. That year, Turner Broadcasting began airing a 24-hour marathon—beginning Christmas Eve and playing through Christmas Day—of the 1983 cult classic *A Christmas Story*, a film depicting the quintessential child's perspective of Christmas. Narrated by the adult voice of the main character, a nine-year-old named Ralphie Parker who is singularly focused on obtaining his dream Christmas present (an official Red Ryder Carbine Action 200-Shot Range Model air rifle with a compass in the stock and this thing that tells time), the film follows the ups and downs of life in "kiddom" at the most exciting time of the year. "Christmas was on its way," the narrator says in the opening sequence of the movie. "Lovely, glorious, beautiful Christmas, upon which the entire kid year revolved."

The marathon, airing on Turner's TBS and TNT channels, proved wildly popular, with an estimated 54.4 million tuning in by 2008.[1] "All three airings of the movie on Christmas Eve draw bigger ratings in the 18–49 demographic than anything else on cable," according to the website *A Christmas Story House and Museum* (yes, there is a museum dedicated to the movie, located in Cleveland, Ohio). "In 2013 the 8:00 pm Christmas Eve showing was the most watched, 5.2 million total viewers."[2]

While the movie is loved for its quirky characters and memorably hilarious scenes, the appeal of the film is also in its nostalgic approach to capturing the essence of what Christmas means to children. Although set in the 1940s and containing cultural references that might not be entirely recognizable to those of us who grew up in later decades, somehow everyone can relate to Ralphie and the nearly delirious excitement with which he anticipates the Christmas event. It reminds us that while Christmas means different things to different people, and while its historical significance and spiritual meaning may have evolved over time, to kids, the meaning of the holiday is quite simple: it's the time of year that their wishes are granted, rules are relaxed, and the fulfillment of their desires is parents' primary concern.

Indeed, Christmas has been so well established for so long as a child-centered

114 Part Two—Curious Customs

Depicting a wild party with rambunctious children being catered to by adults, the caption of this 1835 illustration reads, "'At home' in the Nursery, or the masters & misses twoshoes Christmas party." Artist George Cruikshank. Etching, colored by hand (Rijksmuseum, C. Veth Bequest).

occasion that it is difficult to think of it in any other way. The emphasis on the child as the focal point of the holiday was captured as long ago as 1842 when an account in the journal *Brother Jonathan* announced on December 24 that "[t]omorrow will be Christmas, jolly rosy Christmas, the Saturnalia of children." The article noted "how the little rogues long for the advent of this day; for with it comes their generous friend Santa Claus with his sleigh, like the purse of Fortunatus, over-flowing with treasures." It anticipated the "shouts of joy" and the "embraces of love and gratitude" that children would shower their parents with after they discovered their stockings overflowing with toys and candy. "Surely the most cynical could not look upon such a pleasant scene as this," reads the article, "without feeling the frost of his crabbedness gradually melting away."[3]

* * *

The focus on children and their happiness in our modern Christmas celebration, and indeed within society as a whole, has become so ingrained in the popular psyche that people might actually believe that this has been a constant throughout history, that children have always been viewed as vulnerable little people who require special treatment and constant attention, that their needs and desires were tended to by parents who were concerned above all else with their children's happiness. This doting approach to child-rearing, however, is a relatively new phenomenon, with children throughout history often enduring unspeakable hardship and tragedy and finding little comfort in the consolation and tenderness that would be expected of loving parents and other caring adults.

Although fitting in some ways, there is some irony that Christmas has been reminiscently called the "Saturnalia of children," when Saturnalia was not particularly a child-friendly occasion and in fact there was a time when children may have actually been sacrificed to Greek gods such as Kronos and his Roman counterpart Saturn.[4] Child sacrifice was performed for any number of reasons, including something as simple as an offering in exchange for, say, the gods' help in ensuring the safe voyage of a ship, but also at times held an explicitly symbolic and religious meaning. This was particularly the case when it came to the worship of Kronos and Saturn during their festivals of Kronia and Saturnalia.

The Greek and Roman myths of Kronos and Saturn included prophecies that one of his sons would depose him. Acting out of an abundance of caution, Kronos/Saturn ate his first two children moments after each was born, but to prevent this from happening again, Saturn's wife Ops hid his third son, Jupiter, on the island of Crete. Eventually the prophecy was fulfilled, and Jupiter overthrew

This 17th-century illustration depicts the Myth of Kronos/Saturn. "Saturnus," ca. 1630–ca. 1673. Artist L. Richer (Rijksmuseum).

his father, bringing an end to the Golden Age, which was recalled every year during the celebration of Kronia and later Saturnalia. This appears to be why child sacrifices may have been offered to the god, at least in his earlier Greek iteration, to restore the peace, stability and prosperity of the Golden Age when Kronos was king, and to win favor with him by appeasing his desires.

As Roman statesman Marcus Tullius Cicero describes it in his work *On the Nature of the Gods*, published in 45 BCE,

> By Saturn ... they meant him who controlled the course and revolution of periods and times, the god who in Greek bears that actual name, for he is called [Kronos], that is, a period of time. And he was named Saturn because, it was supposed, he was "made full" (*saturo*) with years, for it is because time swallows up the periods of time, and is loaded, without being satisfied, with the years of the past, that Saturn is represented as having been accustomed to devour his own offspring, and it was in order that he might not have an unrestricted course, and that Jupiter might fetter him with the yoke of the stars.[5]

So, Saturn, like his Greek precursor Kronos, had to be *saturated* with offerings, and what better offering than a child? After all, it was his own child—the one he had failed to eliminate—who came to displace him and brought an end to the Golden Age.

Numerous historical accounts suggest, sadly, that this is precisely what they did in the ancient world. "There were no temples of Kronus in Greece," according to 19th-century linguist Charles Anthon, "but there was a chapel of Kronus and Rhea at Athens and sacrifices were made to him on the Kronian Hill at Olympia." Greek and Latin sources recount the offering of children to Kronos by fire in the Punic city of Carthage, which was a Phoenician colony. As historian Paul Mosca describes the horrific practice, "There stands in their midst a bronze statue of Kronos, its hands extended over a bronze brazier, the flames of which engulf the child. When the flames fall upon the body, the limbs contract and the open mouth seems almost to be laughing until the contracted body slips quietly into the brazier."[6]

The use of child sacrifice to honor Kronos appears to have disappeared when the god became worshipped as Saturn by the Romans,[7] as the Romans came to generally view human sacrifice as distasteful and banned the practice in 97 BCE. In later celebrations of Saturnalia, in fact, children were gifted little dolls, which some have speculated may have been a token reminder of the time that kids were sacrificed to the god.[8] Despite the formal ban on sacrifices, however, "ritual killings" continued to take place, including practices such as disposing of deformed infants by placing them in boxes and casting them out to sea or abandoning babies in the wild—practices that may have held symbolic meaning in terms of the Romans' relationship with the gods. The Romans believed that their success and power were attributable to the gods' beneficence, and therefore strove to maintain this bond by continuing the practices that they believed pleased their deities, even after human sacrifice had been prohibited. Historians believe that these ritual killings were done partially to help preserve Roman dominance, but at the same time, by differentiating between ritual killings and human sacrifice, Romans were able to claim moral superiority over other societies.[9] Indeed, even while currying favor with the gods with ritual killings, the Romans eagerly seized on the issue of child sacrifice as propaganda against their ancient rivals the Carthaginians and, consequently, for a long period accounts of child sacrifice by the Carthaginians were dismissed as baseless Roman smears. Recent scholarship has determined however that the practice most likely did take place.

"Children—both male and female, and mostly a few weeks old—were sacrificed by the Carthaginians at locations known as tophets," according to a groundbreaking academic paper published in 2014. Methodically countering the view that claims of child sacrifices were nothing but propaganda used against ancient Carthaginians by their enemies, the academics determined that the practice was indeed carried out at least in Carthage, Sicily, Sardinia and Malta. "Dedications from the children's parents to the gods are inscribed on slabs of stone above their cremated remains," according to the study.[10]

Trying to make sense of this practice and to understand how a parent could do such a thing to his or her own child, Josephine Quinn, an author of the 2014 paper, noted that the high death rate among children meant that their lives may not have been valued quite as highly as they are today. "We have to remember the high level of mortality among children—it would have been sensible for parents not to get too attached to a child that might well not make its first birthday," Quinn said. Paradoxically, while perhaps not wanting to grow too attached to a child who could very well die anyway, parents may have also believed that offering what was most valuable to them was more indicative of their devout beliefs, more pleasing to the gods, and therefore more likely to result in them bestowing favors. According to Quinn, the practice was likely performed "out of profound religious piety, or a sense that the good the sacrifice could bring the family or community as a whole outweighed the life of the child."

This profound sense of piety is alluded to by Cicero:

> And the worship of the gods which is best, and also purest, and holiest, and most full of piety, is that we should always reverence them with a mind and voice that are without stain, and guiltless, and uncorrupt; for religion has been dissociated from superstition not only by philosophers but by our own ancestors as well. I may mention as to these two terms that men who used to spend whole days in prayer and sacrifice in order that their children might survive them.[11]

Even if it was done out of a deep religious belief, history has generally not been kind to societies that practiced human sacrifice, and the treatment of children in particular has long served as a powerful indictment of the moral depravity of pagans, a talking point that Christians have used throughout the ages. The Bible strongly condemns such practices, with the Old Testament specifically referring to the human sacrifices offered to Moloch and Baal—the Phoenician and Canaanite predecessors of both Kronos and Saturn. A passage in the Book of Ezekiel demonstrates how reprehensible the practice was seen in the eyes of the Lord: "When you present your gifts and offer up your children in fire, you defile yourselves with all your idols to this day. And shall I be inquired of by you, O house of Israel? As I live, declares the Lord God, I will not be inquired of by you."

Psalm 106 had these strong words for the pagans:

> They sacrificed their sons and their daughters to the demons; they poured out innocent blood, the blood of their sons and daughters, whom they sacrificed to the idols of Canaan, and the land was polluted with blood. Thus they became unclean by their acts, and played the whore in their deeds. Then the anger of the Lord was kindled against his people, and he abhorred his heritage; he gave them into the hand of the nations, so that those who hated them ruled over them.

Leviticus 18:21 specifically warns against sacrifices to Moloch: "You shall not give any of your children to offer them to Molech, and so profane the name of your God." In total there are some 100 references to human sacrifice in the Bible, with about a dozen specific references to sacrificing children. This indicates not only how heinous the practice was considered by contemporaries but also, regrettably, how common it must have been.

In later years, the practice of child sacrifice served as a powerful tool of conversion, offering a potent reminder of the moral superiority of Christianity. During the Christianization of Europe in the first millennium, tales were told of Christian missionaries rescuing children from being offered to heathen gods, demonstrating the power of Christian virtue and mercy, including the famous story of St. Boniface converting heathens who were preparing to make a sacrifice of a small child at the base of their sacred oak tree. Boniface reached the village on Christmas Eve just as the pagans were preparing to offer the child to Thor, and using his staff, blocked the executioner's blow. Although these tales were long thought to be exaggerated or fabricated as instances of anti-pagan Christian propaganda, archaeology has since confirmed their grim truth. A dig at Trelleborg, Sweden, discovered five wells where skeletons of humans and animals were found together with tools and jewelry. Four of the human sacrifice victims were children between the ages of four and seven.[12]

* * *

Although sacrifice obviously is an extreme example of the different approaches between paganism and Christianity to what today may be called human rights—and specifically the rights of the child—the emphasis on children's general well-being is something that has long been stressed as one of the advantages of following the Christian faith.

A 19th-century theologian named Richard Joseph Cooke, writing about Christianity's impact on the lives of children, describes the dreadful condition of childhood in heathenism before "Christianity began its mission of mercy and beneficence," ultimately blaming pagans' lack of belief in the Christian God as the reason for kids' maltreatment. The decay of family life, he explains, and the neglect of children and the cruelty that they endured, "in utter disregard of the natural feelings of the heart," were all the result of the heathens' lack of faith in God, leading them "to an abandonment of hope in a future life" and "terrible cruelty, or at least indifference, toward helpless childhood." He argues that indifference towards the child was not only due "to the universal corruption of the age or the extreme poverty of the lower classes," but due to paganism itself. "Heathenism could produce nothing better," he wrote. "Whenever and wherever heathenism came to the flower, it tended to repress the better instincts of humanity."[13]

Christians, on the other hand, through their atonement with God for man's Original Sin, are uniquely positioned to raise children properly, according to Cooke. As he explains, "the child possesses tendencies—strong bias toward evil which drives it deeper and deeper into sin without any power of deliverance." But through Christian guidance, benefits may be accrued through the grace of God, offering the child an opportunity to resist the power of evil and strive towards the good. "The child will," he writes, "yield to evil, since through this same atonement the Spirit of God is not a mere Spectator of human life and history, but a helping dynamic power to aid every one coming into the world."[14] Cooke credits this focus on the child not only with promoting children's well-being, but also helping to establish Christianity as the dominant faith of Western civilization. "A religion which stood in no vital relation to childhood could not have wielded other than a limited influence on society or the family," he concludes.[15]

Notwithstanding Cooke's biases in favor of Christianity (he would become a bishop some 20 years after writing his tract on Christianity and childhood), he certainly had a point about the pagans, who were known for many objectionable practices (at least according to modern sensibilities), with child sacrifice being perhaps the most egregious. But it should also be pointed out that even following the widespread adoption of Christianity in Europe, children continued to suffer hardship and were often considered expendable, particularly during hard times. Children were expected to help out with household tasks such as caring for animals and cooking, and expulsion from the household was a common punishment for idle children. Sometimes children were simply abandoned, but luckier boys and girls might be sent to monastic schools or convents. In some cases this may have been done to get rid of children who parents couldn't afford, but it was more often seen as a religious commitment—an offering to God of the most precious things parents had to give.[16] In this sense, the motivation may not have been entirely different than the child sacrifices as practiced by pagans of an earlier era, expressing their piety and devotion to the gods by offering to them what they considered most valuable.

One of the most difficult realities of life in earlier eras prior to modern medicine and basic healthcare standards was that many infants did not live to see their first birthday. It is estimated that in the Middle Ages as many as one-third of babies perished during their first year, while many others were claimed by diseases and accidents before the age of ten. This harsh reality could lead to rather detached parenting styles, with mothers and fathers not wanting to get too attached to children who could die at any time. Since birth control was also not reliable and was frowned upon by the Church, families tended to be large, which meant that less attention would be focused on individual children and that there was little tolerance for laziness and insolence. Young ones quickly learned the importance of being useful.

Stories developed within this context that captured both the harsh realities of life for children and the pagan worldview that continued to influence people's thinking well into the Christian era. The tales of harsh punishments, both in life and death, for children considered lazy or those who died before baptism not only served as cautionary tales to teach kids the value of hard work, but also reflects the fact that during the Middle Ages, newborns were seen as intrinsically evil,[17] as they had not had the opportunity to unburden themselves from Original Sin through the redemption of baptism and worship. These hybrid pagan-Christian stories had particular relevance at Christmas time.

* * *

Perchta, a witch believed to be the guide and guardian of the heimchen, or souls of children who died unbaptized, has been known in various cultures as Frau Holle, Holla, Holda, Berchta, Berta, or Bertha. She was believed to appear during the 12 days of Christmas, and in Germany was thought to be connected to the spirit world through the magic of spinning and weaving. The figure was initially a pre–Christian female goddess, and was sometimes called Frau Frick, leading to speculation that she has some association with Frigg, who is believed to descend from the same Proto-Germanic figure that gave rise to Freyja,[18] the Norse goddess associated with fertility, sex, war, gold, and magic.

Perchta, as she was called in the Alpine regions of southern Germany and Austria, was known as "queen of the heimchen," and was associated with birch trees, watching over the forests and all the wildlife in them. She was the spirit guide who led the dead into the afterlife, but she was also known to roam the countryside at midwinter to pass judgment on lazy and naughty children. Entering homes during the 12 days of Christmas, and especially on the Twelfth Night, she would reward children who had behaved well and worked hard all year with a coin the next day. If they hadn't, she would slit their bellies open, remove their entrails, and stuff the hole with straw and pebbles.[19] The entourage of spirits that she led during the 12 nights was originally understood as spirits of the departed, but as the Church attempted to suppress this belief, her company came to be commonly feared as demons rather than ghosts.

Also connected to Perchta is an Italian legend of an old witch named Befana who gives presents to children throughout Italy on the eve of the Epiphany, the feast day on January 6 commemorating the baptism of Christ. (For bad children, she leaves coal or sticks—not quite as harsh a punishment as stuffing children's bellies with straw and pebbles but still a clear sign of disapproval.) The Befana legend likely dates back to pre–Christian times, perhaps as far back as the Neolithic period, and while some scholars believe that there is connection with Perchta,[20] others point to a Roman deity named Strenia, a goddess of the new year, or to Nicneven, a Queen of the Fairies in Scottish folklore, as being possible inspirations.

Whatever her origins, Befana was rebranded to fit with the Christmas narrative. According to the Christian legend, Befana was asked for directions by the three magi travelling from the east on their quest to find the baby Jesus, but she turned them away because she was too busy cleaning her house. Later, after having a change of heart, she decided to join the search for the infant but was never able to find him. So, some 2,000 years later Befana is still searching in vain and on the eve of the Epiphany, she visits every house where there is a child and leaves a gift. But although Italians consider Befana a "Christian witch," associated closely with the Epiphany, she remains a manifestation of an old winter goddess associated with fertility and agriculture.[21]

Reinforcing the view that the Epiphany-related Befana legend could be an Italian variation of the Perchta myth, the word "Perchta" is Tyrolese for "Epiphany," and has also been defined by Jacob Grimm as "Shining One." Grimm associated Perchta with pagan moon goddesses and like her counterpart Holda, she was believed to have the gift of flight and to lead the Wild Hunt.[22] Her role as guardian of the heimchen was also described by Grimm: "As the Christian god has not made them His, they fall to the old heathen one." In one of the best-known stories about the heimchen, a peasant encountered Perchta's ghostly procession out on Epiphany Eve and noticed a small child wearing an oversized shirt that he kept tripping on. The peasant said to the boy, "oh you poor ragamuffin," for which the boy thanked the peasant—by calling him "ragamuffin," the boy had been "christened" with a name and was no longer unbaptized, thus freeing his soul from eternal nocturnal wandering.[23]

In another story collected by the Grimm brothers, a brother and sister are abandoned in a forest by their parents, where they come across a house made of gingerbread with a roof "coated with fluffy white icing." The house featured "a gum drop door frame ... sopping with sparkling icing sugar," as well as "a lollipop garden ... in front of a large crystallized sugar window." Little did they know that all these sweets were strategically placed as bait to lure them into the house so that the witch who lived there could kidnap and eat them. "There's more candy in here!" the witch said, enticing the children inside. Her plan was to fatten them before eventually devouring them, but the sister outsmarted the witch and killed her in her own oven. The two children then escaped and returned home with the witch's treasure.

This story, known as "Hansel and Gretel," spawned an iconoclastic Christmas symbol and popular tradition among the more ambitious Christmas celebrants. Considered by some a beloved family ritual and others simply a way to pass the afternoon while licking icing from their fingers and popping gum drops in their mouths, the gingerbread house is assembled by using pieces of baked gingerbread dough fastened to one another with melted sugar and decorating the structure with frosting and candies. It is not entirely clear how it became associated with Christmas, but its origins in the "Hansel and Gretel" tale might be a reflection of evolving views of childhood associated with the holiday, and perhaps an unconscious expression of the collective guilt over how children were once treated. The tradition of building replicas of a cannibalistic witch's house in a story about children abandoned by their parents recalls a time when childhood was often quite cruel, and kids often had to learn to fend for themselves to survive. Indeed, scholars believe that the fairy tale may have actually been inspired by true events, specifically a famine that struck Europe in 1314 when mothers widely abandoned their children and sometimes ate them out of desperation. Lasting for seven years, the Great Famine spurred numerous accounts of cannibalism across Europe,[24] with an Estonian chronicle stating in 1315 that "mothers were fed their children" while an Irish chronicler noted that the people "were so destroyed by hunger that they extracted bodies of the dead from cemeteries and dug out the flesh from the skulls and ate it, and women ate their children."[25]

It was this harsh reality that inspired folk tales such as "Hansel and Gretel," and while these are particularly extreme examples of how difficult and treacherous childhood could be in earlier ages, the fact is a child's life in general was often quite brutish. Childhood was anything but the carefree period of growth, enjoyment, learning and play as we think of it today, and indeed it seems that the concept of "childhood" may not have even existed as we now understand it, which is revealed in artwork from Late Antiquity and the Middle Ages. As Philippe Ariès writes in the influential 1960 study *Centuries of Childhood*, "In the tenth century, artists were unable to depict a child except as a man on a smaller scale,"[26] indicating that people generally lacked the capacity to see them as anything other than imperfect adults. Childhood, Ariès argues, is a relatively new concept that emerged around the 17th century, coinciding with a decline in infant mortality and changes taking place in the European educational system.

It was in this context that Christmas evolved into what would later be called "the Saturnalia of children," developing from a largely adult-focused affair characterized alternatively by pious rejoicing in the birth of the Lord and raucous drinking and feasting into a largely child-centered occasion. The harshness of life for children spurred a number of pagan-influenced traditions, some of which can still be identified today.

* * *

One of the most beloved—and controversial—traditions of the medieval Christmas celebration was the "boy bishop" practice. In an adaption of the inversion of social roles that had been a staple of Saturnalia, "boy bishops" were elected on December 6, the feast day of St. Nicholas, to officiate during the Christmas period, and particularly on the Feast of the Holy Innocents on December 28. On this date, churches would commemorate the biblical story of King Herod's massacre of all children under two years old in Bethlehem in his failed attempt to assassinate the infant Jesus. In a practice that is attested at every cathedral in Britain with a surviving medieval archive, choirboys would take the place of the bishop and other higher clergy to conduct services and lead a torchlit procession.[27] They would then be served a dinner and would give a sermon, a tradition that became so well-established that some churches kept child-sized chasubles, staffs and albs for the boy bishops to use for the occasion.[28] Boy bishops, accompanied sometimes by a Lord of Misrule and an entourage of children, were also known to tour the countryside, visiting nearby villages, singing songs and "blessing" those they encountered.[29] The Feast of the Holy Innocents was not all fun and games though: to remind children of the solemnity of the day, a practice in medieval England included children being whipped in bed on the morning of the 28th, a custom that survived into the 17th century.[30]

The boy bishop tradition was quite popular throughout the Middle Ages but had many opponents within the Church, largely on the grounds that it was seen as heathen in nature—a relic of Roman paganism. The tradition of young boys taking on the role of powerful bishops, while apparently justified by the Church as a reminder of Jesus's own lowly and meek status, closely resembled elements of Saturnalia, when slaves and commoners took on false identities, acted high and mighty, and were served meals by their masters. Opponents of the practice recognized these pagan elements, and with the Reformation came its suppression. A proclamation of Henry VIII on July 22, 1541, decreed that "from henceforth all suche superstitions be loste and clyerlye extinghuissched throughowte all this his relmes and domininos, forasmoche as the same doo resemble rather unlawfull superstition of gentilitie [paganism], than the pure and sincere relition of Christe."[31]

But although it had pagan overtones, the custom was generally portrayed by its proponents as a manifestation of Christian doctrines. As Ronald Hutton points out in *Stations of the Sun*, this tradition was "a reaffirmation of Christ's own teaching about the special relationship of children to the kingdom of heaven, and of the Church's especial respect for innocence and purity—a celebration of norms."[32] Whether it was ultimately Christian or heathen in its origins, the fact that the same tradition was considered by some as a reflection of Christian values and others as a relic of paganism could be seen as an indication that both belief systems served similar functions relating to the need for a relaxing of strict social norms, particularly as they related to children, and especially at Christmas time. As social historian J.A.R. Pimlott has argued, much like Saturnalia's misrule, the boy bishop custom "filled a psychological need, whether it was an outlet for youthful high spirits constrained by the normally severe discipline of medieval religious and educational institutions, or as an assertion of human equality at the season when universal goodwill was supposed to prevail."[33]

* * *

Towards the end of the Middle Ages, life started looking up for children, which can be seen in contemporary depictions of household life. A famous painting by Dutch master Jan Steen called *The Feast of Saint Nicholas*, painted in the late 1660s, depicts a family at home on December 5, the night celebrated in The Netherlands as the Feast of Saint Nicholas, or Sinterklaas. In contrast to earlier works of art that depicted children as miniature adults, usually helping perform household chores, in *The Feast of Saint Nicholas* the children are the center of attention. Adults have organized the occasion for the enjoyment of the kids, with little girls holding dolls and others carrying buckets full of toys, while parents help other children to find their hidden gifts.

Steen's painting indicates that as early as the 17th century, the feast of St. Nicholas was already being celebrated as a children's feast. While not precisely related to the nativity, which was observed later in the month, the feast of St. Nicholas

In this painting, Jan Steen incorporates several elements of the Feast of St. Nicholas. Good children have received gifts from the saint, but naughty children, like the sobbing boy on the left, have received only twigs in their shoe. "The Feast of St Nicholas," 1665–68 (detail). Artist Jan Steen. Oil on canvas, 82 cm × 70.5 cm (Rijksmuseum).

would hold great significance in the development of Christmas, and particularly the evolution of the Santa Claus legend. It also helped Christmas develop into a family-centered festival with children as the focal point. As Philippe Ariès observes in *Centuries of Childhood*, by this period, in the late 17th century, "This is no longer a great collective festival, but a quiet family celebration; and consequently this concentration on the family is continued by a concentration of the family around the children."[34]

But while children may have begun receiving more attention and were treated perhaps more appropriately for their age, the common approach towards child-rearing in general and concentrating on their happiness at Christmas time in particular was still very much tempered by rather draconian practices that seemed to combine elements of pagan and Christian beliefs. The old maxim "spare the rod, spoil the child" was taken to heart by many Christians who believed that it was incumbent upon adults to ensure that children learned not to misbehave and to do what they were told, thereby helping to redeem them from Original Sin. At Christmas time, this stern approach to parenting could be seen in the stories of winter demons such as Krampus who was known to haul naughty children off to his lair, as well as the many variations of St. Nicholas figures who simultaneously gave presents and issued corporal punishments.

Characters such as Pelz Nichol, Ruklaus and Aschenklaus all used elements of St. Nicholas's name, but despite St. Nicholas being the patron saint of children—known for centuries as their protector and guardian—these figures were known to beat children as well as shower them with gifts. When a figure like Pelz Nichol would enter the home on the eve of the St. Nicholas feast, he would scatter nuts and apples on the floor and hit children with his rod as they attempted to collect the treats. As Linda Raedisch describes it in *The Old Magic of Christmas*, "In the old days, most children experienced more than just the threat of a beating on St. Nicholas' Eve. Before they could pick up their treats, it was compulsory to feel the sting of those birch twigs across the backs of their fingers."[35]

Perhaps this was done as some kind of harsh lesson to the children, to teach them that while they may temporarily be the center of attention on this occasion and could expect to receive some gifts and treats, they were still subject to painful and arbitrary punishments at the hands of adults. But there also seems to be some magical folk beliefs attached to the practice, with the birch rod functioning essentially as a magic wand. Raedisch notes that across Europe, apple trees were beaten with birch rods in winter in order to ensure a bountiful harvest in the coming year.[36] Similarly, the recipients of a blow from a birch rod were believed to be blessed with long life, good health and productivity. Furthermore, birch trees in general held special significance in pagan beliefs, with Perchta, "queen of the heimchen," associated with them and branches from birch trees used in Finland during the summer solstice to welcome visitors.

Meanwhile, in America, Christmas was quickly evolving into the celebration of childhood as we know it today. With the advent of softer versions of St. Nicholas—soon to be known simply as Santa Claus—as developed by Washington Irving, Clement Moore and Thomas Nast, the Christmas figure was no longer a stern bishop or a menacing demonic beast, but a friendly elf and later simply a portly old man in a red suit. Some historians point to New York City as the focal point of the transformation

This vintage postcard of Krampus and St. Nicholas demonstrates the dualistic nature of attitudes towards children throughout history. On one hand, children might expect some kindnesses at Christmas, but at the same time they should never forget that they could be subject to cruel and arbitrary punishments by Krampus or other frightening Christmas characters (Dave "Riptheskull" Flickr user, no changes made, CC BY-ND 2.0, https://www.flickr.com/photos/vintagehalloweencollector/3078492517/in/album-72157594429321748/).

of Christmas into today's child-centered occasion. This is not only where many of the stories developed that would deeply impact the development of the Santa Claus myth, including Irving's highly influential *Knickerbocker's History*, but also was seen as the epicenter of Christmas misrule, which provided an impetus to domesticate the holiday with more family-friendly customs. As Judith Flanders speculates in *Christmas: A History*, "Perhaps the rowdy street portions of the holiday, the older topsy-turvy traditions when apprentices shook free of their masters, were being replicated after a fashion as children replaced their parents as the day's star performers."[37]

In this sense, Christmas was truly becoming the Saturnalia of children. With the lowliest members of the household taking on inflated status as the center of attention, empowered by their parents to make wishes for Santa to bring whatever their hearts desired, there were clearly elements of status inversion as the holiday evolved. The focus on the child as the center of the occasion also served to moderate the holiday's rowdier elements and was welcomed by both religious and commercial forces, as a way to both tame Christmas's misrule and expand its business potential.

To kids though, it just meant that Christmas would become the most wonderful time of the year, or as Ralphie put it in *A Christmas Story*, the day "upon which the entire kid year revolved."

10

Ghosts, Goblins and Angels

Between the moonlight and the fire
In winter twilights long ago,
What ghosts we raised for your desire,
To make your merry blood run slow!
How old, how grave, how wise we grow!
No Christmas ghost can make us chill,
Save those that troop in mournful row,
The ghosts we all can raise at will!
—Haven Schauffler,
"Ballade of Christmas Ghosts"

Although perhaps uncommon now, telling ghost stories at Christmas time was once a popular tradition. The formerly widespread nature of the custom is hinted at in Andy Williams's 1963 classic Christmas song "The Most Wonderful Time of the Year," which rattles off several festive traditions associated with the holiday. "There'll be scary ghost stories and tales of the glories of Christmases long, long ago," Williams croons. William Shakespeare also alludes to the tradition in an exchange between Hermione and Mamillus in "The Winter's Tale." When Hermione asks Mamillius to tell a story, he responds, "Merry or sad shall't be?" to which Hermione replies, "As merry as you will." Mamillius then says, "A sad tale's best for winter: I have one of sprites and goblins."[1] And of course we can't forget everyone's favorite holiday story by Charles Dickens, *A Christmas Carol*.

Telling the tale of an elderly miser named Ebenezer Scrooge who is visited by his deceased business partner Jacob Marley and the spirits of Christmas Past, Present and Yet to Come, the book has long been considered an important allegory on the dangers of greed and the joy to be found through goodwill, but it was also intended as a ghost story, which Dickens himself points out. "I have endeavoured in this Ghostly little book," Dickens writes in a brief preface, "to raise the Ghost of an Idea, which shall not put my readers out of humour with themselves, with each other, with the season, or with me. May it haunt their houses pleasantly, and no one wish to lay it." Published on December 19, 1843, as *A Christmas Carol. In Prose. Being a Ghost Story of Christmas*, the novella was an instant success, with the first edition selling out by Christmas Eve. By the end of 1844, 13 editions had been released. Today, it has been adapted hundreds of times for film, television and the stage.

While this was undoubtedly his most popular, Dickens actually wrote several other ghost stories for Christmas, including "The Haunted Man and the Ghost's

Bargain," "The Haunted House," "The Ghost in Master B's Room" and the "The Mortals in the House." In "The Story of the Goblins who Stole a Sexton," published in 1836, Dickens explores a number of similar themes found in *A Christmas Carol*, which would come out about seven years later. In the story, a gin-drinking gravedigger named Gabriel Grub, who is described as "ill-conditioned, cross-grained, and surly," is sent into a rage by a boy singing a Christmas song, prompting Gabriel to beat the boy with his lantern. The curmudgeon goes to work at the cemetery on Christmas Eve to complete an unfinished grave and suddenly hears a voice calling out to him and is startled to see a crowd of shrieking goblins playing leapfrog. The goblins kidnap Gabriel and haul him down into a subterranean lair where he is compelled to watch scenes of the world above, showing the lives of common folk, who despite their everyday struggles, radiate nothing but goodwill and cheer. Gabriel begins to understand the error of his ways and returns to the world a changed man.

Another popular book of this genre is *The Yule Log, for everybody's Christmas Hearth*, published a few years after *A Christmas Carol*, in 1847. Written by Louis Alexis Chamerovzow and illustrated by George Cruikshank, *The Yule Log* features supernatural tales of haunted trees, fairies, sprites, anthropomorphic objects, and malevolent spirits. In one story, the main character, Abel, is being tortured by the Spirit of Yule, who is then joined in the torment by a "multitude of queer-shaped beings" who were "dancing around him, in the darkness, chuckling at him, and making fun of him, in his unfortunate predicament." Despite initially being victimized by these goblins, Abel was so enamored by the fun that they were having that he couldn't help but join them "in shouts of laughter."[2]

This illustration appeared in the 1843 edition of Charles Dickens' *A Christmas Carol*. Although it is generally read as a commentary on the dangers of greed and the joy to be found in generosity, Dickens' tale was written as a Christmas ghost story and included supernatural elements common to the once-popular genre. "Marley's Ghost," 1843. Artist John Leech. From the 1843 edition of Charles Dickens' *A Christmas Carol*. Originally published/produced in London by Chapman & Hall (British Library).

People today might be tempted to attribute these

strange stories of the supernatural to the well-known eccentricities of the Victorian era, but they were actually part of a long tradition of spooky Yuletide tales. A 1658 "history of apparitions," for instance, includes several stories that are linked to Christmas, and *Round about our Coal Fire, or Christmas Entertainment* was a popular collection of ghost stories published in the 1730s, including a tale of a girl who was haunted by a demon.[3] As scholar Jonathan Barry points out, this was an anthology of supposedly true stories, with little discussion of its authenticity or significance, signifying that belief in the reality of the supernatural world of spirits was widespread.[4]

By the 18th century telling ghost stories was considered an obligatory Christmas custom among "countryfolk" in rural areas[5] and by the 19th century, gathering around a fire to tell scary stories became a widely practiced and beloved tradition, which carried on at least into the early 20th century. British writer Jerome K. Jerome collected eight of the most popular ghost stories from the period in his 1891 anthology, *Told After Supper*—stories such as "The Faithful Ghost," "The Haunted Mill," and "My Uncle's Story: The Ghost of the Blue Chamber." In his introduction to the anthology, Jerome notes that while ghosts may appear on other occasions throughout the year, in particular at midsummer and on All Hallows Eve, their favorite occasion is by far Christmas Eve.

"Christmas Eve is the ghosts' great gala night," Jerome writes. "On Christmas Eve they hold their annual fete." Jerome wonders why it is that Christmas Eve, of all nights of the year, was considered the perfect time for sharing stories of the dead. "I never could myself understand," Jerome says, why Christmas Eve would be such a popular time for ghost stories, ultimately chalking it up to the weather. "It is invariably one of the most dismal of nights to be out in—cold, muddy, and wet," he writes. But he also notes that "there must be something ghostly in the air of Christmas—something about the close, muggy atmosphere that draws up the ghosts, like the dampness of the summer rains brings out the frogs and snails."[6]

Here, Jerome is getting closer to the mark. There is indeed something ghostly in the air at Yuletide, or so our ancestors believed in pagan times, which is related to beliefs about increased supernatural activity during the winter solstice. It has long been a widely held belief that nighttime attracts demons and wandering spirits, so naturally, they would be most active on the longest nights of the year. It was also believed that when the sun was at its lowest possible point in the sky, its power was at its weakest and spirits therefore had freer rein at this time of year. Consequently, midwinter was a time when denizens of the otherworld were more active and more easily seen.[7] As religious studies professor Justin Daniels puts it, "The darkest day of the year was seen by many as a time when the dead would have particularly good access to the living."[8]

* * *

In the Balkans, they called the period in between the solstice and the New Year the "unbaptized days," and in Slovenia they were known as "wolf nights." Bulgarians called them "heathen days" and in parts of Central Europe, they are referred to as the "ember nights." As historian Max Dashu has written, "These strange names for the 'Christmas' season" reflect the reality that the midwinter nights are a "time of darkness, when the storm demons nearly swallow the sun, spirits of the dead traverse the heavens, and the ritual hearth fires reassert the sun's power."[9]

Ancient customs of "driving demons away" took place during these nights, with much noise, cracking of whips, ringing of hand bells, and parades of figures in frightening masks. In other customs, farmers have carried incense and sprinkled holy water around the buildings and the farmyard. It is a common theme of this time of the year, and this is why certain traditions, such as the use of bells and evergreens, are so ubiquitous at Christmas time, even to this day—these items were believed to hold magical powers to keep away evil spirits.

In *Christmas Customs and Traditions,* Clement Miles writes, "While Christmas Eve is the night par excellence of the supernatural, the whole season is charged with it."[10] The departed souls were believed to return and visit the living during midwinter, which is why in folk practices, there is both affection shown for the departed, with efforts shown to make them comfortable, but also dread and fear, with people taking pains to avoid the sight of them. The Yule log was a practice related to this veneration of the dead but in some cases may have also be used to keep spirits from entering the home through the chimney. "Ancestral spirits, it seems, were once believed to be imminent in the fire that burned on the hearth, and had to be propriated with libations, while elsewhere the souls of the dead were thought to return to their old homes at the New Year," according to Miles.[11]

In folklore, the Yuletide has long been seen as potentially dangerous, particularly between St. Thomas's Day and New Year's Eve, when it was ill-advised to be out after nightfall. Throughout the Teutonic world, pagans held beliefs in a "raging host" of sprits that rushed through the air on stormy nights. In England the procession of ghosts has been known as the "heathen hounds," while in Iceland it has been called the "Yule host." Miles describes it as the "train of unhappy souls of those who died unbaptized, or by violent hands, or under a curse." In Scandinavia, it is simply Odin's Wild Hunt. In a 1742 study, scholar Johann Peter Schmidt claims that "no one is unaware of the senseless belief held by countless folk, especially some hunters, that the time around Christmas and on the eve of the Carnival (Fastel-Abend) is when the one called Woor or Goor the Wild Huntsman passes." The widely held belief at the time was that it was the Devil who organized a hunt with a troop of rapping spirits, but Schmidt traced the origins of the belief to Norse folklore, and in particular Odin. The company of ghosts is sometimes called Odin's Army, Schmidt points out.[12]

Scandinavians had a particularly pronounced sense of the supernatural during the winter solstice, with trolls and spirits of the dead feared as especially active and aggressive during this period. *Lussinatta*, or the Lussi Night, was considered particularly dangerous to be out, with a witch known as Lussi believed to take away children who had been naughty. Marked in Sweden on December 13, *Lussinatta* is widely believed to be the pre–Christian inspiration for the later St. Lucia Day observation on the same date,[13] in which young children wear crowns of candles and sing Christmas hymns. Before the tradition was Christianized by ascribing it to a fourth-century Christian martyr, it was known as the darkest of all nights when the evil spirits were out. There were legends of wild sorcerers riding in the air, led by a woman with fluttering hair. The entourage of evil spirits was believed to topple houses or abduct people who were foolhardy enough to be out, so most stayed inside. Even the animals felt the evil and the darkness, and it was thought that they could speak on this night.[14]

Christmas Eve, meanwhile, was thought of as a time when the dead revisit their old homes. "The living prepare for their coming with mingled dread and desire to

This illustration from the late 19th century imagines what Odin's Wild Hunt may have looked like. "Odin and the Valkyries." Artist Henri Rivière (Cleveland Museum of Art, Gift of Elizabeth Carroll Shearer in memory of Robert Lundie Shearer 2000).

make them welcome," writes Miles. "When the Christmas Eve festivities are over, and everyone has gone to rest, the parlour is left tidy and adorned, with a great fire burning, candles lighted, the table covered with a festive cloth and plentifully spread with food, and a jug of Yule ale ready." Some might even considerately prepare a warm bath, thinking that the ghosts might like to wash themselves before their meal.[15]

* * *

Among the many uncanny beings that are known to roam the forests and visit homes during the Christmas period are the Tomte Gubbe in Sweden, Pere Fourettard in France, and Knecht Ruprecht and Pelz Nichol in Germany. Samichlaus is a winter demon known to beat bad children and haul off babies in Switzerland.[16]

Around the Alps, and especially in Austria, a half-goat, half-demon monster called the Krampus punishes misbehaving children with birch rods. A horned, demonic-looking beast, Krampus is said to be the son of Hel in Norse mythology and shares characteristics with creatures in Greek mythology, including satyrs and fauns.[17] Anthropologist John J. Honigmann observed in 1975 that the Saint Nicholas festival in Austria "incorporates cultural elements widely distributed in Europe, in some cases going back to pre–Christian times." Austrians, he said, were aware of heathen elements being blended with Christian elements in their Christmas traditions. "They believe Krampus derives from a pagan supernatural who was assimilated to the Christian devil," Honigmann wrote.[18]

In Greece and throughout southeastern Europe, there are legends of a Christmas goblin known as the kallikantzaros, which is said to dwell underground but comes to the surface during the 12 days of Christmas. Closely associated with the werewolf, the kallikantzaros had red eyes and a long tongue, and was covered in black hair. According to folklore, all year round the kallikantzaroi would spend their time sawing the world tree so that it collapses, in order to hasten the end of the world, but once they were able to emerge during the dark days of midwinter, they would abandon their task of sawing the world tree and come out to torment the mortals above ground. When the sun started moving again on January 6, they returned underground to continue their sawing, but by then the world tree had healed itself, so they had to start from scratch. This cycle repeated itself every year.[19]

Kallikantzaroi travelled in packs, hiding from dawn until sunset when they would come out and wreak havoc. A house that was unprepared against their coming would be targeted for pillage and destruction. They would swarm in, either through the door or down the chimney, to eat whatever food they could find, with a particular fondness for sweets, and would often ransack the house—overturning furniture, breaking things and befouling the water and wine—before making their exit. To protect themselves against the kallikantzaros, people would mark their houses with a black cross on Christmas Eve

Vintage postcard depicting the long-tongued Krampus preparing to haul terrified children off to his lair. Krampus postcard, early 1900s. Artist unknown (*Public Domain Review*. https://publicdomainreview.org/).

and would burn incense in an invocation of the Holy Trinity.[20] Its origins have been traced to the winter festival of Dionysus, specifically the masquerades that formed part of the festival, and to a group of child-eating demons called lamiae, who were believed to feast on unbaptized babies. Therefore, to prevent the kallikantzaroi from eating infants, a piglet was left for them as an offering.[21]

In Serbia, a similar creature called karakondžula was believed to attack people at night during the unbaptized days and would particularly target adulterers. Known as a heavy, squat, and ugly creature, the karakondžula would jump on people's backs, and make them carry it wherever it wanted. This torment would only come to an end only when roosters announced the dawn, at which point the creature would release its victim and run away. Out of fear of attracting the attention of the karakondžula people would avoid going out at night during the 12 days when demonic forces were considered to be more active and dangerous.[22]

In northern parts of Norway, Sweden, Finland and the Kola Peninsula, the Sámi people, historically known as Laplanders, believed that invisible, evil creatures known as joulustaalo roamed the earth on Christmas Eve. The joulustaalo would spend the night on a sled being pulled around by various animals of the forest, with the smallest such as shrews and mice at the front and the largest such as wolves and bears at the back. Anyone blocking the path of the joulustaalo would be killed. He would even kill people for failing to keep the areas around their homes tidy or if he heard children making too much noise. Children, especially, had to be very careful around Christmas not to offend the joulustaalo because he was known to bash in their skulls and eat their brains if they were naughty. Children had to avoid going out alone on Christmas and refrain from making too much noise, because if the joulustaalo heard them, he would surely eat them.[23]

Icelanders believed that at Christmas elves moved freely in and out of their world and would sometimes meet to dance all night long on people's farms. They would aggressively demand offerings from the humans and according to Icelandic legend, when a family would go to church for Midnight Mass, one individual was typically designated the dangerous job of guarding the homestead. Tasked with protecting the farm against the onslaught of invading nature spirits known as "hidden folk," the brave watchmen would often vanish during the night or would be found dead the next morning.[24]

Meanwhile, in southern Sweden, a glowing sow known as Gloso was known to appear during the 12 days of Christmas. With eyes of fire and sparks springing from her bristles, she was believed to be an apparition of a murdered child who was never buried or sometimes interpreted as the supernatural guardian of a church. People offered the beast gruel and fish to ensure that she would not harm anyone.[25]

* * *

These stories of hideous and frightening supernatural beings terrorizing people at Christmas time might come as a surprise to those who associate ghosts and goblins more with Halloween than with Christmas. In many countries, however, belief in the paranormal, and particularly ghosts visiting at Christmas, linger on. In Norway, Latvia, Estonia, and Lithuania, old folk beliefs about Christmas spirits continue, and in the German region of Bavaria, some people believe that restless spirits walk abroad during the "Knocking Nights" of Advent. In this tradition, similar to trick-or-treating on Halloween, costumed children go from house to house knocking on doors, reciting rhymes, ringing bells, cracking whips, and rattling tin cans to frighten off the wandering spirits who perform acts of mischief on Thursday (Thor's day) nights during Advent. In exchange for their services in countering this demonic activity, the children are given small presents.[26]

In this 16th-century depiction of Gabriel announcing to Mary that she would bear the Son of God, the Holy Family is surrounded by angels and are blessed by God the Father and the Holy Spirit in the form of a dove overhead. "The Annunciation," ca. 1503–05. Artist Albrecht Dürer. Woodcut (Cleveland Museum of Art, Dudley P. Allen Fund).

But while many might consider the association of ghosts and goblins at Christmas to be unusual, there is also a supernatural element to the more "mainstream" Christmas celebrations that is often overlooked. Adorning Christmas trees and appearing on greetings cards, the use of angels as a Christmas symbol is so common that people might not give much thought to its implications, but of course, these are supernatural beings as well. The popular perception of angels tends to characterize them as compassionate, merciful and gracious, but despite their harmless reputation, they also share some characteristics with other uncanny Christmas figures and have not always been considered unambiguously benign. In fact, in biblical stories, they were known to terrify people who encountered them, and a closer examination of angelology reveals that the origins of angels are essentially a hybrid result of blending Egyptian, Sumerian, Babylonian and Persian supernatural beings.[27]

Angels' relationship to Christmas goes back to the nativity account in the Gospel of Matthew, where they appear on three separate occasions—once to announce Mary's pregnancy, once to warn of King Herod's intentions to kill all the babies of Bethlehem in an attempt to assassinate Jesus, and once again to inform Joseph of Herod's death. In Luke's account of the nativity, the angel Gabriel appeared to inform Mary of the miraculous nature of her pregnancy, telling her that she would bear a child by the Holy Spirit. Then, on the night of Jesus's birth, an angel appeared to inform shepherds in a nearby field of the good news. "An angel of the Lord appeared to them," according to Luke, "and the glory of the Lord shone around them, and they were terrified. But the angel said to them, 'Do not be afraid. I bring you good news that will cause great joy for all the people. Today in the town of David a Savior has been born to you; he is the Messiah, the Lord." Following Gabriel's message, "a great company of the heavenly host appeared with the angel, praising God and saying, 'Glory to God in the highest heaven, and on earth peace to those on whom his favor rests.'"

The way this story is perceived today, and how it fits into the general Christmas motif, is largely influenced by our modern-day conceptions of angels, but in earlier times many equated them with elves and gods, and they were not necessarily all benevolent. Angels were associated with duties such as conception, thunder, forests, music and poetry, which is not unlike the way that pagan gods were empowered over functions such as fertility and abundance. It was for this reason that particular angels were invoked in ceremonial magic and cabalistic magical rites. Miracles, heavenly visitations, and feats of magic were often attributed to them, leading some religious figures to cite their magical powers as proof of Christ's divinity.[28] Many angels, however, even those considered heavenly and holy, were impressed into the service of practitioners of black magic,[29] appearing in manuals for witchcraft such as *The Book of Black Magic and of Pacts* and *The Lesser Key of Solomon*.

Throughout the Bible, angels serve as God's primary liaison with humans, delivering messages and carrying out important divine tasks. But to pagans and Christianized people who retained many of their pre–Christian beliefs, angels were just one of many categories of otherworldly entities that performed this role. As Grimm writes in *Teutonic Mythology*, "daemonic beings, such as angels, elves, [and] giants" fill "the gap between God and man." Under paganism, he notes, messengers of the gods were considered gods themselves,[30] and angels were venerated along with other supernatural beings. Some angels were considered one and the same as heathen gods,

In this 1919 illustration for the *East Mississippi Times,* an angel, holding an olive branch, hovers over children playing with toys. Angel Christmas illustration in the *East Mississippi Times,* December 12, 1919 (Library of Congress).

with Camael, an archangel of strength and courage in Judeo-Christian tradition tasked with patrolling the heavenly pathways for demonic activity, identified as a god of war in Celtic mythology.[31] The archangel Michael was associated with the Greek god Hermes, the Egyptian god Thoth, the Roman god Mercury, and the Celtic god Lugh.[32] The Church banished these earlier pagan deities, but the various powers of the gods were absorbed into Michael's attributes. For example, a pre–Christian myth about an ancient god called Marduk slaying a dragon-like goddess called Tiamat may have been adapted under Christianity as the legend of Michael and the Dragon, in which the archangel slays a seven-headed beast representing the seven deadly sins.[33]

And while today we generally consider angels to be heavenly and pure beings diametrically opposed to the demons of the underworld, which are considered dark forces of evil, these clearly drawn distinctions are not as plain when angels are examined more closely. For instance, in the second triad of the angel hierarchy are the Powers, commanded by Camael. Consisting of 144,000 angels of destruction, punishment, vengeance and death, it is not entirely clear whether these beings serve God or the Devil. Their task is to transform humans' everyday understanding into a unity with the divine source, but as Malcolm Godwin explains it in *Angels: An Endangered Species*, "Being in charge of our souls gives the Powers an intriguing, far-ranging and often capricious, territory." Godwin notes that most of the fallen angels—those rebellious celestial beings that led a mutiny against God and were cast out of heaven— came from the ranks of the Powers. Indeed, it was because of the ambiguous nature of angels that ancient texts such as the Chronicles of Enoch, which described a penal area of Heaven being guarded by enormous angels known as Grigori, were declared apocryphal by the Church in the fourth century.[34]

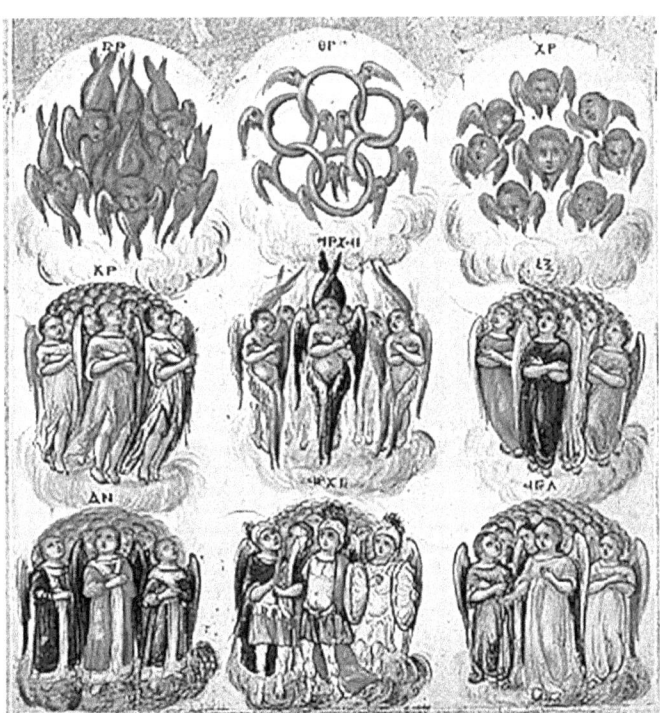

Detail from an icon depicting the nine orders of angels, possibly from the 18th century. The top sphere consists of seraphim, cherubim and ophanim, all of which are described in Scripture as having strange and somewhat frightening physical attributes. Artist unknown.

The perception of angels is further clarified by examining the etymology of the word that we use to describe them. In the Hebrew scriptures, the word used for angels was *malakh*, meaning messenger. When the scriptures were translated from Hebrew to Greek, the authors chose the word *angelos*, meaning "messenger, envoy, one that announces," instead of another Greek word, *daimon*, because according to Greek mythology, *daimons* referred to a lesser deity that exercised both good and evil influences over people.[35] The ancient Greeks called the "good" ones *eudaemon*s and the "bad" ones *cacodaemons*, but all *daimons* were essentially intermediary spirits between humanity and the gods. As Plato put it in his *Symposium*, they were tasked with "[i]nterpreting and transporting human things to the gods and divine things to men; entreaties and sacrifices from below, and ordinances and requitals from above." In the *Apology of Socrates*, Plato noted that his teacher claimed to have demons that often warned him if he was about to make a mistake, but never told him how to act.[36]

According to religious scholar Dale Martin, most ancient Jews (including Jesus's followers) saw angels and demons as distinct "species" of the same being and the original Hebrew words covered various types such as goat-man gods; disease-causing gods; and abstract gods such as Fate or Fortune, but the original translation from Hebrew to Greek lost some of the nuances of the original. Martin notes that what they all had in common was that they were seen as pagan gods that were falsely worshiped, and they were all translated as *daimons* due to pagan conceptions of the word. He points out that the Hebrew *malak* (messenger) could have just as easily been translated as *daimon*, as the functions of the supernatural beings were similar, but the translators instead chose to use the word for "messenger," *angelos*.[37] (Incidentally, Angelos also happened to be the name of a deity of the underworld in the ancient Greek religion.) The original Greek translation was done at a time at which interest in angels was very high, so the translators also added attributes that were not in the original Hebrew, for example describing them as "angels of God" rather than just "angels."[38]

Furthermore, while today's popular representations of angels generally depict them as beautiful, winged people wearing flowing white robes, biblical angels were

An illustration depicting Ezekiel's "chariot vision," with a four-headed cherub in the center. The cherubim are high-ranking angels with human, animal, and birdlike characteristics. Ezekiel's vision, 1670. Artist unknown.

often very weird-looking and frightening creatures. Sometimes they could appear as purely human, with or without wings, but at other times, they could range from human-animal hybrids to floating wheels with eyes. Cherubs are described in the Book of Ezekiel as having four wings and bull hooves for feet, as well as four faces: a lion's, an ox's, an eagle's, and a human's. The Seraphim, another angelic being, has six wings, two of which are for flying and the rest for covering their heads and feet, and may have also had the attributes of a snake. The archangel Metatron, according to the Chronicles of Enoch, has 36 wings, countless flaming eyeballs, and eyelashes of lightning.[39] Gabriel, the angel that announced the virgin birth of the Messiah to Mary, has been described as having 600 wings.[40]

A coin featuring winged Nike, holding a wreath. Early Christian artists used the figure of Nike, the Greco-Roman goddess of victory, as a model for angels. Nike coin, ca. 336–323 BCE. Greece (Cleveland Museum of Art, Gift of Mrs. H.H. Brittingham, 1938).

Angels struck fear into the hearts of those who saw them, which is why the account in the Gospel of Luke notes that the shepherds were "terrified" when Gabriel appeared to share the news of Jesus's birth. The way that they developed their more pleasant appearance, enabling people to incorporate them into their Christmas decorations, was by incorporating attributes of pagan deities like Cupid and Nike. Early Christian artists patterned their depictions of angels on familiar motifs found in Greek and Roman mythology,[41] which likely explains why the image of angels evolved from their terrifying descriptions in Scripture to the more Christmas-friendly version that we know today. So, in other words, even this quintessential "Christian" aspect of the Christmas celebration is in some ways deeply influenced by paganism.

In a broader sense, what the references to angels in the general Christmas motif recall is that Christianity, much like paganism, is imbued with belief in supernatural beings who reside in other dimensions but sometimes interact with humans. Whether or not clear distinctions can be drawn between angels, demons, pagan gods, elves, fairies, goblins, sprites, or spirits, what they all have in common is that they belong to the broad category of "paranormal others." Belief in these beings, which was once considered uncontroversial, is still relatively widespread to one degree or another, with public opinion surveys showing that more than seven in ten Americans believe that angels do in fact exist.[42] Their prominence at Christmas time is a reminder of this widespread belief, which in some respects, does not differ substantially from beliefs of pre–Christian pagans.

Part Three
Enduring Legacies

11

Legacy of Miracles

I summon today
All these powers between me and those evils,
Against every cruel and merciless power
that may oppose my body and soul,
Against incantations of false prophets,
Against black laws of pagandom,
Against false laws of heretics,
Against craft of idolatry,
Against spells of witches and smiths and wizards,
Against every knowledge that corrupts man's body and soul
   —The Prayer of Saint Patrick

Christmas has always been associated with magic and miracles—closely related but not synonymous concepts, as the Church has tried to make clear over the centuries. It wasn't until 1374 that magic was officially declared heresy by Pope Gregory XI based on the belief that it was performed with the aid of demons,[1] but long before that, religious leaders sought to draw distinctions between magic (said to be performed by witches and pagan sorcerers) and miracles (said to be performed by saints or, simply, by God). The distinction, however, was always tenuous, and with old attitudes firmly entrenched, popular belief often blurred the lines between religion, superstition, magic, and miracles.[2] With much overlap between the beliefs, magic was tolerated by the Church but increasing efforts were placed on focusing popular attention on divine forms of supernatural intervention in human affairs, rather than demonic manipulation, a distinction that was particularly relevant for the celebrations of Yule and Christmas.

The midwinter period was already linked with miracles by the time of Jesus's birth, largely thanks to the Jewish tradition of Hanukkah that predated the rise of Christianity by a couple hundred years. A central component of Hanukkah is the nightly lighting of the menorah candle to symbolize a miracle that took place after Judah Maccabee's small force of Jewish guerrillas defeated the much larger and better-equipped Greco-Syrian army of Emperor Antiochus IV. Antiochus had prohibited the study of Torah, as well as other Jewish practices such as ritual circumcision and observance of the Sabbath, and without the Maccabees' victory and the preservation of Jewish sacred texts, Judaism may not have survived—nor its offshoot Christianity which would emerge two centuries later. When Judah's forces recaptured Jerusalem from Antioch, they demolished statues of Zeus and rededicated the

Temple to God. Although Judah only had enough oil to fuel the Temple's eternal light for one day, somehow it lasted for eight, considered by Jews a miracle of God.[3] This miracle is commemorated every year for eight days, starting on the 25th day of Kislev according to the Hebrew calendar, which may occur at any time from late November to late December.

There are also stories from ancient times of false miracles, such as the Old Testament account of Nimrod. Sometimes cited as a possible inspiration for the modern-day Christmas tree, Nimrod's story is also blamed for spawning worldly apostasy and he is widely considered the first of many false prophets foisted upon the world by Satan. He is referred to in the Book of Genesis and Books of Chronicles as a great grandson of Noah who founded the first world empire at Babel, later known as Babylon. Following Nimrod's death around 2167 BCE, his wife and mother Semiramis claimed that she saw a full-grown evergreen tree spring out of the roots of a dead tree stump, supposedly on December 25, symbolizing the rebirth of Nimrod as a god. Nimrod's spirit would visit the tree on the winter solstice and leave gifts under it, Semiramis claimed. Some consider Nimrod and the Roman god Saturn to be one and the same,[4] and believe that the supposed miracle that was represented by the evergreen sprouting from a dead tree stump was actually the work of the Devil. The Babylonian "mystery religion" inspired by Nimrod "was replete with cultic rituals of prostitution, idol worship, child sacrifice, magic, divination, and animal sacrifice," according to Finding Hope Ministries. "Priests, diviners, magicians, and prostitutes all participated regularly in these cultic rituals."[5]

While these miracle stories are sometimes associated with midwinter in general, the Christmas season is most commonly associated with miracles due to the nativity story itself. Ever since Luke recounted how God sent the archangel Gabriel to tell Mary that the Holy Spirit would conceive Jesus in her womb and the three magi followed a star to Bethlehem to pay homage to the infant, what is sometimes referred to as "the first Christmas" has always prominently featured both miracles and magic. From the immaculate conception to the astrology associated with the magi, the story continues to deeply influence the celebration of Christmas among the Christian faithful, serving as a reminder of the possibility of divine intervention in human affairs and imbuing the season with a sense of holiness and magic. Retold for centuries through Christmas plays, cribs and hymns, the nativity story is widely considered a fundamental Christian doctrine, but also shares themes from pagan mythologies that were dominant at the time the Gospels were written.

* * *

"In the sixth month the angel Gabriel was sent by God to a town in Galilee called Nazareth, to a virgin engaged to a man whose name was Joseph, of the house of David," reads the Gospel of Luke. "The angel said to her, 'Do not be afraid, Mary, for you have found favor with God. And now, you will conceive in your womb and bear a son, and you will name him Jesus.'" Mary was perplexed and said, "How can this be, since I am a virgin?" to which Gabriel replied, "The Holy Spirit will come upon you, and the power of the Most High will overshadow you; therefore the child to be born will be holy; he will be called Son of God." Matthew focuses on the story from Joseph's perspective, indicating his surprise to find out that Mary was pregnant since they hadn't had carnal relations at that point and noting that he planned to "dismiss" her. But then an angel appeared and said, "Joseph, son of David, do not be afraid to take Mary as your wife, for the child conceived in her is from the Holy Spirit." The angel instructed him to name the boy Jesus, "for he will save his people from their sins."

Belief in this story is largely seen as a test of faith among Christians, with people either choosing to believe the accounts in the Gospels of Luke and Matthew as the literal truth or interpreting the stories as myth, but skeptics of course have found ample reason to doubt their veracity. Besides the obvious biological reality that the fertilization of an egg can only take place when it comes into contact with sperm, there is also a good deal of circumstantial evidence that indicates a possible embellishment of the story by Luke and Matthew. For one thing, there is a logical disconnect between the way that the gospel writers emphasize the genealogy of Joseph, to whom Mary was betrothed, despite simultaneously emphasizing that Jesus was not Joseph's biological son. In Matthew 1:2–16, for example, Jesus's ancestry is traced back to Abraham through Joseph's lineage, but the gospel conveniently glosses over the immaculate conception in the last line: "and Jacob [was] the father of Joseph, the husband of Mary, and Mary was the mother of Jesus who is called the Messiah."

As Paul Frodsham highlights in *From Stonehenge to Santa Claus*, "Both Luke and Matthew trace Jesus's ancestors back through King David to Abraham and in Luke's case, to Adam," but if Mary conceived Jesus through the Holy Spirit, then Joseph's ancestry becomes irrelevant. Frodsham concludes that "to claim that Jesus was not the biological son of Joseph, but is nevertheless entitled to claim descent from David *through* Joseph is clearly nonsense."[6] The reason that the gospel writers provide the context for Jesus to trace his lineage to Abraham, but at the same time tell the contradictory story of the virgin birth, appears to be related to their perceived need to fulfill a number of Old Testament prophesies to ensure that first-century readers were convinced that Jesus was indeed the Messiah.

The story of the immaculate conception should also be viewed within the context that the gospels were written, at a time when stories of gods impregnating mortal women were widespread. There is even a term for the offspring of gods and mortals, called demigod, which is a common theme in Greek and Roman mythology. In Greek myths, some of the most well-known demigods were Achilles, Hercules, Theseus, Perseus, and Helen of Troy. According to legend, the founders of Rome, Romulus and Remus, were twin brothers conceived by the god Mars and a priestess named Rhea Silvia. Some Roman emperors claimed descent from demigods and Roman author Cassius Dio designated the emperor Julius Caesar a demigod himself.[7] Demigods can also be found in a variety of other pagan mythologies, including the Celtic legend of a warrior named Cú Chulainn, who is the son of the god Lugh and the mortal princess Deichtine. In Norse mythology, Odin had a son, Vali, by Rinda, the mortal daughter of King Billing of Ruthenia.

So, although today belief in the story of the virgin birth is seen as a measure of one's faith as a devout Christian, in the context that the story was first told, it was not particularly unique nor implausible, and in fact this similarity could have even helped to persuade some pagans to convert to Christianity. Similarly, the story of the star which led the magi to find Jesus was not difficult to believe since this was also a common theme in legends of the time, with kings and other notable figures often said to be born under a bright star. The magi who followed this star to find the infant Jesus have always been something of a mystery, with many asking over the centuries who they may have been. The Gospel of Matthew tells the story of how these foreigners are said to have visited Jesus bearing gifts: "And when they were come into the house, they saw the young child with Mary his mother, and fell down, and worshipped him and when they had opened their treasures, they presented unto him gifts; gold, and frankincense and myrrh." Few details are provided by Matthew, declining to even give their number, with subsequent interpretations extrapolating that there must have been three of them based on the number of gifts that they brought. Luke doesn't mention the magi at all.

The magi themselves may have been practitioners of magic, as their name suggests. Deriving from the Greek *magos*, the word magi basically means "skilled magicians, astrologers," and in Old Persian is simply translated as "magician." They were hereditary priests who followed Zoroastrianism and worshipped the supreme god Ahura Mazda, tasked with performing ceremonies and other Zoroastrian rituals. Some magi were known as *daevayasna*, or devil worshippers, and were viewed as sorcerers and witches. Those accused of sorcery could have molten metal poured over their tongue to determine their guilt.[8]

It is not entirely clear in the biblical accounts how the magi were able to pinpoint the location of the infant Jesus, but apparently, they interpreted some sort of astronomical event—possibly the conjunction of Jupiter and Saturn in seven BCE, as modern scholars have speculated[9]—using astrology. The gifts they brought, although probably obtainable at any trading post on the way from Babylon to Bethlehem,[10] were considered luxury items that were known to have magical properties. Although some point to the biblical prophecy of Isaiah, who shared a vision of nations rendering tribute to the Lord with gifts such as gold and frankincense,[11] it is worth noting that frankincense and myrrh were considered important ingredients for incense, used to ward off evil spirits and enable contact with gods and goddesses.[12] Frankincense is also found in a Greek magical spell along with other ingredients such as "the dung of a dog-faced baboon" and "two eggs of an ibex."[13] Incense has been used to sanctify buildings and to drive out demons from the possessed.[14] Myrrh was considered a miraculous substance that could extend life beyond death, and for this reason was used by the ancient Egyptians for embalming.[15]

The allusions to magic in the nativity story, and particularly the nature of the magi who came bearing magical gifts, have been downplayed over the centuries, as magic is frowned upon in the Bible and the magi's possible association with sorcerers and devil worshippers was problematic to the early Church. In Deuteronomy, practitioners of magic are called an abomination: "There shall not be found among you any one that maketh his son or his daughter to pass through the fire, or that useth divination, or an observer of times, or an enchanter, or a witch, Or a charmer, or a consulter with familiar spirits, or a wizard, or a necromancer. For all that do these things are an abomination unto the Lord: and because of these abominations the Lord thy God doth drive them out from before thee." As Leviticus 19:31 warns, "Regard not them that have familiar spirits, neither seek after wizards, to be defiled by them: I am the Lord your God." Verse 20:6 of Leviticus reads, "And the soul that turneth after such as have familiar spirits, and after wizards, to go a whoring after them, I will even set my face against that soul, and will cut him off from among his people." A passage of Exodus proved to be disastrous for thousands who would later be executed under suspicions of witchcraft: "Thou shalt not suffer a witch to live."

With the nativity story incorporating elements of magic, however, and particularly the magi's use of astrology to lead them to their destination, Church leaders had to come up with an explanation to ease the concerns of Christian believers. So, the faithful were reassured that any demonic powers that the magi may have possessed were dispelled by the sacred purpose of their journey,[16] and attempts were

The unspecified number of gift-bearing magi evolved over time into the "Three Kings." Although initially believed to be astrologers skilled in the magical arts, in subsequent centuries the magi were reinterpreted as kings. "Three Kings," c. 1675–1740. Artist Isaac Vincentsz. van der Vinne (Rijksmuseum).

11. Legacy of Miracles

made to rebrand them. Early Church leader Tertullian attempted to link the magi to Old Testament prophecies about kings worshipping the Lord and bearing gifts, and perhaps troubled by the term magi's implications of magic, he chose to call them "kings" instead. "For the East generally regarded the magi as kings," Tertullian writes in *Contra Marción*. "[H]aving discovered Him and honoured Him with their gifts, and on beaded knee adored Him as their God and King, through the witness of the star which led their way and guided them, became the spoils of Samaria, that is to say,

This 17th-century illustration depicts the Jesus miracle stories from the Gospels. "The Miracles of Jesus Christ: Christ Delivering the Possessed," 17th century. Artist Claude Vignon (Cleveland Museum of Art, John L. Severance Fund, 1991).

of idolatry, because, as it is easy enough to see, they believed in Christ."[17] And hence the story of the "three kings" was born.

Considering that miracle stories were so integral to the narrative of Jesus's life, much of which was spent healing the sick and performing miracles—not to mention the many miracles that were said to be performed by saints—Christian theologians became increasingly preoccupied with defining the differences between miracles and magic.[18] They drew from passages in the Bible that offered some guidance, for example John the Baptist's advice on how to tell a spirit of God from a spirit of the antichrist—namely by asking if it confesses that Jesus Christ has come in the flesh, with its denial of this belief serving as proof of its demonic character. The Acts of the Apostles also tell the story of sorcerer Simon Magus, known as "the Great Power of God" by many people of Samaria, a story that proved useful as a way to distinguish magic from miracles. Revered for his well-known magical powers, Simon became an admirer of Christian evangelization and, according to the Acts of the Apostles, requested baptism from Philip the Deacon. After becoming a Christian, Simon offered to purchase supernatural powers of transmitting the Holy Spirit, leading to a harsh rebuke from St. Peter. The biblical account concludes with Simon's repentance and apparent reconciliation with Christianity.

Since the time that Christianity began to develop as a religion, some doubters had suggested that Jesus was a skilled magician not unlike Simon, claiming that he was no more than a sorcerer adept at levitation and other magic tricks. In the Gospels' miracle stories, Jesus not only walks on water and turns water into wine, but he also casts out demons from those who are possessed, heals the sick, gives sight to the blind, and even brings back to life a man who had been dead for three days. The early Christian writers therefore forced a distinction between Christ as God incarnate and Simon as a wizard, or even a demon or heretic.[19] As opposed to Simon's magic tricks, Jesus's acts of healing were not simple sorcery, but miraculous signs of the compassion of God that characterizes the kingdom which his son has come to make available to all of humanity.

* * *

As Ramsay MacMullen explains in *Christianizing the Roman Empire*, this belief in the miraculous power of the Christian God was largely responsible for the mass conversions to Christianity from 100–400 CE. Rather than a rising tide of Christian piety, pagans who adopted the new religion were motivated by the appeal of miracles and the promise of worldly advantages that would come through devout belief in Christianity and the ritualistic practices associated with the religion.[20] Indeed, it was this view that inspired Emperor Constantine to convert to the Roman Empire to Christianity in the first place, believing that currying favor with the Christian God by placing crosses on the shields of his soldiers, for example, would help him achieve success on the battlefield. His son, Emperor Constantius II, in the mid-fourth century used the promise of the material gain that could be attained through divine intervention in urging pagans to convert to Christianity, assuring his subjects that "to people who are zealous in those [Christian] beliefs, all good things in abundance are accustomed to fall, and whatever they set their hand to will answer to their highest hopes."[21] In this world of widespread belief in divine intervention, there was nothing unusual or shameful about appealing to supernatural powers for assistance in worldly affairs.

Following conversion to Christianity, the appeals of the faithful for divine assistance could sometimes closely resemble the magical practices of paganism. Despite the Bible's admonitions against magic, the early Church tolerated the use of these magical practices, including the charms, rituals and incantations that were used by priests to offer blessings, and the amulets worn by early Christians to ward off evil and heal illness.[22] As an indication of how pagan and Christian magical beliefs often intersected in those times, a sixth-century amulet featured New Testament imagery on one side—including angels, the three magi, and depictions of Christ's healing miracles—and on the reverse side a winged male figure believed to be the Egyptian god Horus-Shed holding four scorpions, surrounded by magic symbols.[23] Another Egyptian amulet, also from the sixth century, harnessed the miraculous powers of Christ in assisting with women's menstrual problems. The amulet was made of hematite, derived from the Greek word for "blood," in allusion to its red color and the popular belief that it was able to promote cardiovascular health. With an image of a woman kneeling before Christ, the inscriptions identify the subject as "the Woman with the Issue of Blood," as referred to in the Gospels of Mark and Luke.[24] In addition to Jesus, the ancient Egyptian deity Bes, venerated as a protector of households, was also commonly found on amulets worn by early Christians. Bes was a popular oracle god who Coptic Christians equated with Christ.[25]

Although initially tolerant of such practices, Church leaders grew preoccupied with drawing distinctions with Christianity and paganism, and correspondingly sought to clarify its position on magic, which increasingly became a taboo. In the early fifth century, Augustine of Hippo's *City of*

Invoking the miraculous powers of Jesus Christ, this sixth-century amulet was intended to provide protection against women's menstrual problems. The words inscribed on the amulet were meant to be recited aloud which would increase their magical powers. Amulet Carved in Intaglio (Incised), 6th–7th century, made in Byzantine Egypt, Coptic. Medium: Hematite, silver mount (The Metropolitan Museum of Art, Gift of J. Pierpont Morgan, 1917).

God, a seminal Christian tract, taught that whether they realized it or not, magicians were drawing upon satanic power when they practiced their sorcery. Determined to separate Christianity from paganism, Augustine took a hard line on magic, and his views came to dominate Christian doctrine for the next thousand years.[26] The magical arts, according to Augustine, "are performed according to the teaching and by the power of demons." The magician might justify this by claiming that the demons are needed to present incantations to the gods, but for Christians' prayers to reach the true God, Augustine argues, magic must be shunned. "What kind of prayers of men does he suppose are presented to the good gods by the demons?" he asks. "By no possibility can men be reconciled to good gods by demons, who are the slaves of vice, and who delight in and patronize what good and wise men abhor and condemn, the blasphemous fictions of poets, theatrical exhibitions, and magical arts."[27]

Based largely on Augustine's influential views, as Christianity spread across Europe, ceremonial magic was relegated to the margins of the Viking and Celtic worlds, where supernatural powers continued to be wielded by sorcerers and magicians. In the Christian world, magic lost its legitimacy with magicians increasingly associated with Devil worship and believed to practice *maleficium*, or evil deeds. Punishments for these acts grew increasingly severe, with Emperor Charlemagne declaring the penalty of death for practitioners of magic in 789.[28] Legitimate supernatural powers, meanwhile, came to become the purview of saints, who were believed to be aided by the power of God, and their miraculous abilities were therefore justifiable.

As traditional magic fell out of favor, a Christian version emerged of supernatural manipulation which focused on miracles and the power of guardian angels. Because theologians recognized the need to replace pagan diviners with Christian healers, a field of study emerged to delineate powers held by demons and those held by angels. The functions of pagan *daemons* were assigned to both Christian angels and demons, with the former only assuming attributes compatible with Christianity,[29] and "angel magic" emerging as a practice that included rituals such as fasting, prayer and meditation on images. These practices were believed to purify the soul in order to establish a channel of communication with the heavenly beings but led to some clergy growing increasingly concerned that praying to angels for help was no different than summoning pagan gods.[30] During the period of Christianization, a "cult of relics" also emerged, with believers making pilgrimages to visit holy relics such as fragments of the True Cross, and people beginning to widely believe that Christian symbols such as crosses had the ability to ward off evil influences.[31]

Meanwhile, missionaries and other religious leaders utilized the widespread belief in magic to assist in the work of conversion, with demonstrations of the supernatural power of Christ integral to convincing pagans that Christianity was superior to their heathen beliefs. In an effort to demonstrate the difference between magic and miracles, for example, as part of his campaign to convert pagan Ireland to Christianity in the mid to late 400s, St. Patrick is said to have used divine intervention to show that the power of Christ was stronger than the power of Celtic magicians. He understood that the pagans would not accept Christianity based on theological doctrines alone, and that to win them over it would be necessary to demonstrate Christianity's mysterious and miraculous side. So rather than try to convince them to surrender their beliefs in supernatural beings, he attempted to exploit their fears by recasting their deities as demons and to prove that Christian miracles were more powerful.[32] His biggest obstacle in converting the Irish were the druids, whom Patrick believed possessed strong magical abilities. In order to protect himself against their sorcery, Patrick drew upon the power of God to shield him from "every fierce merciless force that may come upon my body and soul; against incantations of false prophets, against black laws of pagandom, against false laws of heresy, against deceit of idolatry, against spells of witches and smiths and druids."[33]

The stories of Patrick's duels with the druids are legendary—filled with spells that manipulate the weather, infernos being summoned, and the destruction of sacred texts. One biographer from the late 600s, Muirchu, described Patrick challenging druids in contests at Tara, in which each side tried to outdo the other in working magic and miracles before the audience. Invoking demons, a druid brought about a dark fog over the land, and Patrick responded by praying to God and giving his blessing, causing the fog to disperse. And then, according to Muirchu, "through the prayers of Patrick flames of fire consumed the druid," in other words burnt him alive. In a confrontation with a druid named Lochru, who had insulted Patrick and the Christian faith, Patrick looked at him and prayed: "O Lord, who art all-powerful and in whose power is everything, who hast sent me here, may this impious man, who blasphemes thy name, now be cast out and quickly perish." With these words, according to legend, the druid was lifted up into the air and fell down again. As Muirchu describes it, "he hit his brain against a stone, and was smashed to pieces, and died in their presence, and the pagans stood in fear." With this miracle, Patrick converted a Celtic king who immediately announced his adoption of the Christian faith with the words: "It is better for me to believe than to die."[34]

St. Patrick's conversion stories were told throughout the Middle Ages, as Church leaders worked to devise ecclesiastical arguments to distinguish between people who worked miracles and those who practiced magic. It was in this context that miracle plays developed as a genre. Also known as the saint's play, this dramatic portrayal presented a real or invented account of the life and martyrdom of a saint, with a particular emphasis on the miracles he or she performed, specifically re-enacting divine interventions by the saints into the lives of ordinary people. The genre developed from church services during the 10th and 11th centuries to enhance calendar festivals, and over time came to be associated with Christmas because they focused largely on the Virgin Mary and St. Nicholas.[35] A popular 14th-century miracle play was The Pageant of the Shearman and Tailors, which told the story of the annunciation, the nativity, the magi, the Flight into Egypt, and the Massacre of the Innocents.[36]

Over time, these miracle plays and other efforts of the Church helped solidify the concept of a Christmas miracle. Events at Christmas time, whether sacred or profane in nature, often came to be considered miraculous, but to be fair, in the Middle Ages, when people were particularly primed to see signs of God's intervention in human affairs everywhere, it probably wasn't difficult to find Christmas miracles. In those days, a simple flicker of sunlight in an unusual place could be seen as a sign from God,[37] so naturally there was an inclination to identify miracles in particular on the day that angels announced the virgin birth of the Messiah. In an account of the life of an 11th-century religious devotee named Christina of Markyate, for example, she claimed to experience a premonition on Christmas Eve about a dying friend and

Visions of the Virgin Mary have long been reported as a common Christmas miracle. "The Virgin seated on a cloud," 1580–84. Artist Federico Barocci. Medium: Etching with some engraving (The Metropolitan Museum of Art, Joseph Pulitzer Bequest, 1917).

prayed him back to health—crediting her intuition about her ailing friend as a message from God.[38]

The Virgin Mary has also been said to appear to the faithful on Christmas, with a story from 1816 demonstrating the power of this commonly perceived Christmas miracle. Elizabeth Canori Mora, of Italy, was praying in her home on Christmas when the Virgin Mary suddenly appeared. According to Mora's account, Mary was holding baby Jesus in her arms and delivered a message to Elizabeth that she should seek God's justice rather than mercy.[39] On Christmas Eve 1841, the Virgin Mary also reportedly visited a Salish Indian boy to help him learn the prayers and catechism ahead of being baptized.[40]

* * *

11. Legacy of Miracles

What may be the most famous Christmas miracle of all time though was the so-called Christmas Truce, which took place during the first year of World War I. For several weeks leading up to Christmas in 1914, there had been several peace initiatives calling for a pause in the fighting to observe the nativity, with an Open Christmas Letter addressed "To the Women of Germany and Austria" from a group of British women suffragettes, and Pope Benedict XV appealing on December 7 for an official truce between the warring parties. Building upon his earlier denunciation of the war as a suicidal effort of the world's wealthiest nations "to destroy one another with refinements of horror" in which there is "no limit to the measure of ruin and of slaughter,"[41] the Pope asked for a Christmas truce so "that the guns may fall silent at least upon the night the angels sang." But with high levels of distrust on both sides as well as a reluctance to agree to any truce that might prove disadvantageous to their positions, the governments refused to stop fighting.

The common soldiers, however, were more than willing to lay down their weapons in an exchange of goodwill on the battlefield. On Christmas Eve, the temperature dropped and the rain that had been falling in several weeks of wet and dreary weather turned to snow. The German soldiers had received Christmas trees sent by emperor William II to the front in an effort to bolster morale and started setting them up on the parapets of their trenches.[42] The pops, crackles and whistles of guns and mortar fire became more sporadic, then stopped completely. Then, on this frosty and starlit night, songs began to be sung—with the Germans singing "Stille Nacht," and the British, peeking over their trenches and seeing the Christmas trees on the other side, joining with the English version of the song, "Silent Night." Then a shout: "You no shoot, we no shoot!"

British soldier Albert Moren later recalled the magic of the moment:

> It was a beautiful moonlit night, frost on the ground, white almost everywhere; and about 7 or 8 in the evening there was a lot of commotion in the German trenches and there were these lights—I don't know what they were. And then they sang "Silent Night"—"Stille Nacht." I shall never forget it, it was one of the highlights of my life. I thought, what a beautiful tune.

As described by Lance Corporal RS Coulson of the London Rifle Brigade in a letter to his mother,

> On Christmas Eve at about 4pm, we were in a line of advance trenches waiting to be relieved, directly it was dark, when we heard singing and shouting coming from the other trenches at right angles to us which line a hedge of the same field. Then the news filtered down. German and English officers had exchanged compliments and agreed on a truce, and then started giving one another a concert. We all sang every song we could think of, a bonfire was lit and everyone walked about as though it were a picnic. After we were relieved and got back to the breastworks (about 200yds?) behind the firing-lines, we could hear the German band playing Old Folks at Home, God Save the King and Onward, Christian Soldiers.

"First the Germans would sing one of their carols and then we would sing one of ours," recalled Graham Williams of the Fifth London Rifle Brigade, "until when we started up 'O Come, All Ye Faithful' the Germans immediately joined in singing the same hymn to the Latin words Adeste Fideles. And I thought, well, this is really a most extraordinary thing—two nations both singing the same carol in the middle of a war."[43]

The spontaneous singing in the trenches led to widespread fraternization between enemy forces along the Western front. Some two-thirds of German and British troops, approximately 100,000 people, are believed to have participated. Historians disagree over precisely where it began or how it spread, or if, perhaps by some miracle, it occurred simultaneously across the trenches. On Christmas morning, German soldiers emerged from their trenches, calling out "Merry Christmas" in English. Allied soldiers came out warily to greet them and throughout the day, troops exchanged gifts of cigarettes, food, and mementos. There are also stories of pick-up soccer games being played, with German Lieutenant Kurt Zehmisch recalling:

> The English brought a soccer ball from the trenches, and pretty soon a lively game ensued. How marvelously wonderful, yet how strange it was. The English officers felt the same way about it. Thus Christmas, the celebration of love, managed to bring mortal enemies together as friends for a time.

The truce also allowed for soldiers to bury their dead comrades whose corpses were scattered throughout the "No Man's Land" dividing the two sides' trenches. There were joint burial ceremonies and prisoner swaps. "Between the trenches there were a lot of dead Germans whom we helped to bury," recalled a British junior officer. Several of these somber meetings ended in carol-singing, and the emotional intensity of the moment must have been overwhelming for everyone who participated. British Corporal Leon Harris captured it well in a letter home to his parents. "This has been the most wonderful Christmas I have ever struck," he wrote. "Huge fires were going all night and both sides sang carols. It was a wonderful time and the weather was glorious on Christmas Eve and Christmas Day—frosty and bright with moon and stars at night."

Newspapers at the time widely shared the soldiers' accounts of the magical moment, reprinting their letters in full and publishing historic photos of

This 1915 article by Phil Rader about the World War I Christmas Truce is titled "Miracle is Wrought by Christmas Spirit in Hostile Trenches." Article in *Evening Public Ledger* (Philadelphia), March 24, 1915 (Library of Congress).

British and German soldiers standing together on the battlefield.[44] Many treated the event rather matter-of-factly or as a minor curiosity, but there were some journalistic flourishes that noted its "extraordinary" character which "change[d the] perception of the enemy,"[45] and some even likened it to a "Miracle of Noel"[46] or a "Truce of God."[47] Under the headline, "Miracle is Wrought by Christmas Spirit in Hostile Trenches," a United Press article described the incident as "marvelous," noting that the "war's ... horrors wane[d] for a brief space as foemen [met] in amity."[48]

Others, however, were less enthusiastic. The German *Taegliebe Rundschau* newspaper pointed out the danger of fraternization between Germans and French, interpreting the momentary halt in killing as a sign that soldiers didn't take the war seriously enough. "War is no sport," lectures the article, "and we are sorry to say that those who made these overtures did not clearly understand the gravity of the situation."[49]

Today the incident is commonly celebrated as a bona fide Christmas miracle. In an article recalling the event some 100 years later, *The Washington Post* declared: "On a frosty, starlit night, a miracle took place."[50] *The Guardian* used similar language in a 2008 article titled "The Christmas Miracle," which recalled Lance Corporal Henderson's account of the extraordinary event, noting that the Germans and British were singing together, and cheering each side's rendition of popular Christmas carols.[51] A 2017 documentary about the truce is called "The Christmas Miracle of 1914" and *Christian History* magazine's article on the topic is called, simply, "Christmas miracles."[52]

* * *

The World War I Christmas Truce is one of the most well-known and widely cited Christmas miracles, but it is far from the only one. Divine intervention during war appears to be a recurring Christmas theme, in fact, with soldiers telling of seemingly miraculous feats on the battlefield and lives being spared in dire circumstances. During the Korean War on Christmas Day in 1950, for example, a U.S. merchant marine ship somehow managed to pick up more than 14,000 refugees in one trip from a Korean port. The SS *Meredith Victory*'s three-day voyage through mine-infested waters earned the cargo freighter a nickname, "the Ship of Miracles." Several babies were delivered onboard, including Lee Gyong-pil who later explained that due to a lack of basic supplies, the midwife used her teeth to cut his umbilical cord. "People said the fact that I didn't die and was born was a Christmas miracle," Lee said.[53] Captain Leonard P. La Rue, a U.S. Merchant Marine who was on the ship, recalled his awe at the fact that none of the 14,000 rescued people died. "I believe God was with us those three days," he said. "I believe this because by all the laws of logic the loss of life could have been enormous. Yet not a soul perished."[54]

In recent years, a veritable cottage industry of books has sprouted up documenting supposed miracles at Christmas time, with titles such as *Christmas Miracles: Magical True Stories of Modern-Day Miracles*, *A Miracle Under the Christmas Tree: Real Stories of Hope, Faith and the True Gifts of the Season*, and *A Treasury of Christmas Miracles: True Stories of God's Presence Today*. These collections tell stories of help being given in times of need and kindnesses that appear when least expected during the holidays, as well as lives being saved through inexplicable acts attributed to God. Among the stories that writers have explained as examples of divine intervention are tales of a Jewish woman fleeing the Holocaust being spared from a horrible fate on Christmas Eve and how car trouble on Christmas night saved a couple's lives. In *The Magic of Christmas Miracles*, stories are told of a woman walking in the woods visited by an angel and a private plane carrying an unconscious pilot somehow landing safely in an empty field.

Reader's Digest has a collection of "18 True Christmas Miracles That Will Restore Your Hope for the Holidays,"[55] but most of them could be explained by incredulous individuals as coincidences or rather mundane events that may have felt genuinely special to the participants but in all likelihood are probably not cases of actual divine intervention. The collection, for example, highlights stories such as parents finding just enough money to buy Christmas gifts for their children, stranded drivers receiving desperately needed roadside assistance from strangers during snowstorms, and fir trees appearing out of nowhere just in time to decorate for Christmas Eve. Although skeptics would easily dismiss most of these "miracle stories" as little more than random fluke occurrences that have been infused with meaning by superstitious people, the fact that so many identify some sort of divine hand in these incidents is a testament to the enduring myth of a Christmas miracle.

The idea of a Christmas miracle has also been popularized in film, including such mainstays as *Miracle on 34th Street* and *It's a Wonderful Life*, and more recent contributions such as a 2012 movie by the name of *Christmas Miracle*, which tells the story of eight strangers who take refuge in an abandoned church during a storm and learn to work together to overcome a series of challenges. In the 1946 classic *It's a Wonderful Life*, directed by Frank Capra, a frustrated family man named George Bailey, facing financial difficulties, decides on Christmas Eve to end his life by jumping off a bridge into a river, only to be saved by divine intervention. His guardian angel, Clarence Odbody, rescues him from the icy water and proceeds to show George the many ways he has touched the lives of others, and how his community of Bedford Falls would have been a very different place had he not been born. The story ends with George regaining his faith, rediscovering his appreciation for life, renewing his sense of love for his family and his community, and with the angel Clarence finally receiving his wings—indicated by the ringing of a bell hanging from a Christmas tree as the town sings "Auld Lang Syne" together.

In the 1947 American comedy-drama *Miracle on 34th Street*, Kris Kringle discovers that the man playing Santa Claus in the Macy's Thanksgiving Day Parade is drunk, so he ends up taking over as Santa in the parade and then is hired as Macy's Santa at its flagship location in Manhattan. Eventually, Kris is deemed insane and committed to Bellevue Hospital due to his unusually kind-hearted nature, and at a hearing to determine his mental fitness, Kris claims in court that he actually is the real Santa Claus. Eventually, his lawyers prove his case by dumping all the letters addressed to "Santa Claus" from the U.S. Post Office on the desk of the judge, and Kris is released from Bellevue. The "miracle" in the story takes place at the end when one of the characters obtains her dream house, apparently aided by the magic of Kris Kringle. This supposed miracle is a reminder that when people are looking for them, "Christmas miracles" can be seen everywhere.

It's also a reminder of the close relationship between the concepts of magic and miracles, how these beliefs continue to merge with lines blurred during the Christmas season between the supernatural, the sacred and the profane. Despite the efforts of Church leaders and theologians who have long tried to draw distinctions between the two concepts, "magic" and "miracles" for all intents and purposes remain synonymous and manifest themselves in popular culture more or less equally at Christmas time.

12

Legacy of Misrule

Come bring the noise,
My merry, merry boys,
The Christmas log to the firing;
While my good dame, she
Bids ye all be free,
And drink to your heart's desiring.
   —Robert Herrick, "Ceremonies for Christmas"

A friend of mine once remarked that his favorite thing about Christmas is that it's the one time of year that you can drink as much as you want without being judged for it. "The rest of the year," he quipped, "they just call you an alcoholic." His observation was wickedly funny, but there is of course a good deal of truth in it—the Christmas season is widely considered a time to relax and indulge, a time when normal rules and norms, whether related to eating and drinking in moderation or in terms of general social relations, do not strictly apply. This legacy of misrule, largely a relic of pagan celebrations such as Saturnalia and pre–Christian Yule festivities, is well known and has long been appreciated by both secular and religious forces, for better or for worse, as a fact of life during Christmas.

As the Puritans understood, when the Church had decided on December 25 for Jesus Christ's nativity, it was making a compromise—hoping to entice pagans to join the Christian flock by absorbing their traditions into a Christian feast. One of these traditions was that of drinking heavily, which is something that can be traced back to the ways that pagans once celebrated during the holidays of Saturnalia and the winter solstice festivities. Throughout recorded history, from accounts of celebrants stumbling through streets of ancient Rome drinking and singing songs to the Scandinavian expression of "drinking Christmas" (or *drikke jul*), the holiday has been associated with excessive consumption of alcohol and related debaucheries, from raucous wassailing traditions to increased infidelity. In 17th-century colonial America, it was noted that the rate of illegitimate births spiked in September and October, providing a hint of the licentiousness that characterized the Christmas period nine months earlier.[1] Christmas has also been associated with rebelliousness and unrest, leading to both small-scale disturbances and large-scale insurrection, sometimes fueled by alcohol.

As an indication of the deep-seated controversies surrounding the holiday's obstreperous side, a pamphlet was published in 1658 called *The Examination and Tryal of Old Father Christmas* in which Josiah King laid out a satirical legal case

12. Legacy of Misrule 159

against Christmas, accusing it of "devour[ing] all and produc[ing] nothing," as well as teaching "revelling and rebellion." Presented as a transcript of a trial taking place in the Town of Superstition, in the County of Idolatry, the pamphlet offers an indictment of Christmas, alleging that the holiday "incites" people to "Drunkenness, gluttony, & unlawful Gaming, Wantonness, Uncleanness, Lasciviousness, Cursing,

The scene in this 1812 illustration depicts some rather lascivious holiday festivities, with mistletoe overhead and four couples embracing, kissing, or attempting to kiss below. "Christmas Gambols," 1812. Artist Thomas Rowlandson (The Metropolitan Museum of Art, the Elisha Whittelsey Collection, the Elisha Whittelsey Fund, 1959).

Swearing, abuse of the Creatures, some to one Vice, and some to another; all to Idleness." Christmas, the indictment alleges, is "the author of Rebellion and sedition," provoking "wanton fulness and lustful love." Christmas makes people "ready for all evil," teaching "that which the people of the old world practised, only eating and drinking &c such other delights." The pamphlet compared Christmas to "the Idolatrous Israelites" and to the satyrs, the Greek mythological nature spirit with a permanent erection.[2]

Christmas did have defenders at the trial, however. "Peter Poor," testifying on Christmas's behalf, said that "had it not been for old Christmas," he would have been even poorer, "if poorer I could have been." Peter Poor said that without Christmas, his best friend "God-free Giving" might die. "Take away this merry old Gentleman from us, you take away all our joy and comfort that we have on earth," Peter Poor said. "Charles Charity" also testified at the trial, claiming that Christmas "hath done more good in 12 days" than "Schismaticks have done in 12 years." The open heart of Christmas "hath relieved millions of distressed people, whilst the uncharitable hands of his persecutors have destroyed thousands, and fed upon the blood of their best benefactors."

Apparently persuaded by the arguments made of the holiday's benefits for the poor and "distressed people," the jury found Christmas not guilty and he "was released with a great deal of triumph and exaltation." His acquittal, however, did not absolve the holiday of its reputation for inspiring drunkenness and debauchery.

Illustration from Josiah King's *Examination and Tryal of Old Father Christmas*, first published in 1658. This image was used as the frontispiece for the 1658 and 1678 editions. In the book, the caption accompanying the illustration reads, "Behold the majesty and grace of loving cheerful, Christmas face. Whom many thousands with one breath: Cry out let him be put to death. Who indeed can never die: so long as man hath memory." Artist unknown (*Public Domain Review*, https://publicdomainreview.org/).

* * *

Although Christmas has always meant different things to different people, with various social groups observing it in a variety of ways, one of these ways has always had an element of hedonism and bedlam, or as a British newspaper explained, as a time for "Rioting and Drunkenness." Joseph Banks, on Captain James Cook's first expedition to the south Pacific Ocean aboard the HMS *Endeavour*, wrote in 1769 that the crew kept Christmas "in the old fashioned way," with all the crew members "as Drunk as our forefathers used to be upon the like occasion." A Christmas in 1784 was marred by an attack on a Roman Catholic church in Aberdeen, Scotland, by "a riotous assemblage ... stimulated by drink and madness."[3] A man charged with being drunk and disorderly in London in 1831 pleaded for leniency by emphasizing that "it was Christmas time." The magistrate, however, was not impressed by the man's excuses. Finding him guilty, the magistrate pointed out that everyone brought before him for the previous several days had made a similar defense, "appear[ing] to think that they had a right to commit all manner of excesses with impunity at this festive season."[4]

Sometimes the traditions of religiosity and misrule mixed, with pious observances tainted by raucous disorder. Sedate Midnight Mass services, for example, were often disturbed by drunken revelers who seemed to think that the late-night events were just another opportunity for mayhem. In the Rhineland of Germany, Midnight Mass had to be suspended in the 18th century because people tended to view them as just part of their Christmas merrymaking rather than as sacred functions. As described in *Christmas Customs and Traditions*, the congregation at a typical Midnight Mass resembled "a crowd of wild drunken sailors in a tavern" where "the only sober man was the preacher."[5]

An Anglican minister, writing in 1725, while generally supportive of observing Christmas, could not help but acknowledge that the way people celebrated was "a Scandal to Religion, and an encouraging of Wickedness." The Rev. Henry Bourn of Newcastle, England, lamented that the season was little more than "a pretense for Drunkenness, and Rioting, and Wantonness." Through the 12 days of Christmas and all the way up to Candlemas Day on February 2, it was typical "for Men to rise early in the Morning that they may follow strong Drink, and continue until Night, till Wine inflame them," according to Bourn.[6]

When the holiday grew in popularity in 18th-century New England, some observed it with pious devotion and others as a time of feasting, with or without the use of alcohol, but there were many who saw it as a time of misrule, with excessive alcohol use leading to sexual liberties, social inversion and sometimes violence.[7] The Rev. Cotton Mather observed in 1712 that "the Feast of the Christ's Nativity is spent in Reveling, Dicing, Carding, Masking, and in all Licentious Liberty," as well as by "hard Drinking, by lewd Gaming, [and] by rude Reveling."[8] A Christmas Day sermon in 1758 by Presbyterian minister Samuel Davies noted that despite being the day that "the church of Rome" decided "to celebrate in memory of the Prince of Peace, the Savior of men, the incarnate God," instead, "[i]t is generally a season of sinning, sensuality, luxury, and various forms of extravagance; as though men were not celebrating the birth of the holy Jesus, but of Venus, or Bacchus, whose most sacred rites were mysteries of iniquity and debauchery."[9] As a 1769 Boston newspaper succinctly put it, to celebrate the Yuletide is to "keep drunk all the Christmas Holy-days."[10]

Christmas hedonism may have had an enduring impact on American history, with a key victory in the War for Independence attributed, at least in part, to Yuletide overindulgence. In the winter of 1776, General George Washington hoped to turn the tide of the Revolutionary War with a surprise predawn attack on the German Hessian garrison at Trenton, due to the belief that the mercenaries there would have been heartily celebrating Christmas on the night of December 25. As an officer in Washington's staff wrote in his diary before the battle, "They make a great deal of Christmas in Germany, and no doubt the Hessians will drink a great deal of beer and have a dance to-night. They will be sleepy to-morrow morning. Washington will set the tune for them about daybreak." After his famed crossing of the icy Delaware River, Washington launched his surprise attack on the tired Hessian troops quartered at Trenton. The Continental soldiers quickly overpowered the mercenaries, with the victory proving to be a major turning point in the war.[11]

Though he may have exploited the Germans' reputation for Christmas excess, Washington himself was no stranger to holiday indulgence, as his personal recipe for eggnog makes clear. Heavy on both sugar and booze, "George Washington's Eggnog Recipe" was widely circulated at the time, popularized due to the claim that it was penned by the famous Virginian in his own hand. With a quart of cream, a quart of milk and an unspecified number of eggs, the recipe also included "one dozen tablespoons sugar, one pint brandy, ½ pint rye whiskey, ½ pint Jamaica rum, [and] ¼ pint sherry." The first president allegedly advised that after mixing the beverage, it should be set "in cool place for several days," recommending to "[t]aste frequently."[12]

Historians have since raised doubts about whether Washington personally wrote this recipe, but it was nonetheless a popular alcohol-heavy concoction for Christmas revelers in the antebellum American South, where late December was a season of heavy eating and drinking, sexual promiscuity, and general merrymaking. With the harvest complete and little work to be done, the season was a time for blowing off steam, both for planters and slaves, as well as poor whites. A contemporary critic of Christmas called it a "general scene of dissipation and idleness," marked by "[a]pprentice boys and little negroes" firing guns and firecrackers, and everyone drinking hard. People typically started their daily consumption of alcohol at

This 1851 painting depicts Washington's attack on the Hessians at Trenton on December 25, 1776. The mission's success has been partially attributed to the Christmas-related hangovers that the Hessian troops might have had that morning (although some historians dispute this). "Washington Crossing the Delaware." Artist Emanuel Leutze (The Metropolitan Museum of Art, Gift of John Stewart Kennedy, 1897).

breakfast, with "egg-nog, punch and toddy ... freely served to the children," according to one observer.[13]

Christmas misrule even affected austere American institutions such as the Military Academy in West Point, New York. In the so-called Eggnog Riot, also known as the Grog Mutiny, more than one-third of the cadets, including future Confederate States President Jefferson Davis, participated in a drunken Christmas party on December 24–25, 1826, fueled by whiskey that had been smuggled into the academy to make eggnog. The revelry degenerated into window-smashing and widespread insubordination, resulting in nearly two dozen court martials. An investigation by academy officials found that 70 cadets participated in the riot.[14]

* * *

Indeed, Christmas riots, often involving alcohol, are a common theme throughout American history—sometimes inspired by anti–Catholic and anti-immigrant sentiments. In 1806, a Protestant gang attacked Catholic worshippers at St. Peter's Church in New York City on Christmas night, but the churchgoers were prepared to meet them armed with weapons. Nativists and Irish New Yorkers clashed in the streets with dozens of men attacking each other. A participant in the melee, William Otter, recorded the incident in his diary:

> The church was surrounded with a motley crew of Irish and sailors ... engaged in deadly conflict.... The mob fought from the door of the church to Irish town, being the distance of about a fourth of a mile. ... [W]e fell to and drank as much as we pleased, and while we were refreshing ourselves the mob came in and began to break bottles, glasses, pitchers, barrels and all and everything they could find in the shop; and fought on till day light through Irishtown; laying all Irishtown waste; a great deal of property was destroyed by the mob, and a great deal of human blood shed.[15]

As Stephen Nissenbaum describes it in *The Battle for Christmas*, "By 1820 Christmas misrule had become such an acute social threat that respectable New Yorkers could no longer ignore it or take it lightly." Roving mobs of young men would wind their way through the streets, no longer restricting their revelries to their own neighborhoods, but going wherever they pleased, including the city's wealthy areas. They often wore disguises, a holdover of the mumming tradition in England, and included elements of street gangs. They were known to target the homes of the rich and powerful, with one such mob terrorizing the home of the city's mayor in 1826, stopping at his Broadway estate where they "enacted ... a scene of disgraceful rage," as a local newspaper put it.[16]

More than a thousand people took over the streets of New York on New Year's Eve, 1827–28, in a riot that "moved from one end of the city to the other, making the most hideous noises, committing many excesses, and for several hours in succession, disturbing neighborhoods," according to one contemporary account.[17] A mob in New York invaded an upscale restaurant on New Year's Eve, 1851–52, and destroyed the furniture, smashed dishes and assaulted the owner, his wife, and their staff. Other disturbances around the city that night led to the arrests of some 100 men, in what the New York *Tribune* described as "a Saturnalia of discord, by Callithumpian and Cowbellian bands, by musketry and fire-crackers, by bacchanal songs and noisy revels, which for two hours after midnight made sleep not a thing to be dreamed of." At the root of the anarchy, according to the *Tribune*, was alcohol. The *Tribune* reported that "an unusual number of men were arrested for drunkenness, creating a mob, exciting a riot, insulting females, and other offenses to which men of low breeding, when intoxicated, are addicted."[18]

* * *

Christmas misrule also affected the slavocracy of the antebellum South. There, the rebelliousness was not just a display of bravado and hooliganism, but a direct challenge to the established order, and specifically to the cruel injustice of human bondage. One in three of the 70 slave uprisings from the mid–17th century to the early 19th century took place (or were planned to take place) in December.[19] These included both major insurrections and smaller outbreaks that might be confined to a single plantation, and while they may have frightened the ruling caste, ultimately did not overturn the existing order. Further south, however, a Christmas rebellion directly contributed to the abolition of slavery.

The so-called Christmas Uprising in Jamaica, also known as the as the Baptist War and the Great Jamaican Slave Revolt of 1831–32, involved up to 60,000 slaves— one-fifth of the island's 300,000 enslaved people. Beginning on December 25, 1831, the uprising was led by a black Baptist deacon, Samuel Sharpe, who believed that the Bible taught that slavery was morally wrong and preached whites had no more right to hold blacks in bondage than the other way around. Christmas Day 1831 fell on a Sunday, which was a rest day, so Sharpe and his followers argued that the slaves were entitled as compensation to both Monday (Boxing Day) and the following Tuesday off.[20] They began a campaign of passive resistance during the holidays, denying their labor with a demand that the enslaved black workers be given more freedom and a wage for their labor of "half the going wage rate."[21]

The general strike escalated when slaves set fire to Kensington estate, in the hills above Montego Bay, sparking a full-scale rebellion which led to the deaths of 14 whites and 207 blacks. Hundreds more were hanged as a result of the trials afterwards. Although Sharpe was executed in 1832, the Christmas Uprising is credited with promoting the cause of emancipation; in 1834 the Abolition Bill was passed by the British Parliament and full emancipation for everyone in the British colonies was granted on August 1, 1838.[22]

Being sparked by the slaveholders' denial of the full break from work to which the slaves felt entitled, the uprising in Jamaica illustrated that while Christmas could lead to insurrection, it could also be an important buffer against it. As many slave owners in the United States understood, providing slaves some freedom at Christmas time helped prevent rebellions the rest of the year. The great abolitionist Frederick Douglass, who had been raised a slave before escaping in 1838, argued that the holidays were "among the most effective means in the hands of the slaveholder in keeping down the spirit of insurrection." Noting that if slaveholders stripped away Christmas privileges, "it would lead to an immediate insurrection among the slaves," Douglass said that the holidays served as "safety valves" against rebellion.[23]

Throughout the American South, slaves were widely granted broad liberties at Christmas that were unheard of the rest of the year. For most slaves, Christmas meant a relaxation of the rules and norms, and involved a good deal of revelry, including eating, drinking, and dancing. Slaves were released from their obligation to work, usually for several days and in some cases for up to a full month, although sometimes

Depiction of the burning of the Roehampton Estate during the Christmas Uprising in Jamaica, January 1832. "Destruction of the Roehampton Estate," 1833. Artist Adolphe Duperly.

slave owners would withhold Christmas privileges from slaves who had displeased them throughout the year.[24] Douglass described it as a time for "such sports and merriments as playing ball, wrestling, running foot-races, fiddling, dancing, and drinking whisky," noting that "it was deemed a disgrace not to get drunk at Christmas." As former slave Solomon Northup described Christmas on the plantation, it was a "carnival season with the children of bondage," the only time "when they are allowed a little restricted liberty, and heartily indeed do they enjoy it." A white Southerner called Christmas "the time of the blacks' high carnival," and several contemporary accounts compared it to the Roman Saturnalia. A report in *Harper's New Monthly Magazine* called Christmas "the great gala season of the negro," noting that "[i]t may be likened to the saturnalia of the Romans." The poet and Unitarian minister John Pierpont compared it to "bacchanal feasts and amusements of antiquity" and another writer called it a "grand Saturnalia," a time when "all society seems resolved into chaos."[25]

* * *

Indeed, particularly when it comes to the matter of slavery, it is difficult to avoid the parallels with ancient Rome. Just like the American slavers in the antebellum South, the Roman elite lived in a state of fear that their slaves would rebel and kill them, and the respite offered by the Saturnalia celebration and its attendant traditions of social inversion and misrule provided an important safety valve for the established order.

The rulers of ancient Rome built scores of holidays into the calendar year, with Cicero specifically insisting that slaves should get regular breaks from their labors— and no month was as restful as December, including a total of 14 holidays punctuated by the weeklong celebration of Saturnalia followed by Dies Natalis Solis Invicti and Kalends. This was based on the idea, expressed by ancient sources such as Justinus, Macrobius, and Seneca, that treating slaves too harshly only makes them disloyal and ultimately dangerous. "Please remember that the person you call your slave rose from the same seeds, enjoys the same sky and equally breathes, lives and dies," according to Seneca in his *Moral Epistles*, published in 65 CE. He advises slave owners to deal with their inferiors the way they would want their superiors would deal with them[26] and notes in particular the importance of Saturnalia's social inversion practices in reinforcing good relations in a household.

"Set aside a certain number of days," Seneca advises, "during which you shall be content with the scantiest and cheapest fare, with coarse and rough dress." While slaves enjoy the festivities of Saturnalia, Seneca tells slave owners that they should eat "hard and grimy" bread to test themselves and to learn the lesson "that a man's peace of mind does not depend upon Fortune; for, even when angry she grants enough for our needs." Seneca warns however that slave owners should not "think that you are doing anything great," since in reality they are "merely be doing what many thousands of slaves and many thousands of poor men are doing every day."[27]

Historian Fanny Dolansky describes the social role of Saturnalia as a domestic rite that served a variety of purposes, one of which was to provide a safe space for negotiating the complex dynamics of the upper-class household by addressing and diffusing tensions and anxieties. "The Saturnalia," she writes, "possibly even more than any other domestic rite, functioned in this way; yet at the same time, it also offered a fruitful opportunity for instilling in young and new household members, and reinforcing in others, normative social values and beliefs." She notes that in elite Roman households, there was a genuine fear among slave owners for their personal safety, pointing out that excessive cruelty against slaves often pushed them to their limits, resulting in the murder of slave owners. Pliny the Younger, she points out, wrote extensively about slaves killing their owners and Columella advocated a balance between excessive indulgence and excessive cruelty. "With little recourse on a daily basis for dealing with the tensions that resulted from their condition, aside from passive forms of resistance such as stealing or wasting time," Dolansky writes, "the Saturnalia was therefore critical for providing a space expressly for releasing some of the anger and resentment many surely possessed."[28] At the same time, because the role reversal was temporary and artificial, the divergence from the social order helped to reinforce the hierarchical structure experienced the rest of the year.

In this sense, the customs of irreverence, rebellion and permissiveness may have been an important tool of social control, providing a needed outlet for slaves to voice frustrations and live out fantasies of being free, but they also may have provided the backdrop for later Christmas celebrations characterized by misrule and debauchery, or even rebellion and revolt. This connection was drawn by some of the holiday's most vocal critics, such as the Rev. Increase Mather, who argued against Christmas in 1687 by pointing out that "amongst Christmas-keepers in some parts of the World, there use to be such Masters of Misrule." He cites both Protestant and Catholic writers who have acknowledged that the Christmas holidays succeeded "the Old Saturnalia of the Heathen." In that celebration of an earlier age, Mather lamented that "Masters did wait upon their Servants [and] Servants must be Masters."[29] It was this spirit of social inversion and misrule, Mather argues, that has led to "[t]he generality of Christmas-keepers [to] observe that Festival after such a manner as is highly dishonourable to the name of Christ."

* * *

This spirit of misrule in the celebration of Christmas has continued through the centuries and can be seen in popular culture, arguably fulfilling some of the same safety-valve functions that it did in earlier eras. Although people generally don't have it as bad as slaves of ancient Rome or the antebellum American South, there is still a palpable need for some loosening of social norms and even a degree of status inversion which Christmas allows for. Perhaps that is why remnants of Saturnalia traditions endure, with themes found in Christmas movies reminding us that social status is less important than values such as humility, integrity, love and goodwill, as well as serving as reminders that even those at the top of the economic-social order can find themselves brought down to a lowlier state with a simple stroke of fate. Alternatively, in this topsy-turvy world, those at the bottom might just find themselves living in the lap of luxury.

A 1983 Christmas movie called *Trading Places*, for example, explores this theme with a story of a black homeless man named Billy Ray Valentine (played by Eddie Murphy) and a white Wall Street stockbroker named Louis Winthorpe III (played by Dan Aykroyd) switching roles, with the homeless man enjoying all the luxuries of being wealthy and the stockbroker enduring the indignities of poverty. In his newfound role as a rich man, Valentine quickly adapts to his social status and learns to enjoy the finer things, but ultimately unites with Winthorpe to take revenge on the elites at the top. The movie ends with their wealthy adversaries bankrupted, and both Valentine and Winthorpe living comfortably on a tropical island. Similarly, in a 2000 Christmas movie called *The Family Man*, starring Nicolas Cage and Téa Leoni, a rich executive living in a penthouse apartment is given a glimpse of what his life would have been like as a working-class tire salesman if he had made a different decision 13 years earlier, ultimately learning that family is more important than wealth. In yet another twist on this theme, the 1990 hit *Home Alone* tells the story of a young child who is accidentally left in charge of a household during the Christmas holiday, in a throwback to the tradition in ancient Rome of letting the lowliest member of the household serve as Lord of Misrule during the Saturnalia days.

There are also echoes of Saturnalia's social inversion and misrule traditions in real life. In the British army, senior officers to this day continue the tradition of serving food to the junior ranks on Christmas, a custom that appears to be a direct descendant of Roman times. Misrule can also be seen with the chaotic and sometimes violent scenes that break out at malls with customers competing for bargains during the "Black Friday" shopping ritual where individuals generally at the lower end of the economic spectrum are given the opportunity to buy luxury goods that they otherwise might not be able to afford. At office Christmas parties there is often a loosening of the corporate hierarchy, with a sense of equality and comradery that may be absent in the office environment the rest of the year. Basically, there is a general feeling at Christmas that the usual rules don't apply—or at least are a bit more relaxed.

And indeed, when it comes to moderation in drinking, it is clear that social norms are considerably loosened during the holidays. According to a 2018 survey, the average American doubles their alcohol intake at Christmas time,[30] with about a quarter of the distilled spirits industry's annual profits made between Thanksgiving and the New Year,[31] and about 69 percent of Americans saying that they are more likely to overindulge during this time of year than any other.[32] Meanwhile, in the

United Kingdom, a survey found that 61 percent of drinkers admit to overdoing it during the festivities, with 18 percent saying they experience more hangovers during this period.[33] The average Briton consumes about 26 units per day between Christmas Eve and New Year's Day, which is nearly 10 times more than the average units consumed on a regular day, according to one industry survey.[34]

This overindulgence of course has some negative consequences, including a higher rate of alcohol-involved car accidents, violence and petty crimes, as well as employment and relationship issues that stem from embarrassing episodes at alcohol-fueled office parties. Employees have been known on these occasions to allow their inebriation to provide them the false confidence to give their bosses a "piece of their mind" over some perceived injustice, and the occasional shouting match or even physical fight is not unheard of. Alcohol-lubricated office parties are also a dangerous opportunity for employees to make ill-advised sexual overtures toward their colleagues. In the 1950s, critics of the increasingly popular office parties in the United States alleged that they violated the sanctity of the nativity observance, endangered the moral values of family life, and encouraged improper behavior between the sexes.[35] In Denmark they call the post–Christmas period *skilsmissesæson*, or divorce season, due to the high number of divorces filed in January largely as a result of infidelities that occur at office Christmas parties. In the United Kingdom, they call the first business day of January "D-Day," or "Divorce Day," as it is generally considered the busiest of the year for family attorneys. While much of this is because the holidays can sometimes be stressful for a troubled relationship, with families spending more time together than usual, some of it can also be attributed to infidelity.[36]

The debauchery and loosened sexual mores that have long been associated with Christmas can be heard in popular Christmas music, including the 1944 song "Baby It's Cold Outside," which in recent years has spurred an annual controversy about sexual consent. Although the song has long been considered a harmless, flirtatious duet depicting a man trying to convince his lady friend to stay the night, in the era of #MeToo and cancel culture, the lyrics have been criticized as possibly condoning date rape. To be fair, the lyrics do seem to indicate that the guy is ignoring his date's protests and is pressuring her to stay, and perhaps most problematic is when the woman asks, "Say, what's in this drink?" Some have taken this line as a hint that he may have slipped a roofie-like drug into her cup, but it's also possible that she simply meant that she thought that the alcoholic content of her eggnog was a bit too strong.

But "Baby It's Cold Outside" is just one of many tunes hint at the lascivious and carnival side of Christmas. Jimmy Boyd's 1952 hit "I Saw Mommy Kissing Santa Claus," with its paganish lyrics about mistletoe and smooching with a bearded elf, has been covered by everyone from The Jackson 5 to John Mellencamp to Amy Winehouse to Jessica Simpson, becoming a perennial Christmas favorite over the generations. Another one is Rufus Thomas's "I'll Be Your Santa Baby," which begins with the suggestive lines "I'll slide down your chimney / And bring you lots of joy." Less well known but perhaps even more explicit in its sexual content is "Christmas Balls" by Ben Light and his Surf Club Boys, which came out in 1936. "Christmas Balls" uses "trimming the tree" as a double entendre for sex, and as the song progresses, Light continues with the increasingly obvious innuendo. "Let me hang my balls on your Christmas tree," the song goes, because "I've got the nicest balls that you ever did see."

As Ronald Lankford writes in *Sleigh Rides, Jingle Bells, and Silent Nights: A Cultural History of American Christmas*, "Christmas Balls," like other sexually suggestive Christmas tunes, "was an early example of the carnival side of the holiday song, a style that drew from older carnival practices that rejected or simply ignored the Christmas tradition of home, children, and charity along with any religious connotations." This was a thumbing of the nose at mainstream cultural mores, a rebelliousness, Lankford points out, that had roots in festivals such as Saturnalia, Kalends, and Yule.[37]

Santa Claus under a mistletoe, being kissed by two young women, as illustrated on the cover of *Puck* magazine in 1902. "Christmas 1902." Artist Frank Arthur Nankivell. *Puck* 52, no. 1344 (December 3, 1902) (Library of Congress).

Considering this background, it may seem sometimes that debauchery is more central to the Christmas celebration than the more Hallmark-friendly themes of "peace on earth" and "goodwill towards men." Indeed, hints of debauchery can be seen everywhere during the Christmas season, even in the expression that is commonly used during the holiday season as a generic greeting, "Merry Christmas," which contains an element of hedonism and excess. As opposed to simply feeling "happy," being "merry" means overcome with excited feelings of enjoyment and implies a degree of revelry that is missing from the quiet contentment of happiness. Being merry implies a lot of drinking, dancing, eating rich food and playing games, and was actually used as slang for being drunk in the 18th and 19th centuries.[38] Another slang term from the late 1700s was "merry-bout," which meant an act of sexual intercourse,[39] providing a hint of the lewdness that has historically been associated with the term "Merry Christmas" and the holiday season in general.

It was for this reason that the term "Merry Christmas" fell out of favor with the British upper classes, who considered it vulgar, and preferred to say "Happy Christmas," which implies sensibly enjoying the holiday with quiet contentment. In the first radio broadcast of a royal Christmas message in 1932, King George V pointedly wished his subjects a "Happy Christmas," and his successor Queen Elizabeth II continued to do so. Perhaps as a result of this royal preference, "happy" overtook "merry" in Britain during the 1930s, but according to some observers, the term "Merry Christmas" is making a comeback in merry old England.[40]

As we have seen, the push and pull between decency and morality on one hand, and debauchery and merriment on the other, has long characterized the holiday season—ever since Bishop Asterius of Amasea gave a sermon in the year 400 railing against how the raucous Christmas/Saturnalia festival "render[ed] the city a place to be shunned rather than visited."[41] This reality has continued over the centuries to be a source of friction between the more pious religious elements and those who see the holidays as a winter carnival, a chance to let their hair down and gorge themselves on food and drink. None of this debauchery is particularly Christian in nature, of course. As a 16th-century Anglican bishop put it, "Men dishonour Christ more in the 12 days of Christmas, than in all the 12 months besides."[42]

But while perhaps not very Christian, the celebration is very much Christmas.

13

The Halloween Connection

Some merry, friendly, country-folks,
Together did convene,
To burn their nits, and pou their stocks,
And haud their Halloween
   —Robert Burns, "Halloween"

Easily the most beloved holiday on the calendar, Christmas of course does have its detractors, and one of the most common complaints is that the season just lasts too long. In the United States, the Christmas season begins in earnest with the chaotic shopping ritual of Black Friday the day after Thanksgiving, but in actuality, the season could be said to begin a month before that, when Christmas displays of Santa and Frosty begin replacing Halloween displays of ghosts and witches in stores on November 1. In recent years, these aggressive strategies have made their way across the Atlantic, leading to growing discontent in Europe over American-style marketing that many believe initiates the Christmas season too early. Germans, in particular, appear to be aggravated by this trend, with a 2014 survey finding that one in three believe the government should step in to regulate when stores can start selling Christmas goods, with most respondents saying that the date should be set at November 30.[1]

But while complaints are common that there should be more demarcation between the holidays and that marketers should stop trying to "shove Christmas down our throats" so early, historically speaking the season has always been a fairly long, drawn-out process beginning in early November, and despite the common assumption that Halloween and Christmas are two distinct holidays, a closer look reveals a number of surprising connections between the two. With a better understanding of the close relationship between Halloween and Christmas, it makes sense that there would be some overlap between them, and therefore some of the animosity towards shops for premature Yuletide marketing might be misplaced.

Like Christmas, Halloween of course is a hybrid holiday combining elements of pagan belief with Christian religious doctrine, rooted in the changing seasons and the annual cycle of the sun. While some folklorists have traced its origins to the Roman feast of Pomona, known as the goddess of fruits and seeds, or to the festival of the dead called Parentalia, it is most often linked to the ancient Celtic festival Samhain (pronounced SAH-win), meaning summer's end. The date was important on the calendar as a "quarter day" between the vernal equinox and the winter solstice, and also had significance for agricultural reasons, as a time of harvest and when the

A vintage Halloween postcard, printed in 1908. "Merry Halloween" (Dave "Riptheskull" Flickr user, no changes made, CC BY-ND 2.0, https://www.flickr.com/photos/vintagehalloweencollector/1348644336/in/album-72157600713983531/).

animals were sheltered for the winter. The tenth-century Gaelic text Tochmarc Emire mentions Samhain as the day "when the summer goes to its rest."[2]

As an agricultural rite, Samhain was an important practical opportunity for reorganizing communities for the winter months, but was also a period of intense supernatural activity, with forces of darkness said to be abroad, emerging from the ancient mounds of the countryside. To ward off these spirits, the Irish invoked the help of the gods by sacrificing animals and perhaps humans as well.[3] The question of whether or not human sacrifice was involved in Samhain is a contentious one, with most claims to this effect coming from detractors of the druids such as the ancient Romans, and few references to human sacrifice in the ancient Irish sagas. Geoffrey Keating, a 17th-century historian, noted in his *History of Ireland* that on the eve of Samhain, it was customary to make offerings to the Fomorians, a supernatural race in Irish mythology who represent chaos, darkness, death, blight and drought. It is not clear, however, whether or not these tributes involved blood sacrifices.[4]

What is clear is that Samhain was a time of dark omens, when summer has returned to the underworld and night has come to overwhelm day. It was a time when the physical world was teeming with spiritual beings, when ghosts and goblins abounded, elves emerged from the ground, and the boundaries were erased between the physical world and the supernatural.[5] Taking place between the equinox and the solstice, it was seen as a moment of ritual transition and altered states. It represented a time out of time, a brief interval "when the normal order of the universe is suspended" and "charged with a peculiar preternatural energy," according to Celtic scholar Proinsias Mac Cana.[6]

13. The Halloween Connection

In pre–Christian times and during the era of Christianization, the beginning of Yule was marked at Samhain, which was later consecrated by the Church as All Saints Day.[7] The ancient Celts recognized November 1 as the beginning of winter and associated this time of year with the dead,[8] with Samhain considered the most important of the four Celtic festivals, ushering in "the dark half of the year" and celebrated with copious amounts of alcohol consumed, especially mead and beer,[9] as well as eating generous portions of pork, which Celts thought helped them commune with the otherworld.[10] Celebrants believed that the barriers between the physical world and the spirit world disintegrate during Samhain, allowing more interaction between humans and uncanny beings who reside in other realms.[11] (The fact that our ancestors marked the beginning of winter in early November helps explain why the term "midwinter" has historically been used to describe the Yule and Christmas festivals, while in our modern conception of the calendar, December 25 would more properly be called "early winter.")

Lasting for three days,[12] Samhain was the time of year when the sun was believed to descend into the realm of the underworld and uncanny forces were on the rise. Unfettered from celestial control, the lord of the underworld walked the earth accompanied by other creatures such as ghosts and fairies.[13] The prevalence of spiritual activity is experienced from early November through late December,[14] which is why ghost stories were once common at Christmas but are today more commonly associated with Halloween—historically, ghost stories characterized the entire season.

The ancient Celts believed that the night of October 31 marked a spiritual conversion for those who had died during the previous year as they began their transition to the next world and signaled the coming winter and the dark nights ahead.[15] It therefore came to be seen as an important ritual to assist the powers of life against those of pestilence, offering a chance to pray for the dead, as well as for the return of the sun. Samhain's rituals and ceremonies provided assurances that the deceased would successfully transition to the otherworld and that the sun would in fact come back. Ancient Celts built ceremonial fires in honor of the sun goddess Tlachtga, which helped protect the light and warmth against the growing darkness of winter, as well as to symbolize the sun itself.[16] A hill named after Tlachtga was the site of an ancient religious rite known as the Great Fire Festival which signaled the onset of winter. The ceremonies celebrated the sun goddess and offered guarantees to the people that the powers of darkness would be overcome.[17]

* * *

While Halloween may have developed specifically from the Irish celebration of Samhain and the Christian feasts superimposed over these pagan rituals, the spiritual significance of the beginning of winter was not limited to Ireland and the British Isles. Across the North Sea, in Scandinavia, pagans marked the transition from summer to winter as *vetrnætr*, Old Norse for "winter nights." The *vetrnætr* were the three days which begin the winter season,[18] and were observed at the end of October and beginning of November. Marking the beginning of winter at this time was based on the traditional understanding of the seasonal cycles as belonging to two seasons instead of four, with the *vetrnætr* considered the half-way point between the vernal equinox and the solstice.

The way that the ancient Norse split the seasons can be seen on the Swedish and Norwegian wooden runic calendar, the front half of which represents the winter period and the back half represents the summer. Marking special days like solstices and equinoxes, the winter half of the runic calendar starts on the Winter Nights at the beginning of November and continues through to May Day, which marks the beginning of the summer half of the year.[19] All three of these occasions—the beginning of winter, midwinter and the beginning of the summer season—were observed by offering sacrifices, with the winter cosmologically dominated by women, death and magic, and the summer ruled by men and defined by trade and war.

The Winter Nights were observed with rituals such as *álfablót* and *dísablót*, which were essentially sacrifices to the elves and to female spirits known as the *dísir*. The sacrifices were believed to help enhance the harvest, with one made at the beginning of winter for a good year and one in the middle of winter for a good crop. It is likely that the *álfablót* was part of the harvest feast, just as the *dísablót* was part of the Winter Nights feast, with *dísablót* performed as a public sacrifice and *álfablót* a private one held at individual homesteads for the local spirits. With strangers explicitly prohibited, the Winter Nights were centered on a feast to which friends and relations were invited, and it was common to also hold weddings at this time. The association of marriage rites with the Winter Nights may be related to the supposed powers of the *dísir* to promote fertility. Other customs associated with this occasion were gathering mistletoe and lighting bonfires.[20]

In his *Heimskringla*, Snorri Sturluson provides an account of the reign of King Haakon the Good, which includes a reference to a large-scale blood sacrifice that

This illustration depicts a dísablót, a ceremony that was held in honor of female deities called dísir in order to enhance the coming harvest. Artist Johan August Malmström.

took place in Hlaoir, near present-day Trondheim, at the time of the Winter Nights. Sturluson notes that "it was their tradition to hold a sacrifice in the autumn and celebrate the coming of winter, another in the middle of winter, and then a third in the summer to celebrate the coming of summer." These sacrifices were all eventually transferred to Christian feasts, and early Scandinavian law books confirm that King Haakon not only implemented the legally enforced brewing of ale at Christmas, but also applied the same principle to All Hallows Mass, mandating that ale was brewed during the Winter Nights.[21] Indeed, there are so many similarities between All Hallows Mass and Christmas, scholar Terry Gunnell has concluded that many of the characteristics of the Winter Nights festival seem to have been simply "moved" to the Christmas period.

As Gunnell observes, "we see the recurring idea of supernatural figures gradually moving in on settlements as Christmas approaches, even to the point of taking over the farm itself." At both the Winter Nights and the midwinter, Gunnell points out, the outdoors was considered charged with supernatural powers, with elves and trolls about, and the *disir* out riding horses during the Winter Nights similar to Odin's Wild Hunt at Yule. The fact that little occurred at Halloween in Scandinavia during the Middle Ages, as compared to the observances taking place in the British Isles, could be explained by the fact that many of the traditions associated with the Winter Nights were simply absorbed into the Yule celebration that took place a couple months after Halloween.[22] It is perhaps for this reason that Irish and Scottish immigrants settling in America are most often credited with launching the modern Halloween celebration, rather than Scandinavian immigrants.

* * *

Nevertheless, the parallels between the Viking and Celtic observances are striking. Both the Irish and Scandinavian pagans believed not only that the transition from summer to winter was a time of intense spiritual activity, but that sacrifices were in order to appease the gods, spirits and elves. It is also noteworthy that according to both belief systems, the festivals lasted for three days and the intensified spiritual activity beginning at Samhain in Ireland or the Winter Nights in Scandinavia continued throughout the season and reached a zenith at the winter solstice. The ancient Celts believed that Cailleach Bheur, or the Queen of Winter, would appear at Samhain and would rule until the onset of spring. Portrayed as a one-eyed old woman with bad teeth and matted hair, the hag is known as a bringer of storms, and the longest night of the year marked the height of her reign as Queen of Winter. Similarly, in Scandinavia, the Winter Nights marked the beginning of Odin's Wild Hunt. Starting in late October and lasting until the return of spring, the Wild Hunt was believed to be most active during the midwinter period when certain protective measures were taken to protect against Odin's army of the dead, including smudging rituals and the burning of juniper.

In both the Norse and Celtic belief systems, those who had died within the previous year made their transition to the next world during the period of midwinter which started at the beginning of November, and in both beliefs, the dead were known to visit at this time. The view that Samhain was a festival of the dead was popularized by James Frazer, who wrote in 1890 that "the night which marks the transition from autumn to winter" was also the time when the deceased would return "to

This image is from *Wonder tales from Scottish myth & legend*, published in 1917. The text in the book accompanying the illustration reads, "The aged Beira [Bheur] was fearsome to look upon. She had only one eye, but the sight of it was keen and sharp as ice and as swift as the mackerel of the ocean. Her complexion was a dull, dark blue, and this is how she sanor about it:—o Why is my face so dark, so dark? So dark, oho! so dark, ohee! Out in all weathers I wander alone In the mire, in the cold, ah me!" (Internet Archive).

warm themselves by the fire and to comfort themselves with the good cheer provided from them in the kitchen or the parlour by their affectionate kinfolk."[23]

In the Celtic tradition, which began with Samhain and was passed on to All Souls' Day and still recognized today in celebrations of the Day of the Dead, candles would be left burning for the visiting ghosts and in some cases, the living would sleep on the floor so that the dearly departed could have a comfy bed to sleep in. In Scandinavia, this practice may have been associated with the late autumn *álfablót* and *dísablót* observances, but later the custom was absorbed into Yule, and became a prevalent feature of the general Christmas celebration throughout Europe.[24]

These historical practices of honoring the dead at Christmas and Halloween indicate that the spiritual charge was common to both observances, which is likely related to the significance attached to the seasonal and solar changes taking place—with Christmas falling at the winter solstice and Halloween falling at the quarter day in between the equinox and the solstice. But while Halloween's supernatural charge might be attributable to Samhain and the pagan beliefs of the ancient Celts, most of its actual ritual practices were developed in relation to All Souls' and All Saints' Day, also known as All Hallows.

* * *

All Souls' and All Saints' Days developed in conjunction with each other from around the year 650 and, by the end of the 12th century, the linked festivals were well-established days on the Christian calendar. Sometimes called the Commemoration of All the Faithful Departed and the Day of the Dead, All Souls' Day is a day of prayer and remembrance for those who have died and is observed on November 2. The beginning of the season of darkness and cold was transformed by the Church into an opportunity to confront the fear of death and the corresponding Christian fear of damnation. Beginning with this solemn occasion of remembrance of the dead on All Souls' Day, the season would proceed to the fasting of Advent, with sedate anticipation of the coming of the lord, and finally would give way to the merriment of Christmas.[25]

During the Middle Ages, All Souls' and All Saints' Days were considered among the most important feast days, designated as one of the six days of obligation, alongside occasions such as Christmas and Ascension Day. Marked by high masses and prayers, its rituals were intended to prevent hauntings and to assist souls in purgatory. As night fell and All Souls' Day arrived, bells were rung for the souls being purified by purgatorial fire, as well as to keep away demons.[26] In England, the king dressed in purple velvet and his courtiers in black, the colors of mourning, to remember the dead.[27] It was also common to build bonfires in graveyards to ward off malevolent spirits. There are accounts of people setting a lighted lamp or candle and a meal on the table before they go to bed for the wandering spirits to enjoy. In Sicily, there was a belief that the family dead brought presents to children on All Sous' Eve, stealing toys and new clothes from rich shopkeepers and leaving them for good boys and girls.[28]

The jack-o'-lantern tradition of carving scary faces in pumpkins emerged from this Christianized version of Samhain, believed to have originated in the 17th century with a legend of a man known as Stingy Jack. Jack had foolishly played a number of tricks on the Devil, and when he eventually passed away, found out that God would not allow him into heaven and the Devil, still smarting from being tricked, would not allow him into hell. Jack was then sent off into the dark night with just a burning coal to light his way, which he placed into a carved-out turnip. Condemned to roam the Earth with this makeshift lantern, the Irish began referring to the ghost as "Jack of the Lantern," or, simply, "Jack O'Lantern." They started carving their own turnips and potatoes and placing them in windows and doors to keep away Stingy Jack and other wandering spirits. When immigrants brought the tradition with them to the United States, they discovered that pumpkins, a fruit native to America, make perfect jack-o'-lanterns, and began using those instead of turnips.[29]

While the jack-o'-lantern tradition may have emerged during the Christian era and incorporates Christian beliefs such as heaven, hell, God and the Devil, the spiritual basis for the legend seems to be rooted in Samhain. The legend of this ghostly apparition wandering the Earth at All Hallows Eve is not unlike earlier beliefs associated with Samhain—or the Scandinavian Winter Nights—about supernatural forces being abroad at this particular time of year. The practice of lighting a lantern to frighten off the ghost of Stingy Jack also has a number of similarities with practices at Christmas time that were once commonly performed to keep away evil spirits and witches around the winter solstice when the veil between our world and the spirit world was at its thinnest. Hanging mistletoe on the door, for example, was believed to keep away witches and juniper was burned to purge the home of ghosts and goblins,[30] while bonfires were historically lit at this time of year to frighten off demons. The traditional Christmas decoration of holly was also once used to thwart witches, with holly gathered on Christmas Day believed to be particularly effective in this regard. Frankincense and holy water were used to scare off Christmas goblins such as the kallikantzaros.[31] Although these customs are not precisely the same as placing a candle inside a carved pumpkin, the idea behind them are similar: by engaging in certain rituals, people felt that they were taking sensible precautions to protect their homes from evil forces and wandering spirits at a particularly uncanny time of year.

Another striking parallel between Christmas and Halloween is in the traditions of social inversion and misrule. Known in England as All Hallows Eve or Hallowtide, the eve of All Saints' Day inaugurated the season of mumming and misrule that characterized Christmas. An account from 1598 notes that the Lords of Misrule "begin their rule at Allhallond Eve, continued the same till the morrow after.... Candlemas Day,"[32] in other words from October 31 to February 3. During this time, choristers would become boy bishops, mock-mayors would replace urban leaders, and mummers decked with ribbons and bells would parade through towns and the churchyards "with such a confused noise that no man can heare his own voice," according to one contemporary named Philip Stubbs.[33] Much like the wassailers of Christmas time, these Hallowtide mummers demanded tributes from townspeople and those who refused were "mocked and flouted at shamefully ... and otherwise most horribly abused." Closely associated with the role reversals and social inversion practices that had been passed down to Christmas from Saturnalia, Hallowtide was, as Stubbs describes it, a time of "subtle disguisings, masks, and mummeries" in which a "Ground Capitaine of mischeef whom they innoble with the tide of my Lorde of Misserule" would engage in "Heathenerie, Devilrie," and "Drunkennesse."[34]

The similarities with Christmas misrule has not been lost on historians. As Stephen Nissenbaum points out in *The Battle for Christmas*, the way that Christmas was once observed, with aggressive wassailing and home invasions, was "like Halloween today—when, for a single evening, children assume the right to enter houses of neighbors and even strangers, to demand of their elders a gift (or 'treat') and to threaten them, should they fail to provide one, with a punishment (or 'trick')."[35] Although this sort of trick-or-treat ritual is largely non-existent at Christmas today, it was once quite common, with wassailers issuing explicit threats if they weren't given something by the owners of the homes they were invading. One surviving wassail song contains a warning of what would happen if their demands were not met: "We've come here to claim our right ... / And if you don't open up your door, / We will lay you flat upon the floor."[36]

At Halloween, the threat of violence or other reprisals for those who refused to provide a "treat" was quite real, and the public menace posed by Halloween revelers was once considered so acute that some cities took steps to ban the holiday. In the 19th century, common Halloween tricks included relatively harmless pranks such as tipping over outhouses, placing wagons and livestock on barn roofs, uprooting vegetables in backyard gardens, and opening gates to allow livestock to escape. This latter prank was so common that October 31 became known as "Gate Night." But pranks grew increasingly dangerous and sometimes devolved into violence, leading to a newspaper in 1902 advising residents of Arlington Heights, Illinois, to "load their muskets or cannon with rock, salt or bird shot and when trespassers invade your premises at unseemly hours upon mischief bent, pepper them good and proper so

In this promotional poster for a "Halloween Roller Skating Carnival," young people are invited to bring their skates and told that prizes will be given for costumes. It was common in the 1930s for cities and municipalities to organize community events on Halloween as a way to keep kids out of trouble. "Halloween Roller Skating Carnival" poster. New York, 1936, Federal Art Project (Library of Congress).

they will be effectually cured and have no further taste for such tricks." Elsewhere, people fought back with live rounds instead, with a prankster in Tucson, Arizona, for instance shot dead in 1907 after tripping a pedestrian with a wire. During the Great Depression of the 1930s, malicious violence and looting came to be such a widespread problem at Halloween that religious authorities and community organizations decided to organize parties, carnivals and parades on Halloween in an effort to keep kids out of trouble.[37]

* * *

Not surprisingly, the Puritans of early New England despised Halloween—the only question is whether it or Christmas was detested more. Increase Mather called it an "abominable shame" that anyone would celebrate "so vile a piece of heathenism." He approved of the general ban on saints' days and considered Halloween to be an unnecessary concession to the antichrist.[38] While Christmas was disparaged by the Puritans as simply a holdover of pagan holidays that distracted Christians from the work of personal salvation and dishonored Christ with its debaucheries, Halloween was viewed as downright evil. The Devil has long been seen as being intimately involved with the Halloween revelries, believed to personally lead witches on this unholy night in orgiastic frenzies. There are many accounts of the Devil dancing with witches on Halloween night, including a case in 1597 which resulted in a Scot named Thomas Leyis being burned alive. Leyis was accused of being guided by the Devil on Halloween night in "playing before them on his kind of instruments, when they all danced about."[39] Many fortune-telling charms were also performed on Halloween in the name of the Devil, who was seen as the consort and leader of the witches.

While the opposition of devout Christians to Christmas has by and large subsided in the modern era (or been redirected into complaints about the "secularization" of a "sacred" holiday) Christian opposition to Halloween has largely continued unabated. Many Christians vocally object to this holiday, which is seen as pagan at best and satanic at worst. In the 1980s, fundamentalist Christian groups began referring to Halloween as "the Devil's birthday," and many evangelicals took it upon themselves to root out Satan from popular culture, including by attacking heavy metal music and the celebration of Halloween. Christians that would deny the pagan influences over Christmas continue today to cite Halloween's roots in paganism. An article at *ChristianAnswers.net*, for example, argues that Halloween is "closely connected with worship of the Enemy of this world, Satan" and is "a holiday that generally glorifies the dark things of this world, rather than the light of Jesus Christ, The Truth."[40]

More moderate voices within Christianity try to find a middle ground, recognizing that Halloween has become a beloved tradition and not wishing to alienate millions of people who enjoy the holiday, but simultaneously attempting to emphasize the supposed Christian aspects of the tradition. The Roman Catholic Church, for instance, actively encourages acts of piety associated with All Saints' Day, but keeps a distance from the revelries of October 31. A group of French bishops severely condemned the manifestations of Halloween, claiming they undermined the dignity and respect owed to the Communion of Saints.[41] Similarly, an American bishop in 2018 stressed that it is important to recall the "the Catholic meaning and purpose of all holy days," noting that "the cultural customs surrounding Halloween have nonetheless drifted from the feast's intended meaning and purpose." Catholics should "intentionally avoid those things that are contrary to our Catholic faith but have become popularized through the secular adaptation of Halloween," said Bishop David Konderla. "Turning to the Catechism of the Catholic Church, we want to refrain from glamourizing or celebrating anything involving superstition, witches, witchcraft, sorcery, divinations, magic, and the occult."[42]

The problem, of course, is that these concepts are at the very core of Halloween. While some Christians to this day continue to claim that the holiday has no pagan origins whatsoever, the historical context in which Halloween developed is fairly clear: a Christian feast was imposed on a longstanding pagan ritual as part of the Church's policy—as stated by Pope Gregory II in 601—to neutralize heathen sacrificial feasts by turning them into Christian festivals. Much like Christmas, however, Halloween has by and large lost its spiritual aspects and is generally celebrated as a secular affair, even though its origins are anything but.

14

From Pagan to Secular

So now is come our joyful feast,
Let every man be jolly;
Each room with ivy leaves is dressed,
And every post with holly.
Though some churls at our mirth repine,
Round your foreheads garlands twine,
Drown sorrow in a cup of wine,
And let us all be merry.
—George Wither, "A Christmas Carol"

Calls for remembering the true "reason for the season" sometimes seem as ubiquitous in December as Wham's 1985 hit "Last Christmas." Evangelicals often lament the "secularization" of the holiday and yearn for a return to a time that it was celebrated sedately and piously, with Jesus Christ's nativity at the forefront of our thoughts. They tend to rue the central role played by Santa Claus, concerned that he has usurped Jesus as the holiday's focal point, and decry the crass commercialism that seems to have taken the place of reverence and worship during this holy time.

"With the lights, trees and presents, as well as the myriad of familial commitments, it is easy to lose track of what is really important this Christmas season: the birth of Jesus," laments a Christian blogger in a typical grievance. "Remember the Truth and importance of what the Nativity means and why this meaning must be preserved. After all, that's what Christmas is really all about."[1] Another blogger urges people to enjoy the gift-giving and other simple pleasures of Christmas, but argues that they should also remember that all of the festivities are rooted in the celebration birth of Jesus. "The reason for this season of celebration is, always has been, and will be forevermore, that Jesus came to save his people from their sins," he writes. "God became a man; he became the savior of sinners so these sinners could by faith become the children of God and inherit eternal blessings all for the glory of God."[2]

The insistence of many Christians on emphasizing Jesus's nativity and expressing discontent over the perceived secularization of the holiday is sometimes made visible with billboards dotting highways at Christmas time declaring that "Jesus Is the Only Reason for the Season" or reminding us to "Keep Christ in Christmas." In the age of social media, this messaging has gone virtual with memes cropping up in December utilizing hashtags such as #HappyBirthdayBabyJesus. Some social media users will drive the point home by declaring "Merry CHRISTmas" in their posts, just in case it wasn't already obvious that the word "Christ" was featured in the

Photograph of billboard proclaiming "Keep Christ in Christmas" in New Jersey. December 20, 2005 (Jackie "Sister72" Flickr user, no changes made, CC BY-ND 2.0, https://www.flickr.com/photos/sis/75748104/in/album-1360972/).

name of the holiday. The tone that some religious celebrants take indicate a level of hostility and disdain for how people have seemingly forgotten why we are observing the holiday, with public opinion polls confirming that there is a common perception that religious aspects of Christmas are emphasized less today than they were in the past. Some 56 percent of Americans say that they have noticed a decline of outward displays of Christmas's Christian character in the public sphere, according to a Pew survey, with about 30 percent saying they are bothered by this trend.[3]

What these views indicate is an apparently widespread assumption that Christmas was at one time a far more "Christian" occasion, and that it is only relatively recently that it began to lose its focus as a celebration of Jesus's birth. People seem to believe that anti–Christian secularists are systematically dismantling what was once a sedate religious occasion marked by pious observances of Christ's nativity. As we have seen, however, the idea that there was previously a time that Christmas was a purely religious affair is simply not based in historical reality, and therefore the longing for a simpler, more reverent observance of Christmas is very much based on an illusion. The fact is, this holiday, which supplanted pagan observances of the winter solstice and ancient Roman feasts celebrating Saturn and Sol, has always been a syncretic blend of pagan and Christian customs and was never truly the pure and pious Christian feast that evangelicals might imagine. From the raucous displays of rioting and wassailing to arcane traditions steeped in magical beliefs, references abound in the historical record providing ample evidence that the pagan influences have always been at least as strong as the Christian influences, often to the chagrin of religious leaders over the centuries.

Indeed, while people today might dispute Christmas's pagan roots and insist that it is a quintessential Christian holiday based on well-grounded religious doctrines and legitimate beliefs about the birth of Christ taking place on December 25, the heathen origins of the holiday were widely understood even as it was becoming accepted as both a religious and secular celebration in 19th-century America. An 1839 report on Christmas Eve in Texas, for example, remarked that "the way the votaries of that jolly god Bacchus are 'humping' it is curious," in a reference to the Roman god of agriculture, wine and fertility.[4] *Harper's Monthly* published an article by O.M. Spencer in 1872—two years after Christmas was declared a national holiday in the United States—which noted that the "decoration and illumination of our Christian churches recall the temples of Saturn radiant with burning tapers and resplendent with garlands," and detailed many of Christmas's pagan elements, including "its mirth and festivity, its jesting and feasting, its frolic and license."[5] Likewise, in 1891, lawyer and orator Robert Green Ingersoll wrote a widely circulated article for *The Evening Telegram* which stated that "the good part of Christmas is not always Christian—it is generally Pagan; that is to say, human, natural." He noted matter-of-factly that it "may have done some good by borrowing from the Pagan world the old festival called Christmas."[6] Two decades later, an article in *The Leon Reporter* pointed out that "the conflict of Christianity with heathenism" often played out at Christmas time, "which happened to correspond with the Yuletide festival at the time of the winter solstice."[7]

These casual mentions of the holiday's pagan influences indicate that in the not-too-distant past, Christmas was understood to be rooted in heathen traditions and was appreciated as much as a secular occasion as it was a religious occasion. And while the complaints from evangelicals today may give the impression that Christmas has only recently begun to lose its Christian character, it seems, on the contrary, that this trend has existed for quite some time. The assumption is that the Christian Christmas was corrupted by the pernicious influences of modernity, secularism and

Believed to be the first-ever commercially printed Christmas card, the greeting shows an image of revelers feasting and drinking wine. Vintage greetings card, 1843. Artist John Callcott Horsley.

commercialism, but in fact, it appears that it might be the other way around: religiosity in general and the Christian character of Christmas in particular were given a boost in the modern era, with many people seeking solace from the sweeping changes in society by recalling a Godlier time based on a chimerical view of the past.

The evolution of Christmas cards, which grew in popularity in the mid–19th century, is instructive in this regard. The general lack of religious devotion at Christmas time was evident in early representations of Christmas cards, with later iterations adopting more overtly religious imagery. Indeed, the very first Christmas card, designed by John Callcott Horsley in 1843, featured not scenes of the nativity or the three magi but a feast with plentiful food and drink. In fact, the card caused a bit of a scandal in Victorian England because it depicted children drinking alcohol. With a caption that reads "A Merry Christmas and a Happy New Year to You," the picture features several family members holding glasses of wine with a young child (aided by a relative) taking a large gulp.[8]

This trend of emphasizing Christmas's non–Christian aspects in Christmas cards continued through the 19th century. As one historian discovered after cataloguing a collection of more than 100,000 cards printed before 1890, most showed images of holly, mistletoe, Christmas pudding, Santa Claus, Christmas trees, bells, robins, food, and festivity. Only occasionally would one of these cards contain a religious element, usually a church as part of a snowy wintry landscape,[9] and many cards were downright bizarre. Eccentric Victorians of the 19th century enjoyed artwork depicting anthropomorphized animals and insects performing strange activities, such as one popular design featuring an army of black ants attacking an army of red ants with a small caption reading, "The compliments of the season." Mice riding lobsters, dancing frogs, creepy clowns, and roosters biting turtles were rather typical subjects for Christmas cards printed in the late 1800s and early 1900s.[10] Only later would religious elements grow more prominent.

In Christmas cards from 1900 to 1960, the theme of the three magi began to appear more frequently, particularly starting in the 1910s, with depictions of the wise men riding camels on their way to Bethlehem or kneeling down offering gifts to the infant Jesus.[11] In explaining the rising popularity of this quintessential Christian-themed card, historian Kenneth Ames points out that the early 20th century was a period of "rapid modernization accompanied by often highly disruptive and unsettling change." As an "age of anxieties," with "[a]nti-modern sentiments, fears of dissolution of community, weakening of emotional bonds, and the lessening of meaning in modern life," there were general "yearnings for 'authentic' experience," which expressed itself in a revival of both Christian piety and interest in "the Orient," both of which were satisfied with the magi-themed Christmas cards.[12] Overall though, these magi images remained a distinct minority, with most Christmas cards from the 20th century featuring secular and domestic motifs such as family gatherings, Christmas trees, Santa Claus, Christmas carolers, holly, and candles.

Church attendance also belies the notion that there was a time when society was far more devout and celebrated Christmas more reverently, only to be corrupted by secularists pushing an anti–Christian agenda. A census of religious attendance in England in 1851 determined that only between a third and half of the population attended church on any given Sunday. Similarly, in the United States, a 1939 survey found that 43 percent of Americans claimed to attend church regularly, which is

A typically bizarre Christmas card from the late 19th century. Depicting a rooster that is biting a turtle that is biting a duck, the greeting reads, "A hearty Christmas to you all! May good digestion wait on appetite" (The New York Public Library, Miriam and Ira D. Wallach Division of Art, Prints and Photographs: Picture Collection).

almost certainly inflated.[13] While church attendance may have increased at times like Easter and Advent, ironically, it was in many ways the attempts of fundamentalists such as the Puritans and Calvinists to suppress the largely pagan custom of Christmas that ensured its evolution into a more secular tradition. By prohibiting observances of Christmas within churches during their anti–Christmas crusades during the 16th and 17th centuries, the reformers forced Christmas enthusiasts to observe the holiday at home and in taverns where they drank and made merry behind closed doors, which further undermined the ecclesiastical elements of the feast and ensured that the day became even more secular.[14]

* * *

Some aspects of Christmas that are seen as "secular," however, are actually not exactly secular based on the true meaning of the word. Defined as "of or relating to worldly things or to things that are not regarded as religious, spiritual, or sacred,"[15] the word "secular" does not strictly apply to these customs, at least not with a deeper understanding of their origins and meaning. Many of these origins are well known and have been understood for hundreds of years. Others are less recognized, due largely to the loss of knowledge of ancient beliefs that has taken place over the passage of time, or, in some cases, due to the suppression of paganism and its offshoot witchcraft in the late Middle Ages and early modern period.

14. From Pagan to Secular

While the early Church had been grudgingly tolerant of magic, with missionaries and reformers working to absorb elements of paganism between the sixth and the ninth centuries by instilling old rites and customs with ecclesiastical meanings, as time went on, the space for this tolerance continuously shrank. Paganism was suppressed with laws that royal officials and especially bishops were expected to enforce. Charlemagne the Great, for example, had sought to root out paganism in conquered areas of Saxony in modern-day Germany through a 786 law that prohibited the worship of pagan gods. This was accompanied by forced conversions and with harsh punishments for those who refused to convert or who after conversion resisted such Christian practices as tithing.[16]

The Christianization of Europe continued along this increasingly draconian path. It may have started benignly enough, with compromises made between Christians and pagans to allow for the worship of pagan gods and the continuation of certain customs, but in the early 10th century, a ruling of the Church known as *Canon Episcopi* declared that everything in the universe blossomed from divine providence and that those who denied God by definition were adherents to Satan, doomed to damnation and having no place in a Christian society. Witchcraft and magic became increasingly linked with heresy, and practitioners were ostracized as epitomes of

This 17th-century engraving portrays a bare-breasted witch concocting an evil brew in the company of strange beasts. She stands within a "magic circle" scratched into the ground, pouring a horn into cauldron. Two streams of ash spew forth from pipes held in the anus of a flipping demon at left. "The Witch (Night Piece)," 1626. Artist Jan van de Velde (Cleveland Museum of Art, Mr. and Mrs. Lewis B. Williams Collection).

wickedness. As Jacob Grimm described Christianization in *Teutonic Mythology*, it entailed "the gradual transformation of the gods into devils, of the wise women into witches, of the worship into superstitious customs." Heathen myths from goddesses and gods were transferred to Mary and the saints, from elves to angels, and "heathen festivals and customs were transformed into Christian," Grimm observed.[17]

By the late Middle Ages, and particularly following the Reformation, a new era of persecution and repression had begun. Because Christians considered God and Satan polar opposites, those who recognized non–Christian gods were seen as effectively in league with the Devil. The integrity of Christendom and the honor of Christ had to be defended against threats that seemed quite real, which meant that witchcraft—largely a holdover from pagan beliefs—came to be seen as manifestly evil and was treated accordingly.

This growing intolerance culminated in a wave of mass executions of suspected witches, reaching a frenzied height from 1450 to 1750, when an estimated 50,000 people—the vast majority women—were executed, mostly by being burned at the stake.[18] Witch panics started to spread across Europe, with the largest witch trials taking place in Trier (1581–1593), Fulda (1603–1606), Bamberg (1626–1631), and Würzburg (1626–1631). Many were killed on the flimsiest of suspicions and following unfair trials where torture was used routinely. A common practice was to fasten suspected witches in a contraption known as a ducking stool which was used to submerge them under water—if they didn't drown, they were deemed to be witches and summarily executed, typically by being burned alive.[19] A common site during this period was to see forests of blackened stakes, a grim testament to the hysteria gripping much of Europe.

In early 1621 a witch trial took place in Vardø, Norway, that provided a glimpse of how pagan and Christian beliefs could intersect in peculiar ways at Christmas time. Following an interrogation under torture, a woman named Mari Jørgensdatter claimed that Satan came to visit her on Christmas Eve 1620, and together with her neighbor Kirsti Sørensdatter, the group flew to a Christmas party near the city of Bergen, about a thousand miles away. On the top of Lydhorn mountain the Devil's Christmas party was celebrated with dancing and drinking. Mari also claimed that witches had been responsible for a great storm on Christmas three years earlier, in 1617. Another woman corroborated Mari's story, claiming that at Christmas 1617, witches had tied a fishing rope three times, spat at it and untied it, after which "the sea rose like ashes and people were killed." Many of the women pointed to Kirsti Sørensdatter as the ringleader of the witches. After these confessions, Kirsti was arrested, interrogated and sentenced to be burned at the stake along with ten other accused witches.[20]

Another case, from Devon, England, demonstrates how a simple disagreement between neighbors could result in a charge of witchcraft. As Sarah Byrd testified in court, a poor villager named Dorothy East had visited her on Christmas 1692 begging for alms, but Sarah declined. Dorothy, "in a discontented manner," said that it would have been better for Sarah if she had given her something. Then a few days later, Sarah's husband "had very ill fortune with his Cattle," leading Sarah to believe that Dorothy "might [have done] them some mischief."[21] It is unclear from the historical record whether Dorothy East was convicted and put to death, but the incident underlines that even acting strangely or suspiciously, as Dorothy had when she was refused a Christmas donation, was enough to be put on trial. At a time when a simple accusation could get someone arrested and tortured into a confession, those who may have dabbled in the black arts consequently kept their activities increasingly covert.

During this period of religious zealotry and persecution of suspected witches, many seemingly innocuous practices, such as eating roast beef, plum pudding or mince pies for Christmas, were denounced as "carnal abominations"[22] and became associated with paganism. As the poet John Taylor bitterly complained in his *Christmas In and Out*, published in 1652, to the anti–Christmas extremists of his time, "Plumb-Pottage was meer Popery, that a Coller of Brawn was an obhomination, that Roast Beef was Antichristian, that Mince-Pies were Reliques of the Whore of Babylon, and a Goose, a Turkey, or a Capon, were marks of the Beast."[23]

Consequently, many customs that were pagan in origin were either suppressed, baptized as "Christian," or relegated to being "secular," even if the concept didn't truly apply. Due to the growing need for secrecy, many of the practices that once had a basis in pagan beliefs became stripped of their meaning and took on the appearance of being secular, even though the origins were anything but. For example, the decorating of Christmas trees, as we have seen, while not specifically religious, in fact harkens back to very ancient and deeply spiritual customs practiced by pre–Christian peoples who venerated trees. The same goes for the use of bells, which were once considered endowed with magical powers, and Santa Claus, who is largely considered a secular figure today but in fact may have origins in pagan gods such as Odin and Thor, not to mention St. Nicholas, who seems to be a Christian representation of the Greek god Poseidon. Regardless of his specific origin, which is shrouded in myth, Santa can be seen in reality as a modern-day representation of a god and is therefore not a secular figure in the strict sense of the word.

Even Christmas presents, which could today be considered among the secular, materialist aspects of Christmas, were once considered portents for ensuring plentitude in the coming year. The practice of gift exchange had a basis in magical beliefs which were described by a monk writing around the year 1400. Alsso of Brevnov complained that gifts were given at Christmas time not in the spirit of God's gift to mankind, but because those who do not offer gifts will be unlucky in the coming year. Money, he said, instead of being given to the poor, is laid on the table to augur wealth, and people open their purses so that luck and good fortune may enter. Alsso lamented that instead of using fruit as a symbol of Christ, people used it to predict the future. While his assumption was that the way that these practices were carried out was a perversion of Catholic sacraments, it is possible in fact that he had it backwards: these were pagan customs that had been given a veneer of ecclesiastical symbolism, over time taking on the appearance of being secular.[24]

Eating in abundance at Christmas may also have roots in pre–Christian beliefs, associated in pagan times with religious rejoicing and communion with their deities. The pagan feast ordinarily would involve a sacrific and consuming the flesh of an animal was done in the belief that they were feasting together with the gods. "When men meet their god they feast and are glad together, and whenever they feast and are glad they desire that the god should be of the party," explains William Robertson Smith in *Lectures on the Religion of the Semites*. This view was based on the conviction that "they and the deity they adore are good friends, who understand each other perfectly and are united by bonds not easily broken."[25] Because they were in communion with gods during feasts such as Yule, it was important to eat and drink plentifully and offer many toasts, as well as make solemn oaths. This was the religious basis of feasting before Christianization and explains why Pope Gregory the Great in the early seventh century so strongly emphasized the importance of transforming such pagan sacrifices and feasts into eating meat in the "praise of God" and in "thanks to the Giver of all for their abundance."[26]

* * *

It is also clear that what some modern-day Christians may now think of as a religious aspect of Christmas, for example the singing of certain Christmas carols, had previously been considered secular and may have had pagan origins. Rooted in the tradition of wassailing, in which revelers went door to door drinking to the health of their neighbors and expressing goodwill to their social betters in exchange for gifts, the practice appears to date back to pre–Christian fertility rites when villagers sang and shouted to drive away any spirits that might inhibit the growth of crops. Caroling wasn't done in churches until much later—in some cases apparently as a way to provide an alternative to the popular practice of drinking and singing in pubs.[27] In the 18th and 19th centuries antiquarians started collecting these folk songs and touching them up, sometimes attempting to infuse them with deeper biblical meaning, with the versions constantly changing. The many variations of these songs make tracing their origins difficult, but it appears that at least some carols were adapted from pre–Christian songs. The melodies of folk tunes were repurposed for praise, which could be why they don't make a lot of sense when you think about them.

The song "I Saw Three Ships," for example, has a reference to ships sailing into Bethlehem, but the nearest body of water is the Dead Sea about 20 miles away. While some have tried to explain the ships as a metaphor for the camels that the three magi were presumably riding through the desert or claim that the original lyrics referred to three ships taking the supposed skulls of the wise men to Cologne cathedral in Germany, ultimately no one really knows the origins of the lyrics. The words were likely written by wandering minstrels as they traveled through England and were adapted to give them a stronger religious meaning, which is hinted at by the different variations of what the three ships are carrying. In one version "Our Saviour Christ and his lady" is in the ships, while in another version it is "Joseph and his lady." In yet another version it is "three pretty girls" that are in the ships.[28]

The popular Christmas hymn "What Child is This" is also an adaptation of a pre-existing folk song with possible pagan connotations, called "Greensleeves."[29] A traditional English tune that has been in circulation since 1580, "Greensleeves" appears to be about a man who is infatuated with a promiscuous young woman, perhaps a prostitute. "May good fortune prosper thee," goes one of the many versions of the song, "For I am still thy lover true / Oh, come once again and love me." Another version starts with the lines

> Alas my love you do me wrong
> To cast me off discourteously;
> And I have loved you oh so long
> Delighting in your company.

In 1865, the suggestive lyrics of "Greensleeves" were replaced with

What child is this, who, laid to rest
On Mary's lap is sleeping?
Whom angels greet with anthems sweet
While shepherds watch are keeping?

"The Holly and the Ivy" is another carol likely originating in pre–Christian times, with some versions containing religious elements but others that are just about holly and ivy, and elements of nature such as the rising sun and running deer. The song reflects on the nature of the world and humans' place within it, with holly and ivy representing the male and the female. Its lyrics found in hymn books juxtapose the nativity with "the holly bear[ing] a blossom as white as lily flower," stressing that "Mary bore sweet Jesus Christ to do poor sinners good,"[30] but other versions emphasize the "Shining Moon" and "the weary, worn Hunter" instead.[31]

Despite the deeper origins of Christmas carols, when folklorists began collecting these songs and compiling them in publications, they often glossed over their pagan, folk and secular history. William Hone's *Every-Day Book* presented Christmas carols as something that readers would be entirely unfamiliar with and explained their origins as church-based. "Anciently," he wrote, "bishops carolled at Christmas amongst their clergy." R.R. Chope's 1894 *Carols for the Use in Church* claimed to "restore" carols to use in "divine service." He claimed that carols had been "commonly sung in churches" in earlier times, ignoring the fact that they had long been seen as generally secular in nature,[32] and that at one time churches actually frowned upon them. In the introduction to Chope's collection, S. Baring-Gould claimed that "the first carols" were sung at the praesepio, or crib displays at churches. "There may have been stray Christmas hymns in the vernacular before," Baring-Gould wrote, "but it was not till the Christmas crib was set up in Minorite chapels, and from thence spread to all Christian churches, that they burst forth throughout the length and breadth of Western Christendom."[33] This narrative however downplays the secular nature of carols and obscures their possible pagan origins.

* * *

The development of Christmas as a secular affair was given a boost by a man who is sometimes credited with "inventing" the modern holiday—not a Church figure but an author and renowned social critic motivated more by a hatred of poverty than by religious convictions. Often struggling financially himself, Charles Dickens wrote stories that reflected the reality of life as he had experienced it in Victorian England. Born in 1812, he left school as a boy to work in a factory after his father fell ill and was sent to a debtors' prison, providing the young Dickens an early lesson in some of the shortcomings and injustices of unfettered capitalism. At the age of 12, he was working ten hours a day in a shoe-blacking warehouse.

Later in life he travelled to America to campaign against slavery and toured some English mines where he was mortified by the miserable conditions under which children were forced to work.[34] Early in 1843, Dickens read a parliamentary report about children in the workforce, which contained testimony from young laborers about their long days, low wages, and dangerous working conditions. Later that year, he visited schools for the poor in the slums, known as "ragged schools" due to the torn and tattered clothes of many attendees, where he encountered children who lived as thieves and prostitutes to survive.[35] He was so appalled that he resolved to do whatever was in his power to bring attention to the reality of life for these young victims of the Industrial Revolution and decided that the most effective way that he could deliver "something that would come down with sledgehammer force," as he promised in a speech to a charity in Manchester, was to write a short story "that would strike the heaviest blow in my power."[36] He published *A Christmas Carol* shortly thereafter.

With a focus on social justice and goodwill, *A Christmas Carol* is arguably more humanitarian in nature than it is religious. Dickens emphasizes the importance of Christmas as a family occasion, providing an opportunity for loved ones to enjoy a good meal and play games together, but also stresses the need for society to transform in order to provide a basic quality of life for the lower classes. By giving a raise to his employee Bob Cratchit at the end of the story and ensuring that his ailing son Tiny Tim receives the health care that he needs to survive, the transformation of Scrooge is symbolic of the transformation needed of the entire economic system.

Religion is not entirely absent from *A Christmas Carol*, with an appeal in the story to the "Christian cheer of mind" and passing references to God as well as the three Wise Men, but for the most part the story is generally secular. Despite Dickens' own Christian beliefs, *A Christmas Carol* avoids religious themes and focuses on practical social issues instead. The story hit a raw nerve in Victorian society and drew immediate praise from social reformers, with Lord Francis Jeffrey saying that Dickens had "done more good by this little publication, fostered more kindly feelings, and prompted more positive acts of benevolence, than can be traced to all the pulpits and confessionals in Christendom."[37]

Following the Judeo-Christian tradition of tithing, in which giving is intended to be a joy and a blessing, *A Christmas Carol* fed into a growing desire in society for streamlining charity, which provided an impetus of developing a system of supporting the destitute through institutions such as the Salvation Army. The "Christmas box," a package containing cash and gifts that had previously been handed out personally by the well-to-do on Boxing Day, was gradually replaced by seasonal donations and Christmas charities that provided for the genuinely needy. Sometimes these charities were church-based and sometimes they were secular. In New York City, as Stephen Nissenbaum points out, the major charitable institutions fell into two categories: municipal agencies and arms of the city's churches, with several church missions becoming quasi-autonomous operations.[38]

Responding to the growing enthusiasm of their parishioners to engage in charitable giving at Christmas time, some Christian denominations began lifting their long-held objections to the celebration of Christmas. Despite their reservations about a holiday that was pagan in origin and couldn't be found anywhere in Scripture, church leaders yielded to this popular demand for Christmas largely based on the holiday's humanitarian impulses which were attractive to many Christians. As Christmas grew in popularity, it drew on both secular humanitarianism and the traditional beneficence of Christianity. Central to this development were practices that sometimes resembled ancient Roman customs when masters and slaves exchanged places, and the wealthy paid rent for the destitute. At a Christmas dinner served to "1,500 hoboes" in 1913, for example, at the St. Louis House of Delegates, the aldermen served as waiters and busboys who waited on the down-and-out diners in an echo of the social inversion practices of Saturnalia.[39]

Other holdover traditions from Saturnalia might include the tradition of granting pardons at Christmas time, which follows the ancient Roman custom of releasing prisoners and slaves,[40] and ensuring that no criminals could be convicted during Saturnalia festivities. This practice appears to date back to even earlier times, stemming from a tradition of prisoner release during ancient Greek celebrations such as the festival of Dionysus known as the Dionysia.[41] Similarly, secular leaders in modern times have issued high-profile pardons at Christmas in the spirit of humanitarianism and reconciliation. On December 25, 1868, for example, President Andrew Johnson pardoned all former Confederate soldiers who had taken up arms against the United States in the American Civil War. "To secure permanent peace, order, and prosperity throughout the land, and to renew and fully restore confidence and fraternal feeling among the whole people," Johnson declared "a full pardon and amnesty for the offense of treason against the United States."[42] Following in this tradition, nearly a century later, General Douglas MacArthur granted a Christmas amnesty to Japanese war leaders in December 1949.

* * *

Closely linked with secularism, commercialism has been blamed for corrupting the religious aspects of Christmas, but while it is true that heavy-handed marketing practices have come to dominate much of the holiday period, what many see as the excessive materialism of Christmas can serve an important function to enable loved ones to express their appreciation for each other when words simply don't do the trick. As writer Harlan Miller once put it, "the reason we all go so haywire at Christmas time with the endless unrestrained and often silly buying of gifts is that we don't quite know how to put our love into words." This inability to fully express our affection for each other is what marketers often appeal to when pitching their products, sometimes quite explicitly. Love and generosity are likened to an almost mystical "spirit of Christmas," which shoppers can experience when they open their purses and put selflessness ahead of frugality. A 1934 newspaper ad, for example, depicted a goddess-like being blessing shoppers with a wand to infuse them with "the magic touch of Christmas." She claims that through the centuries she has brought to mankind the supreme joy of generosity by awakening the spirit of giving. "Where the merry gift-laden shoppers throng, there I am," the ad reads. "By me the thoroughfares of business are transformed into avenues of Remembrance."[43]

Commercialism has also had an enduring and positive impact on Christmas by contributing some of the most iconic and beloved themes and characters, such as Rudolph the Red-Nosed Reindeer who joined Clement C. Moore's team of eight reindeer in 1939. That year, the retail chain Montgomery Ward mass-produced a pamphlet for its customers' children that introduced Rudolph as the ninth reindeer, ostracized by his companions for his unusual nose, which was "red as a beet" and "twice as bright," until Santa recruited the misfit to help guide his sleigh. Written by Robert Lewis May, the underdog story resonated widely in Great Depression-struck America, and Maxton Books published the first mass-market edition of the story in 1947. In 1949, May's brother-in-law Johnny Marks set Rudolph's story to music. Singing cowboy Gene Autry recorded the song, which went on to become one of the best-selling tunes of all time.[44] The Rudolph story was later adapted as a stop-motion animation film and became an integral part of

This Great Depression–era newspaper advertisement reads, "I awake the Spirit of Giving. The very first Christmas knew me! And down the centuries I have brought to mankind the supreme joy. For mine is the gladness of unselfish giving. Where the merry gift-laden shoppers throng, there I am. By me the thoroughfares of business are transformed into an avenue of Remembrance. I have a share in every Christmas surprise. I help to safeguard every bursting Christmas secret. By my magic touch the Christmas garlands are hung ... the Christmas tree is decked ... the Christmas stockings are filled. I am measured not by the purse but by the heart ... not by the gift but by the giver. I am the Spirit of Christmas!" Advertisement in *The Indianapolis Times*, December 20, 1934 (Library of Congress).

the overall Christmas tradition, thanks entirely to a marketing ploy by a department store chain.

We can also thank commercialism, and particularly the Coca-Cola Company, for popularizing the jolly and personable version of Santa Claus that we know today through an advertising campaign the company launched in 1931.[45] By the early 20th century, Santa had become, according to one American magazine, "our biggest captain of industry,"[46] and Coca-Cola saw his strong potential for selling soda. While the beverage company did not invent Santa, as is often falsely claimed, it certainly helped develop his persona as a smiling, kind, red-suited, pleasantly plump, white-bearded man—rather than the spooky little elf that he had been previously depicted as. Haddon Sundblom's series of paintings for Coca-Cola from 1931 to 1964 cemented his image with depictions of Santa delivering toys, warming his feet by the fire, relaxing in an easy chair, reading letters left by children, and getting busted by kids as he raids refrigerators.

By mid-century, Santa had become a fixture at shopping centers and department stores, providing parents an opportunity to have their children's photos taken at displays such as Santa's Grotto or House of Santa while doing some Christmas shopping. Although the crass commercialism of connecting a gift-giving, miracle-performing saint with merchandising may have been distasteful to some devout Christians, the growing trend of Christmas as a child-centered, family-friendly occasion—as opposed to the unruly period of misrule that it had been in earlier times—surely could be seen as an improvement from a religious perspective.

And while some have criticized Santa's role in the commercialization of Christmas throughout the years, even from an evangelical point of view he plays an important part. Sure, Christmas has become a commercial bonanza and advertisers love to use Santa's imagery in selling products, but if it wasn't for Santa, marketers would likely use some other icon in their marketing campaigns. With this in mind, it is probably better for Santa to push products like Coke than Jesus or even the ecclesiastical version of St. Nicholas. By providing a separate space for secularism and marketing, Santa helps keep the religious space free of the corrupting influence of commercialism.

Furthermore, it is primarily due to aggressive marketing practices that Christmas became a month-long midwinter celebration rather than a stand-alone day at the end of December. In the early American practice of celebrating the holiday, its duration was limited to just a day or two, but under the weight of commercial forces that exploited the festival for merchandising purposes, Christmas regained its seasonal character as a midwinter festival—generally starting from Thanksgiving and ending at New Year's Day, or for some celebrants, on Epiphany Day on January 6.[47] Thanks largely to marketing, Christmas became linked with adjacent holidays and became "the Christmas season" rather than just Christmas Day. While some may lament Christmas displays appearing in stores seemingly earlier and earlier every year, most of us seem to enjoy on some level the weeks of that warm, fuzzy Christmas feeling that characterize the month of December—thanks largely to marketers that milk the holiday for everything it's worth.

But, of course, this isn't to say that Christmas's commercial aspects don't have a negative side. As one American commentator puts it, with mobbed shopping malls and frenzied purchasing, the season has turned into "a breakneck race by anyone and

THE TOY DEPARTMENT.
"Bring the little ones; let them enjoy this wonderful Christmas Carnival to their hearts' content."
—*Extract from a Department Store Adv.*

This 1913 magazine illustration shows a crowd of parents and children in the toy section of a department store at Christmas, with Santa Claus surrounded by a group of parents. The caption reads, "Bring the little ones; let them enjoy this wonderful Christmas Carnival to their hearts' content." Artist L.M. Glackens. Cover art from *Puck* 74, no. 1920 (December 17, 1913) (Library of Congress).

everyone to create the 'ideal' Christmas, formed in the minds of Americans by unrealistic movies and TV shows which portray romantic, unrealistic ideas that involve a roaring fireplace or a brightly decorated tree."[48] The obsession with buying and consuming is blamed for causing people to lose sight of what should really matter at Christmas, whether that's rejoicing in the birth of Jesus, spending quality time with loved ones, or helping the less fortunate. Not only does the excess inspired by commercialism distract from these values, but it can also have a negative effect on people's finances and on the natural environment. As a post at the Organization for Economic Cooperation and Development's *Environment Focus* blog points out, "the carbon footprint of Santa's operations (including toy production and distribution by a sleigh pulled by reindeer) is at around 70 million tonnes of CO2e."[49] Christmas is also known to produce "mountains of waste," with garbage increasing by 30 percent in the United Kingdom, according to one study, as well as high levels of toxic chemicals produced in the manufacturing of some toys and huge amounts of food thrown away.

To counter these trends, the World Wildlife Fund offers advice for more sustainable Christmas celebrations, including buying less, cutting out material presents and instead gifting experiences such as tickets to concerts or "adopting" animals in the wild, and reducing food waste. They also recommend avoiding toys that require batteries and offer other common-sense tips such as recycling and reusing shopping bags, as well as using LED lights on Christmas trees.[50] Others go further, with a "Christmas Climate Strike" movement emerging in recent years calling on people to commit to forgo buying presents and accepting gifts from others. Whether or not Christmas celebrants elect to opt out of gift-giving, there is clearly a desire for promoting a bit more simplicity and sustainability—not to mention sanity—in the Christmas festival.

15

Reason for the Season

Gifts don't need
To be extravagant
A little praise is often enough
Sharing food
And something to drink
Has secured many friendships
—Hávamál (Words of Odin)

Brushing his teeth the day after Christmas in 1956, Theodor Geisel looked at himself in the mirror and noticed a sour look on his face that led him to question whether something was wrong with him, or perhaps, if something had gone wrong with Christmas. Frustrated by the growing materialism that he felt diminished the spirit of togetherness and charity that represented Christmas at its finest, he set out to counter this trend by doing what he did best: making a children's rhyme. Better known as Dr. Seuss, Geisel wrote the book *How the Grinch Stole Christmas*, he later recalled, to see "if I could rediscover something about Christmas that obviously I'd lost."[1] But despite Geisel being brought up with a strong religious background and notwithstanding the fact that some Christians hold up *How the Grinch Stole Christmas* as a parable of Christ's teachings,[2] there is not a single identifiable allusion to Christianity in the story.

In the book, the Grinch is a furry, green, misanthropic creature who lives in a cave with his dog. He hates Christmas and is constantly annoyed by the raucous festivities that take place in nearby Whoville. With a "heart [that] was two sizes too small," the Grinch is driven mad by the "Noise! Noise! Noise! Noise!" and what he hates most of all is how the Whos would "stand close together, with Christmas bells ringing" and then "would start singing." So he hatches a plan to stop Christmas by stealing all the presents, decorations and food. Disguised as Santa Claus, he sneaks into the homes of Whoville and takes all the "Pop guns! And bicycles! Roller skates! Drums! Checkerboards! Tricycles! Popcorn! And plums!" as well as "The ribbons! The wrappings! The tags! And the tinsel!" The Grinch then waits for the Whos to awaken Christmas morning, eagerly anticipating their chorus of sad cries, but instead he hears them singing a joyous Christmas song. Puzzled, the Grinch then realizes that "[m]aybe Christmas doesn't come from a store," but perhaps "means a little bit more!" Then, suddenly filled with Christmas joy, his heart "grew three sizes" and he brings back all the toys and food. The story ends with the Grinch participating in the Christmas feast and "he himself ... carved the roast beef!"

15. Reason for the Season

In an interview with *Redbook*, Geisel later said that *How the Grinch Stole Christmas* was the easiest book that he every wrote largely because he was channeling his own frustrations with the commercialization of the holiday. The hardest part, he said, was coming up with a believable and meaningful ending. He wanted to redeem the Grinch without sounding "like a second-rate preacher or some bible thumper," and so, after going through "thousands of religious choices" over a period of three months, he finally settled on ending the story with the Grinch and the Whos together at a table, with the Grinch carving the roast beef. The choice was appropriate. By eschewing an overtly religious message and focusing instead on a community brought together by a feast of food and drink, Geisel was probably closer to capturing the spirit of Christmas than he would have been by ending the story in a church listening to a sermon.

While avoiding Christian overtones, the story features a couple of pagan ones, whether intentional or not, including a reference to "hanging a mistletoe wreath." The Grinch—although based loosely on the author, as Geisel claimed in his interview with *Redbook*—resembles a number of Christmas goblins with roots in pagan folklore, such as the Krampus and Belsnickel. The way the Grinch sneaks into homes to make mischief and steal things rather than leave presents is also not unlike the widely held beliefs about the dualistic nature of elves in pre–Christian time and shares some similarities with the Greek kallikantzaroi. The focus on Christmas as primarily an occasion for feasting and making "Noise! Noise! Noise! Noise!" is also in keeping with the holiday's pagan origins, and specifically the concept of misrule at the heart of Saturnalia.

Geisel's focus on the holiday's carnival side reflects a general tendency to understate the religious aspects of Christmas, a tendency that is widely seen throughout the genre of stories and films that explore the elusive "meaning of Christmas." While some classic stories, such as "The Gift of the Magi," published by O. Henry in 1905, contain references to the biblical story of the nativity, the general themes relate more to concepts of love, joy and generosity rather than specifically Christian themes of salvation through belief in the Lord or a focus on celebrating Jesus's birth. A central theme is also the concept of gift-giving, which is seen as potentially problematic but also liberating through the selflessness and expression of love that it can represent.

* * *

In O. Henry's story, an impoverished married couple—Jim and Della Dillingham—have only two possessions that they treasure: Jim's gold pocket watch, a family heirloom, and Della's long, beautiful hair. For Christmas, Della wants to buy Jim a chain for his pocket watch but can't afford it. So, she has her hair cut and sells it to a wigmaker for $20, just enough to buy the chain for Jim's watch. However, Jim, unbeknownst to Della, had sold his watch in order to pay for the gift he had picked out for Della—a pair of pricey decorative combs that she had long admired. They exchange gifts on Christmas Eve, but of course, both gifts were completely useless because she had cut off her hair and he had sold his watch. The story concludes with the narrator rather clumsily comparing Jim and Della's gifts to those that the magi gave to the infant Jesus. Although the couple had "most unwisely sacrificed for each other the greatest treasures of their house," they were ultimately wiser than the magi because their gifts were gifts of love. "Of all who give and receive gifts, such as they are wisest," concludes O. Henry.

By drawing a loose comparison between the gifts of love that Jim and Della gave each other to the gifts of praise that the magi presented to Jesus, the story is only peripherally related to the nativity and indeed it would have been just as poignant had the biblical reference been removed. The magi don't play a central role in the tale, which is more of a secular allegory on gift-giving than it is a religious tract, and although O. Henry claims that the magi "invented the art of giving Christmas presents," gift-giving of course is not exclusively Christian in nature. In fact, gift-giving at this time of year has roots in pagan midwinter customs—considered an important aspect of the Roman Saturnalia as well as the new year's celebration of Kalends, at which greenery dedicated to the goddess Strenia, cakes, honey, and coins were considered traditional gifts.[3]

The pagan origins of gift-giving were well known at the time of O. Henry's writing, alluded to, for example, in Hamilton Mabie's popular early 20th-century work *The Book of Christmas*. Describing the English Boxing Day custom, in which goods were boxed up by the wealthy to give to the less fortunate, Mabie notes that it "carries us back to the Roman Paganalia when earthen boxes in which money was slipped

An article in the *Daily Capital Journal* on December 19, 1917, opens with the line "The custom of exchanging gifts at Christmas is derived from the Romans, who made presents to one another during the Saturnalia, a festival instituted about 497 B.C." The article also attributes the origins of Father Christmas to Virgil and Petronius, a courtier under Emperor Nero. Image of the *Daily Capital Journal*, 1917 (Library of Congress).

through a hole were hung up to receive contributions at these rural festivals."[4] A 1917 newspaper article decisively declared that "[t]he custom of exchanging gifts at Christmas is derived from the Romans, who made presents to one another during the Saturnalia,"[5] and a 1926 historical study of Christmas cards notes that popular gifts among the ancient Romans included fruits, olive branches, "lucky pennies," and terra cotta tablets inscribed with messages such as "A Happy and Prosperous New Year."[6]

Gift-giving continued in early modern Europe, where the wassailing tradition was essentially a form of Christmas begging in which the gentry gifted peasants food, drink and money in exchange for their goodwill. "When Christianity folded these rituals into Christmas," according to an article at *The Christian Science Monitor*, "the justification for bearing gifts was redirected to the Three Wise Men, the Magi, who gave gifts to the infant Jesus."[7] And while O. Henry may have a point that "those who give out of love and self-sacrifice are truly wise because they know the value of self-giving love," there is also a utilitarian aspect of gift-giving, which helps establish good social relations by serving as a valuable investment in a relationship, building bonds of affection and loyalty as a partner, parent, friend, or employer, as well as celebrating life, love, and friendship.

Gift-giving is also a major theme of Charles Dickens' *A Christmas Carol*, which in some ways reflects even more closely some of the paternalistic aspects of the practice in pagan Europe. In Saturnalia, there are accounts of the wealthy paying the month's rent for the indigent, and patrons of the poor would pass along a gratuity, known as a *sigillaricium*, to their dependents to help them buy gifts for the holiday.[8] Similarly, in Dickens' famous tale, Ebenezer Scrooge—following his conversion from a stingy and cold miser to a generous and kind humanitarian—provides his employee's family with a large goose so that they can enjoy a proper Christmas dinner and makes a sizable donation to a charity collecting money for the poor. Without dwelling on Christian doctrines, Dickens' story provided a strong basis for establishing what for many has come to represent the spirit of Christmas—selflessness, charity and goodwill. It also coincided with the modern tradition of employers granting Christmas bonuses to their workers. This custom began in the 19th century with offerings such as turkeys or watches, with cash bonuses first introduced by the F.W. Woolworth Company in 1899. By the mid–20th century, many workers had begun to expect the Christmas bonus as a year-end entitlement.[9]

* * *

A Christmas Carol might be the most explicit in its allusions to these concepts, but they can be found throughout the genre of Christmas stories and films, most of which do not focus at all on the holiday's religious aspects. Indeed, in lists of popular Christmas movies, it is remarkable how many of them continue to recognize Christmas as primarily a secular affair and those that do give a nod to Christianity, tend to do so discreetly. A list of the top 20 Christmas movies at *USA Today*, for example, is heavily dominated by comedies and a few classics like 1940's *The Shop Around the Corner* and 1960's *The Apartment*. Only one of them has anything even close to resembling a religious theme—*It's a Wonderful Life*—and this only tangentially because one of the main characters is an angel sent from heaven to help a suicidal man.[10] Nearly all the others celebrate the holiday's secular, magical and profane aspects.

Similarly, a list of the top 75 Christmas movies at *Today.com* only features a handful that might be considered religious in nature. *The Bishop's Wife*, a 1947 movie about an Episcopal bishop who receives help from an angel when he loses sight of his family while planning an elaborate cathedral, came in at number 51 on the list, while *The Preacher's Wife*, a 1996 reboot starring Denzel Washington and Whitney Houston, came in at number 24. Coming in at number three was *It's a Wonderful Life*. At the tail end of the list, incidentally, is an R-rated film that celebrates Christmas as an opportunity for misrule, the raunchy *Office Christmas Party* starring Jennifer Anniston.[11]

A popular crowdsourced website called *Ranker*, which bills itself as "the definitive source of rankings on everything from film to sports to food," has a list of 127 Christmas movies, ranked from top to bottom. Notably, the three highest-ranked movies are all comedies: 1989's *Christmas Vacation* starring Chevy Chase, 2003's *Elf* starring Will Ferrell, and 1990's *Home Alone* starring Macaulay Culkin. The next three are animated films—*Rudolph the Red-Nosed Reindeer*, *Dr. Seuss' How the Grinch Stole Christmas!*, and *A Charlie Brown Christmas*—followed by *A Christmas Story*, and coming in at eighth place, *It's a Wonderful Life*. The next two favorites are *The Santa Clause*, the 1994 comedy starring Tim Allen, and *Die Hard*, the 1988 action film starring Bruce Willis. Also popular are romances such as 1954's *White Christmas* and 2003's *Love Actually*, as well as horrors such as 1984's *Gremlins* and 2015's *Krampus*, which both explore the darker side of Christmas.

But while heavily skewed towards light-hearted entertainment and "guilty pleasures," the *Ranker* list is actually one of the few that contains a title that is directly related to explicitly Christian aspects of Christmas. *The Nativity Story*, a 2006 epic biblical drama film based on the Gospels' stories, opens with a portrayal of the Massacre of the Innocents, and goes on to depict the annunciation, birth of Jesus, and the magi following the great star to Bethlehem. Receiving mixed reviews and grossing $46.4 million on a reported $35 million budget, *The Nativity Story* holds a 37 percent approval rating on the review aggregator *Rotten Tomatoes*. The "Critics Consensus" at the website states, "*The Nativity Story* is a dull retelling of a well-worn tale with the look and feel of a high-school production."[12] At *Ranker*, the movie comes in at number 56, right after *A Chipmunk Christmas*.[13]

What these informal movie rankings seem to indicate is that to the vast majority of regular people, not to mention most Hollywood producers and professional critics, Christmas is less of a religious occasion for spiritual reflection than it is an opportunity for indulgent pleasure. Indeed, if one were to judge solely on the basis of the ever-growing miscellany of Christmas movies and books, the holiday appears to have little to nothing to do with worship and praise, and almost everything to do with amusement and joy. Of course, many Christmas films do examine serious topics, including such fundamental questions as the meaning of life, but even those that explore these matters do so in a largely secular way. While there is some overlap between themes found in Christmas stories such as *It's a Wonderful Life* and teachings found in the Bible, the reality is that Christmas in film is for all intents and purposes a holiday that transcends religious doctrine. It's almost as if it is generally (if perhaps unconsciously) understood that Christmas is not intrinsically Christian at its core.

Something else that becomes apparent when reviewing Christmas movies and stories is that Christmas sometimes looks like a holiday in a state of existential crisis. For all of its grandeur, its enduring cultural influence, its unique status as perhaps the oldest continuing tradition observed today, and its widespread popularity among people of all walks of life, it seems to be constantly questioning whether it lives up to live up to its ideals. How many books and movies have been written exploring the theme of "the meaning of Christmas," and questioning whether Christmas celebrants are straying from the fundamental principles of the holiday? From classics like Dickens' *A Christmas Carol* to campy Christmas flicks like *Home Alone*, not to mention Dr. Seuss's tale of the Grinch who stole Christmas, holiday stories are constantly examining and re-examining themes of materialism and generosity and asking whether people have lost sight of ideals such as charity and goodwill. As Kris Kringle observes in *Miracle on 34th Street*, it "[s]eems we're all so busy trying to beat the other fellow in making things go faster and look shinier and cost less that Christmas and I are sort of getting lost in the shuffle." This is also a central theme of such perennial favorites as *Elf* and *The Polar Express*, both of which portray the lack of Christmas spirit as a fundamental threat to the holiday.

And this, of course, is not just a Hollywood trope—it is also a common theme in real life, with a certain amount of social pressure to show outward signs of merriment and goodwill, lest one is held responsible for "ruining Christmas." People who fail to display the requisite amount of cheer and generosity are commonly chided by others with the friendly but rather accusatory question, "where's your Christmas spirit?" as if the holiday is so fragile and vulnerable that one person can single-handedly wreck it simply by being in a bad mood.

* * *

On one hand, of course, this constant self-reflection could be considered healthy: by continuously demanding a high level of excellence and examining its adherence to its own ideals, Christmas guards against succumbing to the corrupting influences of modernity, materialism and selfishness. On the other hand, this perpetual questioning of itself could be seen as something of an identity crisis. To the casual observer, it may seem that the holiday is on a constant search for rediscovering its mojo, or fearful that it will lose whatever mojo it has, which gives the impression that Christmas suffers from a case of chronic low self-esteem. This begs the question: where does this self-doubt come from? Could it be the result of the long-running historical battle over the true "reason for the season"? Is there a relationship between the way people today continue to ask what Christmas is really all about and the fact that our pre–Christian ancestors once celebrated this holiday for reasons that have largely been forgotten? Perhaps the historical background of Christmas—being an amalgamation of pagan, Christian, humanist and commercial influences—has caused the holiday to experience a crisis of confidence.

While some might assume that this identity crisis is a modern phenomenon, in fact, it is clear that it is something that Christmas enthusiasts have been grappling with for a very long time. As Mabie writes in the introduction to his 1909 tome on Christmas traditions, after two millennia "Christmas shows no signs of decrepitude or weariness" but it is threatened by "perverted uses and overstimulated activities." Commercialism has "pushed [it] so far that its sentiment often loses spontaneity and charm in excessive organization and prodigal distribution," Mabie observes. "The

Christmas shopper suffers such a perversion of feeling that she hates the season she ought to bless," he continues, "and the modern Santa Claus is so intent on the ingenuity or the cost of his gifts that he overlooks the only gift that warms the heart and translates Christmas into the vernacular." Mabie's prescription for saving Christmas "from desecration" and "forgetfulness" is to revive its sentiments "year by year in the joyful celebration of the old rites."[14] He adds: "We have been so eager of late years to rid ourselves of superstition and 'see things as they are' that we have lost that vision of the large relations of things in which alone their meaning and use is revealed."

This loss of perspective, the ridding of outdated superstitions, the forgetting of the original meanings behind many of our Christmas traditions and the overall identity crisis affecting the holiday, ultimately could be the result of a false narrative promoted by evangelicals and culture warriors who insist that secularists are somehow corrupting what is traditionally a Christian holiday, when, if anything, the opposite is closer to the truth: that this pagan tradition, incorporated by Christianity and promoted as an important date on the Christian calendar despite not being mentioned anywhere in the Bible, has been stripped of its historical context, and succeeded by a seemingly secular celebration that is disconnected from its original spiritual and cultural significance. Perhaps the appropriation of pagan rites marking the end of the harvest year and the rebirth of the sun has created a psychological detachment between what the season originally meant to humans at a time when they were more connected to seasonal cycles.

And perhaps this is why a bourgeoning movement of neopagans, Wiccans and neo-druids has emerged to "reclaim" Christmas's heathen origins, observing not a traditional Christmas but pagan traditions associated with this time of year. To these celebrants, the occasion is not a Christian observance nor a secular festival, but one of the eight annual "sabbats" that represent important points on the "Wheel of the Year." Along with Samhain, Imbolc, the Spring Equinox, Beltane, the Summer Solstice, Lughnasadh and the Autumn Equinox, the Winter Solstice is recognized as an important point on the calendar year, representing the eternal cycle of birth, death and rebirth. In particular, the Winter Solstice is recognized by neopagans as the time that the Holly King overcomes the Oak King, with the Holly King representing darkness and the Oak King representing light. Some groups hold specific rites to mark each of the eight sabbats, with particular customs associated with midwinter.[15] Bonfires are an integral part of most neopagan festivities, which can be used to symbolize the "rebirth" of the sun at the solstice. Some groups may also light giant candles and decorate alternative Christmas trees with magical symbols and a pentacle on top rather than a star or angel.[16]

* * *

Some neo-druids also gather just before Christmas at Stonehenge in south-central England for a ritualistic solstice celebration. At most times of the year, the site is restricted, with visitors roped off and kept far from the stones, but for the solstices and equinoxes the site is opened for those who observe spiritual practices, particularly practitioners of Druidry. A spiritual movement that promotes harmony with nature, neo-druidism originated in Britain during the 18th century as a cultural phenomenon and later gained religious connotations, focusing in particular on reverence for the natural world and the veneration of ancestors.[17] Druidic rituals aim to align participants with the spirit of nature, and typically reflect on the time of year and the changing of the seasons.[18]

An American photographer named Joshua Kristal who documented the annual midwinter gathering in 2011 described ceremonies that included drumming, chanting, knighting and other rituals. "I was surprised and happy to realize the spot definitely emanates a strong spiritual charge," Kristal wrote at his blog. "It's hard to describe the feeling but it was as if I could feel the presence of the ancient societies and the 1000's of years they had practiced their spiritual rituals in this very spot."[19]

For those who wish to share this spiritual experience, a British travel agency called Stonehenge Tours offers packages that allow visitors from around the world to gather at Stonehenge to mark the winter solstice and to see the sunrise above the stones. "Follow the footsteps of your ancestors and exalt in the beauty of Salisbury's hallowed monoliths from within the inner ring; ground rarely trodden but for sacred occasions," reads the pitch on their website. "The sun's celestial machinations have been celebrated at this time of year for thousands of years and it is perhaps the most important time of the year to be at Stonehenge—a truly spiritual experience." Calling Stonehenge "a site of unequaled religious significance," Stonehenge Tours invites people to "watch as the long night is broken by the primordial light of Ostara, or dawn, as she gives her light and colour to the painting of beauty that is Wiltshire's countryside, and it is refracted by those most ancient stones."[20]

Stonehenge is not the only Neolithic site that people gather to experience the winter solstice as ancient druids may have done. Every year, a lottery is drawn to select 60 lucky people who can experience the winter solstice at Newgrange, Ireland. Built around 3200 BCE, Newgrange was designed so that its longest passage and inner chamber illuminate completely during sunrise on the winter solstice. Archaeologists believe that it may have served as a religious or ceremonial center, where feasts were held at midwinter in prehistoric times. Due to COVID-19 restrictions, the in-person gatherings were cancelled in 2020, but the solstice sunrise was livestreamed from within the Newgrange Chamber from December 20 to 22.[21]

Modern-day heathens who would like to experience ancient pagan winter solstice traditions from the comfort of their homes can also do so by participating in online Saturnalia festivities. The popular roleplaying forum Second Life hosts several annual events to celebrate the ancient Roman holiday, including such activities as the "Saturnalia Ritual & Tavern Celebration," where participants can honor Saturn and Sol Invictus by taking part in an online party with virtual dancing, music, and merrymaking. According to *Second Life Newser*, the event offers an opportunity to "party like a Patrician (Even if you're not)!"[22] Second Life also hosts a "Winter Solstice & Yule Market" where role-players can purchase pagan-themed gear for their avatars.

Other neopagan revivals include attempts to resurrect the wassailing tradition, replete with "re-paganized" versions of carols that can be found all over the internet. These songs, some of which work better than others, are purported to be carols that have been restored to their original pagan meanings before they were Christianized during the Middle Ages. But of course, they are mostly based on guesswork, since the actual lyrics of bygone pagan eras have long-since been lost to history, or are simply creative adaptations of Christian songs with new pagan-friendly lyrics imposed on familiar tunes, such as this version of "Oh, Come All Ye Faithful":

Solstice spiral horns, available to purchase at the online role-playing forum Second Life. Developed for the event "SATURNALIA: A Winter Solstice & Yule Market," these horns can be added to Second Life avatars. According to the sales pitch, "The Solstice spiral represents our journey through the year, through the seasons" (Original artwork by Second Life user and content creator A. James [Nama Gearz], https://my.secondlife.com/nama.gearz. Used with permission).

> Oh, come all ye faithful
> Gather round the Yule Fire
> Oh, come ye, oh, come ye,
> To call the Sun!
> Fires within us
> Call the Fire above us
> O, come, let us invoke Him!
> O, come, let us invoke Him!
> O, come, let us invoke Him!
> Our Lord, the Sun![23]

Anyone interested in wassailing while enjoying the traditional beverage associated with the practice can find recipes online. The website *Learn Religions*[24] recommends mixing apple cider, cranberry juice, honey and sugar on low heat, and then adding oranges, cloves, diced apple, allspice, ginger and nutmeg. Mixing eggs, which was done in earlier times to sprinkle over the crops to ensure fertility, is optional. The website also provides several other ideas for celebrating the solstice the old-fashioned way. Describing Yule as one of the eight traditional Wiccan and pagan holidays based on the earth's rotation and seasonal markers, *Learn Religions* offers craft ideas such as making decorative greenery, wreaths, and Yule logs, as well as smudging sticks "to cleanse a sacred space"[25] and incense to "evoke ... the magic of a cold December night."[26]

And while you are engaging in making these crafts, drinking traditional beverages, attending online Saturnalia parties, and singing "restored" pagan songs, instead of wearing that ugly old Christmas sweater, you can wear neo-pagan attire with messages such as "Keep Saturn in Saturnalia" and "Blessed Yule," available to purchase online.

* * *

What these efforts at rekindling traditions of a bygone era show is that there is a widespread awareness of how the original "reason for the season" has been lost, or, perhaps, absorbed by the dominant cultural zeitgeist—and there is a desire to rediscover it. But at the same time, it is important not to overstate the burgeoning neopagan revival nor imply that it is somehow more significant than the spirituality that Christians continue to attach to the season. While some might make the pilgrimage to Stonehenge, others make the journey to Bethlehem instead, or hold Midnight Mass at St. Peter's Basilica in Rome. And despite the vocal minority of neopagans who question the authenticity of the holiday's religious origins, according to a 2019 Gallup survey, 67 percent of Americans continue to observe Christmas as a Christian feast.[27] Another survey, from 2016, found that just three percent of Christmas celebrants said they would be observing the occasion as a winter solstice celebration rather than a celebration of the nativity. On the other hand, although three percent might not sound like much, it is nearly as many as the number of people (4 percent) who were observing Advent that year.[28]

Of course, while viewed by many as a secular occasion and by a few neopagans as an occasion for spiritual revival, Christmas continues to be a season deeply infused with Christian theology, which is seen in the cribs that pop up at churches at Christmas time and felt in the songs that we all know and love. While Christmas movies may generally avoid religious overtones and opt for more light-hearted, family-friendly fare, our tunes don't shy away from the spiritual side of the holiday. Online rankings of popular Christmas songs do tend to skew heavily towards secular favorites such as Mariah Carey's "All I Want for Christmas Is You" and The Pogues' "Fairytale of New York," but they also feature such standards as "Mary's Boy Child" by Harry Belafonte, "Go Tell It on the Mountain" by Mahalia Jackson, and "Joy to the World" by Dolly Parton. Other mainstays of our collective Christmas soundtrack include "Away in a Manger," "The First Noel," "Hark! The Herald Angels Sing," "O Come, All Ye Faithful," "O Holy Night," and of course, the moving "Silent Night." The latter was first performed on Christmas Eve 1818 in Austria as "Stille Nacht" and has since been translated into 140 languages. "Silent Night" is so universally recognized that it was declared an "intangible cultural heritage" by UNESCO in 2011.[29]

The heightened sense of religiosity can also be seen in the general spike in church attendance during the Christmas season. A 2015 survey found six out of

10 Americans typically attend church at Christmas time,[30] compared to about 35 percent who attend regularly during the rest of the year,[31] and about half say they attend church on Christmas Eve or Christmas Day.[32] While some say that they attend church just to be with family and friends or to observe tradition, the vast majority—77 percent according to one survey—say they do it "to honor Jesus."[33]

What these figures reveal is that despite Christmas's historical background as a hybrid pagan-Christian-secular affair, its religious aspects as a Christian feast continue to inspire the holiday. Whether Jesus was actually born on December 25 or not, clearly, the centuries of observing the nativity on this date have had an enduring and possibly permanent impact on how humans mark the midwinter and end-of-year festivities. The selection of this date by the Church way back in the fourth century may very well have been done in order to replace a pagan holiday, but over time it has become inextricably linked with the Christian faith. Although some may continue to push back by trying to restore pagan traditions associated with the winter solstice and despite the fact that much of the Christmas season—at least judging by Hollywood fare—is far more secular than it is religious, the Christian aspects of the holiday are indeed alive and well.

Yet, perhaps even among Christian observances there is room to recognize the varied and multi-layered origins of the holiday. Attending a 2021 Christmas Day church service in Denmark, I was pleasantly surprised to hear the priest acknowledge that Jesus's birth is not the only "reason for the season." He talked specifically about the winter solstice, reminding the congregation that the shortest day of the year had just passed and that the coming longer days were a cause for celebration. What the season represents, he recalled, is not just the birth of the Savior, but the ending of one yearly cycle and the initiation of a new one. Indeed, this is why the Christmas season resonates so widely, the priest said, reminding us that the celebration of the coming of the Lord coincides (perhaps not coincidentally) with the earth's seasonal cycle.

Six months after listening to this sermon, at the summer solstice in June, I was reminded once again of how these traditions and beliefs overlap. Much as their heathen ancestors did, Danes celebrate the longest day of the year by lighting bonfires, singing songs and drinking beer. But while these activities are steeped in pagan traditions, they were long ago incorporated into the Christian faith by assigning them to the feast of St. John on June 24, and today are observed largely as a secular celebration of summer. St. John's Eve, or Sankt Hans Aften as it is called in Denmark, is a reminder that important turning points in the year have always been celebrated by pagans and Christians alike, but ultimately, to most people the origins of these traditions are not particularly important. What's important is that we continue to celebrate them.

16

War Over Christmas

So, stick up ivy and the bays,
And then restore the heathen ways.
Green will remind you of the spring,
Though this great day denies the thing
   —Henry Vaughan, "The True Christmas"

How Christmas is celebrated may vary from individual to individual and from family to family, but at the end of the day, no one escapes it. While some folks immerse themselves in Christmas traditions, making crafts and gingerbread houses and spending a small fortune on decorating their homes, others may observe it more piously by participating in church events and donating time or money to charities. Some participate passively, grudgingly attending office parties and barely getting their Christmas shopping done in time, while still others perhaps reject the celebration altogether for one reason or another. Jehovah's Witnesses, Seventh-Day Adventists and adherents to Islam, Judaism and other faiths may abstain because of religious beliefs, while atheists may resent what they see as an imposition of Christian beliefs. Likewise, some evangelical Christians may object to the commercialism of the holiday and to its "secular" elements like Santa Claus, but whether they like it or not, everyone participates on one level or another. This is simply by virtue of being a member of a society that is thoroughly absorbed in the Christmas celebration for a month every year. As author Garrison Keillor once put it, "A lovely thing about Christmas is that it's compulsory, like a thunderstorm, and we all go through it together."[1]

Indeed, whatever one's spiritual beliefs may be, it is impossible to elude the Christmas festival due to its all-encompassing nature—Christmas is simply everywhere during December, from merchandising displays in stores to commercials on television to Christmas-themed movies to ubiquitous decorations to Christmas music being played on intercoms to friends and family posting Christmas-related messages on social media. The only way to truly avoid Christmas would be to not leave your home during December and not turn on your TV or radio, or to go online. Even then, you might receive a Christmas card or a Christmas-themed catalogue in the mail, so you better not check your mailbox either. Basically, it is impossible to avoid Christmas or being affected by it in some way.

And, according to surveys, nearly everyone does partake on some level. A Pew poll found in 2017 that about 90 percent of Americans celebrate Christmas, with some 46 percent recognizing it as a religious holiday, 33 percent as primarily a cultural holiday, and nine percent celebrating as both a religious and a cultural occasion. Only eight percent say they don't celebrate at all.[2] What is striking about this is not so much that there are so many who celebrate Christmas, but that it is the only holiday that is so universally recognized. While every country has some sort of national day, and America arguably has two—Independence Day and Thanksgiving—the significance of these days is obviously limited to the individual countries. And while some customs may have more significance in the belief systems of Christianity, for example Easter, none of them approaches the cultural significance of Christmas.

This, ultimately, is due to the long-standing historical role of Christmas, predating its consecration as a "Christian feast." When people engage in Christmas traditions, they are participating in very ancient beliefs that are related to the spiritual and cultural significance of the winter solstice, augmented over the centuries with Christian teachings and secular humanist beliefs. The yearly celebration fulfills a need—not only providing some respite from the gathering cold and darkness and offering an opportunity to joyously reunite with loved ones, but also to reconnect with ancestors and rediscover their ancient wisdom. By hanging mistletoe and wreaths, decorating trees, and engaging with myths like Santa Claus and elves, we are taking part in primeval practices that would otherwise be forgotten.

Over the centuries, these ancient pagan traditions have been infused with a spirit of charity and benevolence that is grounded in the teachings of Jesus but is also humanist in nature. The result is a wonderful hybrid holiday full of rich traditions, selfless generosity, hedonistic pleasure and deep spiritual meaning. It is truly a magical time of year and one that is responsible for creating countless treasured memories and for serving as a powerful annual reminder of the importance of family, tradition and goodwill, as well as recalling the elusive promise of peace on earth. But despite this rich and layered history, and notwithstanding the influences the holiday has always enjoyed from its pagan origins, to many people, Christmas has come to primarily embody Christian doctrines and is a time that is designated to rejoice in the birth of Jesus. Not only do they insist that the holiday is fundamentally Christian, but they also insist that everyone else recognize it as such. This divisive and strident approach has led to highly politicized culture-war arguments that have over the years grown increasingly absurd.

*　*　*

As an illustration of how asinine the controversies have become, since at least 2015, one of the main—and unlikeliest—battlegrounds in the so-called War on Christmas has been the Starbucks coffee chain. That year, the company unveiled its annual "holiday cup," which had for the previous 18 years featured what Starbucks called "symbols of the season," including holly, stars, reindeer, snowflakes, Christmas trees, and doves. When the company debuted a simple two-tone design in November 2015, eschewing the usual iconic images and going instead for a minimalist approach of a plain bright red cup with the green Starbucks logo in the center, people freaked out. With no seasonal symbols at all, the cup sparked outrage across conservative media, with the right-wing website *Breitbart*, for example, declaring that the "Starbucks red cups are emblematic of the Christian culture cleansing of the West."[3]

Culture warriors and evangelicals took to the internet to voice their discontent and within days, both #RedCups and #MerryChristmasStarbucks were trending on social media sites. In a viral Facebook post that received more than 10 million views, Joshua Feuerstein fumed: "Starbucks REMOVED CHRISTMAS from their cups because they hate Jesus." (Never mind the fact that some of the iconography that Starbucks had used in previous years, such as holly, were clearly pagan in origin and none of them were overtly religious.) Feuerstein posted an accompanying video urging people to go into Starbucks and give their names as "Merry Christmas" so that unsuspecting baristas would write "Merry Christmas" on the cups—and then might actually be tricked into *saying* the words when they called out the "name" of the customer when his or her gingerbread latte was ready.[4] Some also began posting videos of themselves drawing pictures on the plain red cups, including depictions of explicitly Christian themes such as manger scenes.[5]

In subsequent years, Starbucks developed more "Christmassy" motifs, even opening up their design process to competition from around the world—a rather ingenious PR move that simultaneously democratized the process, publicized their product and potentially insulated themselves from criticism if customers didn't like the cups. ("Hey, you guys came up with these designs, not us," they could say if people complained again.) The 2016 cup featured 13 customer-created designs with white hand-drawn seasonal scenes against a red background[6] and within a couple years, conservatives were gloating that Starbucks had buckled under pressure. "Starbucks' new coffee cups are beginning to look a lot like Christmas," Dom Calicchio wrote at Fox News, but complained nevertheless that "they don't name the holiday." Instead of saying "Merry Christmas," the cups said "Merry Coffee," Calicchio grumbled, warning that the company was risking "more War on Christmas backlash."[7]

Clearly, the Starbucks controversy is particularly dumb, but unfortunately it is all too typical of the larger, deeply politicized absurdities that have come to surround the holiday. The issue of whether or not to say the words "Merry Christmas" is fundamental to the annual controversy. Despite the fact that the more inclusive greeting "Happy Holidays" has been in use since at least 1863,[8] the term "Merry Christmas" has become something of a litmus test for conservatives judging whether a company or an individual is perpetuating an anti–Christian political correctness and promoting secular multiculturalism. The conservative American Family Association targets companies every year that decline to use the word "Christmas" in their marketing communications, claiming that "secular forces in our country ... hate Christmas because the word itself is a reminder of Jesus Christ." The group claims that secularists "want to eradicate anything that reminds Americans of Christianity."[9]

Donald Trump waded into the controversy as a candidate running for president in 2016, promising not only to make America great again but to also make it safe to say "Christmas" again. "When I started 18 months ago, I told my first crowd in Wisconsin that we are going to come back here some day and we are going to say 'Merry Christmas' again," he declared in December 2016, a little over a month after winning the election.[10] A year later, Trump was claiming that thanks to him, people were saying "Merry Christmas" all over the country. At 10 p.m. on Christmas Eve in 2017, Trump took to Twitter to declare victory in the so-called War on Christmas. "People are proud to be saying Merry Christmas again," he tweeted. "I am proud to have led the charge against the assault of our cherished and beautiful phrase. MERRY CHRISTMAS!!!!!"[11] It was a theme that he continued to revisit for the duration of his presidency. "When I first started campaigning, people were not allowed, or—in some cases—foolishly ashamed, to be using on stores, 'Merry Christmas, Happy Christmas.' They would say 'Happy Holidays,'" Trump claimed at a National Day of Prayer service at the White House in May 2019. "Take a look at your stores nowadays. It's all 'Merry Christmas,' again."[12]

Of course, the idea that there is some kneejerk aversion to the word "Christmas" is largely a right-wing myth, and the reason that some people say "Happy Holidays" is not just because they are trying to be culturally sensitive and politically correct. Yes, some people may believe that it is more inclusive to say "Happy Holidays" out of respect to those who celebrate Hanukkah instead or don't recognize Christmas for one reason or another, but it is also simply a recognition that there are many holidays taking place at roughly the same time. In the United States, the period from Thanksgiving to New Year's Day is considered the "holiday season," which is similar to how the ancient Romans recognized the celebration of Saturnalia, Opalia, Dies Natalis Solis Invicti, and Kalends at roughly the same time. This, of course, is rooted in the reality that all of these celebrations are related in some way to underlying seasonal cycles—Thanksgiving, like Saturnalia, was initially a harvest festival; and Christmas, like Dies Natalis Solis Invicti, is related to the birth of the Sun of Righteousness, or as the Roman pagans believed, the Unconquered Sun, both of which related to the solstice. Kalends was a year-end celebration not unlike modern-day New Year's revelries. At their core, the holidays simply mark the end of the yearly cycle—harvest, solstice and rebirth—and this is why it makes sense to acknowledge them together with the simple alternative phrase "Happy Holidays."

It should also be appreciated that, despite the conservative caricature of anti–Christian secular zealots hell-bent on removing the word "Christmas" from our lexicon, even those who don't necessarily consider themselves Christians have long accepted the term "Christmas" and use it routinely. One of the most well-known and popular Christmas songs is by John Lennon, who considered himself as much of a

A billboard in Pitman, N.J., says "Keep Saturn in Saturnalia." The billboard was erected by the Freedom from Religion Foundation in response to a "Keep Christ in Christmas" banner that was displayed in the town. In this photograph, a protester dressed as Santa Claus is holding a sign that reads, "For Christ sake [sic], it's Christmas not Obamass" and lawn signs are planted in the ground saying "Keep Christ in Christmas" (Freedom From Religion Foundation / FFRF.org. Used with permission).

Buddhist as a Christian and deeply lamented how organized Christianity has distorted the teachings of Jesus with what he disparagingly called the "Onward Christian soldiers bit."[13] Yet, despite being widely considered "anti–Christian," Lennon wrote a song that unabashedly and repeatedly used the word "Christmas"—the 1970 hit "Happy Xmas (War Is Over)."

Doubling as a protest song against the Vietnam War, the song celebrates Christmas as a family-centered occasion to be cherished with loved ones but also a time of personal introspection and hope. Lennon is urging people to bring peace to the world through the force of will, declaring "war is over, if you want it," and pleas for racial harmony. But in spite of the clear left-leaning messages of the song and Lennon's own reservations about Christianity and organized religion, he uses the word "Christmas" 16 times in the lyrics.

As John Lennon's Christmas anthem makes clear, the aversion to using the word "Christmas," even among those on the political left or among critics of organized religion, is far from universal. However, it has become an unfortunate reality that due to how controversialized the holiday has become, whether someone says "Merry Christmas" or "Happy Holidays" as a greeting has become something of a political statement, even for those who would rather avoid politics.

* * *

As language specialist Melissa Mohr explains it, neither "Happy Holidays" nor "Merry Christmas" serves the traditional function of what linguists call "phatic speech." These are expressions that are intended to establish and maintain good social relations, greetings such as "hello" and "nice to see you," which signal the speaker's goodwill and puts people at ease without necessarily communicating any information. In contrast, the choice between using "Merry Christmas" and "Happy Holidays" is fraught with difficulties and one's choice could be seen as a signal of political ideology rather than friendliness. As a 2016 Public Religion Research Institute survey found, 67 percent of Republicans reject the notion that stores and businesses should greet their customers with "Happy Holidays" or "Season's Greetings" out of respect for people of different faiths, while 66 percent of Democrats support the practice. "The person most likely to insist on 'Merry Christmas,'" explains Mohr, "would be a Republican man over 60 who lives in the Midwest; the archetypal 'Happy Holidays' proponent is a young (18 to 29) female Democrat living in the Northeast." Rather than the friendly greeting it ought to be, the function of "Happy Holidays" or "Merry Christmas" is to characterize the speaker's group identification. "'Merry Christmas' advertises that you're likely a conservative and comfortable with Christianity as the default," Mohr writes. "Happy Holidays," on the other hand, often indicates that the person identifies as a liberal who tries hard to be inclusive.[14]

This dilemma has led to a good deal of anxiety during the holidays, which is unfortunate because Christmas can already be stressful enough. It also detracts from the sense of unity and celebration that should be at the core of the holiday, especially considering the fact that nine out of ten Americans celebrate it and most don't particularly care whether they are greeted with "Happy Holidays" or "Merry Christmas."

As an American who has lived in Denmark for many years, it seems to me that the dilemma of how to greet people at Christmas time is rather uniquely American. When I am in the U.S. at Christmas, I am aware that my choice of words when greeting others can potentially impact social interactions, either eliciting annoyance or appreciation, and this very much depends on the worldview of strangers that you come in contact with—something that is generally impossible to know. Personally, I tend to reject the whole premise of the underlying political ramifications and rather consciously alternate my greetings between "Happy Holidays" and "Merry Christmas," and let the chips fall where they may. Celebrating Christmas should not be so politically charged and one's choice of words in greeting others shouldn't be seen as an indication of ideological allegiance, so perhaps the best thing to do is just say both as a way to subvert the assumption that this contrived controversy is even grounded in reality to begin with.

What this drives home is that it is largely a matter of perception whether the anti–Christmas sentiments that are highlighted by the media every year even exist, or whether the controversy is basically a giant misunderstanding. The choice of greeting is either an innocuous wish for a pleasant holiday, or it is a coded signal identifying one's tribal allegiances. Likewise, depending on one's perspective, the "War on Christmas" is either a self-evident fact, demonstrated every year by the unofficial prohibition of the phrase "Merry Christmas" as just one in a litany of examples proving some sort of anti–Christian secular crusade, or it is much ado about nothing, an overblown dispute over symbols and semantics pushed by opportunists seeking to sow division, manufacture outrage, and get clicks and ratings. But while it may look to us as a contemporary conflict unique to our time, one that pits modern secularism against traditional religious values, the dispute actually has its roots in the efforts of the Church to Christianize midwinter celebrations many hundreds of years ago.

Historically, the divide over the proper greeting during the holiday season can largely be attributed to the fact that England changed the name of Yule to "Christmas" during the first millennium. This was an effort to supplant popular pagan traditions but was not universally successful, with Scandinavian countries in particular sticking with the old name. Therefore, when people greet each other in Denmark, they simply say *"glædelig jul,"* which roughly translates as "merry Christmas," but really means "merry Yule," since the Danes never accepted the name change that the Church tried to introduce a thousand years ago. Consequently, there's no problem in Denmark when it comes to what to say, no politically charged split-second decisions about how to greet others, nor any contrived controversies about the "war on Yule." What this illustrates is that America's ongoing battle over how to greet people during the holiday season in some ways is a continuation of that age-old struggle between the Christianizing forces on one hand, and the pagan and secular forces on the other hand.

* * *

Although the conflict over the meaning of Christmas appears to be focused more today on a struggle between religious and secular forces, which has played out largely as a polarized cultural battle over "religious freedom" and "political correctness," there is also still a good deal of wrangling over the pagan origins of Christmas. Arguments continue to be held over the reason that the Church decided on December 25 as Jesus's birthday and how many of our Christmas traditions are actually pagan in nature—for example, the decorating of Christmas trees. Neopagans and secularists are quick to claim that certain customs are pagan, sometimes despite a lack of solid evidence, while evangelicals and culture warriors are just as quick to make ahistorical claims that back up their side of the debate.

What the argument really comes down to is narrative control—who gets to decide what it is that society collectively believes, how it celebrates and who is included in the celebrations. When the culture warriors decry "creeping secularism" and make indignant claims about liberals and multiculturalists waging a "War on Christmas," what they are actually doing is criticizing how and why we celebrate, and implicitly conceding the inability of Christianity to fully establish itself as the dominant force in society and its failure to thoroughly replace ancient heathen customs. While these customs are now mistaken for being "secular," as we have seen, many of them are influenced by pagan beliefs, and their survivals represent the historical failure of efforts to form an exclusively "Christian" holiday during the period of the winter solstice. This can be traced back to the earliest days of Christianity establishing itself as the dominant social, religious and political order of Europe. It is no accident that the adoption of Christianity as Rome's official religion, the declaration of Jesus's birthday as December 25, and the designation of this date as a nativity celebration happened in such quick succession—in 322, 336, and 350, respectively.

Over the following millennium and a half, the Church continued to struggle in its attempts to suppress heathen gods, beliefs and customs, or to incorporate and adapt them into its catechism, all while attempting to whitewash their pagan origins. The efforts of the Puritans to suppress the holiday altogether in the 17th century were a recognition not only of its pagan origins but the inability of the Church to eliminate its hedonistic tendencies. Many of the "secular" aspects of Christmas that evangelicals and culture warriors now criticize are in fact survivals of these pagan traditions, albeit stripped of their original meaning. The ecclesiastical elements of Christmas, on the other hand, are impositions on these more ancient celebrations. While the Christian contributions have over time taken on the appearance of long-held religious traditions, for example the practice of singing at manger displays or attending Midnight Mass, there once was a time when these were novel additions to the end-of-year winter solstice celebrations that took place across Europe. Therefore, when people complain about a manger scene being removed from public grounds, they are not really defending the true "reason for the season"—what they are doing is engaging in a very long-running battle to supplant the original reason for the season (the celebration of the return of the sun) with a religious element that has no basis in historical reality, i.e., the birth of Jesus Christ, which almost certainly did not take place on December 25.

It is this ahistorical nature of the "War on Christmas" arguments that should be pushed back against, and this requires an effort being made to correct the general misinformation that surrounds the holiday. When children ask why Christmas is celebrated on December 25, for example, they should not simply be told that this is Jesus's birthday. Ideally, they should be told that this is the date that was celebrated for many thousands of years to mark the winter solstice and to give thanks to ancient gods associated with the sun, seen by our ancestors as the giver of life. Of course, children can also be taught that this is the date that Christians have chosen to celebrate the nativity of their Savior, but to tell them that this is the day that Jesus was actually born gives them the false impression that the celebration grew organically as an authentic Christian feast. This is not only a fabrication, but it is also far less interesting than the truth, simplifying its historical richness and denying the holiday the spirit of magic and misrule that stems from its pagan origins.

* * *

Perpetuating these sorts of myths and falsehoods can have palpable effects on society, with the ignorance of history easily exploited by powerful interests to highlight dividing lines for political purposes. Many scholars have explored the subject of the misteaching of history and how the stories that children are told can be used to enforce a certain ideology and suppress ideas that don't conform to the paradigm of values and doctrines dominant in society, thus distorting cultural understanding and blocking social progress. Howard Zinn's 1980 book *A People's History of the United States*, for example, sought to offer a corrective for generations of books that gave a top-down version of history. Rather than presenting a simplistic view of how "great men" shaped the world, *A People's History* told America's story from the point of view of women, Native Americans, African Americans, and industrial workers, and the powerful role they played in shaping the world we live in. It was an attempt to reclaim a rich historical narrative that had been overly simplified for generations.

A 1995 book called *Lies My Teacher Told Me* by sociologist James Loewen, built on this theme by critically examining 12 popular American high school history textbooks. Loewen concluded that they not only propagate mythologized and chauvinistic views of American history, but actually offer students historical accounts that are demonstrably false. For example, in discussing the history of America's "discovery," textbooks give credit to Christopher Columbus as the first explorer to ever stumble upon the "New World," glossing over the fact that it had already been settled by peoples who had migrated on foot from Asia thousands of years earlier, and entirely ignoring the fact that Columbus's voyage was not even the second to "find" America. By omitting evidence that Viking, Irish, and African explorers had in fact found it hundreds of years before Columbus set sail, the textbooks give students a frankly erroneous account of the New World's discovery.

Similarly, children are given an inaccurate view of history when they are told that "the first Christmas" took place when three wise men travelled from the east to bring gifts to a newborn baby named Jesus. Assuming that this biblical story happened as the Gospels claim, it probably wasn't at the end of December and therefore it cannot be considered the first Christmas—especially considering the fact that the Church didn't declare the holiday until three and a half centuries later.

None of this is to say that Christmas should not be recognized a Christian feast, or that Christians have not been instrumental in the holiday's development. Obviously, there is a strong Christian element, which is seen in the very fact that the holiday's name now contains the word "Christ," at least in the English version. Christians have contributed wonderful traditions to the holiday, developing an unruly heathen festival into a family-friendly occasion and infusing it with a deeply spiritual element summed up with the maxim "peace on earth." This line, of course, comes from the Bible's nativity story in the Gospel of Luke: "And suddenly there was with the angel a multitude of the heavenly host praising God, and saying, Glory to God in the highest, and on earth peace, good will toward men."

But while appreciating the Christian aspect of Christmas as important to the holiday's development and its significance to many believers, it must be acknowledged that this aspect has never been the central component of the holiday and is not an indispensable element. In fact, in most ways, the holiday might be celebrated exactly the same had the Church not declared December 25 as Jesus's birthday back in the fourth century. It wouldn't be called Christmas and it wouldn't have all of the same songs and symbols, but many elements would probably be the same—for example, the use of evergreens, the exchanging of gifts, and the custom of eating and drinking in abundance. This, of course, is due to the historical reality that these customs were not originally Christian.

What it all comes down to is that the modern Christmas holiday is the result of merging various traditions and beliefs, some of which are fundamentally contradictory in nature. The magical arts practiced by pre–Christian pagans, which eventually went underground as witchcraft, subsequently were rebranded as a harmless, largely metaphorical concept of "Christmas magic" and the "Christmas miracle." The pagans' beliefs in powerful gods led to the development of the Santa Claus figure. The misrule of Saturnalia evolved into the hedonistic pleasure associated with the secular celebration that is enjoyed today. Over the centuries, as we have seen, these contradictory elements have led to serious disagreements within the Church—falling down largely on Protestant vs. Catholic lines—about whether the holiday should be celebrated at all. Not only have some religious leaders objected on principle to the way that the holiday absorbed pagan elements or the fact that no reference to it can be found in Scripture, but the way that the holiday has been celebrated has been condemned as highly dishonorable to Christ.

Therefore, when Christians insist on displaying nativity scenes on government property, a practice which, disturbingly, most Americans say they support,[15] it is not simply an expression of faith—it is a political act geared towards defining the Christmas holiday not as the secular occasion that it is to so many, but as an explicitly Christian occasion. It is a continuation of an effort that has been underway for nearly 1,700 years to Christianize the celebration of the winter solstice. The effect that this has is to make the midwinter end-of-year observance an exclusive celebration rather than the inclusive occasion that it should be—for example by giving Muslims, Jews and others the false impression that there is some reason that they can't participate. With a deeper historical understanding of these traditions, it is clear that there is absolutely no reason why it should be seen as an exclusively Christian occasion. It is by its nature an inclusive end-of-year celebration of the world's natural life cycle.

In order to ensure that everyone can enjoy this celebration, which honestly does not belong to any one particular culture or religion, perhaps it is time to declare a truce in the War over Christmas. After all, if the warring parties in the First World War were able to lay down their weapons in the spirit of the season and join together in song and celebration, then surely the culture warriors of today can do the same. For the sake of all of us who just want to enjoy the holiday and feel the warmth of Christmas on the darkest days of the year, let's all just give it a rest.

In the immortal words of John Lennon, war is over if you want it.

Chapter Notes

Introduction

1. "Christmas." *Encyclopedia Britannica*, https://www.britannica.com/topic/Christmas. Accessed March 30, 2021.

2. Miltimore, Jon. "Red and Green Colors 'Not Appropriate' During the Holiday Season, University Says." *Intellectual Takeout*, https://www.intellectualtakeout.org/article/red-and-green-colors-not-appropriate-during-holiday-season-university-says/. Accessed July 4, 2021.

3. MacMullen, Ramsay. *Christianity and Paganism in the Fourth to Eighth Centuries*. New Haven: Yale University Press, 1997, p. 155.

4. Rodríguez, Ángel Manuel. "Should Adventists Celebrate Christmas?" Seventh-Day Adventist Church Biblical Research Institute, https://adventistbiblicalresearch.org/materials/should-adventists-celebrate-christmas/. Accessed March 30, 2021.

Chapter 1

1. MacMullen, Ramsay. *Christianity and Paganism in the Fourth to Eighth Centuries*. New Haven: Yale University Press, 1997, p. 4.

2. Flanders, Judith. *Christmas: A History*. London: Picador, 2017, p. 7.

3. Dickman, Laurel. "Christmas Isn't Christian: The Pagan Roots of the Winter Holiday." December 2, 2016. *Wear Your Voice*, https://www.wearyourvoicemag.com/christmas-pagan-roots-winter-holiday/. Accessed August 20, 2021.

4. Kageyama, Ben. "The History of Christmas." December 3, 2020. *History of Yesterday*, https://historyofyesterday.com/the-history-of-christmas-bd2703487989. Accessed August 20, 2021.

5. Vinje, Judith Gabriel. "Don't Take Odin out of Yule." December 18, 2014. *The Norwegian American*, www.norwegianamerican.com/dont-take-odin-out-of-yule/. Accessed June 21, 2021.

6. Page, Nick. *Christmas: Tradition, Truth and Total Baubles*. London: Hodder & Stoughton, 2020, p. 10.

7. Simmons, Kurt M. "The Origins of Christmas and the Date of Christ's Birth," *Journal of the Evangelical Theological Society* 58.2 (June 2015): 302.

8. Harvey, Geoff. "Why Christmas Is Not Pagan." The Good Shepherd Orthodox Church, December 16, 2018, www.thegoodshepherd.org.au/why-christmas-not-pagan. Accessed June 21, 2021.

9. O'Donnell, Hugh. "The 25th of December Pagan Feast or Patristic Tradition?" October 22, 2020. *Inside the Vatican*, https://insidethevatican.com/magazine/lead-story/the-25th-of-december-pagan-feast-or-patristic-tradition/. Accessed June 21, 2021.

10. "Christmas." *Encyclopedia Britannica*, https://www.britannica.com/topic/Christmas. Accessed June 21, 2021.

11. "On Idolatry." *Early Christian Writings*, www.earlychristianwritings.com/text/tertullian02.html. Accessed June 21, 2021.

12. Hijmans, Steven. "Sol Invictus, the Winter Solstice, and the Origins of Christmas," *Mouseion* 47/3 (2003): 379–80.

13. *Ibid.*, p. 587.

14. Miles, Clement A. *Christmas Customs and Traditions: Their History and Significance*. New York: Dover 1976 (republication of a book published in 1912), p. 23.

15. Mather, Increase. *A Testimony Against several Prophane and Superstitious Customs, Now Practised by some in New-England, The Evil whereof is evinced from the Holy Scriptures, and from the Writings both of Ancient and Modern Divines*. University of Michigan Digital Collections, https://quod.lib.umich.edu/e/eebo2/A50236.0001.001?rgn=main;view=fulltext. Accessed June 21, 2021.

16. Bauckham, Richard. *Jesus: A Very Short Introduction*. Oxford: Oxford University Press, 2011, p. 16.

17. Romey, Kristin. "The Real Story Behind the 'House of Jesus' Apostles' Discovery." *History*, National Geographic, May 3, 2021, www.nationalgeographic.com/history/article/jesus-bible-apostles-bethsaida-israel-archaeology. Accessed June 22, 2021.

18. Frodsham, Paul. *From Stonehenge to Santa Claus: The Evolution of Christmas.* Stroud, Gloucestershire: The History Press, 2008, p. 68.
19. Flanders, Judith. *Christmas: A History.* London: Picador, 2017, p. 6.
20. "New Theory Says Jesus Born in Summer of Year 12 B.C.," Associated Press. December 19, 1985.
21. St. Bede the Venerable. *Bede: The Reckoning of Time.* Liverpool: Liverpool University Press, 1999, p. 53.
22. Nordberg, Andreas. *Jul, disting och förkyrklig tideräkning: Kalendrar och kalendariska riter i det förkristna Norden.* Uppsala: Kungliga Gustav Adolfs Akademien, 2006. https://www.academia.edu/1366945/Jul_disting_och_f%C3%B6rkyrklig_tider%C3%A4kning. Accessed June 21, 2021.
23. "The Sun." *OpenBible,* https://www.openbible.info/topics/the_sun. Accessed April 24, 2021.
24. "John Chrysostom—Homily on the Date of Christmas, sections 1 and 2." *Early Church Texts,* https://earlychurchtexts.com/public/john_chrysostom_homily_in_diem_natalem_domini_nostri_jesu_christi.htm. Accessed June 14, 2021.
25. Spier, Jeffrey. "The Emergence of Christian Art." *Picturing the Bible: The Earliest Christian Art.* New Haven: Yale University Press, 2007, pp. 51–52.
26. Curtiss, Frank Homer. *The Pattern Life: Order of Christian Mystics.* Los Angeles: Willing, 1943, p. 40.

Chapter 2

1. Rubin, Miri. *The Middle Ages: A Very Short Introduction.* Oxford: Oxford University Press, 2014, p. 59.
2. "Summary." *Christianity and Paganism in the Fourth to Eighth Centuries* by Ramsay MacMullen. New Haven: Yale University Press, 1997, pp. 150–160. JSTOR, www.jstor.org/stable/j.ctt32bfqt.7. Accessed April 24, 2021.
3. Tertullian, *The Sacred Writings of Tertullian, Volume 1.* Jazzybee Verlag, 2017, p. 81.
4. *Book of Ancient Rome.* Bournemouth: Imagine, 2015, p. 116.
5. Hutton, Ronald. *Pagan Britain.* New Haven: Yale University Press, 2015, p. 232.
6. "Nero's Rome burns." November 13, 2009. *History.com,* https://www.history.com/this-day-in-history/neros-rome-burns. Accessed June 21, 2021.
7. Graves, Dan, MSL. "The First Recorded Celebration of Christmas." October 23, 2020. *Christianity.com,* Salem Web Network, www.christianity.com/church/church-history/timeline/301-600/the-1st-recorded-celebration-of-christmas-11629658.html. Accessed June 21, 2021.
8. Salzman, Michele Renee. *On Roman Time: The Codex-Calendar of 354 and the Rhythms of Urban Life in Late Antiquity.* Oakland: University of California, 1991, p. 45.
9. Conybeare, F.C. "The History of Christmas." *The American Journal of Theology* 3.1 (January 1899): 1–2.
10. "Epiphany (Christian)." New World Encyclopedia, www.newworldencyclopedia.org/entry/Epiphany_(Christian). Accessed June 21, 2021.
11. Wold, Rev. Kristian. "Advent: A Brief History." November 13, 2020. Hope Lutheran Church, https://www.hopelutheran.ca/news/advent-a-brief-history. Accessed May 4, 2021.
12. Curtiss, Frank Homer. *The Pattern Life: Order of Christian Mystics.* Los Angeles: Willing, 1943, p. 40.
13. Thurston, H. "Natal Day." *Catholic Encyclopedia.* Robert Appleton Company, 1911. www.newadvent.org/cathen/10709a.htm. Accessed March 1, 2021.
14. Jones, Cheslyn, Geoffrey Wainwright, Edward Yarnold, and Paul Bradshaw, eds. *The Study of Liturgy,* rev. ed. New York: Oxford University Press, New York, 1992, p. 474.
15. Kelly, Joseph F. "The Birth of Christmas." Center for Christian Ethics at Baylor University, https://www.baylor.edu/content/services/document.php/159119.pdf. Accessed April 29, 2021.
16. *Book of Ancient Rome.* Bournemouth: Imagine, 2015, p. 103.
17. Rawson, Beryl, ed. *A Companion to Families in the Greek and Roman Worlds.* Hoboken: Blackwell, 2010, p. 493.
18. Ibid., 491.
19. *Book of Ancient Rome.* Bournemouth: Imagine, 2015, p. 103.
20. Flanders, Judith. *Christmas: A History.* London: Picador, 2017, p. 9.
21. Sheldon, Natasha. "Io Saturnalia! The Origins and Celebration of a Favorite Roman Midwinter Festival." August 31, 2019. *History and Archaeology Online,* https://historyandarchaeologyonline.com/io-saturnalia-the-origins-and-celebration-of-a-favorite-roman-midwinter-festival/. Accessed June 22, 2021.
22. "Saturnalia." https://penelope.uchicago.edu/~grout/encyclopaedia_romana/calendar/saturnalia.html. Accessed June 22, 2021.
23. *Moral letters to Lucilius* (Epistulae morales ad Lucilium) by Seneca, translated by Richard Mott Gummere. Loeb Classical Library edition. https://en.wikisource.org/wiki/Moral_letters_to_Lucilius. Accessed April 30, 2021.
24. Rawson, Beryl, ed. *A Companion to Families in the Greek and Roman Worlds.* Hoboken: Blackwell, 2010, p. 491.
25. Kelly, Joseph F. "The Birth of Christmas." Center for Christian Ethics at Baylor University, https://www.baylor.edu/content/services/document.php/159119.pdf. Accessed April 29, 2021.
26. Sheldon, Natasha. "Io Saturnalia! The

Origins and Celebration of a Favorite Roman Midwinter Festival." August 31, 2019. *History and Archaeology Online,* https://historyandarchaeologyonline.com/io-saturnalia-the-origins-and-celebration-of-a-favorite-roman-midwinter-festival/. Accessed June 22, 2021.

27. Cartwright, Mark. "Saturnalia." *Ancient History Encyclopedia,* www.ancient.eu/Saturnalia/. Accessed June 21, 2021.

28. The Works of Lucian of Samosata. Translated by H.W. and F.G. Fowler. Oxford: Clarendon, 1905. http://lucianofsamosata.info/wiki/doku.php?id=home:texts_and_library:dialogues:saturnalia. Accessed June 22, 2021.

29. Cartwright, Mark. "Saturnalia." *Ancient History Encyclopedia,* www.ancient.eu/Saturnalia/. Accessed June 21, 2021. E

30. Del Re, Gerard, and Patricia. *The Christmas Almanac,* 2d ed. New York: Random House, 2004, pp. 66–67.

31. The History of Christmas, https://www.english-heritage.org.uk/christmas/the-history-of-christmas/. Accessed June 21, 2021.

32. Grimfrost Academy—Viking Religion, https://www.youtube.com/watch?v=ruQw7ieoGJM. Accessed June 21, 2021.

33. Cooke, Richard Joseph. *Christianity and Childhood: Or the Relation of Children to the Church.* London: Forgotten Books, 2018 (republication of a book published in 1891), p. 9.

34. Palmer, Robert E.A. *Rome and Carthage at Peace.* Franz Steiner, 1997, pp. 63–64.

35. Curran, J.R. *Pagan City and Christian Capital: Rome in the Fourth Century.* Oxford: Clarendon, 2000, p. 222.

36. "Sol Invictus, the Winter Solstice, and the Origins of Christmas," *Mouseion* 47/3 (2003): 377–98.

37. Salzman, Michele Renee. *On Roman Time: The Codex-Calendar of 354 and the Rhythms of Urban Life in Late Antiquity.* Oakland: University of California, 1991, p. 13.

38. Weiser, Francis X. *Handbook of Christian Feasts and Customs.* San Diego: Harcourt, 1958, p. 62.

39. *Ibid.*

40. Salzman, Michele Renee. *On Roman Time: The Codex-Calendar of 354 and the Rhythms of Urban Life in Late Antiquity.* Oakland: University of California, 1991, p. 120.

41. Curran, J.R., *Pagan City and Christian Capital: Rome in the Fourth Century.* Oxford, 2000. p. 229.

42. *Ibid.,* p. 323.

43. Kelly, Joseph F. "The Birth of Christmas." Center for Christian Ethics at Baylor University, https://www.baylor.edu/content/services/document.php/159119.pdf. Accessed April 29, 2021.

44. "Christianity becomes the religion of the Roman Empire—February 27, 380." *Deutsche Welle,* https://www.dw.com/en/christianity-becomes-the-religion-of-the-roman-empire-february-27-380/a-4602728. Accessed May 4, 2021.

45. "John Chrysostom—Homily on the Date of Christmas, sections 1 and 2." *Early Church Texts,* https://www.earlychurchtexts.com/public/john_chrysostom_homily_in_diem_natalem_domini_nostri_jesu_christi.htm. Accessed April 25, 2021.

46. Salzman, Michele Renee. *On Roman Time: The Codex-Calendar of 354 and the Rhythms of Urban Life in Late Antiquity.* Oakland: University of California, 1991, p. 239.

47. Hutton, Ronald. *Stations of the Sun: A History of the Ritual Year in Britain.* New York: Oxford University Press, 2001, Chapter 1.

48. Sheldon, Natasha. "Io Saturnalia! The Origins and Celebration of a Favorite Roman Midwinter Festival." August 31, 2019. *History and Archaeology Online,* https://historyandarchaeologyonline.com/io-saturnalia-the-origins-and-celebration-of-a-favorite-roman-midwinter-festival/. Accessed June 22, 2021.

49. "Bah! Humbug! Complaining about Holiday Gifts 1600 Years Ago." December 27, 2020. *Medievalists.net,* www.medievalists.net/2014/12/bah-humbug-complaining-holiday-gifts-1600-years-ago/. Accessed June 24, 2021.

50. Asterius of Amasea. "On the Festival of the Calends." *Early Christian Writings,* http://www.earlychristianwritings.com/fathers/asterius_04_sermon4.html. Accessed June 24, 2021.

51. "Saturnalia: The origins of the debauched Roman 'Christmas.'" *History Extra,* https://www.historyextra.com/period/roman/how-did-the-romans-celebrate-christmas/. Accessed April 5, 2021.

52. MacMullen, Ramsay. *Christianity and Paganism in the Fourth to Eighth Centuries.* New Haven: Yale University Press, 1997.

53. Weiser, Francis X. *Handbook of Christian Feasts and Customs.* San Diego: Harcourt, 1958, p. 62.

54. Watts, Edward J. *The Final Pagan Generation: Rome's Unexpected Path to Christianity.* Berkeley: University of California Press, 2020.

Chapter 3

1. Gill, N.S. "Greek Winter Solstice Celebrations in Honor of Poseidon." *ThoughtCo,* www.thoughtco.com/greek-winter-solstice-celebrations-120989. Accessed June 22, 2021.

2. Simek, Rudolf. *A Dictionary of Northern Mythology.* Suffolk: Boydell and Brewer, 2008, p. 220.

3. St. Bede the Venerable. *Bede: The Reckoning of Time.* Liverpool: Liverpool University Press, 1999, p. 53.

4. Della-Piana, Patricia. *Witch Daze: A Perennial Pagan Calendar.* Morrisville, NC: Lulu.com, 2010, p. 22.

5. Vulcănescu, Romulus, ed. *Romanian Mythology*. Bucharest: Academiei, 1985, p. 382.
6. Frodsham, Paul. *From Stonehenge to Santa Claus: The Evolution of Christmas*. Stroud, Gloucestershire: The History Press, 2008, p. 46.
7. Miles, Clement A. *Christmas Customs and Traditions: Their History and Significance*. New York: Dover, 1976 (republication of a book published in 1912), p. 182.
8. Foley, Daniel. *The Christmas Tree*. Boston: Chilton Book Co., 1961, p. 24.
9. Alberge, Dalya. "Stonehenge was built on solstice axis, dig confirms." September 8, 2013. *The Guardian*, https://www.theguardian.com/culture/2013/sep/08/stonehenge-ice-age-solstice-axis. Accessed June 21, 2021.
10. Frodsham, Paul. *From Stonehenge to Santa Claus: The Evolution of Christmas*. Stroud, Gloucestershire: The History Press, 2008, pp. 24–25.
11. *Ibid.*, p. 47.
12. Hutton, Ronald. *Pagan Britain*. New Haven: Yale University Press, 2015, pp. 171–72.
13. *Ibid.*, p. 175.
14. *Ibid.*, p. 229.
15. *Ibid.*, p. 235.
16. *Ibid.*, p. 236.
17. Hutton, Ronald. *The Rise and Fall of Merry England: The Ritual Year 1400–1700*. New York: Oxford University Press, 1994, p. 15.
18. "Saint Augustine of Canterbury (604)." May 28, 2016. *Catholicism.org*, https://catholicism.org/saint-augustine-of-canterbury-604.html. Accessed June 24, 2021.
19. Hutton, Ronald. *Pagan Britain*. New Haven: Yale University Press, 2015, pp. 292–93.
20. Grig, Lucy, ed. "Interpreting the Kalends of January: A Case Study for Late Antique Popular Culture?" *Popular Culture in the Ancient World*. Cambridge: Cambridge University Press, 2016, pp. 237–56.
21. Müller-Ebeling, Claudia, and Christian Rätsch. *Pagan Christmas: The Plants, Spirits, and Rituals at the Origins of Yuletide*. Rochester, VT: Inner Traditions, 2006, p. 11.
22. "Anglo-Saxons: a Brief History." The Historical Association, www.history.org.uk/primary/resource/3865/anglo-saxons-a-brief-history. Accessed June 25, 2021.
23. Del Re, Gerard, and Patricia. *The Christmas Almanac*, 2d ed. New York: Random House, 2004, pp. 66–67.
24. Hutton, Ronald. *The Pagan Religions of the Ancient British Isles: Their Nature and Legacy* (reprint edition). Hoboken: Wiley-Blackwell, 1993, p. 265.
25. *Ibid.*
26. Hutton, Ronald. *Pagan Britain*. New York: Yale University Press, 2015, p. 322.
27. *Ibid.*, p. 327.
28. Roesdahl, Else. *The Vikings*. London: Penguin, 1999, p. 147.
29. Weiser, Francis X. *Handbook of Christian Feasts and Customs*. San Diego: Harcourt, 1958, p. 63.
30. Pertz, G.H., ed. "Capitulare Paderbrunnense." *MGH, Leges, I*. Hannover, 1835, reprinted 1963, p. 48.
31. "The Heliand: A Germanic Account of Jesus Written to Suit the Saxon World." February 17, 2019. *Ancient Origins*, https://www.ancient-origins.net/artifacts-ancient-writings/heliand-germanic-portrait-jesus-0011498. Accessed July 20, 2021.
32. Frassetto, Michael. *The Early Medieval World: From the Fall of Rome to the Time of Charlemagne*. Santa Barbara: ABC-CLIO, 2013, p. 306.
33. Murphy, G. Ronald. *The Saxon Savior: The Germanic Transformation of the Gospel in the Ninth-Century Heliand*. New York: Oxford University Press, 1989, pp. 51–52.
34. Dodwell, C.R. *The Pictorial Arts of the West, 800–1200*. New Haven: Yale University Press, 1993, p. 79.
35. Assarsson, Berndt David. "Retrospective History of the Mission in Sweden." *St. Ansgar's Scandinavian Catholic League of New York Bulletin* 25 (1926). http://www.saintansgars.com/download/pdf/1926%20-%20Bulletin%20No.%2025.pdf. Accessed May 1, 2021.
36. Damaschin, Liliana. "Slavic mythology." *Academia.edu*, https://www.academia.edu/10255821/Slavic_mythology?auto=download&email_work_card=download-paper. Accessed May 3, 2021.
37. *Ibid.*
38. *Ibid.*
39. Grimm, Jacob. *Teutonic Mythology* (translated from the 4th ed. with notes and appendix by James Steven Stallybrass). London: George Bell and Sons, 1882, p. 4.
40. *Ibid.*, p. 43.
41. *Ibid.*, p. 51.
42. Blind, Karl. "The Boar's Head Dinner at Oxford, and a Teutonic Sun-God." *Saga-Book* 1 (October 1892–December 1896), Viking Society for Northern Research, p. 93.
43. Byghan, Yowann. *Sacred and Mythological Animals: A Worldwide Taxonomy*. Jefferson, NC: McFarland, 2020, p. 130.
44. Frith, Alex. *Illustrated Norse Myths*. London: Usborne, 2012, p. 279.
45. Nordberg, Andreas. *Jul, disting och förkyrklig tideräkning: Kalendrar och kalendariska riter i det förkristna Norden*. Uppsala: Kungliga Gustav Adolfs Akademien, 2006, p. 156. https://www.academia.edu/1366945/Jul_disting_och_f%C3%B6rkyrklig_tider%C3%A4kning. Accessed June 21, 2021.
46. *Ibid.*
47. Henriksson, Göran. "The pagan Great Midwinter Sacrifice and the 'royal' mounds at Old Uppsala." Uppsala University website, https://www.astro.uu.se/archast/Henriksson.pdf. Accessed June 25, 2021.

48. "What is the Origin of Yule?" *Jolablot*, https://jolablot.com/origin-of-yule/. Accessed August 24, 2021.

49. Gunnell, Terry. "The Season of the Disir: The Winter Nights, and the Disablot in Early Medieval Scandinavian Belief." *Cosmos* 16 (2000): 126.

50. Foley, Daniel. *The Christmas Tree.* Boston: Chilton Book Co., 1961, p. 29.

51. Miles, Clement A. *Christmas Customs and Traditions: Their History and Significance.* New York: Dover, 1976 (republication of a book published in 1912), p. 181.

52. Tetzner, Noah. "A Tale of Two Yules." *Medievalists.net*, https://www.medievalists.net/2020/12/medieval-yule/. Accessed May 24, 2021.

53. "St. Lucia's Day." *Encyclopedia Britannica*, https://www.britannica.com/topic/St-Lucias-Day. Accessed June 28, 2021.

54. Hollander, M. Lee, trans. *Heimskringla: History of the Kings of Norway.* Austin: University of Texas Press, 2007, p. 107.

55. Keyser, Rudolph. *The Religion of The Northmen.* Translated by Barclay Pennock. New York: Charles B. Norton, 1854.

56. Lothursdottir, Alfta Svanni. "The Religious Practices of the Pre-Christian and Viking Age North." 2003. Northvegr.org, https://web.archive.org/web/20070927235136/http://www.northvegr.org/northern/book/religious017.php. Accessed May 9, 2021.

57. Grimm, Jacob. *Teutonic Mythology* (translated from the 4th ed. with notes and appendix by James Steven Stallybrass). London: George Bell and Sons, 1882, p. 11.

58. Roesdahl, Else. *The Vikings.* London: Penguin, 1998, p. 149.

59. MacMullen, Ramsay. *Christianizing the Roman Empire: A.D. 100–400.* New Haven: Yale University Press, 1984.

60. Müller-Ebeling, Claudia, and Christian Rätsch. *Pagan Christmas: The Plants, Spirits, and Rituals at the Origins of Yuletide.* Rochester, VT: Inner Traditions, 2006, p. 25.

61. MacDonald, Fiona. *Christmas: A Very Peculiar History.* Brighton: Book House, 2010, p. 143.

62. Plotnikova, A.A. "Чесница." In Svetlana Mikhaylovna Tolstaya and Ljubinko Radenković, eds., Словенска митологија: енциклопедијски речник [Slavic mythology: encyclopedic dictionary]. Belgrade: Zepter Book World, 2001, pp. 577–78.

Chapter 4

1. Rubin, Miri. *The Middle Ages: A Very Short Introduction.* Oxford: Oxford University Press, 2014. p. 60.

2. Grimm, Jacob. *Teutonic Mythology* (translated from the 4th edition with notes and appendix by James Steven Stallybrass). London: George Bell and Sons, 1882, p. 4.

3. Gillan, Joanna. "Saint Patrick: When the True Story is More Exciting than the Legend." *Ancient Origins*, https://www.ancient-origins.net/history-ancient-traditions/st-patrick-ireland-001455. Accessed March 26, 2021.

4. Godkin, James. *Ireland and Her Churches.* London: Chapman and Hall, 1867, p. 26.

5. Ellis, Peter Berresford. *A Brief History of the Druids.* Philadelphia: Running Press, 2002, pp. 133–34.

6. Bede, *The Venerable Bede's Ecclesiastical History of England.* Nabu Press. lib. i. cap. 30., edited by J.A. Giles (London, 1843), vol. ii, p. 142.

7. Hollander, M. Lee, trans. *Heimskringla: History of the Kings of Norway.* Austin: University of Texas Press, 2007, p. 106.

8. Gunnell, Terry. "The Season of the Disir: The Winter Nights, and the Disablot in Early Medieval Scandinavian Belief," *Cosmos* 16 (2000): 123.

9. Derry, T.K. *A History of Scandinavia: Norway, Sweden, Denmark, Finland, and Iceland.* Minneapolis: University of Minnesota Press, 1979, p. 27.

10. Williams, Gareth, Peter Pentz, and Matthias Wemhoff, eds., *Vikings: Life and Legend.* London: The British Museum Press, 2014, p. 165.

11. Roesdahl, Else. *The Vikings.* London: Penguin, 1998, p. 158.

12. Ibid.

13. Ibid., p. 152.

14. Ibid., p. 159.

15. Bingham, Joseph. *The Antiquities of the Christian Church.* London: Henry G. Bohn, 1843, p. 357.

16. Alvarez, Sandra. "Advent in the Middle Ages." *Medievalists.net*, https://www.medievalists.net/2015/12/63132/. Accessed March 22, 2021.

17. "Feast of Fools." *Encyclopedia Britannica*, https://www.britannica.com/topic/Feast-of-Fools. Accessed July 19, 2021.

18. "St. Lucia's Day." *Encyclopedia Britannica*, https://www.britannica.com/topic/St-Lucias-Day. Accessed March 22, 2021.

19. Hutton, Richard. *Stations of the Sun: A History of the Ritual Year in Britain.* New York: Oxford University Press, 2001, Chapter 4.

20. Gill, Robin D. *Topsy-Turvey 1585: 611 Ways Europeans & Japanese are Contrary* (translated from *Tratado* by Luis Frois S.J.). Key Biscayne, FL: Paraverse Press, 2004, p. 331.

21. Frodsham, Paul. *From Stonehenge to Santa Claus: The Evolution of Christmas.* Stroud, Gloucestershire: The History Press, 2008, p. 100.

22. Chambers, Robert. *The Book of Days: A Miscellany of Popular Antiquities in Connection with the Calendar: Including Anecdote, Biography, & History, Curiosities and Literature, and Oddities of Human Life and Character.* London: W&R Chambers, 1863, p. 753.

23. Miles, Clement A. *Christmas Customs and Traditions: Their History and Significance.* New York: Dover, 1976 (republication of a book published in 1912), p. 185.

24. Nissenbaum, Stephen. *The Battle for Christmas: A Social and Cultural History of Our Most Cherished Holiday.* New York: Vintage, 1997, p. 5.

25. Flanders, Judith. *Christmas: A History.* London: Picador, 2017, p. 7.

26. Ludovicus, J.R. Milis, ed. *The Pagan Middle Ages.* Woodbridge: The Boydell Press, 1998, p. 23.

27. Rubin, Miri. *The Middle Ages: A Very Short Introduction.* Oxford: Oxford University Press, 2014, p. 61.

28. Margetson, Stella. "Medieval Nativity Plays." *History Today* 22, no. 12 (December 1972). https://www.historytoday.com/archive/medieval-nativity-plays. Accessed March 26, 2021.

29. Cartwright, Mark. "A Medieval Christmas." *World History Encyclopedia*, https://www.ancient.eu/article/1288/a-medieval-christmas/. Accessed March 26, 2021.

30. Ridenour, Al. *The Krampus and the Old, Dark Christmas: Roots and Rebirth of the Folkloric Devil.* Port Townsend, WA: Feral House, 2016.

31. Foley, Daniel. *The Christmas Tree.* Boston: Chilton Book Co., 1961, p. 39.

32. Miles, Clement A. *Christmas Customs and Traditions: Their History and Significance.* New York: Dover, 1976 (republication of a book published in 1912), p. 300.

33. Hutton, Ronald. *The Rise and Fall of Merry England: The Ritual Year 1400–1700.* New York: Oxford University Press, 1994, p. 9.

34. Chambers, Robert. *The Book of Days: A Miscellany of Popular Antiquities in Connection with the Calendar: Including Anecdote, Biography, & History, Curiosities and Literature, and Oddities of Human Life and Character.* London: W&R Chambers, 1863, p. 789.

35. Margetson, Stella. "Medieval Nativity Plays." *History Today* 22, no. 12 (December 1972). https://www.historytoday.com/archive/medieval-nativity-plays. Accessed March 26, 2021.

36. "The History of Fortunatus." February 6, 2014. The British Library, www.bl.uk/collection-items/the-history-of-fortunatus. Accessed June 27, 2021.

37. Dekker, Thomas. *The pleasant comedie of old Fortunatus As it was plaied before the Queenes Maiestie this Christmas, by the Right Honourable the Earle of Nottingham, Lord high Admirall of England his seruants.* London: S. Stafford,1600, p. 53.

38. *Ibid.*, p. 60.

39. "St. Francis of Assisi." *New Advent*, https://www.newadvent.org/cathen/06221a.htm.

40. "A History of Christmas Hymns and Carols." *The Hymns and Carols of Christmas*, http://www.hymnsandcarolsofchristmas.com/HTML/History_of_Hymns_and_Carols.htm. Accessed March 26, 2021.

41. Frodsham, Paul. *From Stonehenge to Santa Claus: The Evolution of Christmas.* Stroud, Gloucesteshire: The History Press, 2008, p. 106.

42. Athanassakis, Apostolos N. (trans., intro., and notes) *The Homeric Hymns.* Baltimore: Johns Hopkins University Press 1976 (updated in 2004).

43. Lenzi, Alan, ed. *Reading Akkadian Prayers & Hymns: An Introduction.* Atlanta: Society of Biblical Literature, 2011, pp. 381–82.

44. "The Hymns and Carols." Women for Faith and Family, http://archive.wf-f.org/Hymns-carols.html. August 11, 2021.

45. Terry, Sir Richard Runciman. *A Medieval Carol Book: The Melodies Chiefly from MMS.* London: Burns Oates & Washbourne, 1932, pp. 22–23.

46. *Ibid.*, p. 39.

47. Husk, William Henry. *Songs of the Nativity.* London: John Camden Hotten, 1868.

48. Frodsham, Paul. *From Stonehenge to Santa Claus: The Evolution of Christmas.* Stroud, Gloucestershire: The History Press, 2008, p. 109.

49. Flanders, Judith. *Christmas: A History.* London: Picador, 2017, p. 56.

50. Derry, T.K. *A History of Scandinavia: Norway, Sweden, Denmark, Finland, and Iceland.* Minneapolis: University of Minnesota Press, 1979, p. 94.

51. Pallesen, Birgitte Duelund. "Thomas Kingo." *Forfatterweb*, https://forfatterweb.dk/oversigt/kingo-thomas. Accessed March 26, 2021.

52. Nissenbaum, Stephen W. "Christmas in Early New England, 1620–1820: Puritanism, Popular Culture, and the Printed Word." *Proceedings of the American Antiquarian Society* 106, American Antiquarian Society, Worcester, MA, 2012, p. 136.

53. *Ibid.*, p. 137.

Chapter 5

1. Nissenbaum, Stephen. *The Battle for Christmas: A Social and Cultural History of Our Most Cherished Holiday.* New York: Vintage, 1997, p. 6.

2. "Seven Medieval Christmas Traditions." December 19, 2019. *Medievalists.net*, www.medievalists.net/2012/12/seven-medieval-christmas-traditions/. Accessed June 26, 2021.

3. *Ibid.*

4. "Troels-Lund: Om Julen i 1500-Tallet." Aarhus University, https://danmarkshistorien.dk/leksikon-og-kilder/vis/materiale/troels-lund-om-julen-i-1500-tallet/. Accessed June 26, 2021.

5. Salisbury, Eve. *The Trials and Joys of Marriage.* Kalamazoo: Medieval Institute Publications, 2002.

6. Ludovicus, J.R. Milis, ed. *The Pagan Middle Ages*. Woodbridge: The Boydell Press, 1998, p. 6.
7. Thorisson, Jon, ed. *The Viking Gods*. London: Gudrun, 1995, p. 11.
8. Nedelius, Sabina. "Fun Etymology Special—Jul." September 17, 2019. *The Historical Linguist Channel*, https://thehistoricallinguistchannel.com/fun-etymology-tuesday-jul/. Accessed June 26, 2021.
9. "Jolly (Adj.)." *Etymonline*, https://www.etymonline.com/word/jolly. Accessed June 26, 2021.
10. Simek, Rudolf. *A Dictionary of Northern Mythology*. Suffolk: Boydell and Brewer, 2008, pp. 379–80.
11. Lund, Troels Frederik. *Dagligt Liv i Norden i det sekstende Aarhundrede / Bog VII*. Gyldendal, 1900, p. 23.
12. Kindtler-Nielsen, Emrah Sütcü, and Bue. "Hvordan blev jul fejret i middelalderen?" December 22, 2020. *Historienet.dk*, https://historienet.dk/jul/hvordan-blev-jul-fejret-i-middelalderen. Accessed June 26, 2021.
13. Hutton, Ronald. *The Rise and Fall of Merry England: The Ritual Year 1400–1700*. New York: Oxford University Press, 1994, p. 9.
14. "Wassailing." *Historic UK*, www.historic-uk.com/CultureUK/Wassailing/. Accessed June 26, 2021.
15. Hutton, Ronald. *Pagan Britain*. New Haven: Yale University Press, 2015, p. 372.
16. Hutton, Ronald. *The Rise and Fall of Merry England: The Ritual Year 1400–1700*. New York: Oxford University Press, 1994, p. 14.
17. Rickert, Edith. *Ancient English Christmas Carols: 1400–1700*. London: Chatto & Windus, 1914, pp. 134–35.
18. Flanders, Judith. *Christmas: A History*. London: Picador, 2017, p. 67.
19. Nissenbaum, Stephen. *The Battle for Christmas: A Social and Cultural History of Our Most Cherished Holiday*. New York: Vintage, 1997, p. 9.
20. "Puritanism." *Encyclopedia Britannica*, www.britannica.com/topic/Puritanism. Accessed June 26, 2021.
21. Thomas, Keith. *Religion and the Decline of Magic: Studies in Popular Beliefs in Sixteenth and Seventeenth-Century England*. London: Weidenfeld and Nicolson, 1971, p. 65.
22. Durston, Chris. "Lords of Misrule: The Puritan War on Christmas 1642–60." *History Today* 35, no. 12 (December 1985). https://www.historytoday.com/archive/puritan-war-christmas. Accessed June 26, 2021.
23. http://www.olivercromwell.org/faqs4.htm.
24. Miles, Clement A. *Christmas Customs and Traditions: Their History and Significance*. New York: Dover, 1976 (republication of a book published in 1912), p. 185.
25. "Christmas Abolished!" *Oliver Cromwell—FAQ 4*, The Cromwell Association, www.olivercromwell.org/faqs4.htm. Accessed June 26, 2021.
26. "Plum Pudding Riot." December 17, 2015. *The History Jar*, https://thehistoryjar.com/tag/plum-pudding-riot/. Accessed June 27, 2021.
27. "Plymouth Rock." *Encyclopedia Britannica*, www.britannica.com/topic/Plymouth-Rock-United-States-history. Accessed June 27, 2021.
28. Barnett, James H. *The American Christmas: A Study in National Culture*. New York: Macmillan, 1954, p. 3.
29. Ibid., p. 4.
30. Nissenbaum, Stephen. *The Battle for Christmas: A Social and Cultural History of Our Most Cherished Holiday*. New York: Vintag, 1997, p. 4.
31. Marling, Karal Ann. *Merry Christmas! Celebrating America's Greatest Holiday*. Cambridge: Harvard University Press, 2000, p. 44.
32. Flanders, Judith. *Christmas: A History*. London: Picador, 2017, p. 47.
33. Coldwell, Chris. "The Religious Observance of Christmas and 'Holy Days' in American Presbyterianism—Naphtali Press." Originally published in *The Blue Banner* 8, nos. 9–1 (September/October 1999). Republished by Naphtali Press, December 17, 2016, www.naphtali.com/articles/chris-coldwell/the-religious-observance-of-christmas-and-holy-days-in-american-presbyterianism/. Accessed June 27, 2021.
34. Barnett, James H. *The American Christmas: A Study in National Culture*. New York: Macmillan, 1954, p. 8.
35. Ibid., p. 5.
36. Hervey, Thomas Kibble. *The Book of Christmas; Descriptive of the Customs, Ceremonies, Traditions, Superstitions, Fun, Feeling, and Festivities of the Christmas Season*. Pierce Press, 2011 (reprint of a book published in 1888), p. 33.

Chapter 6

1. Goody, Jack. *The Culture of Flowers*. Cambridge: Cambridge University Press, 1993, p. 201.
2. Foley, Daniel. *The Christmas Tree*. Boston: Chilton Book Co., 1961, p. 23.
3. Welscher, Alexander. "Was the First Ever Christmas Tree Put up in the Baltics?" December 25, 2020. *Baltic Business Quarterly*, www.lrt.lt/en/news-in-english/19/1302535/was-the-first-ever-christmas-tree-put-up-in-the-baltics. Accessed June 25, 2021.
4. Foley, Daniel. *The Christmas Tree*. Boston: Chilton Book Co., 1961, pp. 42–43.
5. Perry, Joe. *Christmas in Germany: A Cultural History*. Chapel Hill: University of North Carolina Press, 2010, p. 32.
6. Elia. "The Christmas Tree." H. Harbaugh, ed. *The Guardian* 16 (January 1865), p. 222.
7. Perry, Joe. *Christmas in Germany: A*

Cultural History. Chapel Hill: University of North Carolina Press, 2010, pp. 31–32.

8. Foley, Daniel. *The Christmas Tree*. Boston: Chilton Book Co., 1961, p. 45.

9. Hutton, Ronald. *Pagan Britain*. New Haven: Yale University Press, 2015, p. 37.

10. Ellis, Peter. *A Brief History of the Druids*. London: Little, Brown, 2002, p. 39.

11. Miles, Clement A. *Christmas Customs and Traditions: Their History and Significance*. New York: Dover, 1976 (republication of a book published in 1912), p. 269.

12. Hutton, Ronald. *Stations of the Sun: A History of the Ritual Year in Britain*. New York: Oxford University Press, 2001, pp. 312–13.

13. Davies, Owen. *Paganism: A Very Short Introduction*. Oxford: Oxford University Press, 2011, p. 28.

14. "Ash Mythology and Folklore." March 5, 2021. *Trees for Life*, https://treesforlife.org.uk/into-the-forest/trees-plants-animals/trees/ash/ash-mythology-and-folklore/. Accessed June 25, 2021.

15. "Yggdrasil—Livets Træ—En Odins Fortælling." December 17, 2018. *Yggdrasil—Livets Træ*, www.odinsklinge.dk/da/odins-fortael linger/yggdrasil-livets-trae.html. Accessed June 25, 2021.

16. Williams, Gareth, Peter Pentz, and Matthias Wemhoff, eds. *Vikings: Life and Legend*. London: The British Museum Press, 2014, p. 167.

17. https://www.odinsklinge.dk/da/odins-fortaellinger/yggdrasil-livets-trae.html.

18. Keyser, Rudolph. *The Religion of The Northmen*. Trans. Barclay Pennock. New York: Charles B. Norton, 1854, p. 118.

19. Țenche-Constantinescu Alina-Maria, Varan Claudia, Borlea Fl., Madoşa E., Szekely G. "The symbolism of the linden tree." *Journal of Horticulture, Forestry and Biotechnology* 19, no. 2 (2015): 237–42. tm.ro/romana/2015/Lucrari%20PDF/Lucrari%20PDF%2019(2)/41Tenche%20Alina%202.pdf. Accessed May 1, 2021.

20. Williams, Rose. *The Clay-Footed Superheroes: Mythology Tales for the New Millennium*. Wauconda, IL: Bolchazy-Carducci, 2010, p. 56.

21. Frazer, James George. *The Golden Bough: A Study in Magic and Religion*. Third Edition, Vol. 2 of 12. Project Gutenberg. Chapel Hill: University of North Carolina Press, 2019, pp. 122–23.

22. Paul Roche, *Lucan: De Bello Civili, Book 1*. Oxford: Oxford University Press, 2009, p. 296.

23. Grimm, Jacob. *Teutonic Mythology* (translated from the 4th ed. with notes and appendix by James Steven Stallybrass). London: George Bell and Sons, London, 1882, p. 69.

24. *Ibid.*, p. 72.

25. Davies, Owen. *Paganism: A Very Short Introduction*. Oxford: Oxford University Press, 2011, pp. 22–23.

26. Weninger, Father Francis Xavier. "St. Martin, Bishop of Tours." *Catholic Harbor of Faith and Morals*, http://catholicharboroffaith andmorals.com/St.%20Martin%20of%20Tours.html. Accessed March 26, 2021.

27. Foley, Daniel. *The Christmas Tree*. Boston: Chilton Book Co., 1961, p. 28.

28. Miles, Clement A. *Christmas Customs and Traditions: Their History and Significance*. New York: Dover 1976 (republication of a book published in 1912), p. 264.

29. Frodsham, Paul. *From Stonehenge to Santa Claus: The Evolution of Christmas*. Stroud, Gloucestershire: The History Press, 2008, p. 183.

30. Van Dyke, Henry. *The First Christmas Tree*. The Project Gutenberg eBook. https://www.gutenberg.org/files/16134/16134-h/16134-h.htm#1. Accessed April 28, 2021.

31. "Saint Boniface." *Encyclopedia Britannica*, https://www.britannica.com/biography/Saint-Boniface. Accessed April 28, 2021.

32. Müller-Ebeling, Claudia, and Christian Rätsch. *Pagan Christmas: The Plants, Spirits, and Rituals at the Origins of Yuletide*. Rochester, VT: Inner Traditions, 2006, p. 25.

33. "History of Christmas Trees." October 27, 2009, updated December 2, 2020. History.com, https://www.history.com/topics/christmas/history-of-christmas-trees. Accessed January 2, 2021.

34. Barnes, Alison. "The First Christmas Tree." *History Today* 56 (December 12, 2006). https://www.historytoday.com/archive/history-matters/first-christmas-tree. Accessed April 28, 2021.

35. Higgins, Jim. "Book Explores Culture's Route to 'Inventing the Christmas Tree.'" *Journal Sentinel*, https://archive.jsonline.com/entertainment/arts/book-explores-cultures-route-to-inventing-the-christmas-tree-7s7pjne-181572861.html/. Accessed June 25, 2021.

36. Frodsham, Paul. *From Stonehenge to Santa Claus: The Evolution of Christmas*. Stroud, Gloucestershire: The History Press, 2008, p. 184.

37. "Christmas tree." *Encyclopedia Britannica*, https://www.britannica.com/plant/Christmas-tree. Accessed April 29, 2021.

38. Brunner, Bernd. *Inventing the Christmas Tree*. New Haven: Yale University Press, 2012, p. 90.

39. Perry, Joe. *Christmas in Germany: A Cultural History*. Chapel Hill: University of North Carolina Press, 2010, p. 32.

40. Miles, Clement A. *Christmas Customs and Traditions: Their History and Significance*. New York: Dover, 1976 (republication of a book published in 1912), p. 265.

41. Frodsham, Paul. *From Stonehenge to Santa Claus: The Evolution of Christmas*. Stroud, Gloucestershire: The History Press, 2008, p. 187.

Chapter 7

1. Walker, Barbara. *The Woman's Encyclopedia of Myths and Secrets*. New York: Harper and Row, 1983, pp. 725–26.

2. Hurt, Carla. "Saint Nicholas through the Ages." December 24, 2013. *Found in Antiquity*, https://foundinantiquity.com/2013/12/24/saint-nicholas-through-the-ages/. Accessed August 26, 2021.

3. Flanders, Judith. *Christmas: A History*. London: Picador, 2017, p. 100.

4. "Who Is St. Nicholas?" St. Nicholas Center, https://www.stnicholascenter.org/who-is-st-nicholas. Accessed June 28, 2021.

5. Seal, Jeremy. *Nicholas: The Epic Journey from Saint to Santa Claus*. New York: Bloomsbury, 2005.

6. Tsolakidou, Stella. "What Do Santa Claus, St. Nicholas and Poseidon Have in Common?" January 25, 2021. *GreekReporter.com*, https://greece.greekreporter.com/2012/12/27/what-do-santa-claus-st-nicholas-and-poseidon-have-in-common/. Accessed June 28, 2021.

7. Swartz, Jr., B.K. "The Origin of American Christmas Myth and Customs." http://www.arthuriana.co.uk/xmas/swartz/American%20Christmas%20Origins.htm. Accessed June 28, 2021.

8. Makris, A. "Temple of Poseidon Found in Sozopol." January 26, 2021. *GreekReporter.com*, https://eu.greekreporter.com/2012/12/16/temple-of-poseidon-found-in-sozopol/, Accessed June 28, 2021.

9. Hurt, Carla. "Saint Nicholas through the Ages." December 24, 2013. Found in Antiquity, https://foundinantiquity.com/2013/12/24/saint-nicholas-through-the-ages/. Accessed June 28, 2021.

10. Hawkins, Paul. *Bad Santas: Disquieting Winter Folk Tales for Grown-Ups*. London: Simon & Schuster, 2013, p. 32.

11. Hawkins, Paul. *Bad Santas: Disquieting Winter Folk Tales for Grown-Ups*. London: Simon & Schuster, 2013, pp. 33–34.

12. Dixon-Kennedy, Mike. *Encyclopedia of Russian and Slavic Myth and Legend*. Santa Barbara: ABC-CLIO, 1998, p. 178.

13. Barnett, James H. *The American Christmas: A Study in National Culture*. New York: Macmillan, 1954, p. 10.

14. Raedisch, Linda. *The Old Magic of Christmas: Yuletide Traditions for the Darkest Days of the Year*. Woodbury, MN: Llewellyn, 2013, p. 89.

15. Jerman, Tom A. *Santa Claus Worldwide: A History of St. Nicholas and Other Holiday Gift-Bringers*. Jefferson, NC: McFarland, 2020, p. 6.

16. *Ibid.*, p. 121.

17. Swartz, Jr., B.K. "The Origin of American Christmas Myth and Customs." http://www.arthuriana.co.uk/xmas/swartz/American%20Christmas%20Origins.htm. Accessed May 29, 2021.

18. "Father Christmas." St. Nicholas Center, https://www.stnicholascenter.org/who-is-st-nicholas/origin-of-santa/father-christmas. Accessed June 28, 2021.

19. Jones, Charles W. "Knickerbocker Santa Claus." October 1954. *The New-York Historical Society Quarterly*, https://www.stnicholascenter.org/who-is-st-nicholas/origin-of-santa/knickerbocker. Accessed June 28, 2021.

20. Raedisch, Linda. *The Old Magic of Christmas: Yuletide Traditions for the Darkest Days of the Year*. Woodbury, MN: Llewellyn, 2013, p. 87.

21. Lecouteux, Claude. *Encyclopedia of Norse and Germanic Folklore, Mythology, and Magic*. Rochester, VT: Inner Traditions, 2014.

22. Vinje, Judith Gabriel. "Don't Take Odin out of Yule." December 18, 2014. *The Norwegian American*, www.norwegianamerican.com/dont-take-odin-out-of-yule/. Accessed June 21, 2021.

23. Stacey Baker, Menzel, Cara Okleshen, and Robert Mittelstaedt. "Santa Claus Does More than Deliver Toys: Advertising's Commercialization of the Collective Memory of Americans." *Consumption, Markets and Culture* 4, no. 3 (2001): 216.

24. Raedisch, Linda. *The Old Magic of Christmas: Yuletide Traditions for the Darkest Days of the Year*. Woodbury, MN: Llewellyn, 2013, p. 73.

25. Siefker, Phyllis. *Santa Claus, Last of the Wild Men: The Origins and Evolution of Saint Nicholas, Spanning 50,000 Years*. Jefferson, NC: McFarland, 2006, pp. 171–73.

26. Harris, Karen. "Odin And Santa: The Norse God Delivered Gifts with an Eight-Legged, Flying Horse." *History Daily*, https://historydaily.org/odin-and-santa. Accessed June 12, 2021.

27. Müller-Ebeling, Claudia, and Christian Rätsch. *Pagan Christmas: The Plants, Spirits, and Rituals at the Origins of Yuletide*. Rochester, VT: Inner Traditions, 2006, p. 16.

28. Spencer, O.M. "Christmas Throughout Christendom." *Harper's New Monthly Magazine* 46 (1873): 241–57.

29. Harris, Kathleen. "How Joulupukki, the Finnish Santa, went from naughty to nice." December 22, 2015. *Ink Tank*, https://inktank.fi/how-joulupukki-the-finnish-santa-went-from-naughty-to-nice/. Accessed April 8, 2021.

30. Weiser, Francis X. *Handbook of Christian Feasts and Customs*. San Diego: Harcourt, 1958.

31. Harris, Karen. "Odin And Santa: The Norse God Delivered Gifts with an Eight-Legged, Flying Horse." December 9, 2019. *History Daily*, https://historydaily.org/odin-and-santa. Accessed June 28, 2021.

32. Mavromataki, Maria. *Greek Mythology and Religion*. Athens: Haitalis, 1997, pp. 103–04.

33. Nissenbaum, Stephen. *The Battle for Christmas: A Social and Cultural History of Our Most Cherished Holiday*. New York: Vintage, 1997, p. 93.

34. Flanders, Judith. *Christmas: A History*. London: Picador, 2017, p. 118.

35. Belk, Russell W. "Materialism and the Modern U.S. Christmas," in SV–Interpretive Consumer Research, eds. Elizabeth C. Hirschman.

Provo: Association for Consumer Research, 1989, pp. 115–35. https://www.acrwebsite.org/volumes/12180. Accessed June 28, 2021.
  36. Bowler, Gerry. *Santa Claus: A Biography*. Toronto: McClelland & Stewart, 2007.
  37. Nissenbaum, Stephen. *The Battle for Christmas: A Social and Cultural History of Our Most Cherished Holiday*. New York: Vintage, 1997, p. 93.
  38. Johnston, LD. "Classical Origins of Christmas Customs," p. 94, PhD thesis, University of Illinois, 1936.
  39. Main, Douglas. "Magic Mushrooms May Explain Santa & His 'Flying' Reindeer." *LiveScience.com*, https://www.livescience.com/25731-magic-mushrooms-santa-claus.html. Accessed June 13, 2021.
  40. *Ibid.*
  41. Page, Nick. *Christmas: Tradition, Truth and Total Baubles*. London: Hodder & Stoughton, 2020, p. 11.
  42. Harris, Richard. "Did 'Shrooms Send Santa and His Reindeer Flying?" December 23, 2010. National Public Radio, https://www.npr.org/2010/12/24/132260025/did-shrooms-send-santa-and-his-reindeer-flying?t=1628828388315. Accessed August 13, 2021.
  43. "Santa Banished from Zion; Great Fraud, Voliva Declares." December 24, 1921. *New-York Tribune*, https://chroniclingamerica.loc.gov/lccn/sn83030214/1921-12-24/ed-1/seq-1/. Accessed June 28, 2021.
  44. Clough, Martin F. *Hartford Courant*, December 26, 1949.
  45. Belk, Russell W. "Materialism and the Modern U.S. Christmas," in SV–Interpretive Consumer Research, eds. Elizabeth C. Hirschman. Provo: Association for Consumer Research, 1989, pp. 115–35. https://www.acrwebsite.org/volumes/12180. Accessed June 28, 2021.
  46. Watkins, Terry. "Santa Claus: The Great Impostor." Jesus Is Savior, https://jesus-is-savior.com/False%20Religions/Other%20Pagan%-20Mumbo-Jumbo/santa_claus.htm. Accessed June 28, 2021.
  47. Littlejohns, Richard, and Sara Soncini, eds. *Myths of Europe* 107 (2007): 74.
  48. Flanders, Judith. *Christmas: A History*. London: Picador, 2017, p. 163.
  49. "Are Santa Claus & the Easter Bunny Welcome at Church?" November 2019. National Association of Evangelicals, https://www.nae.net/is-santa-claus-welcome-at-church/. Accessed June 28, 2021.
  50. *Ibid.*

Chapter 8

  1. DK. *A History of Magic, Witchcraft and the Occult*. Foreword by Suzannah Lipscomb. London: Dorling Kindersley, 2020, p. 31.
  2. *Ibid.*, p. 23.
  3. Gaskill, Malcolm. *Witchcraft: A Very Short Introduction*. Oxford: Oxford University Press, 2010, p. 17.
  4. Said, Miriam. "Mesopotamian Magic in the First Millennium B.C." December 2018. The Metropolitan Museum of Art, https://www.metmuseum.org/toah/hd/magic/hd_magic.htm. Accessed June 28, 2021.
  5. Reese, Thomas. "Beyond Halloween: Witches, devils, trials and executions." October 25, 2017. *National Catholic Reporter*, https://www.ncronline.org/news/opinion/beyond-halloween-witches-devils-trials-and-executions. Accessed June 28, 2021.
  6. DK. *A History of Magic, Witchcraft and the Occult*. Foreword by Suzannah Lipscomb. London: Dorling Kindersley, 2020, p. 43.
  7. *Ibid.*, p. 82.
  8. Gaskill, Malcolm. *Witchcraft: A Very Short Introduction*. Oxford: Oxford University Press, 2010, p. 10.
  9. DK. *A History of Magic, Witchcraft and the Occult*. Foreword by Suzannah Lipscomb. London: Dorling Kindersley, 2020, p. 32.
  10. "Magic." OpenBible, https://www.openbible.info/topics/magic. Accessed June 28, 2021.
  11. Thomas, Keith. *Religion and the Decline of Magic: Studies in Popular Beliefs in Sixteenth and Seventeenth-Century England*. London: Weidenfeld and Nicolson, 1971, p. 178.
  12. Davies, Owen. *Magic: A Very Short Introduction*. Oxford: Oxford University Press, 2012, p. 32.
  13. *Ibid.*, p. 33.
  14. *Ibid.*, p. 34.
  15. Frith, Alex. *Illustrated Norse Myths*. London: Usborne, 2012, pp. 26–28.
  16. Williams, Gareth, Peter Pentz, and Matthias Wemhoff, eds. *Vikings: Life and Legend*. London: The British Museum Press, 2014, p. 175.
  17. *Ibid.*, p. 117.
  18. Thomas, Keith. *Religion and the Decline of Magic: Studies in Popular Beliefs in Sixteenth and Seventeenth-Century England*. London: Weidenfeld and Nicolson, 1971, p. 47.
  19. *Ibid.*, p. 48.
  20. *Ibid.*, p. 239.
  21. Mabie, Hamilton W. *The Book of Christmas*. New York: Macmillan, 1909, pp. 60–61.
  22. Miles, Clement A. *Christmas Customs and Traditions: Their History and Significance*. New York: Dover, 1976 (republication of a book published in 1912), p. 104.
  23. *Ibid.*, p. 288.
  24. Müller-Ebeling, Claudia, and Christian Rätsch, *Pagan Christmas: The Plants, Spirits, and Rituals at the Origins of Yuletide*. Rochester, VT: Inner Traditions, 2006, p. 15.
  25. "Christmas Traditions in Agnone." *Dooid It Magazine*, https://magazine.dooid.it/en/interests-en/events/christmas-traditions-agnone/. Accessed June 28, 2021.

26. Gulevich, Tanya. *Encyclopedia of Christmas & New Year's Celebrations*. Detroit: Omnigraphics, 2003, p. 54.
27. "Tools of Wiccan Ritual: The Bell." *Wicca Living*, https://wiccaliving.com/wiccan-bell/. Accessed June 28, 2021.
28. "Bells in Witchcraft." Occult World, https://occult-world.com/bells-in-witchcraft/. Accessed June 28, 2021.
29. "Devils—Afraid of Bells." *Encyclopedia.com*, https://www.encyclopedia.com/science/encyclopedias-almanacs-transcripts-and-maps/devils-afraid-bells. Accessed June 28, 2021.
30. Gulevich, Tanya. *Encyclopedia of Christmas & New Year's Celebrations*. Detroit: Omnigraphics, 2003, p. 53.
31. Armstrong, Patti Maguire. "An Exorcist Explains Why the Devil Hates Bells So Much." October 1, 2019. National Catholic Register, https://www.ncregister.com/blog/an-exorcist-explains-why-the-devil-hates-bells-so-much. Accessed June 28, 2021.
32. Cohen, I. Bernard. *Benjamin Franklin's Science*. Cambridge: Harvard University Press, 1990, p. 119.
33. Raedisch, Linda. *The Old Magic of Christmas: Yuletide Traditions for the Darkest Days of the Year*. Woodbury, MN: Llewellyn, 2013, p. 87.
34. Alexander, Maria. "The Witches of Winter." December 15, 2016. *Tor.com*, https://www.tor.com/2016/12/15/the-witches-of-winter/. Accessed June 28, 2021.
35. Flanders, Judith. *Christmas: A History*. London: Picador, 2017, p. 59.
36. Miles, Clement A. *Christmas Customs and Traditions: Their History and Significance*. New York: Dover, 1976 (republication of a book published in 1912), p. 300.
37. Flanders, Judith. *Christmas: A History*. London: Picador, 2017, p. 65.
38. Miles, Clement A. *Christmas Customs and Traditions: Their History and Significance*. New York: Dover, 1976 (republication of a book published in 1912), p. 272.
39. Müller-Ebeling, Claudia, and Christian Rätsch, *Pagan Christmas: The Plants, Spirits, and Rituals at the Origins of Yuletide*. Rochester, VT: Inner Traditions, 2006, pp. 79–80.
40. Palacios, Surya. "Christmas Eve, the flower of the Aztec warriors that Mexico gave to the world." December 24, 2020. Entrepreneur. https://www.entrepreneur.com/article/362318. Accessed June 28, 2021.
41. "Poinsettia Day." December 12, 2021. *Days of the Year*, https://www.daysoftheyear.com/days/poinsettia-day/ Accessed June 28, 2021.
42. "The Legend of the Poinsettia." December 5, 2020. *How Stuff Works*, https://people.howstuffworks.com/culture-traditions/holidays-christmas/inspirational-christmas-stories10.htm. Accessed June 28, 2021.
43. McCoy, Daniel. "The Death of Baldur." June 29, 2018. *Norse Mythology for Smart People*, https://norse-mythology.org/tales/the-death-of-baldur/. Accessed June 29, 2021.
44. "Merry Berry: Magical Mistletoe." October 28, 2019. *National Trust*, www.nationaltrust.org.uk/features/merry-berry-magical-mistletoe. Accessed June 29, 2021.
45. Perry, Leonard P. "Mistletoe Myths and Medicines." University of Vermont, https://pss.uvm.edu/ppp/articles/mistlmyths.html. Accessed June 29, 2021.
46. Flanders, Judith. *Christmas: A History*. London: Picador, 2017, p. 50.
47. *Ibid.*, pp. 84–85.
48. Frazer, James George. *The Golden Bough: A Study in Magic and Religion*. Third Edition, Vol. 2 of 12. Project Gutenberg. Chapel Hill: University of North Carolina Press, 2019, p. 358.
49. "Remembering the magic of mistletoe." December 8, 2019. *The Hazel Tree*, https://www.thehazeltree.co.uk/2019/12/08/remembering-the-magic-of-mistletoe/. Accessed June 29, 2021.
50. Fay, Michael F., Jonathan R. Bennett, Kingsley W. Dixon, and Maarten J.M. Christenhusz. "Parasites, Their Relationships and the Disintegration of Scrophulariaceae Sensu Lato." *Curtis's Botanical Magazine* (2010): 299.
51. *Ibid.*
52. Lecouteux, Claude. *Encyclopedia of Norse and Germanic Folklore, Mythology, and Magic*. Rochester, VT: Inner Traditions, 2014.
53. Roesdahl, Else. *The Vikings*. London: Penguin, 1999, p. 152.
54. Rouă, Victor. "Huldufólk (Elves) in Icelandic and Faroese Folklores." May 28, 2016. *The Dockyards*, http://www.thedockyards.com/huldufolk-icelandic-folklore/. Accessed June 29, 2021.
55. Ellis, Peter. *A Brief History of the Druids*. London: Little, Brown, 2002, p. 130.
56. Raedisch, Linda. *The Old Magic of Christmas: Yuletide Traditions for the Darkest Days of the Year*. Woodbury, MN: Llewellyn, 2013, p. 32.
57. *Ibid.*, pp. 32–33.
58. Piø, Iørn. *Nissen*. Copenhagen: Gyldendal, 2018, p. 13.
59. Flanders, Judith. *Christmas: A History*. London: Picador, 2017, p. 154.
60. "Legends of the Tomte." *Skandium*, https://www.skandium.com/blogs/news/legends-of-the-tomte. Accessed June 29, 2021.
61. Radford, Benjamin. "A History of Elves." November 1, 2017. *Live Science*, https://www.livescience.com/39689-history-of-elves.html. Accessed June 29, 2021.
62. Elf on the Shelf website, https://elfontheshelf.com/. Accessed June 29, 2021.
63. Tuttle, Kate. "You're a Creepy One, Elf on the Shelf." December 6, 2012. *The Atlantic*.

Chapter 9

1. "'A Christmas Story' marathon slated for 13th year on TBS." December 24, 2009. *Examiner.com*.

2. "Viewership." A Christmas Story House and Museum, https://www.achristmasstoryhouse.com/a-christmas-story-movie-facts/viewership/. Accessed April 22, 2021.

3. "Our Weekly Gossip." *Brother Jonathan* 3, no. 17 (December 24, 1842): 494.

4. Mosca, Paul. *Child Sacrifice in Canaanite and Israelite Religion*. Harvard University (PhD thesis, 1975), p. 22.

5. Cicero, Marcus Tullius. *De Natura Deorum* [On the Nature of the Gods]. 45 BCE. Trans. P.G. Walsh (reissue ed.). Oxford: Oxford University Press, 2008, pp. 69–70.

6. Anthon, Charles. *A Classical Dictionary: Containing an Account of the Principal Proper Names Mentioned in Ancient Authors, and Intended to Elucidate All the Important Points Connected with the Geography, History, Biography, Mythology, and Fine Arts of the Greeks and Romans Together with an Account of Coins, Weights, and Measures, with Tabular Values of the Same* Harper & Brothers, 1842, p. 1197.

7. Rives, James B. "Tertullian on Child Sacrifice." *Museum Helveticum* 51, no. 1 (1994): 54. https://www.jstor.org/stable/24818326?seq=1. Accessed April 22, 2021.

8. Bowler, Gerry. *Santa Claus: A Biography*. Toronto: McClelland & Stewart, 2007.

9. Carver, Dawn F., Jasmine Watson, Jason Curtiss, Jr. "Ritual Killing in Ancient Rome: Homicide and Roman Superiority" *El Rio: A Student Research Journal* (Spring 2018). https://mountainscholar.org/bitstream/handle/10217/190858/STUP_RIO_2018_Carver.pdf?sequence=1. Accessed April 23, 2021.

10. "Ancient Carthaginians really did sacrifice their children." January 23, 2014. *University of Oxford News and events*, https://www.ox.ac.uk/news/2014-01-23-ancient-carthaginians-really-did-sacrifice-their-children. Accessed April 22, 2021.

11. Cicero. *On the Nature of the Gods*. Francis Brooks English Translation. https://www.informationphilosopher.com/solutions/philosophers/cicero/nature_of_the_gods.html.

12. DK. *A History of Magic, Witchcraft and the Occult*. Foreword by Suzannah Lipscomb. London: Dorling Kindersley, 2020, p. 66.

13. Cooke, Richard Joseph. *Christianity and Childhood: Or the Relation of Children to the Church*. London: Forgotten Books, 2018 (republication of a book published in 1891), p. 18.

14. *Ibid.*, p. 98.

15. *Ibid.*, p. 34.

16. Cybulskie, Danièle. "Childhood in the Middle Ages." *Medievalists.net*, https://www.medievalists.net/2018/11/childhood-middle-ages/. Accessed April 25, 2021.

17. "In the Middle Ages there was no such thing as childhood." January 5, 2019. *The Economist*, https://www.economist.com/special-report/2019/01/03/in-the-middle-ages-there-was-no-such-thing-as-childhood. Accessed June 29, 2021.

18. Grundy, Stephan. "Freyja and Frigg," in Sandra Billington and Miranda Green, eds., *The Concept of the Goddess*. Oxfordshire: Routledge, 1998, pp. 56–66.

19. "Frau Perchta, the Belly-Slitter." December 9, 2019. *Bone & Sickle*, https://www.boneandsickle.com/2019/12/09/frau-perchta-the-belly-slitter/. Accessed July 12, 2021.

20. Müller-Ebeling, Claudia, and Christian Rätsch. *Pagan Christmas: The Plants, Spirits, and Rituals at the Origins of Yuletide*. Rochester, VT: Inner Traditions, 2006, pp. 173–74.

21. Raedisch, Linda. *The Old Magic of Christmas: Yuletide Traditions for the Darkest Days of the Year*. Woodbury, MN: Llewellyn, 2013, pp. 190–91.

22. Alexander, Maria. "The Witches of Winter." December 15, 2016. *Tor.com*, https://www.tor.com/2016/12/15/the-witches-of-winter/. Accessed June 28, 2021.

23. Ridenour, Al. *The Krampus and the Old, Dark Christmas: Roots and Rebirth of the Folkloric Devil*. Port Townsend, WA: Feral House, 2016.

24. Johnson, Ben. "The Great Flood and Great Famine of 1314." *History Magazine*, https://www.historic-uk.com/HistoryUK/HistoryofEngland/The-Great-Flood-Great-Famine-of-1314/. Accessed June 29, 2021.

25. Williams, Joseph. "Discover the Truly Grim History Behind the Fairy Tale of Hansel and Gretel." January 23, 2020. *All That's Interesting*, https://allthatsinteresting.com/hansel-and-gretel-true-story. Accessed June 29, 2021.

26. Ariès, Philippe. *Centuries of Childhood: A Social History of Family Life*. Trans. from French by Robert Baldick. New York: Vintage, 1965, p. 10.

27. Cartwright, Mark. "A Medieval Christmas." *World History Encyclopedia*, https://www.ancient.eu/article/1288/a-medieval-christmas/. Accessed March 26, 2021.

28. Flanders, Judith. *Christmas: A History*. London: Picador, 2017, p. 12.

29. Hutton, Ronald. *The Rise and Fall of Merry England: The Ritual Year 1400–1700*. New York: Oxford University Press, 1994, p. 12.

30. "Feast of the Holy Innocents." *Encyclopedia Britannica*, https://www.britannica.com/topic/Feast-of-the-Holy-Innocents. Accessed March 26, 2021.

31. Miles, Clement A. *Christmas Customs and Traditions: Their History and Significance*. New York: Dover, 1976 (republication of a book published in 1912), p. 308.

32. Hutton, Richard. *Stations of the Sun: A History of the Ritual Year in Britain*. New York: Oxford University Press, 2001, Chapter 9.

33. Frodsham, Paul. *From Stonehenge to Santa Claus: The Evolution of Christmas*. Stroud, Gloucestershire: The History Press, 2008), pp. 111–12.

34. Ariès, Philippe. *Centuries of Childhood: A Social History of Family Life*. Trans. from French by Robert Baldick. New York: Vintage, 1965, p. 359.

35. Raedisch, Linda. *The Old Magic of Christmas: Yuletide Traditions for the Darkest Days of the Year*. Woodbury, MN: Llewellyn, 2013, p. 83.

36. *Ibid.*

37. Flanders, Judith. *Christmas: A History*. London: Picador, 2017, p. 116.

Chapter 10

1. Shakespeare, William. "The Winter's Tale." *Open Source Shakespeare*, https://www.opensourceshakespeare.org/views/plays/play_view.php?WorkID=winterstale&Act=2&Scene=1&Scope=scene. Accessed May 26, 2021.

2. Chamerovzow, Louis Alexis. *The Yule Log, for everybody's Christmas Hearth, showing where it grew, how it was cut and brought home, and how it was burnt*. London: T.C. Newby, 1847, pp. 123–24.

3. Barry, Jonathan, Owen Davies, and Cornelie Usborne, eds. *Cultures of Witchcraft in Europe from the Middle Ages to the Present*. Cham, Switzerland: Springer International, 2017, p. 192.

4. *Ibid.*, p. 179.

5. Flanders, Judith. *Christmas: A History*. London: Picador, 2017, p. 238.

6. Jerome, Jerome K. *Told After Supper*. The Project Gutenberg eBook, 1999 (reproduced from 1891 Leadenhall Press edition). http://www.gutenberg.org/cache/epub/1993/pg1993-images.html. Accessed June 29, 2021.

7. Flanders, Judith. *Christmas: A History*. London: Picador, 2017, p. 32.

8. Eschner, Kat. "Why Do People Tell Ghost Stories on Christmas?" December 23, 2016. *Smithsonian Magazine*, https://www.smithsonianmag.com/smart-news/why-do-ghost-stories-go-christmas-180961547/. Accessed June 30, 2021.

9. Dashu, Max. "The 'Pagan Days.'" 2007. *Matri Focus* Vol. 6–2 http://www.matrifocus.com/IMB07/scholar.htm. Accessed June 30, 2021.

10. Miles, Clement A. *Christmas Customs and Traditions: Their History and Significance*. New York: Dover Publications, 1976 (republication of a book published in 1912), p. 239.

11. *Ibid.*, p. 181.

12. Lecouteux, Claude. *Encyclopedia of Norse and Germanic Folklore, Mythology, and Magic*. Rochester, VT: Inner Traditions, 2014.

13. Strömberg, Håkan. *Lucia: den svenskaste av alla traditioner*. Stockholm: Carlsson Bokförlag, 2017, p. 36.

14. Nordentoft, Bodil Iversdatter. *Lucia: Lys i Mørket*. Risskov, Denmark: Klematis, 1996, p. 6.

15. Miles, Clement A. *Christmas Customs and Traditions: Their History and Significance*. New York: Dover, 1976 (republication of a book published in 1912), p. 235.

16. Flanders, Judith. *Christmas: A History*. London: Picador, 2017, p. 33.

17. Basu, Tanya. "Who is Krampus? Explaining the horrific Christmas beast." December 5, 2018. *National Geographic*, https://www.nationalgeographic.com/news/2018/12/131217-krampus-christmas-santa-devil/. Accessed June 30, 2021.

18. Honigmann, John J. "The Masked Face." Autumn 1977. *AnthroSource*, https://anthrosource.onlinelibrary.wiley.com/doi/abs/10.1525/eth.1977.5.3.02a00020. Accessed June 30, 2021.

19. "Kallikantzaros." *Hellenica World*, http://www.hellenicaworld.com/Greece/Info/en/Kallikantzaros.html. Accessed June 30, 2021.

20. Miles, Clement A. *Christmas Customs and Traditions: Their History and Significance*. New York: Dover, 1976 (republication of a book published in 1912), p. 245.

21. Raedisch, Linda. *The Old Magic of Christmas: Yuletide Traditions for the Darkest Days of the Year*. Woodbury, MN: Llewellyn, 2013, p. 198.

22. Vuković, Milan T. "Божићни празници". Народни обичаји, веровања и пословице код Срба [Serbian folk customs, beliefs, and sayings] (in Serbian) (12 ed.). Belgrade: Sazvežđa, 2004, p. 94.

23. Hawkins, Paul. *Bad Santas: Disquieting Winter Folk Tales for Grown-Ups*. London: Simon & Schuster, 2013, p. 102.

24. Gunnell, Terry. "The coming of the Christmas Visitors ... Folk legends concerning the attacks on Icelandic farmhouses made by spirits at Christmas." *Northern Studies* 38 (2004). https://www.ssns.org.uk/wp-content/uploads/2019/09/Gunnell_2004_Vol_38_pp_51_76.pdf. Accessed June 26, 2021.

25. Lecouteux, Claude. *Phantom Armies of the Night: The Wild Hunt and the Ghostly Processions of the Undead*.

26. "Knocking Nights." *The Free Dictionary*, https://encyclopedia2.thefreedictionary.com/Knocking+Nights. Accessed June 30, 2021.

27. Godwin, Michael. *Angels: An Endangered Species*. London: Simon & Schuster, 1990, p. 19.

28. Davidson, Gustav. *A Dictionary of Angels Including the Fallen Angels*. New York: The Free Press, 1967, p. xxiv.

29. Davidson, Gustav. *A Dictionary of Angels Including the Fallen Angels*. New York: The Free Press, 1967, p. 2.

30. Grimm, Jacob. *Teutonic Mythology* (translated from the 4th edition with notes and appendix by James Steven Stallybrass). London: George Bell and Sons, 1882, pp. 340–41.

31. Godwin, Michael. *Angels: An Endangered Species*. New York: Simon & Schuster, 1990, p. 33.

32. *Ibid.*, p. 25.
33. *Ibid.*, p. 41.
34. *Ibid.*, p. 9.
35. Gulevich, Tanya. *Encyclopedia of Christmas & New Year's Celebrations*. Detroit: Omnigraphics, 2003, p. 30.
36. Joyal, M. "To Daimonion and the Socratic Problem," *Apeiron* 38, no. 2 (2005).
37. Martin, Dale. "When Did Angels Become Demons?" *Journal of Biblical Literature* (2010): 194.
38. Jones, David Albert. *Angels: A Very Short Introduction*. Oxford: Oxford University Press, 2011, p. 6.
39. Scholem, Gershom G. *Major Trends in Jewish Mysticism*. New York: Schocken Books, 1995, p. 67.
40. "Jibrīl, archangel." *Encyclopedia Britannica*, https://www.britannica.com/topic/Jibril. Accessed July 15, 2021.
41. Martin, Therese. "The Development of Winged Angels in Christian Art." *Historia del Arte Espacio*. Tiempo y Forma, Serie VII t. 14. 2001, p. 11.
42. Newport, Frank. "Most Americans Still Believe in God." June 29, 2016. *Gallup*, https://news.gallup.com/poll/193271/americans-believe-god.aspx. Accessed April 9, 2021.

Chapter 11

1. "The witch hunts." *Encyclopedia Britannica*, https://www.britannica.com/topic/witchcraft/The-witch-hunts. Accessed June 30, 2021.
2. Gaskill, Malcolm. *Witchcraft: A Very Short Introduction*. Oxford: Oxford University Press, 2010, p. 17.
3. Markoe, Lauren. "How Christmas is linked to Hanukkah." December 8, 2017. *Religion News Service*, https://religionnews.com/2017/12/08/how-christmas-is-linked-to-hanukkah/. Accessed April 9, 2021.
4. "What the Bible says about Nimrod." *Bible Tools*, https://www.bibletools.org/index.cfm/fuseaction/Topical.show/RTD/cgg/ID/388/Nimrod.htm. Accessed June 30, 2021.
5. "Nimrod in Prophecy: The Mystery Religion of Babylon." *Finding Hope Ministries*, https://findinghopeministries.org/nimrod-in-prophecy-the-mystery-religion-of-babylon/. Accessed June 30, 2021.
6. Frodsham, Paul. *From Stonehenge to Santa Claus: The Evolution of Christmas*. Stroud, Gloustershire: The History Press, 2008. p. 71.
7. Hansen, William. *Classical Mythology: A Guide to the Mythical World of the Greeks and Romans*. New York: Oxford University Press, 2005, p. 199.
8. DK *A History of Magic, Witchcraft and the Occult*. Foreword by Suzannah Lipscomb. London: Dorling Kindersley, 2020, p. 31.
9. Frodsham, Paul. *From Stonehenge to Santa Claus: The Evolution of Christmas*. Stroud, Gloucestershire: The History Press, 2008, p. 73.
10. *Ibid.*, p. 79.
11. Isbouts, Jean-Pierre. "Who were the three kings in the Christmas story?" December 24, 2018. National Geographic, https://www.nationalgeographic.com/culture/article/three-kings-magi-epiphany. Accessed June 30, 2021.
12. Müller-Ebeling, Claudia, and Christian Rätsch. *Pagan Christmas: The Plants, Spirits, and Rituals at the Origins of Yuletide*. Rochester, VT: Inner Traditions, 2006, p. 14.
13. DK *A History of Magic, Witchcraft and the Occult*. Foreword by Suzannah Lipscomb. London: Dorling Kindersley, 2020, p. 33.
14. Müller-Ebeling, Claudia, and Christian Rätsch. *Pagan Christmas: The Plants, Spirits, and Rituals at the Origins of Yuletide*. Rochester, VT: Inner Traditions, 2006, p. 105.
15. *Ibid.*, p. 182.
16. Davies, Owen. *Magic: A Very Short Introduction*. Oxford: Oxford University Press, 2012, p. 4.
17. Martínez, Antonio Marco. "Some Notes on the 'Magi,' the Three Wise Men." January 7, 2015. *History of Greece and Rome*, www.antiquitatem.com/en/the-three-wise-men-epiphany-jesus/. Accessed June 25, 2021.
18. Reese, Thomas. "Beyond Halloween: Witches, Devils, Trials and Executions." October 25, 2017. *National Catholic Reporter*, www.ncronline.org/news/opinion/beyond-halloween-witches-devils-trials-and-executions. Accessed June 25, 2021.
19. Gaskill, Malcolm. *Witchcraft: A Very Short Introduction*. Oxford: Oxford University Press, 2010, p. 16.
20. MacMullen, Ramsay. *Christianizing the Roman Empire: A.D. 100–400*. New Haven: Yale University Press, 1984, p. 14.
21. Liebman, Sheldon W. *The Great Betrayal: Christians and Jews in the First Four Centuries*. Eugene, OR: Wipf and Stock, 2018, p. 146.
22. Dospěl, Marek. "Early Christian Amulets: Between Faith and Magic." October 1, 2018. *Biblical Archaeology*, https://www.biblicalarchaeology.org/daily/biblical-artifacts/inscriptions/early-christian-amulets-between-faith-and-magic/. Accessed July 1, 2021.
23. "Amulet." The British Museum. Museum number 1938,1010.1 https://www.britishmuseum.org/collection/object/H_1938-1010-1. Accessed July 1, 2021.
24. "Amulet Carved in Intaglio (Incised) 6th-7th century." The Metropolitan Museum of Art. Accession Number: 17.190.491. https://www.metmuseum.org/art/collection/search/464456. Accessed August 2, 2021.
25. Hornung, Erik. *The Secret Lore of Egypt: Its*

Impact on the West. Ithaca: Cornell University Press, 2002, p. 75.

26. DK. *A History of Magic, Witchcraft and the Occult*. Foreword by Suzannah Lipscomb. London: Dorling Kindersley, 2020, p. 102.

27. St. Augustine of Hippo. *The City of God*, Book VIII, "Conspect." https://www.documentacatholicaomnia.eu/03d/0354-0430,_Augustinus,_De_Civitate_Dei_Contra_Paganos,_EN.pdf .Accessed July 1, 2021.

28. DK. *A History of Magic, Witchcraft and the Occult*. Foreword by Suzannah Lipscomb. London: Dorling Kindersley, 2020, p. 62.

29. Keck, David. *Angels and Angelology in the Middle Ages*. New York: Oxford University Press, 1998, p. 18.

30. DK. *A History of Magic, Witchcraft and the Occult*. Foreword by Suzannah Lipscomb. London: Dorling Kindersley, 2020, p. 103.

31. *Ibid.*, p. 102.

32. "Patrick the Saint." Christian History Institute, https://christianhistoryinstitute.org/magazine/article/patrick-the-saint. Accessed July 1, 2021.

33. *Ibid.*

34. "Muirchú's text in English." *St. Patrick's Confessio,* https://www.confessio.ie/more/muirchu_english#. Accessed July 1, 2021.

35. "Miracle play." *Encyclopedia Britannica*, https://www.britannica.com/art/miracle-play. Accessed July 1, 2021.

36. Flanders, Judith. *Christmas: A History.* London: Picador, 2017, p. 11.

37. Justice, Steven. "Did the Middle Ages Believe in Their Miracles?" *Representations* 103, no. 1 (Summer 2008), p. 4.

38. *Ibid.*, p. 16.

39. Ewing, Jeannie. "This Is the Most Complete List of Marian Apparitions." The Mystical Humanity of Christ Publishing, https://www.coraevans.com/blog/article/this-is-the-most-complete-list-of-marian-apparitions. Accessed May 8, 2021.

40. Pronechen, Joseph. "Exactly 310 Years After Guadalupe, Our Lady Appeared to Indians in the Present-Day U.S." March 5, 2021. National Catholic Register, https://www.ncregister.com/blog/montana-marian-apparition. Accessed May 8, 2021.

41. Philpot, Terry. "World War I's Pope Benedict XV and the pursuit of peace." *National Catholic Reporter*. July 19, 2014.

42. Brockell, Gillian. "The Christmas Truce miracle: Soldiers put down their guns to sing carols and drink wine." December 24, 2017. *The Washington Post,* https://www.washingtonpost.com/news/retropolis/wp/2017/12/24/the-christmas-truce-miracle-soldiers-put-down-their-guns-to-sing-carols-and-drink-wine/. Accessed July 1, 2021.

43. *Ibid.*

44. Cole, Kate. "The story of the 1914 Christmas Truce, as reported by WWI newspapers." December 19, 2014. *The British Newspaper Archive Blog,* https://blog.britishnewspaperarchive.co.uk/2014/12/19/the-story-of-the-1914-christmas-truce-as-reported-by-ww1-newspapers/. Accessed July 1, 2021.

45. "Christmas truce changes perception of the enemy." December 31, 1914. *The Winnipeg Tribune,* https://www.newspapers.com/clip/24455924/christmas-truce-changes-perception-of/. Accessed July 1, 2021.

46. Rader, Phil. "Miracle is Wrought by Christmas Spirit in Hostile Trenches," March 24, 1915. *Evening Public Ledger,* https://chroniclingamerica.loc.gov/lccn/sn83045211/1915-03-24/ed-1/seq-4/. Accessed August 5, 2021.

47. "The Christmas Truce: An Incident of the Great War." January 9, 1915. *The Guardian,* https://www.newspapers.com/clip/24455878/the-christmas-truce-an-incident-of-the/. Accessed July 1, 2021.

48. Rader, Phil. "Miracle is Wrought by Christmas Spirit in Hostile Trenches," March 24, 1915. *Evening Public Ledger*, https://chroniclingamerica.loc.gov/lccn/sn83045211/1915-03-24/ed-1/seq-4/. Accessed August 5, 2021.

49. "Germans and the Christmas Truce." National WWI Museum and Memorial, http://exhibitions.theworldwar.org/christmas-truce/incidents/23/germans-and-the-christmas-truce. Accessed July 1, 2021.

50. Brockell, Gillian. "The Christmas Truce miracle: Soldiers put down their guns to sing carols and drink wine." December 24, 2017. *The Washington Post,* https://www.washingtonpost.com/news/retropolis/wp/2017/12/24/the-christmas-truce-miracle-soldiers-put-down-their-guns-to-sing-carols-and-drink-wine/. Accessed July 1, 2021.

51. "The Christmas miracle." November 10, 2008. *The Guardian*, https://www.theguardian.com/world/2008/nov/10/first-world-war-christmas-truce. Accessed March 27, 2021.

52. "Christmas miracles." Christian History Institute, https://christianhistoryinstitute.org/magazine/article/christmas-miracles-worldwars. Accessed July 1, 2021.

53. Bicker, Laura. "The U.S. Ship of Miracles that saved 14,000 North Korean refugees." December 24, 2019. BBC News, https://www.bbc.com/news/world-asia-50805106. Accessed August 4, 2021.

54. La Rue, Leonard P., and David Lester. "I Witnessed a Christmas Miracle." *Evening Star.* December 11, 1960. Chronicling America: Historic American Newspapers. Library of Congress. https://chroniclingamerica.loc.gov/lccn/sn83045462/1960-12-11/ed-1/seq-133/. Accessed August 4, 2021.

55. Specktor, Brandon. "18 True Christmas Miracles That Will Restore Your Hope for the Holidays." December 20, 2019. *Reader's Digest*, https://www.rd.com/list/christmas-miracles/. Accessed April 1, 2021.

Chapter 12

1. Flanders, Judith. *Christmas: A History.* London: Picador, 2017, p. 63.
2. King, Josiah. *The Examination and Tryal of Old Father Christmas Together with His Clearing by the Jury, at the Assizes Held at the Town of Difference in the County of Discontent: Written According to Legal Proceeding.* London, 1678. https://www.hymnsandcarolsofchristmas.com/Poetry/examination__and__tryal_of.htm. Accessed July 1, 2021.
3. Flanders, Judith. *Christmas: A History.* London: Picador, 2017, p. 72.
4. Ibid., p. 73.
5. Miles, Clement A. *Christmas Customs and Traditions: Their History and Significance.* New York: Dover, 1976 (republication of a book published in 1912), pp. 98–99.
6. Nissenbaum, Stephen. *The Battle for Christmas: A Social and Cultural History of Our Most Cherished Holiday.* New York: Vintage, 1997, p. 7.
7. Ibid., p. 38.
8. Ibid., p. 7.
9. Coldwell, Chris. "The Religious Observance of Christmas and 'Holy Days' in American Presbyterianism." *The Blue Banner* 8, nos. 9–10, September/October 1999. https://www.naphtali.com/articles/chris-coldwell/the-religious-observance-of-christmas-and-holy-days-in-american-presbyterianism/. Accessed March 28, 2021.
10. Flanders, Judith. *Christmas: A History.* London: Picador, 2017, p. 72.
11. "The Battle of Trenton." *American Revolutionary War Battles for 1776,* https://revolutionarywar.us/year-1776/battle-of-trenton./ Accessed April 5, 2021.
12. "George Washington's Christmas Eggnog." December 16, 2020. The Old Farmer's Almanac, https://www.almanac.com/george-washingtons-christmas-eggnog. Accessed May 16, 2021.
13. Nissenbaum, Stephen. *The Battle for Christmas: A Social and Cultural History of Our Most Cherished Holiday.* New York: Vintage, 1997, p. 261.
14. Bowler, Gerry. "Eggnog Riot." *The World Encyclopedia of Christmas.* Toronto: McClelland & Stewart, 2000, p. 73.
15. "The Christmas Riot of 1806: Anti-Catholic violence mars the holiday." December 19, 2016. *The Bowery Boys New York City History,* https://www.boweryboyshistory.com/2016/12/christmas-riot-1806-anti-catholic-violence-mars-holiday.html. Accessed March 28, 2021.
16. Nissenbaum, Stephen. *The Battle for Christmas: A Social and Cultural History of Our Most Cherished Holiday.* New York: Vintage, 1997, p. 54.
17. Ibid., p. 94.
18. Ibid., p. 98.
19. Flanders, Judith. *Christmas: A History.* London: Picador, 2017, p. 68.
20. Wooten, Andre. "Samuel Sharpe (ca. 1780–1832)." August 16, 2013. *Black Past,* https://www.blackpast.org/global-african-history/sharpe-samuel-ca-1780-1832/. Accessed March 28, 2021.
21. Blackburn, Robin. *The Overthrow of Colonial Slavery, 1776–1848.* New York: Verso, 2011, p. 432.
22. "The Slavery Abolition Act of 1833." *The History Press,* https://www.thehistorypress.co.uk/articles/the-slavery-abolition-act-of-1833/. Accessed March 28, 2021.
23. Douglass, Frederik. *Narrative of the Life of Frederick Douglass.* Boston: The Anti-Slavery Office, 1849, p. 74.
24. Gulevich, Tanya. *Encyclopedia of Christmas & New Year's Celebrations.* Detroit: Omnigraphics, 2003, p. 22.
25. Nissenbaum, Stephen. *The Battle for Christmas: A Social and Cultural History of Our Most Cherished Holiday.* New York: Vintage, 1997, pp. 266–67.
26. "Seneca on the Treatment of Slaves," *Sententiae Antiquae.* January 28, 2018. https://sententiaeantiquae.com/2018/01/28/seneca-on-the-treatment-of-slaves/. Accessed March 28, 2021.
27. Seneca, Letter 18: On Festivals and Fasting. https://www.lettersfromastoic.net/letter-18-on-festivals-and-fasting/. Accessed May 16, 2021.
28. Rawson, Beryl, ed. *A Companion to Families in the Greek and Roman Worlds.* Hoboken: Blackwell, 2010, p. 497.
29. Mather, Increase. *A Testimony against Several Prophane and Superstitious Customs, Now Practiced by Some in New-England.* London, 1687, p. 35.
30. Newhart, Beth. "Americans double their drinking during the holidays." December 19, 2018. *Beverage Daily,* https://www.beveragedaily.com/Article/2018/12/19/Americans-double-their-drinking-during-the-holidays-dampen-work-productivity?utm_source=copyright&utm_medium=OnSite&utm_campaign=copyright. Accessed March 28, 2021.
31. "Tis the season to be jolly: Christmas should be protected from advertising which promotes harmful drinking." , December 20, 2019. The BMJ, https://blogs.bmj.com/bmj/2019/12/20/tis-the-season-to-be-jolly-the-public-health-harms-of-excess-alcohol-consumption-at-christmas/. Accessed March 28, 2021.
32. Newhart, Beth. "Americans double their drinking during the holidays." December 19, 2018. *Beverage Daily,* https://www.beveragedaily.com/Article/2018/12/19/Americans-double-their-drinking-during-the-holidays-dampen-work-productivity?utm_source=copyright&utm_medium=OnSite&utm_campaign=copyright. Accessed March 28, 2021.
33. Hancock, Edith. "This is how much the average brit drinks on Christmas Day." December

5, 2019. https://www.thedrinksbusiness.com/2019/12/this-is-how-much-the-average-brit-drinks-on-christmas-day/. Accessed March 28, 2021.

34. Eads, Lauren. "Britons to consume six billion units of alcohol this Christmas." December 21, 2018. *The Drinks Business*, https://www.thedrinksbusiness.com/2018/12/britons-to-consume-six-billion-units-of-alcohol-this-christmas/. Accessed March 28, 2021.

35. Barnett, James H. *The American Christmas: A Study in National Culture.* New York: Macmillan, 1954, p. 141.

36. Hosie, Rachel. "Divorce Day: January 8 most popular day to start legal proceedings to dissolve marriages." January 3, 2018. *The Independent*, https://www.independent.co.uk/life-style/love-sex/divorce-day-date-january-8-marriage-end-start-legal-proceedings-most-popular-lawyers-solicitors-a8139251.html. Accessed April 9, 2021.

37. Lankford, Ronald D. *Sleigh Rides, Jingle Bells, and Silent Nights: A Cultural History of American Christmas Songs.* Gainesville: University Press of Florida, 2013, p. 96.

38. Mohr, Melissa. "Using Merry Christmas or Happy Holidays is no longer about putting a stranger at ease." December 23, 2019. *NBC News*, https://www.nbcnews.com/think/opinion/using-merry-christmas-or-happy-holidays-no-longer-about-putting-ncna1106181. Accessed March 28, 2021.

39. "Merry-Bout." *Words and Phrases from the Past.* July 22, 2015. https://www.wordsandphrasesfromthepast.com/bull-blog/merry-bout. Accessed March 28, 2021.

40. Mohr, Melissa. "'Merry' versus 'Happy' Christmas." December 20, 2018. *Christian Science Monitor*, https://www.csmonitor.com/The-Culture/In-a-Word/2018/1220/Merry-versus-Happy-Christmas. Accessed April 25, 2021.

41. Asterius of Amasea. "Sermon 4: On the Festival of the Calends." *Early Christian Writings*, http://www.earlychristianwritings.com/fathers/asterius_04_sermon4.html. Accessed March 28, 2021.

42. Nissenbaum, Stephen. *The Battle for Christmas: A Social and Cultural History of Our Most Cherished Holiday.* New York: Vintage, 1997, p. 7.

Chapter 13

1. de Pommereau, Isabelle. "Germans join 'War on Christmas'—pre-Christmas commercialism, that is." *Christian Science Monitor*, https://www.csmonitor.com/World/Europe/2014/1005/Germans-join-War-on-Christmas-pre-Christmas-commercialism-that-is, Accessed June 15, 2021.

2. Rogers, Nicholas. *Halloween: From Pagan Ritual to Party Night.* Oxford: Oxford University Press, 2003, p. 11.

3. *Ibid.*, p. 24.

4. *Ibid.*, p. 29.

5. Rees, Alwyn and Brinley. *Celtic Heritage: Ancient Tradition in Ireland and Wales.* London: Thames and Hudson, 1961, p. 84.

6. Mac Cana, Proinsias. *Celtic Mythology.* Feltham: Hamlyn, 1970, p. 127.

7. Miles, Clement A. *Christmas Customs and Traditions: Their History and Significance.* New York: Dover, 1976 (republication of a book published in 1912), p. 181.

8. Frodsham, Paul. *From Stonehenge to Santa Claus: The Evolution of Christmas.* Stroud, Gloustershire: The History Press, 2008, p. 49.

9. Markale, Jean. *The Pagan Mysteries of Halloween: Celebrating the Dark Half of the Year.* Rochester, VT: Inner Traditions, 2001, p. 24.

10. *Ibid.*, p. 29.

11. "Samhain." November 3, 2020. *History.com*, https://www.history.com/topics/holidays/samhain. Accessed April 23, 2021.

12. Markale, Jean. *The Pagan Mysteries of Halloween: Celebrating the Dark Half of the Year.* Rochester, VT: Inner Traditions, 2001, p. 20.

13. Gilroy, John. *Tlachtga: Celtic Fire Festival.* Pikefield, 2000.

14. Miles, Clement A. *Christmas Customs and Traditions: Their History and Significance.* New York: Dover, 1976 (republication of a book published in 1912), p. 181.

15. Rogers, Nicholas. *Halloween: From Pagan Ritual to Party Night.* Oxford: Oxford University Press, 2003, p. 23.

16. Mullally, Erin. "Samhain Revival." *Archaeology* 69, no. 6 (November/December 2016): 35.

17. Gilroy, John. *Tlachtga: Celtic Fire Festival.* Pikefield, 2000.

18. Zoega, Geir T. *A Concise Dictionary of Old Icelandic.* Toronto: University of Toronto Press, 2004.

19. Gunnell, Terry. "The Season of the Disir: The Winter Nights, and the Disablot in Early Medieval Scandinavian Belief." *Cosmos* 16 (2000): 127.

20. *Ibid.*, p. 129.

21. *Ibid.*, p. 125.

22. *Ibid.*, p. 136.

23. Frazer, James. *The Golden Bough*, 13 vols. London: Macmillan, 1911, 10:225.

24. Raedisch, Linda. *The Old Magic of Christmas: Yuletide Traditions for the Darkest Days of the Year.* Woodbury, MN: Llewellyn, 2013, p. 105.

25. Hutton, Ronald. *The Rise and Fall of Merry England: The Ritual Year 1400–1700.* New York: Oxford University Press, 1994, p. 45.

26. Rogers, Nicholas. *Halloween: From Pagan Ritual to Party Night.* Oxford: Oxford University Press, 2003, p. 23.

27. Hutton, Ronald. *The Rise and Fall of Merry England: The Ritual Year 1400–1700.* New York: Oxford University Press, 1994, p. 45.

28. Miles, Clement A. *Christmas Customs and Traditions: Their History and Significance*, New

York: Dover, 1976 (republication of a book published in 1912), p. 192.

29. "How Jack O'Lanterns Originated in Irish Myth." October 21, 2020. *History.com,* https://www.history.com/news/history-of-the-jack-o-lantern-irish-origins. Accessed May 6, 2021.

30. Raedisch, Linda. *The Old Magic of Christmas: Yuletide Traditions for the Darkest Days of the Year.* Woodbury, MN: Llewellyn, 2013, p. 217.

31. *Ibid.,* p. 199.

32. Morton, Lisa. *Trick or Treat: A History of Halloween.* London: Reaktion Books, 2019, p. 19.

33. Stubbs, Philip. *The Anatomy of Abuses in Ailgna.* London, 1583, pp. 92–93.

34. *Ibid.*

35. Nissenbaum, Stephen. *The Battle for Christmas: A Social and Cultural History of Our Most Cherished Holiday.* New York: Vintage, 1997, p. 11.

36. *Ibid.,* p. 10.

37. Klein, Christopher. "Halloween Was Once So Dangerous That Some Cities Considered Banning It." October 27, 2020. *History.com,* https://www.history.com/news/halloween-was-once-so-dangerous-that-some-cities-considered-banning-it. Accessed May 6, 2021.

38. Rogers, Nicholas. *Halloween: From Pagan Ritual to Party Night.* Oxford: Oxford University Press, 2003, p. 49.

39. Morton, Lisa. *Trick or Treat: A History of Halloween.* London: Reaktion Books, 2019, p. 23.

40. "Should Christians Participate in Halloween?" *ChristianAnswers.net,* https://christiananswers.net/q-eden/halloween.html. Accessed May 6, 2021.

41. Markale, Jean. *The Pagan Mysteries of Halloween: Celebrating the Dark Half of the Year.* Rochester, VT: Inner Traditions, 2001, p. 4.

42. "Bishop Konderla issues Memorandum on the Celebration of Halloween Within the Diocese." Diocese of Tulsa and Eastern Oklahoma, https://dioceseoftulsa.org/news/bishop-konderla-issues-memorandum-on-the-celebration-of-halloween-within-the-diocese. Accessed May 6, 2021.

Chapter 14

1. **Notes to** "Keep the Christ in Christmas—What It Really Means." *Conversation of Our Generation,* https://conversationofourgeneration.com/2017/12/20/keep-the-christ-in-christmas-what-it-really-means/. Accessed July 3, 2021.

2. Chavis, James. "Jesus Is the Reason for the Season." *HealthKeepers.com,* http://www.healthkeeperz.com/blog/jesus-is-the-reason-for-the-season. Accessed June 14, 2021.

3. Lipka, Michael, and David Masci. "5 facts about Christmas in America." December 18, 2017. Pew Research Center, https://www.pewresearch.org/fact-tank/2017/12/18/5-facts-about-christmas-in-america/. Accessed April 9, 2021.

4. Webb, W.P. "Christmas and New Year in Texas," *Southern Historical Quarterly* 44, no. 365 (July 1940–April 1941).

5. Spencer, O.M. "Christmas Throughout Christendom." *Harper's New Monthly Magazine* 46 (January 1873): 241–57.

6. Ingersoll, Robert Green. "Christmas Sermon." December 19,1891. *The Evening Telegram* (reproduced by *The Secular Web*), https://infidels.org/library/historical/robert_ingersoll/christmas_sermon.html. Accessed July 16, 2021.

7. "First Christmas Tree." December 26, 1912. *The Leon Reporter,* https://chroniclingamerica.loc.gov/lccn/sn87057096/1912-12-26/ed-1/seq-3/. Accessed August 19, 2021.

8. Di Liscia, Valentina. "Did You Know the First Commercial Christmas Card Featured Underage Drinking?" December 9, 2020. *Fooled by Art,* https://fooledby.art/did-you-know-the-first-commercial-christmas-card-featured-underage-drinking/. Accessed August 3, 2021.

9. Flanders, Judith. *Christmas: A History.* London: Picador, 2017, p. 167.

10. Ponti, Crystal. "Some of the Earliest Christmas Cards Were Morbid and Creepy." December 16, 2019. *History.com,* https://www.history.com/news/victorian-christmas-cards. Accessed August 4, 2021.

11. Ames, Kenneth L. *American Christmas Cards, 1900–1960.* New Haven: Yale University Press, 2011, p. 90.

12. *Ibid.,* p. 91.

13. Flanders, Judith. *Christmas: A History.* London: Picador, 2017, pp. 162–63.

14. *Ibid.,* p. 47.

15. "Secular." *Dictionary.com,* https://www.dictionary.com/browse/secular. Accessed July 3, 2021.

16. "Charlemagne." *Encyclopedia.com,* https://www.encyclopedia.com/people/history/french-history-biographies/charlemagne. Accessed July 3, 2021.

17. Grimm, Jacob. *Teutonic Mythology* (translated from the 4th edition with notes and appendix by James Steven Stallybrass). London: George Bell and Sons, 1882, p. 11.

18. Reese, Thomas. "Beyond Halloween: Witches, devils, trials and executions." October 25, 2017. *National Catholic Reporter,* https://www.ncronline.org/news/opinion/beyond-halloween-witches-devils-trials-and-executions. Accessed June 28, 2021.

19. DK. *A History of Magic, Witchcraft and the Occult.* Foreword by Suzannah Lipscomb. London: Dorling Kindersley, 2020, p. 179.

20. Hagen, Rune Blix. "The Witches' Sabbath at Yuletide." *UiT Norges arktiske universitet,* http://ansatte.uit.no/rune.hagen/christma.htm. Accessed March 30, 2021.

21. Waddell, Brodie. "A seventeenth-century Christmas: mince pies, jollity and witchcraft."

Many Headed Monster, https://manyheadedmonster.com/2012/12/24/a-seventeenth-century-christmas-mince-pies-jollity-and-witchcraft/. Accessed July 3, 2021.

22. Garrard, Thomas. *Edward Colston, the Philanthropist, His Life and Times: Including a Memoir of His Father; The Result of a Laborious Investigation into the Archives of the City.* London: Forgotten Books, 2016 (republication of a book published in 1852), p. 155.

23. Winick, Stephen. "In Comes I, Old Father Christmas: Surprising History of a Christmas Icon." December 20, 2018. *Library of Congress Blog,* https://blogs.loc.gov/folklife/2018/12/in-comes-i-old-father-christmas-surprising-history-of-a-christmas-icon/. Accessed July 3, 2021.

24. Miles, Clement A. *Christmas Customs and Traditions: Their History and Significance.* New York: Dover, 1976 (republication of a book published in 1912), p. 183.

25. Smith, William Robertson. *Lectures on the Religion of the Semites.* 1894 Elibron Classics (reprint of a 1894 edition by Adam and Charles Black, London), p. 255.

26. Bede, *The Venerable Bede's Ecclesiastical History of England.* Nabu Press. lib. i. cap. 30., edited by J.A. Giles (London, 1843), vol. ii, p. 142.

27. Forsyth, Mark. "The surprising origins of famous Christmas carols." December 20, 2016. *BBC.com,* https://www.bbc.com/culture/article/20161220-the-surprising-origins-of-famous-christmas-carols. Accessed July 3, 2021.

28. Crane, Walter. *The Baby's Opera: A Book of Old Rhymes with New Dresses.* Frederick Warne & Co., 1877, pp. 18–19.

29. Wigington, Patti. "What Songs Should I Sing at Yule?" November 13, 2019. *Learn Religions,* https://www.learnreligions.com/singing-at-yule-2562984. Accessed July 17, 2021.

30. "The Holly and the Ivy." *The Hymns and Carols of Christmas,* www.hymnsandcarolsofchristmas.com/Hymns_and_Carols/holly_and_the_ivy.htm. Accessed June 27, 2021.

31. Iles, Norman. *Pagan Carols Restored.* Morecambe, United Kingdom. https://www.patheos.com/blogs/viviannecrowley/2013/12/reclaiming-christmas-lets-party-like-pagans/. Accessed July 3, 2021.

32. Flanders, Judith. *Christmas: A History.* London: Picador, 2017, p. 184.

33. Baring-Gould, S. *For R. R. Chope, Carols for Use in Church.* London: William Clowes & Sons, 1894. https://www.hymnsandcarolsofchristmas.com/Hymns_and_Carols/Images/Chope/introduction.htm. Accessed July 3, 2021.

34. Frodsham, Paul. *From Stonehenge to Santa Claus: The Evolution of Christmas.* Stroud, Gloucestershire: The History Press, 2008, pp. 170–71.

35. Kettler, Sara. "Charles Dickens Wrote 'A Christmas Carol' in Only Six Weeks." December 15, 2020. *Biography.com,* www.biography.com/news/charles-dickens-a-christmas-carol?li_source=LI&li_medium=m2m-rcw-biography. Accessed June 27, 2021.

36. Sutherland, John. "The origins of *A Christmas Carol.*" May 15, 2014. The British Library, https://www.bl.uk/romantics-and-victorians/articles/the-origins-of-a-christmas-carol. Accessed August 28, 2021.

37. Frodsham, Paul. *From Stonehenge to Santa Claus: The Evolution of Christmas.* Stroud, Gloucestershire: The History Press, 2008, p. 172.

38. Barnett, James H. *The American Christmas: A Study in National Culture.* New York: Macmillan, 1954, p. 232.

39. *Ibid.,* p. 75.

40. Harrison, Jane Ellen. *Themis: A Study of the Social Origins of Greek Religion.* Cambridge: Cambridge University Press, 2010, p. 224.

41. Merritt, Robert L. "Jesus Barabbas and the Paschal Pardon." *Journal of Biblical Literature* 104, no. 1 (March 1985).

42. Gaughan, Anthony. "The Christmas Amnesty of 1868." December 27, 2018. *The Faculty Lounge,* https://www.thefacultylounge.org/2018/12/the-christmas-amnesty-of-1868.html. Accessed July 3, 2021.

43. *The Indianapolis Times.* December 20, 1934. Chronicling America: Historic American Newspapers. Library of Congress, https://chroniclingamerica.loc.gov/lccn/sn82015313/1934-12-20/ed-1/seq-20/. Accessed July 22, 2021.

44. Lankford, Ronald D. *Sleigh Rides Jingle Bells & Silent Nights: A Cultural History of American Christmas Songs.* Gainesville: University Press of Florida, 2013, p. 86.

45. "Did Coca-Cola Create Santa Claus?" The Coca-Cola Company, https://www.coca-colacompany.com/faqs/did-coca-cola-invent-santa. Accessed July 3, 2021.

46. Flanders, Judith. *Christmas: A History.* London: Picador, 2017, p. 132.

47. Barnett, James H. *The American Christmas: A Study in National Culture.* New York: Macmillan, 1954, p. 130.

48. Kyllonen, Claire. "Spirit of Christmas Lost to Commercialism." December 16, 2013. *The Roar,* https://lhsroar.com/opinions/editorials/spirit-of-christmas-lost-to-commercialism/. Accessed July 4, 2021.

49. Cox, Anthony. "What is the environmental footprint of Christmas?" December 24, 2019. *OECD Environment Focus,* https://oecd-environment-focus.blog/2019/12/24/what-is-the-environmental-footprint-of-christmas/. Accessed April 9, 2021.

50. "Top Tips for a Sustainable Christmas." World Wildlife Fund, https://www.wwf.org.uk/top-tips-sustainable-christmas. Accessed April 9, 2021.

Chapter 15

1. Witter, Brad. "Who Was Dr. Seuss' Inspiration for the Grinch? Himself!" November 7, 2018. Biography.com, https://www.biography.com/news/dr-seuss-grinch-inspiration. Accessed July 4, 2021.
2. Karnick, S.T. "Dr. Seuss: Christian Author?" August 8, 2008. *The American Culture*, http://theamericanculture.org/dr-seuss-christian-author/. Accessed July 4, 2021.
3. "Kalends." *The Free Dictionary*, https://encyclopedia2.thefreedictionary.com/Kalends. Accessed March 28, 2021.
4. Mabie, Hamilton W. *The Book of Christmas*. New York: Macmillan, 1909, pp. 47–48.
5. "The First Giving of Gifts at Christmas Time." *Daily Capital Journal*, December 19, 1917, p. 16.
6. Chase, Ernest Dudley. *The Romance of Greeting Cards: An Historical Account of the Origin, Evolution, and Development of Christmas Card, Valentine, and Other Forms of Engraved or Printed Greetings from the Earliest Days to the Present Time*. Cambridge, MA: The University Press for E. D. Chase, 1926, p. 10.
7. Llana, Sara Miller. "Christmas: How did gift-giving and caroling get started?" *The Christian Science Monitor*, https://www.csmonitor.com/World/2013/1221/Christmas-How-did-gift-giving-and-caroling-get-started.
8. Versnel, Hank S. "Saturnus and the Saturnalia." December 1, 1992. *Inconsistencies in Greek and Roman Religion, Volume 2: Transition and Reversal in Myth and Ritual*, pp. 148–149.
9. Dooley, Chrissy Nicholas. "A History of the Holiday Bonus—When Did Cash Bonuses Become Big for Business?" November 21, 2016. Recruiting Blogs, https://recruitingblogs.com/profiles/blogs/a-history-of-the-holiday-bonus-when-did-cash-bonuses-become-big. Accessed July 17, 2021.
10. Truitt, Brian. "The 20 best Christmas movies of all time, ranked (from 'Happiest Season' to 'Scrooged')." *USA Today*, https://usatoday.com/story/entertainment/movies/2020/11/05/best-christmas-movies-ranked-wonderful-life-home-alone-die-hard/6170245002/. Accessed April 1, 2021.
11. "Here are the 75 best Christmas movies of all time for the holidays." November 28, 2019. *Today*, https://www.today.com/popculture/75-best-christmas-movies-all-time-2019-holidays-ranked-t168135. Accessed April 1, 2021.
12. "The Nativity Story—Rotten Tomatoes." *Rotten Tomatoes*, https://www.rottentomatoes.com/m/nativity_story. Accessed April 1, 2021.
13. "The Best Christmas Movies of All Time." December 16, 2020. Ranker, https://www.ranker.com/crowdranked-list/best-christmas-movies-of-all-time. Accessed July 4, 2021.
14. Mabie, Hamilton W. *The Book of Christmas*. New York: Macmillan, 1909.
15. Butler, Jenny. "The Neopagan Ritual Year." *Cosmos: The Journal of the Traditional Cosmology Society* 18 (2002): 122.
16. *Ibid.*, p. 127.
17. Cooper, Michael T. "The Roles of Nature, Deities, and Ancestors in Constructing Religious Identity in Contemporary Druidry." *The Pomegranate: The International Journal of Pagan Studies* 11, no. 1 (2009): 58–73.
18. Bowman, Marion. "Contemporary Celtic Spirituality." In Joanne Pearson, ed., *Belief Beyond Boundaries: Wicca, Celtic Spirituality and the New Age*. Milton Keynes: Open University, 2002, pp. 55–101.
19. Kristal, Joshua. "Stonehenge and its Neo-Druids at Winter Solstice." March 17, 2002. *Joshua Kristal, Photographer*, https://machupicchuthis.wordpress.com/2012/03/17/stonehenge-and-its-neo-druids-at-winter-solstice/. Accessed July 4, 2021.
20. "Stonehenge Winter Solstice Tour." Stonehenge Tours, https://stonehengetours.com/stonehenge-winter-solstice-tour.htm. Accessed July 4, 2021.
21. "Newgrange Winter Solstice 2020." Boyne Valley Tours, https://www.boynevalleytours.com/winter-solstice-2020.htm. Accessed April 2, 2021.
22. Shuftan, Bixyl. "Roma's Saturnalia Festival." December 26, 2013. *Second Life Newser*, https://slnewser.blogspot.com/2013/12/romas-saturnalia-festival.html. Accessed August 6, 2021.
23. Reed, Ellen. "Oh, Come All Ye Faithful." *Willow Firesong's Pagan Yule Carol Collection*, https://members.tripod.com/~Willow_Firesong/YulCarls/OhComeAl.html. Accessed April 2, 2021.
24. Wigington, Patti. "Yule Wassail Recipe and History" December 4, 2018. *Learn Religions*, https://www.learnreligions.com/go-a-wassailing-for-yule-2562973. Accessed April 1, 2021.
25. Wigington, Patti. "Yule Craft Projects for the Winter Solstice" October 13, 2018. *Learn Religions*, https://www.learnreligions.com/yule-craft-projects-4147322. Accessed April 3, 2021.
26. Wigington, Patti. "Winter Nights Yule Incense" June 25, 2019. *Learn Religions*, https://www.learnreligions.com/winter-nights-yule-incense-2562153. Accessed April 3, 2021.
27. Hrynowski, Zach. "More Americans Celebrating a Secular Christmas." December 20, 2019. *Gallup News*, https://news.gallup.com/poll/272378/americans-celebrating-secular-christmas.aspx. Accessed July 4, 2021.
28. Cox, Daniel, and Robert P. Jones P. "'Merry Christmas' vs. 'Happy Holidays': Republicans and Democrats are Polar Opposites." December 19, 2016. PRRI, https://www.prri.org/research/poll-post-election-holiday-war-christmas/. Accessed July 4, 2021.
29. "Silent Night: The story of the Christmas

carol." December 24, 2013. BBC News, https://www.bbc.com/news/av/world-europe-25471256. Accessed April 4, 2021.

30. "No Place Like Church for the Holidays." December 14, 2015. Lifeway Research, https://lifewayresearch.com/2015/12/14/no-place-like-church-for-the-holidays/. Accessed April 2, 2021.

31. "Religion: Gallup Historical Trends." *Gallup News,* https://news.gallup.com/poll/1690/religion.aspx. Accessed April 2, 2021.

32. "Americans Say Religious Aspects of Christmas Are Declining in Public Life." December 12, 2017. Pew Research Center, https://www.pewforum.org/2017/12/12/americans-say-religious-aspects-of-christmas-are-declining-in-public-life/. Accessed July 4, 2021.

33. "No Place Like Church for the Holidays." December 14, 2015. Lifeway Research, https://lifewayresearch.com/2015/12/14/no-place-like-church-for-the-holidays/. Accessed April 2, 2021.

Chapter 16

1. Ratcliffe, Susan, ed. *Oxford Treasury of Sayings and Quotations.* Oxford: Oxford University Press, 2011, p. 78.

2. "Americans Say Religious Aspects of Christmas Are Declining in Public Life." December 12, 2017. Pew Research Center, https://pewforum.org/2017/12/12/americans-say-religious-aspects-of-christmas-are-declining-in-public-life/. Accessed July 4, 2021.

3. Kassam, Raheem. "War on Christmas: Starbucks Red Cups Are Emblematic of the Christian Culture Cleansing Of The West." November 5, 2015. Breitbart.com, https://www.breitbart.com/europe/2015/11/05/war-on-christmas-starbucks-new-red-cups-are-emblematic-of-the-christian-culture-cleansing-of-the-west/. Accessed August 29, 2021.

4. Wattles, Jackie. "Starbucks' plain red holiday cups stir up controversy." November 9, 2015. *CNN Business,* https://money.cnn.com/2015/11/08/news/companies/starbucks-red-cups-controversy/. Accessed July 4, 2021.

5. "Starbucks Unveils 2016 Holiday Red Cups." November 9, 2016. *Starbucks Stories & News,* https://stories.starbucks.com/stories/2016/starbucks-red-cups-2016/. Accessed July 4, 2021.

6. "20 Years of Starbucks Cups." November 9, 2017. *Starbucks Stories & News,* https://stories.starbucks.com/stories/2017/20-years-of-starbucks-holiday-cups/. Accessed July 4, 2021.

7. Calicchio, Dom. "Starbucks 'Merry Coffee' cups look a lot like Christmas—without saying it." November 7, 2019. Fox News, https://www.foxnews.com/food-drink/starbucks-risks-more-war-on-christmas-backlash-with-merry-coffee-cups. Accessed July 4, 2021.

8. Aldrich, Jeremy. "History of 'Happy Holidays.'" *Hburgjeremy.com,* http://www.hburgjeremy.com/2011/12/history-of-happy-holidays.html. Accessed July 18, 2021.

9. Stack, Liam. "How the 'War on Christmas' Controversy was Created." December 19, 2016. *The New York Times,* https://www.nytimes.com/2016/12/19/us/war-on-christmas-controversy.html. Accessed February 23, 2021.

10. *Ibid.*

11. Hayes, Liz. "Trump Declares Victory in Fake 'War on Christmas.'" December 26, 2017. Americans United for Separation of Church and State's *Wall of Separation Blog,* https://www.au.org/blogs/wall-of-separation/trump-declares-victory-in-fake-war-on-christmas. Accessed July 4, 2021.

12. Cathey, Libby. "Trump, at Florida rally, suggests he's fighting a new 'War on Thanksgiving.'" November 27, 2019. *ABC News,* https://abcnews.go.com/Politics/trump-florida-rally-suggests-fighting-war-thanksgiving/story?id=67345066. Accessed July 4, 2021.

13. "1980 *Playboy* Interview with John Lennon And Yoko Ono." *John-Lennon.com,* https://www.namedat.com/1980-playboy-interview-with-john-lennon-and-yoko-ono/. Accessed February 27, 2021.

14. Mohr, Melissa. "Using Merry Christmas or Happy Holidays is no longer about putting a stranger at ease." December 23, 2019. *NBC News,* https://www.nbcnews.com/think/opinion/using-merry-christmas-or-happy-holidays-no-longer-about-putting-ncna1106181. Accessed July 4, 2021.

15. "Americans Say Religious Aspects of Christmas Are Declining in Public Life." December 12, 2017. Pew Research Center, https://www.pewforum.org/2017/12/12/americans-say-religious-aspects-of-christmas-are-declining-in-public-life/.bowller Accessed July 4, 2021.

Bibliography

A wide variety of sources were used for this book, some primary and some secondary, some that deal with Christmas history and others that deal more broadly with the history of paganism and the Christianization of Europe. Utilizing several historical studies of the holiday itself, this book also benefits from many histories of pre–Christian religions and ancient Rome; sociological examinations of childhood; scholarly studies of the Bible; collections of Norse, Greek and Roman mythologies; cultural histories of magic and witchcraft, and other related topics.

For general histories of Christmas, the works by Judith Flanders, Paul Frodsham, Clement A. Miles, and Stephen Nissenbaum are must-reads. For those interested in the supernatural side of Christmas—its ghosts, goblins and strange superstitions—the books by Al Ridenour, Linda Raedisch, Paul Hawkins, Claudia Müller-Ebeling, and Christian Rätsch are among the best. Specific aspects of Christmas customs such as Santa Claus, Christmas cards, and Christmas trees are covered well by authors such as Kenneth Ames, Gerry Bowler, Daniel Foley, Tom Jerman, and Phyllis Siefker. For general studies of paganism and the Christianization of Europe, anything by Ronald Hutton is highly recommended. Also worth reading are Edward J. Watts' *The Final Pagan Generation: Rome's Unexpected Path to Christianity*, Ramsay MacMullen's *Christianity and Paganism in the Fourth to Eighth Centuries*, and Jacob Grimm's *Teutonic Mythology*.

Please see below for a carefully selected bibliography for further reading. Citations for other materials appear in the Chapter Notes.

Ames, Kenneth L. *American Christmas Cards, 1900–1960*. New Haven: Yale University Press, 2011.

Ariès, Philippe. *Centuries of Childhood: A Social History of Family Life*. Translated from French by Robert Baldick. New York: Vintage, 1965.

Barnett, James H. *The American Christmas: A Study in National Culture*. New York: Macmillan, 1954.

Bauckham, Richard. *Jesus: A Very Short Introduction*. Oxford: Oxford University Press, 2011.

Bede the Venerable. *Bede: The Reckoning of Time*. Liverpool: Liverpool University Press, 1999.

Bowler, Gerry. *Santa Claus: A Biography*. Toronto: McClelland & Stewart, 2007.

Bowler, Gerry. *The World Encyclopedia of Christmas*. Toronto: McClelland & Stewart, 2000.

Chambers, Robert. *The Book of Days: A Miscellany of Popular Antiquities in Connection with the Calendar: Including Anecdote, Biography, & History, Curiosities and Literature, and Oddities of Human Life and Character*. London: W&R Chambers, 1863.

Cooke, Richard Joseph. *Christianity and Childhood: Or the Relation of Children to the Church*. London: Forgotten Books, 2018 (republication of a book published in 1891).

Curran, J.R. *Pagan City and Christian Capital: Rome in the Fourth Century*. Oxford: Oxford University Press, 2000.

Curtiss, Frank Homer. *The Pattern Life: Order of Christian Mystics*. Los Angeles: Willing, 1943.

Davidson, Gustav. *A Dictionary of Angels Including the Fallen Angels*. New York: The Free Press, 1967.

Davies, Owen. *Paganism: A Very Short Introduction*. Oxford: Oxford University Press, 2011.

Del Re, Gerard, and Patricia. *The Christmas*

Almanac, 2d ed. New York: Random House, 2004.

Derry, T.K. *A History of Scandinavia: Norway, Sweden, Denmark, Finland, and Iceland*. Minneapolis: University of Minnesota Press, 1979.

DK. *A History of Magic, Witchcraft and the Occult*. Foreword by Suzannah Lipscomb. London: Dorling Kindersley, 2020.

Dixon-Kennedy, Mike. *Encyclopedia of Russian and Slavic Myth and Legend*. Santa Barbara: ABC-CLIO, 1998.

Ellis, Peter Berresford. *A Brief History of the Druids*. Philadelphia: Running Press, 2002.

Flanders, Judith. *Christmas: A History*. London: Picador, 2017.

Foley, Daniel. *The Christmas Tree*. Boston: Chilton Book Co., 1961.

Frassetto, Michael. *The Early Medieval World: From the Fall of Rome to the Time of Charlemagne*. Santa Barbara: ABC-CLIO, 2013.

Frazer, James George. *The Golden Bough: A Study in Magic and Religion*, 3d ed., Vol. 2 of 12. Project Gutenberg. Chapel Hill: University of North Carolina Press, 2019.

Frodsham, Paul. *From Stonehenge to Santa Claus: The Evolution of Christmas*. Stroud, Gloucestershire: The History Press, 2008.

Gaskill, Malcolm. *Witchcraft: A Very Short Introduction*. Oxford: Oxford University Press, 2010.

Godwin, Michael. *Angels: An Endangered Species*. New York: Simon & Schuster, 1990.

Grimm, Jacob. *Teutonic Mythology*. Translated from the 4th edition with notes and appendix by James Steven Stallybrass. London: George Bell and Sons, 1882.

Gulevich, Tanya. *Encyclopedia of Christmas & New Year's Celebrations*. Detroit: Omnigraphics, 2003.

Hansen, William. *Classical Mythology: A Guide to the Mythical World of the Greeks and Romans*. New York: Oxford University Press, 2005.

Harrison, Jane Ellen. *Themis: A Study of the Social Origins of Greek Religion*. Cambridge: Cambridge University Press, 2010.

Hawkins, Paul. *Bad Santas: Disquieting Winter Folk Tales for Grown-Ups*. London: Simon & Schuster, 2013.

Hervey, Thomas Kibble. *The Book of Christmas; Descriptive of the Customs, Ceremonies, Traditions, Superstitions, Fun, Feeling, And Festivities of the Christmas Season*. Pierce Press, 2011 (reprint of a book published in 1888).

Hollander, M. Lee, trans. *Heimskringla: History of the Kings of Norway*. Austin: University of Texas Press, 2007.

Hutton, Ronald. *Pagan Britain*. New Haven: Yale University Press, 2015.

Hutton, Ronald. *Stations of the Sun: A History of the Ritual Year in Britain*. New York: Oxford University Press, 2001.

Hutton, Ronald. *The Pagan Religions of the Ancient British Isles: Their Nature and Legacy* (reprint edition). Hoboken: Wiley-Blackwell, 1993.

Hutton, Ronald. *The Rise and Fall of Merry England: The Ritual Year 1400–1700*. New York: Oxford University Press, 1994.

Jones, David Albert. *Angels: A Very Short Introduction*. Oxford: Oxford University Press, 2011.

Jerman, Tom A. *Santa Claus Worldwide: A History of St. Nicholas and Other Holiday Gift-Bringers*. Jefferson, NC: McFarland, 2020.

Keck, David. *Angels and Angelology in the Middle Ages*. New York: Oxford University Press, 1998.

Keyser, Rudolph. *The Religion of The Northmen*. Trans. Barclay Pennock. New York: Charles B. Norton, 1854.

Lankford, Ronald D. *Sleigh Rides, Jingle Bells, and Silent Nights: A Cultural History of American Christmas Songs*. Gainesville: University Press of Florida, 2013.

Lecouteux, Claude. *Encyclopedia of Norse and Germanic Folklore, Mythology, and Magic*. Rochester, VT: Inner Traditions, 2014.

Ludovicus, J.R. Milis, ed. *The Pagan Middle Ages*. Woodbridge: The Boydell Press, 1998.

Mabie, Hamilton W. *The Book of Christmas*. New York: Macmillan, 1909.

Mac Cana, Proinsias. *Celtic Mythology*. Feltham: Hamlyn, 1970.

MacDonald, Fiona. *Christmas: A Very Peculiar History*. Brighton, United Kingdom: Book House, 2010.

MacMullen, Ramsay. *Christianity and Paganism in the Fourth to Eighth Centuries*. New Haven: Yale University Press, 1997.

Markale, Jean. *The Pagan Mysteries of Halloween: Celebrating the Dark Half of the Year*. Rochester, VT: Inner Traditions, 2001.

Mavromataki, Maria. *Greek Mythology and Religion*. Athens: Haitalis, 1997.

Miles, Clement A. *Christmas Customs and Traditions: Their History and Significance*. New York: Dover, 1976 (republication of a book published in 1912).

Morton, Lisa. *Trick or Treat: A History of Halloween*. London: Reaktion Books, 2019.

Müller-Ebeling, Claudia and Rätsch, Christian. *Pagan Christmas: The Plants, Spirits, and Rituals at the Origins of Yuletide*. Rochester, VT: Inner Traditions, 2006.

Murphy, G. Ronald. *The Saxon Savior: The Germanic Transformation of the Gospel in the Ninth-Century Heliand*. New York: Oxford University Press, 1989.

Nissenbaum, Stephen. *The Battle for Christmas: A Social and Cultural History of Our Most Cherished Holiday*. New York: Vintage, 1997.

Page, Nick. *Christmas: Tradition, Truth and Total Baubles*. London: Hodder & Stoughton, 2020.

Perry, Joe. *Christmas in Germany: A Cultural*

History. Chapel Hill: University of North Carolina Press, 2010.

Raedisch, Linda. *The Old Magic of Christmas: Yuletide Traditions for the Darkest Days of the Year*. Woodbury, MN: Llewellyn, 2013.

Rawson, Beryl, ed. *A Companion to Families in the Greek and Roman Worlds*. Hoboken: Blackwell, 2010.

Rees, Alwyn, and Brinley. *Celtic Heritage: Ancient Tradition in Ireland and Wales*. London: Thames and Hudson, 1961.

Ridenour, Al. *The Krampus and the Old, Dark Christmas: Roots and Rebirth of the Folkloric Devil*. Port Townsend, WA: Feral House, 2016.

Roesdahl, Else. *The Vikings*. London: Penguin, 1999.

Rogers, Nicholas. *Halloween: From Pagan Ritual to Party Night*. Oxford: Oxford University Press, 2003.

Rubin, Miri. *The Middle Ages: A Very Short Introduction*. Oxford: Oxford University Press, 2014.

Salzman, Michele Renee. *On Roman Time: The Codex-Calendar of 354 and the Rhythms of Urban Life in Late Antiquity*. Oakland: University of California, 1991.

Seal, Jeremy. *Nicholas: The Epic Journey from Saint to Santa Claus*. New York: Bloomsbury, 2005.

Siefker, Phyllis. *Santa Claus, Last of the Wild Men: The Origins and Evolution of Saint Nicholas, Spanning 50,000 Years*. Jefferson, NC: McFarland, 2006.

Simek, Rudolf. *A Dictionary of Northern Mythology*. Suffolk: Boydell and Brewer, 2008.

Thomas, Keith. *Religion and the Decline of Magic: Studies in Popular Beliefs in Sixteenth and Seventeenth-Century England*. London: Weidenfeld and Nicolson, 1971.

Watts, Edward J. *The Final Pagan Generation: Rome's Unexpected Path to Christianity*. Berkeley: University of California Press, 2020.

Weiser, Francis X. *Handbook of Christian Feasts and Customs*. San Diego: Harcourt, 1958.

Index

Abbot Mellitus 47
Abbot of Misrule *see* Lord of Misrule
Abolition Bill of 1834 164
Abraham 144
Achilles 144
Acts of the Apostles 148
Adam of Bremen 30, 43–44, 48, 72
Advent 31, 48, 51–52, 58, 54, 69, 73, 104, 133, 177, 186, 207
aes sidhe 109
Æsir *see* Norse pantheon of gods
Ahura Mazda 145
Ajax 10
Akkadians 99
alcohol 43, 58–59, 61, 92, 158, 162–163, 167–168, 173, 185
Alexandrinus, Clemens 15
álfablót 108, 174, 176
álfar 88, 108; *Dökkálfar* 88; *Ljósálfar* 88
Alfheim 88
All Hallows Eve *see* All Saints Day
All Hallows Mass 175
All Saints Day 173, 177–178, 180
All Souls Day 176–177; *see also* All Souls Day
Alsso of Brevnov 189
Ambrose of Milan 31
The American Christmas (Barnett) 65
American Family Association 211
Ames, Kenneth 185
Andersen, Hans Christian 56
Andrew (the apostle) 16
Andros, Edmund 65
angelos 137
angels 4, 51, 53, 100, 135–139, 149–153, 188; Grigori 137; Powers 137
Angels: An Endangered Species (Godwin) 137
Angles 38
Anglo-Saxons 17, 34, 38
Anniston, Jennifer 202
Anthon, Charles 116
Antioch 24, 37, 142
Antiochus IV 142

Apollo 19, 50, 69, 73
Apology of Socrates 138
Ariès, Philippe 121, 124
Aschenklaus 124
Asgård 73
Assarsson, Berndt David 40
Assyrians 99
Asterius 32, 170
astral magic 99
astrology 99, 101, 143, 145, 146
astronomy 99
Attica 73
Augustine 33, 36, 39, 45, 149–150
Austria 45, 104, 120, 131, 153, 209
Autry, Gene 193

Baal 27, 30, 117
Babel *see* Babylon
Babylon 143, 145, 189
Babylonians 69, 100
Bacchanalia 63–64
Bacchus 36–37, 45, 50, 90–92, 95–96, 162, 184
Baldur the Beautiful 76, 105
Banks, Joseph 160
Baptist War *see* Christmas Uprising
Baring-Gould, S. 191
Barnett, James Howard 65
Barry, Jonathan 129
The Battle for Christmas (Nissenbaum) 62, 92, 163, 178
Battle of Emesa 26
Bauckman, Richard 15
Bavaria 51, 133
Bay 50, 55
Bede, Venerable 17, 34
Befana 120
Belafonte, Harry 207
Belarus 85
bells 4, 34, 85, 103–105, 111–112, 130, 134, 177–178, 185, 189, 198
Belsnickel 85, 88, 104, 199
Ben Light and his Surf Club Boys 168
Berchta *see* Perchta
berserkers 94, 101
Berta *see* Perchta
Bertha *see* Perchta
Bes 149

Bethsaida 16
Bible 7, 19, 21, 40, 52, 54, 56, 58, 63–66, 78, 100, 117–118, 148, 164, 202, 204, 216; angels' depictions in 135; Book of Ezekiel 117, 139; Book of Genesis 68, 143; Book of Jeremiah 68–69, 73; Book of Psalms 39, 54, 56; Book of Revelation 56; Books of Chronicles 68, 143; Deuteronomy 145; Exodus 146; Fall of Man 51; Gospels 16–17, 53, 68, 95, 135, 139, 143–145, 216; Leviticus 118, 145; magic 100, 145; nativity story 145–146, 151, 199–200, 202, 216; New Testament 19, 39, 149; Old Testament 19, 56, 117, 143–144, 147; prophecy of Malachi 19, 56
Bifrost 73
Billing, King of Ruthenia 144
The Bishop's Wife (film) 202
Black Friday 167, 171
Blessing of the Waters 101
Blitzen 90
blot 47
boggarts 109
The Book of Black Magic and of Pacts 135
The Book of Christmas (Mabie) 200
The Book of Christmas: Descriptive of the Customs, Ceremonies, Traditions, Superstitions, Fun, Feeling, and Festivities of the Christmas Season (Hervey) 66
The Book of Days (Chambers) 53
Bourn, Henry 161
Bowler, Gerry 92
Boxing Day 164, 192, 200
boy bishop custom 122, 178; *see also* Feast of the Holy Innocents
Božić 41
Bradford, William 64
Brother Jonathan 114
Bulgaria 84, 129
Burning the Bush 108; *see also* mistletoe
Byrd, Sarah 188

Cage, Nicolas 167
Cailleach Bheur 175
Calicchio, Dom 211
Camael 137
candelabrum 69
Candlemas Day 161, 178
Capernaum 16
Capra, Frank 156
Caracalla 30
Carey, Mariah 207
Caristia 30
carols 23, 54–57, 61, 153–155, 190–191, 205; *see also* hymns
Carols for the Use in Church 191
Carthage 30, 116–117
Carthaginians 116
Cash, Johnny 3
Catholic Apostolic Church 95
The Catholic Encyclopedia 24
Catholicism 44, 50, 63, 104
Catullus 29
Celts 11, 35, 71, 74, 82, 108, 173, 175, 177
Centuries of Childhood (Aries) 121, 124
Ceremonie upon Candlemas Eve 106
česnica 45
Charlemagne 39, 150, 187
A Charlie Brown Christmas (film) 202
Childebert, Frankish King 51
A Chipmunk Christmas (film) 202
Chorazin 16
Christian and Missionary Alliance 97
Christian History 155
The Christian Science Monitor 201
ChristianAnswers.net 180
Christianization 2, 17, 35–38, 73–75, 88–89, 101, 109, 118, 150, 173, 187–188, 190
Christianizing the Roman Empire (MacMullen) 148
Christina of Markyate 151
Christmas: A History (Flanders) 11, 126
Christmas box 192
Christmas cards 185, 201
A Christmas Carol (Dickens) 127–128, 192, 201
Christmas Customs and Traditions (Miles) 15, 75, 130, 161
Christmas in Germany: A Cultural History (Perry) 71
Christmas In and Out (Taylor) 189
Christmas Lord *see* Lord of Misrule
Christmas Miracles: Magical True Stories of Modern-Day Miracles (Miller, Lewis and Sander) 155
Christmas peace 60
A Christmas Story (film) 113, 126, 202

A Christmas Story House and Museum (website) 113
Christmas: Tradition, Truth and Total Baubles (Page) 12
The Christmas Tree (Foley) 78
Christmas trees 4, 80, 135, 153, 185, 189, 197, 204, 210, 214
Christmas Truce of World War I 153–155
Christmas Uprising 164–165
Christmas Vacation (film) 202
Chronicles of Enoch 137, 139
Chrysostom, Dion 35
Chrysostom, John 14, 19, 31
Chumash 35
Cicero 26, 35, 116–117, 165
circenses 30
Clement, Bishop of Rome 100
Clough, Martin F. 95
Coca-Cola Company 194–195
Codex of 354 24, 30
Columbus, Christopher 216
Columella 166
commercialism 182, 193–197, 203, 209
Commodus 30
Constantine 14, 24, 50, 148
Constantius II 148
Contra Marción 147
Cook, James 160
Cooke, Richard Joseph 118
Coulson, RS 153
Council of Nicaea 84
Council of Saragossa 31
cribs 53, 143, 207
Cú Chulainn 144

daevayasna 145
daimons 138; cacodaemons 138; eudaemons 138
Damaschin, Liliana 41
Daniels, Justin 129
Dannhauer, Johann Konrad 79
Daphne 69
Dashu, Max 129
Davies, Samuel 66, 162
Davis, Jefferson 163
Day of the Dead 176; *see also* All Souls Day
Dažbog 41
Dea Syria 30
Ded Moroz 85–86
Demandt, Alexander 79
de Middleburgo, Paulus 15
demigods 53, 144
demons 98–100, 103–105, 117, 120, 124, 129–133, 137–139, 142, 145, 148, 150–151, 177–178
Denmark 5, 17, 34, 39, 56, 60, 111, 168, 213, 214
the Devil 47, 63, 130, 132, 137, 143, 150, 177–178, 180, 188
de Voragine, Jacobus 104
Diana 73
Dickens, Charles 22, 127–128, 191–192, 201, 203
Dies Natalis Solis Invicti 5, 14, 26, 165

Dio, Cassius 144
Dionysus 90
dísablót 174, 176
disir 174–175
Dr. Seuss *see* Geisel, Theodor
Dr. Seuss' How the Grinch Stole Christmas! 198–199; *see also* Geisel, Theodor
Dolansky, Fanny 166
Dōngzhì Festival 34
Dorset Cursus 35
Douglass, Frederick 164–165
driudecht 36
Druidry 204
druids 35–36, 45, 71, 94, 98, 105–106, 108, 151, 172, 204–205
Durrington Walls 35
dvoeverie 40

East, Dorothy 188
Eastern Orthodox Church 15
Ebenezer Scrooge 127, 201
Egeria 73
Eggnog Riot 163; *see also* misrule
Egypt 24, 36, 54, 79, 99, 149, 151
Elf 1202
Elf on the Shelf 110
Elizabeth I, Queen of England 53
Elizabeth II, Queen of England 170
Elizabethan Religious Settlement of 1559 63
elves 88–90, 95, 108–112, 133–135, 139, 172–175, 188, 199, 210
ember nights 129
Encyclopedia Britannica 4, 78–79, , 228
England 29, 36–39, 50, 53, 55, 59, 61, 64, 81, 101, 104, 122, 130, 161, 163, 170, 177, 178, 185, 188, 190–191, 204, 214
English Civil War 64, 86
Ephrem the Syrian 31
Epiphanius 24
Epiphany 24, 30–31, 48, 120, 195
Eros 90
Eusebius 84
Evangelical Friends Church 96
The Evening Telegram 184
The Examination and Tryal of Old Father Christmas (King) 158

fairies 53, 103, 109, 120, 128, 139, 173
The Family Man (film) 167
The Family's High Times in Olden Days (Gunnarsen) 63
Father Christmas 38, 61, 63, 66, 86–87, 90, 92, 158, 160, 200
Feast of Fools 48–49
Feast of Saint Nicholas 123; *The Feast of Saint Nicholas* (painting) 123

Index

Feast of the Holy Innocents 122
Feast of the Nativity 63
Fenrir 38
Feuerstein, Joshua 211
Finding Hope Ministries 143
The First Christmas: What the Gospels Really Teach About Jesus's Birth (Borg and Crossan) 22
Flanders, Judith 11, 107, 126
Fleming, Jim 17
Flora Britannica (Mabey) 108
Foley, Daniel J. 78
Fomorians 172
Fortunatus 53, 114
Fox News 4, 211
France 48, 131
Franciscan order 48, 131
frankincense 145, 178
Frau Holle *see* Perchta
Frazer, James 108, 175
Frey 41–44, 47, 55
Freyja 44, 73, 76, 120, 50, 76, 79, 121
Frigg 120
Frisians 38–39
Frodsham, Paul 35, 81, 144
From Stonehenge to Santa Claus (Frodsham) 35, 144
Frosty the Snowman (film) 111

Gabriel the archangel 135, 139, 143
Gaels 73
games and circuses 30–31
Gaskill, Malcolm 99
Gate Night 179; *see also* Halloween
Geisel, Theodor 198–199
George V, King of England 170
Germany 39, 45, 66, 69–79, 101, 103, 109, 119–120, 131, 161, 187, 190
Gibson, John 4
gift-giving 6, 17, 23, 32, 35, 43, 65, 96, 182, 195, 197, 199–201
The Gift of the Magi (Henry) 199
gingerbread houses 209
Gloso 133
God 13, 24, 31, 33, 47–48, 50, 54, 56, 58–59, 63, 65, 75–76, 79, 95–96, 100, 117–120, 135–138, 142–156, 162, 177–178, 182, 187–192, 216
Godwin, Malcolm 137
Golby, J.M. 86
The Golden Bough: A Study in Magic and Religion (Frazer) 108
The Golden Legend (de Voragine) 104
Grandfather Frost *see* Ded Moroz
Great Fire Festival 173
Great Flood 52, 100
Great Jamaican Slave Revolt of 1831–32 *see* Christmas Uprising

Greccio 53
Greece 34, 36, 54, 83, 90, 99, 116, 132, 139
Gremlins 202
Grimm, Jacob 41, 46, 120, 188
Grimm brothers 109, 121; The Elves and The Shoemaker 109; Hansel and Gretel 121
The Guardian 155
Gunnell, Terry 175

Haakon 47, 175
Hadrian's Wall 36
Hallowtide *see* All Saints Day
Handbook of Christian Feasts and Customs (Weiser) 71
Happy Xmas (War is Over) 213
Harold Fairhair, king of Norway 43
Harper's New Monthly Magazine 55, 90, 165
Harper's Weekly 80, 92, 110
Harris, Leon 154
Hartford Courant 95
Harvey, Father Geoff 12
heathen days 129
Heckert, Randy 96
heimchen 119–120, 125
Heimskringla 174
Hekate 100
Helen of Troy 144
Heliand 39–40
Helios 19
Henriksson, Goran 43
Henry, O. 199–200
Henry VIII, king of England 122
Hercules 144
Hermes 137
Herod 16, 25, 39, 51, 122, 135
Herrick, Robert 61, 106–107
Hijmans, Steven 14
Hippolytus 13–14, 35
History of Ireland (Keating) 172
History Today 77
Hlaoir 175
Hodur 105
Hökunótt 34
Holda *see* Perchta
Holla *see* Perchta
holly 6, 35, 45, 50, 55, 86, 92, 105, 178, 185, 191, 210
Holly King 204
Home Alone (film) 167, 202
Homeric Hymns 54
Honigmann, John J. 131
Hornklove, Torbjørn 43
Horus-Shed 149
Hoteiosho 86
How the Goode Man Taught Hys Sone 59
How the Goode Wife Taught Hyr Doughter 59
How the Grinch Stole Christmas 198–199
Hræsvelgr 88
Hrafnsmá 43
Hudson, David 96
Huginn and Muninn 90

huldufólk 109
Hutton, Ronald 94, 122
hymns 23, 31, 48, 54–57, 130, 143, 191

incense 112, 130, 133, 145, 207; *see also* frankincense
Ingersoll, Robert Green 184
Interpretatio christiana 45
Inti Raymi 34
Ireland 39, 46–47, 150, 172–175, 205
Irenaeus 13–14
Irving, Washington 87, 93, 124–126; *see also* Knickerbocker's History of New York
Israelites 16, 160
It's a Wonderful Life 156, 201–202
Italy 31, 34, 53, 73, 79, 103, 120, 152
ivy 35, 45, 50, 86, 105, 191

Jackson, Mahalia 207
Jakobsson, Armann 108
James I, King of England 86
Jehovah's Witnesses 7, 209
Jeremiah 51
Jerome, Jerome K. 129
Jesus 1–7, 11–25, 31, 38–41, 45, 47–56, 60, 75, 79–80, 84, 95–96, 105, 120–122, 135, 138–139, 142–152, 162, 180–185, 191, 199–202, 208–217; *see also* Bible
Jesus Is Savior (website) 96
John the Baptist 14, 148
Johnston, L.D. 92
jól 44, 59
jólablót 44
Jólnir 44
Jones, Charles 87
Jørgensdatter, Mari 188
Jotunheim 73
jötunn 88
joulustaalo 133
Journal of the Evangelical Theological Society 12
Judah Maccabee 142
Judaism 68, 142, 209
Julemand 86; *see also* Santa Claus
Julius Caesar 35, 144
Jupiter 27, 30, 36, 38, 73, 115–116
Justinian 30
Justinus 165
Jutes 38

Kalends 5, 17, 26, 28, 32, 36–37, 80, 165, 169, 200, 212
kallikantzaros 132, 178
karakondžula 133
Keating, Geoffrey 172
Keillor, Garrison 209
Keyser, Rudolph 73
Kievan Rus 39, 85
King, Josiah 158

King David 144
Kingo, Thomas 56
Knecht Ruprecht 45, 85, 104, 131
Knickerbocker's History of New York 87, 126; *see also* Irving, Washington
Knocking Nights 133
Konderla, David 181
Korean War 155
Krampus 45, 104, 124–125, 131–132, 199
Krampus (film) 202
Kris Kringle 93, 156, 203
Kronia 115–116
Kronian Hill 116
Kronos 27, 115–117

Laertius, Diogenes 35
lamiae 133
Lankford, Ronald 169
Laplanders *see* Sámi
La Rue, Leonard P. 155
Latimer, Hugh 100
laurel 50, 69, 80
Learn Religions (website) 206–207
Lectures on the Religion of the Semites 189
Lenacea 34
Lennon, John 212–213, 217
Lent 31, 58
Leoni, Téa 167
The Lesser Key of Solomon 135
Lewis, C.S. 6
Leyis, Thomas 180
Libanius 37
Lies My Teacher Told Me (Loewen) 216
linden trees 73
Lindisfarne 38
The Lion, the Witch and the Wardrobe (Lewis) 6
Lithuania 133
Livingston, Henry, Jr. 88
Lochru 151
Loewen, James 216
London Rifle Brigade 153
Lord of Misrule 29, 61, 86, 92, 122, 167
Louis the Pious 39
Lucan 35
Lucian of Samosata 29
Lucifer *see* the Devil
Lucina 34
ludi 30–31
Lugh 137, 144
Luke the Apostle 16–17, 22, 135, 139, 143–145, 216
Lund, Troels Frederik 59
Lussi Night *see* Lussinatta
Lussinatta 130
Luther, Martin 55, 68, 77–78, 80
Lutheranism 50
Lutherbaums 80

Mabey, Richard 108
Mabie, Hamilton 101, 200–204
Mac Cana, Proinsias 172
MacMullen, Ramsay 148
Macrobius 27, 29, 165
magi 22–23, 31–32, 51, 54, 120, 144–149, 151, 185, 190, 199–202
magic 2, 7, 35–36, 44–45, 53, 73, 83, 88–89, 94, 96, 98–112, 119–120, 124, 130, 135, 142–151, 155–157, 174, 181, 187, 189, 193, 216–217
The Magic of Christmas Miracles (Miller) 156
magos 145
malakh 137
maleficium 150
Malta 117
The Man Who Invented Christmas (film) 22
manger displays *see* cribs
Marcus Aurelius 30
Marcus Tullius 116
Marduk 13
Marks, Johnny 193
Mars 30, 36, 144
Martin, Dale 138
Massachusetts Bay Colony 64–65
Massacre of the Innocents 122, 151, 202
materialism 32, 92, 96, 193, 198, 203
Mather, Cotton 162
Mather, Increase 15, 65, 166, 180
Matthew the Apostle 16, 22, 68, 95, 135, 143–145
May, Robert Lewis 193
Mercury 36, 111, 137
SS *Meredith Victory* 155
Mesoamerica 68
Mesopotamia 68, 98
The Metamorphoses (Ovid) 55
Metatron, the archangel 139
Michael the archangel 137; legend of Michael and the Dragon 137
Michaelsmas 47
Midnight Mass 31, 60, 133, 161, 207, 215
Mikulás 86
Miles, Clement 15, 75, 130
The Milk of the Catechism (Dannhauer) 79
Military Academy in West Point 163
Miracle on 34th Street (film) 156, 203
miracle plays 51, 151
A Miracle Under the Christmas Tree: Real Stories of Hope, Faith and the True Gifts of the Season (Sander) 155
misrule 32, 49, 62, 122, 126, 158–170, 178, 195, 199, 202, 216–217
mistletoe 45, 50, 86, 92, 104–108, 168, 174, 178, 185, 199, 210

Mithraism 26
Mithras 17, 26, 30, 36
Modranicht 34
Mokosh 41
Moloch 117–118
Moore, Clement C. 12, 87–94, 124, 193
Mora, Elizabeth Canori 152
Moral Epistles (Seneca) 166
Moren, Albert 153
Morozko 85
Mosca, Paul 116
Moses 51
Muirchu 151
Muller-Ebeling, Claudia 81, 90
mumming 53, 163, 178
Musselburgh 36
myrrh 145
mystery plays 51

Nast, Thomas 87, 91–92, 107, 124
Natale Petri de Cathedra 30
natalis invicti 5
Nathan, Rich 96
nativity plays 51
nativity scenes *see* cribs
The Nativity Story (film) 202
Natural History (Pliny) 100, 105
necromancy 100
nemeton 74
nemus 74
neopaganism 8, 10, 204–207
Neptune 83, 94
Nero 24, 30
The New-York Historical Society Quarterly 87
Nicneven 120
Nifelheim 100
Night of the Mothers *see* Modranicht
Nike 10, 139
Nimrod 95, 143
Nissan 13
Nissenbaum, Stephen 56, 62, 93, 163, 178, 192
nisses 109–111
Noah 52, 100, 143
Nocturnal Procession of the 'Ndocciata 34, 103
Noel Baba 86
Nordberg, Andreas 17
Norse mythology 38, 41–43, 88–89, 93, 100, 105, 131, 144
Northup, Solomon 165
Norway 39, 47, 60, 111, 188
The Norwegian American 12
nymphs 41, 53, 90–91, 103

Oak King 204
Odin 12, 30, 38, 44, 47–48, 76, 89–96, 100, 130–131, 144, 189
O'Donnell, Hugh 13
Office Christmas Party (film) 202
office parties 168, 209
The Old Magic of Christmas (Raedisch) 104, 124

Index

On Idolatry (Tertullian) 23
Opalia 26, 28, 212
Ops 27–28, 115
O'Reilly, Bill 4
Organization for Economic Cooperation and Development 197
Origen, Frater 24
Original Sin 68, 118–119, 124, 125
Orthodox Church 101
Ostara 205
Otter, William 163
Ovid 55

Pagan Christmas (Ratsch and Muller-Ebeling) 81, 90, 103
Page, Nick 12, 94
The Pageant of the Shearman and Tailors 151
Papai Noel 86
paradise plays 78, 82
Parentalia 171
Parton, Dolly 207
Pelz Nichol 124, 131
A People's History of the United States (Zinn) 216
Perchta 119–120, 124
perchten 104
Pere Fourettard 131
Père Noël 86
Perry, Joe 71
Perseus 144
Persia 36, 68, 100
Perun 41
Peter the Apostle 16, 148, 163
Pharaoh 24
Philip the Apostle 16
Philip the Deacon 148
Picts 36
Pierpont, John 165
Pimlott, J.A.R. 122
Plato 138
The Pleasant Comedy of Old Fortunatus 53
Pliny the Elder 100, 105
Pliny the Younger 166
Plum Pudding Riot 64
Poetic Edda 73, 89
Poinsett, Joel Roberts 105
poinsettia 105
The Polar Express (film) 112, 203
Pomona 171
Pope Benedict XV 153
Pope Gregory I 47, 69, 190
Pope Gregory II 77, 181
Pope Gregory XI 142
Pope Julius I 24, 30
Pope Leo I 33
Poseidon 34, 83–84, 91, 94, 96, 189
The Preacher's Wife (film) 202
prophecy of Malachi 19
prophecy of Micah 16
The Prophets (play) 51
Prose Edda 43, 88
Prudentius 312
Purdue, A.W. 86

purgatory 177
Puritans 7, 15, 50, 62–65, 86

Quakers 7
Queen of Winter *see* Cailleach Bheur
Quinn, Josephine 117

Raedisch, Linda 124
Ragnarok 38
Ranker 202
Ratsch, Christian 81, 90
Reader's Digest 156
Redbook 199
Reformation 12, 55, 60, 62, 85, 122, 188
The Religion of the Norsemen (Keyser) 73
Renaissance 35
Richard of Swinfield, Bishop of Hereford 58
Rinda 144
Roman Empire 11, 14, 24–26, 28, 32, 33, 34, 37, 46, 146, 148; Roman occupation of England and Wales 29, 36; Romano-British culture 29, 36
Rose, Carol 108
rosemary 50
Rotten Tomatoes (website) 202
Round About Our Coal Fire, or Christmas Entertainment 129
Ruck, Carl 94
Rudolph the Red-Nosed Reindeer 193, 202
Ruklaus 124
Rural Dionysia 91
Rush, John 93
Russia 85, 100

sacrifice 34–35, 37, 40–41, 43, 44, 47, 63, 76, 80, 90, 98, 105, 108, 116–119, 143, 172, 174–175, 190; of animals 44, 47, 143, 190; of children 76, 116–119, 143; of humans 51, 53, 72, 105, 116–119, 172; and ritual killings 116
The Saga of King Heidrek the Wise 43
Saint Ansgar 39
Saint Boniface 39
Saint Francis of Assisi 53
Saint George and the dragon (legend of) 53
St. John's Eve 47, 208
St. Lucia Day 130
St. Lucia tradition 49
Saint Martin of Tours 75
Saint Nicholas 45, 66, 83–89, 93–94, 96, 124, 151, 189, 195; St. Nicholas's Feast Day 87, 104, 122–124, 131
St. Nicholas Society 96
Saint Patrick 39, 46, 151
St. Peter's Basilica 207
St. Thomas's Day 130
saint's plays *see* miracle plays

Salamis 24
Salibi, Dionysius 5
Salvation Army 96, 192
Samaria 147
Samhain 44, 171–178, 204
Sámi 133
Samichlaus 85, 104, 131
Santa Claus 2, 4, 12, 23, 83–97, 104, 110, 112, 114, 124–126, 156, 168–169, 185, 189, 194, 196, 198, 204, 209, 210, 217; as Bacchus 90–95; and hallucinogenic mushrooms 93; as Odin 89–93; as Saturn 92–93; as Thor 88
The Santa Clause (film) 202
Santa's Workshop (short film) 110
Santi-Chlaus 85
Sardinia 117
Satan *see* the Devil
Saturn 19, 26–27, 29, 93, 96, 115–117, 143, 145, 183–184, 193, 205
Saturnalia 5, 12–14, 17, 23, 26–33, 37, 45, 48, 62–63, 65, 86, 92, 114–116, 121–122, 158, 165–170, 178, 192, 199–201, 205–207, 212, 217
The Saturnalia (Macrobius) 27
Saxons 38–40, 77
Schmidt Peter, Johann 130
Scotland 29, 38, 109, 161
Scriptor Syrus 32
Scripture *see* Bible
Second Life 205
Second Punic War 30
Seneca 29, 165–166; Moral Letters to Lucilius 29
separation of church and state 1, 4
Seraphim 139
Seventh-Day Adventist Church 7
Severus 30
Sextus Julius Africanus 13, 14
Shab-e Yalda 34
Shakespeare, William 127
shamanism 93
Shamash 54
Sharpe, Samuel 164
shepherds' plays 53
Ship of Miracles 155
The Shop Around the Corner (film) 201
Siberia 93–94
Sicily 117, 177
sigillaricium 201
Sigurd 38
Silent Night 153, 207
Simargl 41
Simek, Rudolf 60
Simmons, Kurt 12
Simon Magus 148
Simpson, Jessica 168
Sinterklaas 85, 123
slavery 23, 27–29, 122, 150, 162, 164–167, 191–193

Sleigh Rides, Jingle Bells & Silent Nights: A Cultural History of American Christmas Songs (Lankford) 169
Sleipnir 14, 88–89; *see also* Odin
Smith, William Robertson 189
smudging nights 103
smudging sticks 207
social inversion 29, 126, 162, 165–167, 178, 192
Socrates 138
Sol Invictus 5, 14, 17, 19, 26, 30, 205
sonarblót 43
Sørensdatter, Kirsti 188
Soyal 34
Starbucks 4, 207, 210–211
Stations of the Sun (Hutton) 122
status inversion *see* social inversion
Steen, Jan 123
Stille Nacht *see* Silent Night
Stonehenge 35, 204–207
Stonehenge Tours 205
Strenia 120, 200
Stribog 41
Stubbs, Philip 178
Stumbo, John 97
Sturluson, Snorri 43, 88, 108, 174
Stuttgart Psalter 39–40
Sumerians 54, 99
Sun of Righteousness 14, 19, 56, 212
Sundblom, Haddon 195
Survey of London 50
Svarog 41
Swartz, Benjamin K., Jr. 84
Sweden 30, 39–40, 109, 118, 130–131, 133
Switzerland 104, 131
Syria 5, 30–31, 98, 142

Tacitus 30, 35
Taegliebe Rundschau 155
Tate, Nahum 56
Taylor, John 63, 189
temple of Uppsala 30, 72, 76
Tertullian 13, 23, 147
Teutonic Mythology 39, 41, 46, 135, 188
Teutonic tribes 11, 75, 81
Thanksgiving 156, 167, 171, 195, 210, 212
Theodosius 31, 37, 73
Theseus 144

Thietmar 43
Thomas, Rufus 168
Thor 30, 38, 47–48, 76, 90, 94–96, 118, 189
Thor's Oak 68, 77
Thoth 137
Thunor *see* Thor
Tiamat 137
Tiberias 16
Tlachtga 173
Tochmarc Emire 172
Told After Supper (Jerome) 129
tomte 109
Tomte Gubbe 131
Torah 142
Trading Places (film) 167
A Treasury of Christmas Miracles: True Stories of God's Presence Today (Kingsbury) 155
tree of knowledge 68, 78
tree of life 68, 73
troping 51
True Cross 150
Trump, Donald 211
Tryggvason, Olafur 47
Turkey 83
Turner Broadcasting 113
Twelfth Night 120
Twitter 211

Ukraine 85
unbaptized days 129, 133
UNESCO 207
United States of America 5, 66, 77, 85, 87, 94, 105, 110, 124, 164, 168, 171, 175, 177, 184–185, 191, 193, 210–212
University of Minnesota 4

Valhalla 48, 76
Vali 144
valkyrie 88
Van Dam, Rip 91, 93
Van Dyke, Henry 76
Veðrfölnir 88
vetrnætr see Winter Nights
The Viking Gods (Ludovicus) 59
Vikings 30, 38, 44, 47–48, 51, 59–60, 85, 94, 101, 150, 175, 216
Vinje, Judith Gabriel 12
Virgin Mary 16, 20, 22–23, 51, 53, 97, 102, 135–136, 139, 143–145, 151–152, 188, 191
Voliva, Wilbur Glenn 95

War on Christmas 1, 4, 210–211, 214–215
The War on Christmas: How the Liberal Plot to Ban the Sacred Christian Holiday Is Worse Than You Thought (Gibson) 4
Washington, George 162; Eggnog recipe of 162
The Washington Post 155
wassailing 61–62, 66, 101, 158, 178, 183, 190, 201, 205–206
Wasson, R. Gordon 93
Weiser, Francis 71, 90
Weninger, Francis Xavier 75
Westgothland 40
Wild Hunt 103, 112, 120, 130, 175
William II 153
Williams, Andy 127
Williams, Graham 153
Willis, Bruce 202
Winehouse, Amy 168
Winter Nights 173–175
winter solstice celebrations 2, 11, 34–35, 43–44, 103, 215
witch panics 188
witchcraft 44, 100, 135, 146, 181, 186–188, 217
Woden *see* Odin
wolf nights 129
The Wonders of Santa Claus (poem) 110
world tree 68, 73, 74, 101, 132
World War I 153–155, 217; *see also* Christmas Truce of World War I
World Wildlife Fund 197
wreaths 29, 45, 69–70, 78, 81, 207

Yggdrasil 68, 73–74, 88, 101
Ýlir 44
Yule 11–12, 17, 35, 41–44, 46–47, 59–60, 66, 71, 75, 86, 90, 128–131, 142, 158, 169, 173–176, 190, 205–207, 214; etymology 59; modern observances 205–207; Yule boar 41, 60; Yule log 60, 66, 75, 86, 130; Yule trees 71

Zehmisch, Kurt 154
Zeus 90, 142
Zinn, Howard 216
Zoroaster 100
Zoroastrianism 145
Zurram 34